A Brief History of Is

A BRIEF HISTORY OF ISLAM IN EUROPE

Thirteen Centuries of Creed, Conflict and Coexistence

Maurits S. Berger

Leiden University Press

Cover design: Studio Frederik de Wal

Cover illustration: Louis Haghe, Isle of Graia Gulf of Akabah Arabia Petraea, Feb 27th 1839, Library of Congress Prints and Photographs Division Washington.

Lay-out: TAT Zetwerk, Utrecht

ISBN   978 90 8728 195 3

e-ISBN   978 94 0060 150 5 (ePDF)

e-ISBN   978 94 0060 151 2 (ePub)

NUR   680, 717

This book is distributed in North America by the University of Chicago Press (www.press.uchicago.edu).

Contents

Chapter Two. Crusading Europe (1000–1500 CE)

Chapter Three. Divided Europe (1500–1700 CE)

Chapter Four. Powerful Europe (1700–1950 CE)

Chapter Five. Struggling Europe (1950–)

Foreword

This book is the result of six years teaching my BA class entitled 'The history of Islam in the West' at Leiden University. I want to thank the students for their active participation and comments, which prompted me every year further to refine my arguments, dig deeper into Europe's rich history with Islam, and to become more critical about contemporary references to 'Islam.' Annefieke Bonants was one of the first students who took that class, and she later became my assistant to do the research for this book. Her meticulous and painstaking work, and not least the friendly patience with which she reacted to the flurry of ideas and orders I hurled at her were indispensable to the finishing of the writing of this book. Anniek Meinders, the publisher of the newly established Leiden University Press, was courageous enough to take on this project that did not fit neatly into an academic category. Finally thanks to the advisory board of Leiden University Press and the three peer reviewers who spent their precious time reading the manuscript and dispensing helpful comments: Prof. M. Schrovers of the History department at Leiden University, Prof. J. Nielsen of the Theology Faculty at the University of Copenhagen, and a third reviewer who preferred to remain anonymous.

The Hague, May 2014

Introduction

Islam's recent arrival in Europe by means of migration, violence and media images has kindled a wave of interest in Europe's past and present relations with Islam. Publications on these subjects are prolific, so why another book on 'Islam in Europe'? There are three reasons: to provide the first comprehensive overview of the entire thirteen-century history of Islam in Europe from 700 CE until now (most existing literature covers only a part of this history); to identify the role of 'Islam' during this period; and to look into the impact of this long history on the current discourse and situation of Islam in Europe. My endeavour is to present a framework by which we can conceptualize the notion of 'Islam in Europe' in time (the eighth to the twenty-first centuries CE) and space ('Europe'), and that will allow us to sample and interconnect the enormous corpus of existing knowledge on Islam in Europe and to put it in chronological and thematic order. This framework should provide the reader with novel insights into the history of Islam in Europe.

Given the comprehensiveness of this book, its approach is by default multidisciplinary. The secondary literature used to write it is that of specialists of regions (Europe, Spain, Sicily, the Balkans, the Ottoman Empire, the Mediterranean), periods (Middle Ages, Renaissance, colonial period, modern Europe), and specific disciplinary subjects (religion, economics, social sciences, political sciences, law, art, agriculture). The ambitious set-up that squeezes thirteen centuries into a single volume requires a clear perspective on what story this book wants to tell, how that story is told, and why it needs to be told in the first place. These questions will be addressed in the following.

1. The Link to Today

In discussions nowadays on the role of Islam in Europe, direct or indirect references are often made to events of the past that allude to a history of perpetual conflict whereby 'Europe' and 'Islam' stand for entities that collide because, according to some observers, they represent different value systems or, in the eyes of others, because Islam is by nature aggressive and has put Europe on the defensive ever since the Arab Muslims rode out of the Arab Peninsula in the seventh century in search of conquest. To the proponents of these views the current presence of large numbers of Muslims in Europe is a reason for concern, and they justify their anxieties with references to history.[1] There are also other observers, however, who hold a much more positive historical view on Islamic-European relations, referring to the knowledge that has passed on from the medieval Islamic civilization to Europe: their emphasis is on the intellectual interaction between the two realms rather than on their belligerent relations.[2]

Such opposing views are not reserved for political debates, but have also permeated academic discussions. Two eminent contemporary scholars of Islamic history, the American professors Bernard Lewis and Richard Bulliet, provide a case in point.[3] Bulliet argues that Islam and Christianity share the same cradle of a common civilization from which they parted "as siblings" in the sixteenth century, while Lewis asserts that the two civilizations have always been at loggerheads. Bulliet stresses the similarities in the developments and experiences of the two civilizations, while Lewis emphasizes their differences. Bulliet refers to religion as only one of the many factors that shaped Muslim identity, while Lewis puts religion at centre stage for understanding the Muslim. And Bulliet argues for a legacy of a Christian-Islamic heritage, while Lewis differentiates between an Islamic civilization, on the one hand, and a Judeo-Christian civilization, on the other. Lewis' view has gained popularity since the attacks of 9/11 in 2001 and the subsequent terrorist attacks in Europe, and seems to be corroborated by the mounting reports on the apparent lack of integration of Muslim migrants in Western European societies. Bulliet's view, on the other hand, is shared particularly by many historians of the Middle Ages who point to the parallels between the two civilizations and the ways in which Europe is indebted to Islamic civilization.

As every historian will confirm, history can provide source material that may lead to very different interpretations. In the case of Islam, however, historical facts and terminology are not always a source of academic interplay between rival historians, but are sometimes rewritten in public discourse or, worse, become a demagogic tool against Muslim Europeans. One example is the claim that Europeans are part of a 'Judeo-Christian civilization' (sometimes with the addition of 'Humanist') which, as we have seen, is used as a premise by Bernard Lewis but is a notion challenged by Richard Bulliet. In 2005, however, this academic debate spilled over into political reality when, in the final drafting phase of the new European Union Convention, known as the 'EU constitution', there was deliberation about introducing this term in the preamble.[4] The implicit aim of this political manoeuvring was to put up a wall against the alleged Islamicization of Europe by its expanding Muslim population. The proposed amendment did not come to pass, which was probably the smart thing to do, because such an identity-marker would not only deny the influences of Islamic civilization, but also the value of Greek, Roman, Ottoman and all other non-Judeo and non-Christian elements that have contributed to European civilization.

Collective Memory

The history (by which I mean the amalgam of transnational and transcultural, political, social, economic, intellectual and other forms and disciplines of history) of 'Islam in Europe' provides, from the perspective of current European affairs, therefore, an interesting example of what has been called 'collective memory.' This term received much attention from historians in the 1990s and consequently developed into multiple meanings, but for the purpose of this book we will use this notion to mean the ways in which people construct a conception of the past, and from which they derive an awareness of their present sense of unity and peculiarity.[5] A collective memory provides a people with a common identity that can be traced back into history, regardless of the accuracy of the historical events or the causal connection of these events to the identity of the people holding the collective memory. The concept of a Judeo-Christian heritage to underpin European unity is a perfect illustration of this. In a similar vein Tony Judt analysed how the memory of the wartime experience in continental Europe was "distorted, sublimated, and appropriated, [and] bequeathed to the postwar era an identity that was fundamentally false, dependent upon the erection of an unnatural and unsustainable frontier between past and present in European public memory".[6]

An important aspect of this collective memory, therefore, is the distortion of history into mythology or imagery. Several contemporary medieval historians have made interesting compilations and analyses of the European medieval image of Islam as a threat, whether as a religion, a belligerent ideology or a dominating culture, and argued how this imagery has continued into the present age.[7] The argument these historians by implication make is that present-day Western (and in particular West European) anxieties about Islam are related not only to the recent phenomenon of Muslim immigration and Islamic terrorism, but also to a perpetuating image that is centuries old, an image that often has little to do with reality but all the more with the perception of the Muslim as the embodiment of everything that the Westerner is not.

What, then, are the historical experiences that Europe has had with Islam, and, more importantly, in what form are they lodged in today's collective memory? An example is the Frankish victory at Poitiers against one of the many plunder raids conducted by Spanish Moors: in European collective memory this battle has acquired the historical significance of halting the Muslim onslaught on Europe and consequently saving Europe from Islamic domination. In chapter one we will discuss the historical evidence that proves this analysis to be incorrect. Equally interesting is the obverse of this same question: what are the 'memory holes', or those historical experiences that have been erased from or not admitted into European collective memory? An example is the ample study of the six centuries of Muslim life in Catholic Spain as opposed to the near lack of such interest in the six centuries of Muslim life in Catholic Poland and Lithuania.[8] Another example is the European collective memory of the Barbary corsairs and the hundreds of thousands of Christian slaves they kept, while neglecting the fact that enslavement of Muslims by means of piracy was conducted on a similar scale by the Christian European side.[9] This is not to say that such omissions in our collective memory or in our academic interest happen deliberately; but it is in itself interesting to note that one is selective when discussing 'Islam in Europe'. In this book we therefore want to provide a story of Islam in Europe that is as comprehensive as possible. The purpose is not to single out the distortions and the omissions in our current collective memory of Islam in Europe; the endeavour to give the full story will itself highlight these omissions as the reader may be surprised with events, facts and numbers that were hitherto unknown to him or her.

Of paramount importance when telling these stories and histories is to be aware of who told them then, who tells them now, and who they are addressed to, because the collective memory of a people will resonate with certain stories, but not with others. To Catholics of the sixteenth and seventeenth centuries the 'Turk' was the great enemy, while many Protestants saw more similarities with Islam than with Catholicism and some Protestants even claimed to prefer Ottoman rule to that of the Catholics. Nowadays, on the other hand, most Protestants will feel closer to Catholicism than to Islam. In the seventeenth century, the fall of Vienna might have been a disaster for the Holy Roman Empire, but such event would have been applauded by the Empire's enemy France. Nowadays, on the other hand, Frenchmen may concur with the view that the breaking of the Ottoman siege of Vienna saved Europe from Islamic domination.

This coexistence of different collective memories in the past is recurring again in present-day Europe, not only because of different experiences in the various geographical parts of Europe, but also because of the presence of a relatively large number of immigrants of foreign origin, many of whom are Muslim. Even those among them who are born, raised and educated in Europe have inherited a collective memory that has stored different images, events and notions from that of their fellow Europeans. For instance, when mentioning the battles of Poitiers and Vienna where respectively Moorish and Ottoman armies were defeated, many of my students of Dutch origin nod their heads in recognition of these names, while my Dutch Muslim students of foreign origin will give me blank stares. Conversely, when I mention the battle of Hittin, where Saladin brought defeat to the Crusader armies, my Muslim students look up in recognition while the others do not. The different reactions are remarkable given the fact that all these students have taken the same Dutch state exams, and none of these historical events is part of the Dutch school curriculum. Collective memory, therefore, is powerful, perhaps even more so than acquired knowledge.

2. 'Islam' and 'Europe'

A Methodological Framework

Based on these considerations, the topic of 'Islam in Europe' is more than a story told by stringing together historical events. It is a story about us, Europeans, whether Muslim or non-Muslim, of native or foreign origin, and how we struggle with our past and our present in the continent called Europe, how we shape our identity and, particularly, the uneasy relationship between who we are and who we want to be. In the many years of studying this topic and engaging in public and academic debates on it, I became convinced that the only way to conceptualize the notion of 'Islam in Europe' is to apply a strict framework of notions set within certain timelines that allow us with each event in each epoch to ask ourselves the basic questions: What is the nature of the interaction between 'Europe' and 'Islam'? What do we mean by Islam in this particular instance? To what extent do Muslims or Islam play a role in the events before us? What is real and what is imaginary? The aim of this framework is, in short, to structure our thoughts and arguments when discussing 'Islam in Europe' and to avoid being drawn into the myriad of events and details of thirteen centuries of interaction between Europe and Islam.[10]

In brief, the structure of the framework is as follows: we limit ourselves to the European perspective on Islam, and from that perspective look at thirteen centuries of interaction between Europe and Islam, whereby we can divide this long period into five periods, and for each period provide an analysis of that interaction based on certain categories of interaction and on a limited number (three) of approaches. This all sounds quite abstract, so let us elaborate these different composites of the framework.

First and foremost, it must be emphasized that the object of inquiry in this book is the European perspective on its history with Muslims and Islam. We will, so to speak, pitch our camera on the European continent and from that angle look at European interactions with Muslims and Islam. The Muslim reactions and experiences with Europeans, although equally interesting, will be a story left for others to tell.[11] Also, we will take the 'in' of Islam in Europe quite literally: European relations with Muslims and Islam will be discussed only insofar as they take place on the European continent. European experiences during colonial times with Muslim societies in North Africa or Asia will play only a minor role in this book.

Next we need to be very clear on the terminology that we will use. So far we have used the terms 'Islam' and 'Europe' because they have become quite common in political and public debates of today: 'Europe' is under threat of 'Islam', 'Islam' is an obstacle to integration, 'Islam' is anathema to 'European culture', 'Europe' is indebted to 'Islamic civilization', etc. Even the title of this book alludes to a self-evidence that is actually unwarranted, because the use of the two terms 'Europe' and 'Islam' as individual entities or notions is a highly problematic representation of the interaction (or confrontation) between the two. A clarification of these two terms is therefore in order.

Europe

Defining 'Europe' is the typical headache hurdle for every politician or academic. If one conceives Europe as the heir to the Christian commonwealth of the later Middle Ages, then the question arises how one is to consider Christian Orthodoxy and its geographical realm that extends into Russia and the Middle East. If, on the other hand, one is to conceive of Europe in a modern setting, one may consider an economical-legal entity like the European Union or the geographical and political-legal Council of Europe. Both have their disadvantages for what we want to do here, however: the European Union is geographically too narrow as it does not contain countries like Iceland, Norway, Switzerland, Albania, Serbia or Bosnia-Hercegovina; and the Council of Europe as a frame of reference for 'Europe' is geographically too wide because it includes countries as far east as Turkey, Azerbaijan, Georgia and the Russian Federation.

For the purpose of this book we will first define Europe in accordance with the geographical area bordered by waterways, that is the Polar Sea in the north, the Atlantic in the west, the Mediterranean in the south and the Black Sea and the rivers Dnieper and Volga in the east. We will further use terminology like 'western' or 'south-eastern' Europe with the explicit mention that these are not political but mere geographical indications.

This definition has as a result that, on the one hand, we will restrict our discussion of the Byzantine and Ottoman Empires to their dominions in south-eastern Europe (the 'Balkans') and not those in the Middle East and, on the other hand, that we will include in our account the stories of north-eastern European countries like the Baltic states. These and other eastern European countries have had long encounters with Islam and Muslims, as we will see later, and we have already observed that these interactions have received little academic attention from Western historians. This shows that 'Islam in Europe' is mostly studied and reflected upon from a western Euro-centred point of view – a perspective that is in need of revision if we truly want to do justice to the concept of 'Islam in Europe'.

In addition to Europe as a geographical area we will also consider Europe in its capacity as a single civilization, or a unity of values, or any other uniform identity for its inhabitants. However, as we will see in the following chapters, the unity of these values or identities was not always concrete, let alone existent, as they changed through the centuries. Europe has been perceived in the eyes of its inhabitants as a Christian Commonwealth, gradually transformed into the notion of a 'European Commonwealth' (a term coined by Edmund Burke in the late eighteenth century), and from the nineteenth century onwards Europe was equated by its inhabitants with the highest form of civilization in any sense if its meaning – legally, politically, culturally, technically. Rather than trying to come here to a definition of European identity, we will regard the situation and state of mind of 'Europe' in accordance with each epoch.

Islam

The term 'Islam' is as problematic as 'Europe', as it often includes several representations of Islam that may be different or even mutually exclusive. In this book we conceptualize the term 'Islam' in four meanings: its adherents, the Muslims; Islam as a culture and civilization; Islam as a religion; and Islam as an image.

First, Islam may represent its adherents, the Muslims, either as powers or as individuals and communities. The presence of Muslim *powers* within Europe has been longstanding: 800 years in Spain, 500 years in Greece, 300 years in the Balkans, and more than a century in countries like Sicily, Hungary, Romania. Muslim *people* have sometimes been present longer, for they often stayed on even when Muslim sovereignty had ended. As subjects under non-Muslim rule, Muslims lived in Spain for 800 years (and an additional 100 years in secrecy) and in Sicily 400 years, and they still live in Lithuania and Poland where they have been for over 600 years, as they do in most Balkan countries where they have lived for more than 500 years. In other places, such as Sicily and Spain, on the other hand, the entire Muslim populations have been expelled or forced to convert, while certain elements of their civilization and culture have remained after their disappearance (think of architecture, language, music, customs, food). Since the late sixteenth century very few – if any – Muslims have resided in the European region west of the line Warsaw-Vienna-Trieste (a region that we will hereafter refer to as 'western Europe'). This changed with the large-scale immigration of Muslims in the twentieth century, particularly from the 1970s onwards.

It must be kept in mind that the notion of Muslim as used here is nothing more than an identity marker used by either the European or the Muslim, and does not necessarily relate to the degree of religiousness of that particular person. This brings us to yet another problem of terminology, since from a historical point of view the term 'Muslim' is a novelty. During the Middle Ages reference was made to Saracens, and in Spain more specifically to Moors.* Europeans in the Middle Ages also used names like 'Hagarenes' or 'Ishmaelites', referring to the Arab-Muslim claim to be Abraham's offspring through the line of Hagar and her son Ishmael. Later, with the rise of the Ottoman Empire, the commonly used term was 'Turk' ('turning Turk' was the expression for conversion to Islam). During colonial times, Europeans sometimes referred to Muslims as Musulmans, but more often as Mohammedans, or followers of Mohammad, erroneously analogous to the term 'Christians' as the followers of Christ. And until twenty or thirty years ago, Muslims in Europe were spoken of, and spoke of themselves, in ethnic and national terms: Arabs and Asians, Turks and Pakistanis, Kurds and Berber. The term 'Muslim' is only of very recent date, and it is therefore historically awkward to use twenty-first century terminology to describe people five, ten or thirteen centuries ago, when in those times different, and

---

* While the etymology of Moors is 'dark people', the name Saracene has been given different origins, ranging from the Arabic 'sharqiyin' ('Easterner') to the Greek 'skene' ('tent dweller') or the Greek 'sara kene', meaning 'empty Sarah', referring to Abraham's wife Sarah who gave birth to Isaac, the founding father of the Israelites, and who was therefore not related – 'empty' – to Ishmael, who was fathered by Abraham with his slave woman Hagar, and who is claimed by the Arabs as their founding father.

mostly non-religious, terminology was used. Still, even though we might try to be historically true in terminology, references to 'Muslims' cannot be avoided.

The second representation of 'Islam' is that of a culture and civilization. We can observe this in the institutions of typical Islamic nature, either as physical buildings like mosques, hospitals and *caravanserais*, or as non-physical institutions such as forms of government, judiciary, or a legal or social system. In addition to these institutions, Islam as a culture or civilization can be found in the cultural and scientific achievements of the Muslims, such as irrigation and navigation techniques, sciences, arts. Islam in this sense can also exist long after Muslim presence has disappeared, either as a heritage of forlorn times, as is the case in Spain and Sicily where tour guides advertise 'Islamic civilization', or as a legacy of arts, sciences and technologies that over the centuries have been adopted and assimilated by Europeans.

The third representation of 'Islam' is that of the religion itself, meaning the theological doctrines that can be found in scripture and texts, and the religious practices of Muslims. The historian Hudgson in his seminal *Venture of Islam* had introduced the term 'Islamdom' and the adjective 'Islamicate' to denote Islam as a culture and civilization, separate from the notion of 'Islam' as religious doctrine.[12] Unfortunately, this useful distinction never really caught on. And indeed, one of the unfortunate effects of post-9/11 developments is that the understanding of 'Islam' and the way it is being discussed has become reduced to that of religious doctrine – not only in the West, but also in the Muslim world. By consequence, the religion of Islam is by many considered essential to understanding the Muslim, disregarding all the other aspects that have shaped the identity, character and mind-set of this same Muslim. Equating Muslims with the theological tenets of Islam is even more problematic if we want to make sense of the past thirteen centuries of European interaction with 'Islam', as we will see in the coming chapters.

Finally, there is a fourth notion of Islam, which is its imaginary representation in the minds of either Muslims or Europeans. Such representation may be emanant, in that it reflects something 'out there' like a historical civilization, an apocalyptic threat or a great religion. But more often the representation is immanent in that it reflects a notion of Islam that relates to people personally. For Muslims such immanent representation may take on the form of identity: being a 'Muslim' makes one part of a greater identity called 'Islam', which may take on all kinds of forms, ranging from a great civilization to a global religious community. For non-Muslim Europeans, on the other hand, 'Islam' often takes on the representation of a photo negative of themselves and as such constitutes what is also called the European Other. We will elaborate on this below, since the concept of 'Othering' is one of the central themes in this book.

3. Europe's Interaction with Islam

While these descriptions of the terms 'Islam' and 'Europe' may give us a fair impression of what we are talking about, we must now address their interaction, because that is the main focus of this book: Islam in Europe is not a static situation, but an interaction of the two. Moreover, as we will see in the next chapters, from a European perspective much of the interaction with 'Islam' took place on the level of knowledge, ideas or images, and this was mostly done without any physical Muslim counterpart. In other words, talking and writing about 'Mahomet' and the 'Turk' was mostly done by Europeans who had had no encounters with Muslims themselves. In modern times we see a similar phenomenon, with Europeans conducting heated discussions about Islamic theology or the presence of mosques or Muslims' integration in European societies, but engaging remarkably little with the Muslims themselves, even though they are now physically present. The distinction between the physical encounter with 'Islam', on the one hand, and talking and thinking about Islam, on the other, is therefore essential when discussing Islam in Europe. In the framework of this book we will treat these two forms of interaction separately under the titles of what I suggest calling 'physical' and 'virtual' Islam, respectively.

'Physical' and 'Virtual' Islam

'Physical Islam' is represented by the mere presence of people called Muslims, on the one hand, and the visibility of their presence that can be identified as 'Islamic', on the other. The visibility shows in behaviour of Muslims that can somehow be denoted as, to use Hodgson's terminology, either religiously 'Islamic' or culturally 'Islamicate'. The visibility further shows in the Muslim's material expressions of his or her Islam, such as clothes, arts and buildings, but also the records of intellectual and cultural life and ideas, ranging from the medieval philosophical texts to modern rap clips on youtube. To bring some order to the many manifestations of physical Islam over a period of thirteen centuries, we will limit ourselves in this book to the following forms of interaction: armed conflict like war, raids, piracy; trade and diplomacy; government and rule; and coexistence within a single society (including discrimination and persecution). Interestingly, travel and exploration is not one of these categories: whereas Europeans have travelled extensively into Muslim countries for a variety of reasons, Muslims have done almost no travelling into Europe, for reasons that will be explained in due course.

'Virtual Islam' comprises all immaterial or non-physical aspects of Islam, such as the tenets of Islamic orthodoxy and the culture, ideas, messages and knowledge. Put differently, virtual Islam is all manifestations of Islam that are transmitted by the physical forms of Islam. Virtual Islam therefore also includes the images and visions of what is considered 'Islamic', by Muslims as well as non-Muslims, including imagined or real notions of conflicts between what is considered 'Islamic' and 'European'. For example, a mosque pertains to physical Islam, while the different meanings it may convey – religious grandeur, Muslim domination, symbol of piety – are what we call virtual Islam. In this book we will discuss the following domains of interaction related to virtual Islam: culture (including science and scholarship); the study of Islam; and issues of imagery and identity.

The merit of the distinction between physical and virtual Islam is that it allows us to distinguish between the neutral observation of physical appearances, behaviour and expressions of Muslims, on the one hand, and the assessment of the interpretations, meanings and values thereof, on the other. For instance, the presence of Muslims in contemporary European societies is often expressed in terms of numbers, with the implicit warning that these numbers may reach dangerous levels: "[b]y 2050, the number of Muslims in Europe will reach 20 per cent!"[13] Similarly, the building of mosques, and in particular their height and 'Oriental' architecture, has received severe criticism in contemporary Europe. The distinction between physical and virtual Islam allows us to deconstruct the multiple issues that are condensed in these controversies. From the perspective of physical Islam, we may observe that there is the physical presence of a certain number of people called Muslims that live and work in European societies, manifest their religious beliefs by means of dress or behaviour, and establish certain institutions like a mosque or a *sharia* council. From the perspective of virtual Islam, on the other hand, we will be able to attribute meaning to these manifestations: on what basis are people identified by themselves or others as 'Muslim', how do Europeans form their opinions about these 'Muslims', what are the reasons for supporting or criticizing an 'Oriental' style in modern European mosque architecture?

We have seen that there is already a considerable volume of academic literature on European writings and representations about Muslims and Islam. I will gratefully make use of their findings, but will widen the scope of 'interaction' by posing the question how the themes of this European discourse relate to the practices and experiences of Europeans with Islam and Muslims. The long European history of talking and writing about Muslims, their civilization and their religion is one thing, but the history of Europeans interacting with Muslims through war, diplomacy or by living in the same city is quite another. The two influence each other, of course, but also very often do not. We will see that interaction with Muslims themselves ('physical Islam'), on the one hand, and images and discussions of Muslims and their religion ('virtual Islam'), on the other, often run on parallel but separate tracks.

In addition, rather than looking into a specific period, we will look into these interactions over a timeline of thirteen centuries, to see if there are any patterns that reflect on the situation of today. To do so, we will make use of a chronological narrative, so that we can see whether there is a continuation, accumulation or discontinuation of certain kinds of interactions, images, and the like.

Five Periods

We will see in the next chapters that the position of the Muslim as well as the image of Islam has undergone all kinds of metamorphoses during the thirteen centuries of interaction with Europe. The Muslim has acted on the European stage as a ruler and as a subject, as the antichrist and as an ally, corsair and tradesman, slave and master, terrorist and fellow citizen. The image of Islam has varied accordingly, as a religion that was feared as an enemy or embraced as a partner against heretic Christians, despised as an abomination or admired as a civilization, as a source of violence and of social civility, and studied for missionary, academic, colonial or security purposes. Whether we can speak of a continuing story of Islam in Europe that can be extrapolated into our present age is a question we will leave for discussion in the epilogue.

What we can say beforehand, however, is that the European attitudes and experiences vis-à-vis Muslims and Islam were being shaped by internal European experiences rather than by external Islamic influences. This is in no way meant to argue that Muslims and Islam were mere passive objects of European actions and experiences. On the contrary: Muslims in many instances played a very active role and at times determined the agenda of European history, driven by religious, belligerent or cultural motives. These facts obviously are of huge importance and will be given due attention, but the main objective of this book is the analysis of the interaction by Europeans with the manifestations of Islam in Europe. From that perspective it is my contention that these interactions can be mostly explained by the state of affairs within Europe and the ensuing European mind-set at a given time in its history.

Based on that premise, we can discern five periods, each characterized by specific European relations with and attitudes toward Muslims and Islam: Uncivilized Europe (700–1000), Crusading Europe (1000–1500), Divided Europe (1500–1700), Powerful Europe (1700–1950), and Struggling Europe (1950-now). These periods are admittedly artificial and simplistic, and their names are rather provocative, but it serves our purpose of highlighting how the situation of Europeans at certain times shaped their relations with Islam. We will use this periodization to structure this book, by describing each period in a separate chapter. The chapters will be further divided into three sections: the first will 'set the stage' with a brief overview of the major events and characteristics of that period, followed by a section on European interaction with physical Islam and one on European interaction with virtual Islam.

Three Themes: Religion, Toleration, Othering

So far, we have made the discussion of the thirteen centuries of Islam in Europe manageable by dividing it up into periods, and further into the domains of physicial and virtual Islam. The final part of this book's framework is the use of a specific scope to discuss the historical material. We will do so by using three interrelated approaches that will form the themes of our narrative. Given the subject-matter of this book – 'Islam' – we will raise the question of the religiosity of events and actions relating to 'Muslims' or 'Islam'. Religion is therefore the first theme. The other two themes are related to the notion of interaction: in the case of physical interaction of people we will face the question of (in)tolerance, while in the case of virtual interaction we deal with what has become known as the process of 'Othering'. We will see that in the specific case of Islam in Europe the notions of (in)tolerance and Othering are intrinsically related to religion. These three themes must be briefly introduced to get a firmer grip on the historical narrative in the following chapters.

Religion. We have already remarked that not all that Muslims do can be considered Islam, just as not every act by Europeans can be considered an expression of Christianity. A recurring question in this book will therefore be: to what extent was a particular situation or action related to religion? For instance, modern historians of the European Crusades and of Arab and Ottoman *jihads* have questioned the religiousness of these wars, arguing that the call for a 'holy war' often served practical rather than religious purposes. On the other hand, religious discourse has always been important to some degree in most wars in Europe, up to the Yugoslavian civil wars of the 1990s. One of the issues raised and discussed in the following chapters will therefore be whether it is valid to speak of the presence or absence of religion, as well as the use, misuse or abuse thereof.

But even if at times we are going to dismiss the religiousness of certain actions, our point of departure is to look into interactions that are *prima facie* of a religious nature or justified by religion. We will use the notion of religion in two ways: as a doctrine and as a cultural system. Religion as a theological doctrine claims to be fixed and eternal and in the cases of Islam and Christianity is recorded in Holy Scripture and in the theological manuals of the scholars. Religion as a cultural system consists of the patterns of symbols and power structures produced by the faithful and the ways that this system motivates people to conceptualize their social environment and to move them into action in accordance with that worldview.[14] The two notions of theological doctrine and a cultural system should ideally overlap, but often do not.

From this perspective, religion is not considered absolute in the trans-historical and transcultural sense, but subject to historical and cultural differences. In other words, when we speak of 'Christianity' or 'Islam' it is with the understanding that these notions and their interpretations are specific to their time and place, whether as a doctrine or a cultural system. This is not as self-evident as it may seem. Modern Christians may still identify with their Christian heritage (for instance, when they speak of Christian democracy or the Christian duty to give development aid), but may at the same time be very critical of certain interpretations or dismissive of certain practices that are part of that heritage (such as the persecution of heretics or slavery). The same holds for Muslims. If we want to understand their heritage and presence in Europe, now and in history, we must understand the dynamics of the historical narrative of religion.

An issue that is important to many social scientists who study religion is its meaning to the individual, and how that meaning is expressed in symbols, rituals and societal structures, on both an individual and a communal level. Although interesting in the case of Islam in Europe, this is too wide a range of aspects to be covered for a period of thirteen centuries. Since the purpose of this book is to understand the interaction between 'Islam' and 'Europe', we will conceive the history of European and Christian interaction with the Muslim and Islam as a continuum of delineating each other's space and position. Religion, with its claims on the ultimate worldview and its resulting directives on human behaviour, plays an important – at times the most important – role in this ordering process. Both the conceptualization and the means of ordering society and relationships are rooted in a worldview that is translated into a political, legal and cultural system. In this particular process religion serves as an instrument of power.[15] The stronger party – not necessarily the majority, as we will see – will apply a certain religiously founded logic or conceptualization to how society should be ordered, or how trade or war is to be conducted. These power structures yield questions that are reflected in the other two themes: how to live with others (the notion of tolerance) and how to reflect on those who are 'not like us' (the notion of Othering).

Toleration. Tolerance literally means to bear something, implying that it is something one would prefer not to do. In contemporary Western literature, tolerance has been defined as "a deliberate choice not to interfere with the conduct of which one disapproves".[16] Or, in other words, tolerance is an attitude of putting up with that which one opposes, even when it "shocks, enrages, frightens, or disgusts."[17] The key notion is the verb 'putting up with', which consists of two elements. First, tolerance is mainly exercised in matters involving firmly held beliefs. It implies that the tolerator strongly objects to a certain behaviour or opinion, but decides to accept it.[18] The second element of tolerance is its exercise by someone who has the power also *not* to tolerate the conduct of which he or she disapproves. In other words, when certain behaviour is tolerated or rights are granted, the tolerator merely indulges him- or herself. The important feature of this aspect of tolerance is that it puts tolerance in the context of a power balance. Tolerance is by definition a quality – and often perceived as a virtue – of those in power. Only those holding power have the luxury of being benevolent and tolerant.[19] Those who are subjected to the dominant power do not have the chance to be tolerant, for the simple reason that they are not in the position to decide whether or not they are willing to accept unwanted behaviour by those in power.

An important question is why one would tolerate unwanted behaviour in the first place. The two main arguments used in Western literature when answering this question are pragmatism and moral principle. The pragmatic view holds that the alternative to tolerance is conflict or war. A more cynical variation on this pragmatic view is that, even if those in power are willing to risk violent conflict in order to get rid of an unwanted people or community (and we will see many examples of such desires), the impossibility of such cleansing operation might prompt those in power to settle for second best, which is some form of tolerance, even if it were oppressive. Tolerance, in other words, is the only way to maintain a peaceful coexistence.[20] The principled view, on the other hand, holds that tolerance arises, or should arise, from a moral principle.[21] Tolerance is then a virtue or moral obligation that goes beyond the indifference of merely accepting disagreeable differences, but should engage in a form of recognition.

Religion and toleration make for an interesting concoction. Typical for religions like Christianity and Islam is that they have universal claims (salvation is only for those who embrace that faith) and are exclusive (the world is divided between believers and unbelievers). While many observers explain the alleged confrontation between the two by their universal claim,[22] I would argue that the main conflict is in their exclusive nature, for it divides the world (and the Afterworld, for that matter) into believers and unbelievers, us and them. Even the most tolerant Muslim or Christian will, as a believer, come to the point where he needs to acknowledge that the unbeliever may be a great colleague or friend but nevertheless is missing out on a world view that is essential to him, the believer. During the centuries, as we will see, this acknowledgement has been a reason for war and bloodshed at worst, and tolerant segregation at best. Europe has a long history in this respect with regard to Judaism, Christian heresies and denominational factions, but also in its relation with Muslims and Islam.

We will see in the following chapters that in the case of coexistence – i.e., different communities sharing a single territorial space – Muslims and Christians structured most of their legal, political and social interactions on the basis of religious categories. The exclusive nature of both Islam and Christianity created 'natural' demarcation lines between communities. Only under certain circumstances were deviations from and exceptions to these structures allowed. For instance, Christian and Islamic law does not allow for the non-believer to be in a position of authority over a believer, but there have been Muslim and Christian palace courts where infidels held high positions. Outside the courts, religious differences were often of little consequence and religious communities lived, worked and socialized together. But whenever there was social change or upheaval, the underlying structures prompted people to identify with a religious label, because that label marked their social, political and legal status.[23] And even when the religious categorization was formally abandoned by the Ottoman Empire and European states from the late eighteenth century onwards, we will see that religion remained an important factor of demarcation, whether culturally (Jews, and later Muslims, were not considered by everyone as belonging to the 'Christian' civilization of Europe), or as the schism between the religious and the secular.

Othering. The division between believers and unbelievers in the case of the interaction between Europe and Islam is more than a theological, political, social and legal construct that may be considered discriminatory or tolerant or otherwise. In addition to these practical and theoretical distinctions, there is also a cognitive dimension that gives rise to a perceived division between 'us' and 'them'. This is what in the social sciences is known as the process of 'Othering.' The Other is not merely an indication of a category of persons who are different, but primarily serves as a process to identify and profile oneself as opposed to that other. The Other embodies everything that We are not, and as such represents everything that We scorn or deny or, to put it more mildly, prefer not to be. As we will see in the next chapters, the notion of Othering is very helpful to describe the relationship between Islam and Europe. From a European perspective, Muslims and Islam represented more than a false religion or incidental interactions of warfare, commerce or science; they represented a permanent European Other.

In social sciences, the process of Othering is researched on numerous levels: man versus woman, white man versus black man, sane person versus madman, civilized person versus barbarian, occidental versus oriental, etc. In the context of this book, we find that most relevant research in this context has been conducted in the discipline of International Relations where the notion of Othering is discussed as a factor of interaction among European nation-states as well as the interaction between those states and non-European states.[24] An interesting point made by most of these scholars is that the centuries of Othering *within* Europe – that is, among European nations – have never undermined the prevailing sense of a single and unified European identity. Tony Judt notes the 'curious' characteristic of Europeans that emphasizing their mutual differences is precisely the factor that binds them: "Indeed, drawing distinctions among and between themselves has been one of the defining obsessions of the inhabitants of the continent."[25] This notion of a Europeanness as a diversity-in-unity has resulted in a process of Othering that was mainly directed outward, towards the non-European Other, pitting the 'West' against 'the Rest'.[26] Here, the Other was the primitive or savage, as opposed to the 'civilized' world of Europe. Europe perceived itself as rational, organized and cultured, characteristics that had propelled it into its state of power and prosperity. The notion of the un-civilized Other not only had a "reinforcing effect on the collective of Europe"[27] but has also been elaborated by postcolonial scholarship as "critical for the formation of Western modernity – without it, the West would not have been able to recognize and represent itself as the summit of human history".[28]

In addition to European Othering in terms of nation-states and civilizations, religion played a key role from the early Middle Ages onwards. European Christians divided the world into three categories: Christians, heretics (Christians who had to be brought back into the fold of the true Church) and infidels (non-Christians). This categorization may explain the unity-in-diversity among Europeans: they might fight and hate each other, but would always share the same Christian roots. The real Other was the infidel non-Christian. Christian scholars came to accept the notion of other religions as more or less equal belief-systems only in the eighteenth century, when Enlightenment prompted them to be critical of their own religion and to open their eyes to the world. And even though centuries of religious conflict and religious wars, culminating in the Thirty Years' War (1618–1648), appear to argue the opposite of the unity-in-diversity, the notion of Europe-as-Christendom has been called the 'grand narrative' of European identity: this narrative "possesses a sufficient degree of continuity and coherence to be a powerful factor both in intellectual history and in the collective unconsciousness of contemporary Europeans."[29] Indeed, such grand narratives can hardly be challenged "partly because their greatest power is at the level of the unconscious mind, collective and individual."[30] So powerful is this narrative that it has even survived the secularization of Europe since the nineteenth century. From that moment onwards, the Other was mostly defined in terms of culture and civilization, but Christendom was still considered an intrinsic part, and to some even the main propellant, of that European superior civilization.[31]

The question we want to address by using the approach of Otherness is: does Islam function as the European Other and, if so, how, when, and why at that particular moment, in that place? We will see that the image of Islam as the Other transforms through time, subject to the transformations that Europe is undergoing. And that brings us to another question: is Islam merely another Other in European self-identity, or does it play a special role in European history? At first glance, Islam does not appear to be very different from the other Others: Muslims as well as Islamic civilization have served as the anti-Christian archetype in medieval times and as the uncivilized Other during colonial times, and nowadays Islam is often perceived as the antithesis to modernity and its products of Enlightenment, freedom and democracy. In this respect, Islam is not an exceptional Other compared to the barbaric pagans of medieval Europe, the savages in foreign lands during colonial times, the Soviet Union during the Cold War, or any other form of social or political Othering. However, I would argue that within the notion of European Otherness, Islam takes a special position in several respects. First, its interaction with Europe has not been incidental or contingent, like the Communism or colonialism, but continuous, albeit in different forms for a period of thirteen centuries. Second, as a civilization, Islam has for several centuries been superior to Europe in numerous ways – militarily, economically, technically, intellectually, culturally – and consequently had a position different from that of the conventional Other who is to serve as the lesser alter ego. Third, Islam as a religion has always been a topic of discussion in European polemics, unlike other religions such as Judaism, Hinduism or animism. Moreover, these polemics did not confine themselves to theological dogma, but extended freely into the Islamic 'mind', 'nature' or 'culture' of its believers. The combination of these factors, through a period of thirteen centuries, has given Islam its special position as the European Other.

The aforementioned scholar Bernard Lewis also observes distinct characteristics of Islam that distinguishes it from "the European images of the Chinese or Indian," but for different reasons from those I have just mentioned. The difference, Lewis argues, is that the "Indians, after all, have never invaded Spain or crossed the Pyrenees; the Chinese had never conquered Constantinople or besieged Vienna", they never made attempts to convert Christians to their religious beliefs, and never had they condemned the Bible as obsolete and offered a new scripture to take its place; Europe and Islam, Bernard states, "were old acquaintances, intimate enemies".[32] This imagery represents a widely held European view of Islam but, as the next chapters will make clear, Lewis takes liberties with history, in particular by attributing the Muslims (and hence Islam, for he uses the two terms interchangeably) with an aggressive agency that is not always consistent with the facts.

CHAPTER ONE

Uncivilized Europe
(700–1000 CE)

I. Setting the Stage

Europe encountered Islam shortly after this new religion was established in the Arab Peninsula. The death of the prophet of Islam, Muhammad, in 632 CE caused only a brief period of internal strife among Muslims before the prophet's successors (caliphs) sent small but determined armies northwards, aimed at conquest. Their timing was perfect, although not intentionally so, because the two empires that they met on their way, the Byzantines in the Middle East and North Africa and the Sassanids in Iraq and Iran had by then worn each other out in centuries of military strife. Within years, the Muslim armies had vanquished these two empires and conquered vast territories. When the Islamic caliphate moved its capital from Medina to Damascus in 661 CE, its empire reached from present day Libya to Iran.

The sudden expansion of this new power hardly affected the inhabitants of Europe, however, because the Muslim conquests took place mainly outside the continent, with three exceptions: the (failed) attacks on the Byzantine capital of Constantinople which lies on the European side of the Bosporus, the quick conquest of the Iberian Peninsula in 711 CE and the laborious occupation of Sicily a century later. Villages on the European coastlines of the Mediterranean had to fear pirates, some of them Muslims operating from Tunisia or from one of the many Mediterranean islands. Beyond these regions, Europeans were aware of Muslims and Islam, but only in very vague terms and by means of crude images. The vast majority of Europeans could not care less: they were too busy surviving one of the most insecure and chaotic periods in Europe's history.

1. Europe at the Dawn of the Muslim Conquests

To explain the background to this period we must go back in time, to the fifth century. The collapse of the western part of the Roman Empire with its capital in Rome, in combination with vast migration waves of tribes and peoples from eastern to western Europe, had caused enormous chaos in all aspects of the word.[1] With the disappearance of political, social and economic structures, any sense of coherent life that we might call civilization had broken down. The network of long stretches of brick roads built by the Romans throughout Europe was left in disarray, and a similar fate befell the walls, schools, public baths and sewage systems of the cities. Reading and writing became an obsolete skill, and those who persevered in it had to make use of hides, since papyrus was no longer available. Worse, all knowledge that had once brought about the technical prowess of the Romans had gradually vanished, together with their statecraft, arts, literature and science.

The chapter of what once was the Roman Empire was closed for the peoples of western Europe who were now going through the lengthy and painful process of reinventing and re-establishing themselves. Hence the name Middle Ages, as the period between the Roman and Renaissance eras is called. Only the south-eastern part of the European continent was rescued from this collapse; here, the Byzantine Empire had succeeded the eastern Roman Empire. The Byzantines continued to build and expand a prosperous empire that comprised what is now called the Balkans, Turkey, the Middle East, North Africa and southern Italy.

An issue of debate is the extent to which the Muslim conquests in the late seventh and early eighth centuries were to be blamed for the Western European decline. Some historians have argued that the Muslims' occupation of the lands south of the Mediterranean and their ensuing maritime blockade of the entire Mediterranean deprived Europe of the chance to import vital goods and consequently cut off the main artery of the European economy.[2] This thesis has been contested, however, mainly because Europe's decline had already set in at a much earlier date than the Muslim conquests in the seventh century. Several historians even take the contrary position, arguing that the Muslim conquests had actually contributed to the later social, economic and technological revival of Western Europe rather than having caused its earlier decline.[3]

If any factor played a role in the European economic deterioration, then it was not Islam but Christianity. The Church strongly disapproved of wealth, preaching a return to poverty and ascetic life as the ultimate virtue. At a time when abbeys, churches and monasteries were perhaps the last institutions with capital to spend, the Catholic Church had forbidden all clergy from lending money at interest or trading as professional merchants as early as 325 CE (Council of Nicae). The Church put a ban on usury, which was decreed a crime by worldly leaders like Charlemagne in the late eight century. Consequently, Western Europe for several centuries "was deprived of its financiers, bankers, great merchants, and contractors; in other words, specialists in production and exchange".[4] The strict enforcement of Christian rules regarding usury, capital and wealth was a reason for the continuation, if not the cause, of an early medieval European economy that was in a complete shambles: the use of money had become nearly obsolete and was largely replaced by a barter economy, investment was almost nil due to the strict enforcement of the usury ban; and consequently the development of a financial and economic infrastructure was non-existent. This situation was to change only around 1000 CE, as we will see in the next chapter.

In this early era, two European powers played a key role in the interactions with the new Muslim neighbour. The first was the Byzantine Empire, the eastern part of the former Roman Empire that had started a new life while the western part slumped and collapsed. The Byzantine Empire grew powerful in terms of territory as well as politics, military might and culture. It even managed to retain its power and civilization after the Arab Muslims had usurped most of its territories in the Middle East and North Africa.

The second empire that played an important role in this epoch was that of the Carolingian Franks, with their power base in France. This empire arose from the European debris of the Western Roman Empire, and was of an entirely different nature from the Byzantine Empire because it was, in the words of one historian, "religiously intolerant, intellectually impoverished, socially calcified, and economically primitive".[5] Its pinnacle of success and power was the reign of Charlemagne who ruled from 768 until 814, and who had pledged his allegiance to the Roman papacy as champion of Christianity. He unified large parts of Europe under the Frankish-Christian banner, but his military campaigns were fought with increasing religious fanaticism, aimed at the conversion of the conquered tribes by force of the sword and exercising vengeful ferocity against those who resisted or who reverted to their heathen ways. Even nations that were already Christian fell under the Frankish sword with the allegation that they were not true Christians.[6] All this was done with the blessing of the Pope and with the help of missionary priests who accompanied the Frankish armies.[7]

The Carolingians and Byzantines did not see eye to eye, and there was serious rivalry and even hostility between the two powers. The most conspicuous difference between them was their interpretation of Christianity: the Carolingians in the west followed the Christianity that was Latin in language and rite, with its papal seat in Rome, while the Byzantines in the east followed the Christianity of Constantinople that was Greek in language and rite. Both sides therefore claimed superiority over all Christendom and made a point of not recognizing the supreme leaders of the rival church. Given the close relationship between clerical and worldly power, the claim to power over the Christian flock was not a mere theological issue, but a matter of power and therefore a continual bone of contention. This antagonism was aggravated by considerations of a more material nature. The richness and opulence of the Byzantine Empire, and in particular its capital Constantinople, was a thorn in the side of the impoverished and primitive Western European. The Byzantines also did not miss an opportunity to express their contempt for the intellectual and technological backwardness of the Europeans. This streak of enmity that divided Europe must be kept in mind when we take a closer look at the interactions with the new adversary: Islam.

2. The Islamic Empire

In the period when Europe was still in decline, the Muslims, by contrast, established a thriving empire which they had built with dazzling speed, not only in territorial terms, but also culturally, economically and politically. The relative security within their vast empire brought about a Pax Islamica that stimulated an ever-increasing cultural and economic prosperity, culminating in what became known as the golden age that lasted until the end of the tenth century CE.[8]

After the brief reign of the so-called 'Rightly guided caliphs', the Islamic empire was ruled from 661 to 750 by the Umayyad dynasty from its capital Damascus, which was then replaced by the Abbasid dynasty that moved the capital eastwards, to Baghdad. By then, the empire stretched from Morocco and the Iberian Peninsula to present-day Afghanistan and Central Asia. With the moving of the capital eastward to Baghdad in 762 CE, the focus of the empire gravitated towards Asia, with China and India as the main sources of commerce and knowledge. The Mediterranean basin remained of only marginal importance, being located on the western outskirts of the empire.

Commerce in particular benefited from the security of the Pax Islamica across the vastness of the empire. Trade could now be conducted along routes that stretched from East Asia to West Africa and were dotted with caravanserais, the walled edifices that combined hostel and trade centre. These same routes facilitated the flow of knowledge and technology across the empire.[9] This was particularly important for agriculture, one of the backbones of the prosperity of the inhabitants of the Islamic Empire. Crops that did well in semi-arid areas of India and Mesopotamia were transplanted to other regions in the empire with similar climates and, in combination with new agricultural techniques, allowing for an increase in harvests.[10]

One of the main features of this golden age was the patronage of arts and sciences by the caliphate court. At the heart of this patronage was the collection of scholarly and scientific tracts from all over the empire for study by scholars in Baghdad. A multitude of Greek, Persian and Sanskrit scholarly manuscripts was collected and translated into Arabic, becoming an immense source of knowledge on a range of sciences. The Arab Muslim scholars assigned to study these tracts in turn furthered the theories and sciences they became acquainted with.[11] This scholarly enterprise, which had already started in the eight century when the new Abbasid caliphate had moved its seat to Baghdad, soon became institutionalized in the famous and prestigious 'House of Wisdom', an academic research centre *avant la lettre*.

With the exception of the Iberian Peninsula, the Islamic empire did not seem to care much about Europe at that time: Europe had very little to offer, and in terms of commerce and knowledge the Muslims mostly turned eastwards, toward India and China. The little trade that existed between Europe and the Islamic Empire was mostly a one-way affair based on European demand for goods from the Islamic Empire, and hardly the other way round. Moreover, the Muslims did not venture out to trade across the Mediterranean; they would take their caravans as far as the Byzantine Empire while Constantinople dominated trade further into the Mediterranean basin. Knowledge was not yet in demand by the Europeans – that became a commodity only after the tenth century, as we will see in the next chapter.

II. Physical Islam

1. The Realm of Interaction

Now that we have outlined the division of powers and territories in the period between 700 and 1000, we come to the main question: how did the people of the two sides interact, and what was the role of religion in this interaction? As we have already seen, virtual interaction was very limited: Europeans had no interest in Islam as a religion or civilization, or in its technologies or knowledge. What little we know of the images that Europeans held of Muslims and Islam will be discussed at the end of this chapter. Interaction was mostly of a physical nature, which was of course dominated by battles and raids, but also by diplomacy, trade and, most importantly, by the coexistence of these peoples in three territories: Constantinople, the Iberian Peninsula and Sicily. The situations of these three regions were quite different, and therefore merit separate introductions before we will take a closer look at their inhabitants.

Constantinople and the Byzantine Empire

When the Arab Muslim warriors rode out into the Middle East for the first time in 634 CE, the Byzantine Empire's territories encompassed present-day Sicily, southern Italy, the Balkans, Greece, Turkey, the Middle East and North Africa, and as such had been spared most of the wars and migrations of the European peoples that had ravaged and disrupted the European mainland in the previous centuries. Before the Muslims, the only real threat had come from the east, from the Huns in Central Asia and the rival empire of the Sassanids in Persia, but the Byzantines were able to repel them. However, by the time the Arab Muslim armies emerged in the seventh century the Byzantine Empire was too weakened to put up sufficient military resistance. The Arab Muslim armies swiftly took the larger Byzantine cities in the Middle East, like Jerusalem in 637 CE. The Muslims' victories were aided not only by the Byzantine inability to defend its territories, but also by the little resistance put up by the Byzantine subjects themselves. In several cases, they even welcomed the new Muslim conquerors, because their promise of religious freedom was a much better alternative than the persecution they endured from Constantinople that vehemently opposed their sectarian views of Christianity.[12]

The Muslim conquest of Byzantine territory took place in several stages, spread out over a period of seventy years. The Byzantine Empire lost most of its dominions in the Middle East and North Africa, and was left with its territories on the European continent and with the region what nowadays is Turkey.[13] The Arab Muslim armies even laid siege to the city of Constantinople in 674 CE, and again in 717 CE. The last siege of the city ended in a devastating defeat for the Muslim armies. From that moment onwards, the two powers maintained their territorial positions with continuous skirmishes and raids in the border areas.

The Byzantine loss of most of its territories to the Arab Muslims plunged the remnant of the Byzantine Empire on the European continent into what some historians have called a 'dark age'. Trade between the remainder of the Byzantine Empire and the former Byzantine lands that were now part of the Islamic empire diminished dramatically.[14] The centuries-old economic infrastructure was utterly disrupted now that large portions of the empire were lost. Being cut off from the granaries of Egypt and North Africa was only one of the many problems that Byzantium faced. The despair also showed culturally: "fewer authors wrote, fewer teachers taught, fewer artists and artisans created, and fewer builders built."[15] The demoralization was further reflected in arguments on God's displeasure with the Byzantines, resulting in disputes about religious doctrine.

Al-Andalus: The Emirate and Caliphate of Cordoba

The Muslim conquest of the Iberian Peninsula seems to have been driven by chance rather than by strategy. The peninsula was invaded in 711 CE, less than a century after the Muslim conquests had started, and almost at the same time as, on the other side of the Mediterranean, the Muslims were being repulsed from their siege of Constantinople. The army of twenty thousand warriors was led by general Tariq, who left his name to the mountainous outcropping at the most southern point of the peninsula (Gibraltar, from Gabal Tari', 'mountain of Tariq'). The peninsula at the time was ruled by the Visigoths, one of the Germanic tribes that had moved from eastern Europe during the migration period, and who had converted to Christianity. Several scholars have questioned whether the conquest of the Iberian Peninsula can be called a Muslim conquest, given that the bulk of the invaders were ethnically Berbers who were brought under Arab dominion only several years earlier and whose recent conversion to Islam was probably symbolic at best,[16] but also because the local population did not conceive of the invaders from Morocco in religious terms as a threat to their own Christianity.[17] Their resistance to the invaders was meagre, and the Visigoth kingdom collapsed when its king was killed during the first battle. The easy walk-in by the Muslim army therefore hardly deserves the name of conquest, but was more a take-over, especially with many of the inhabitants applauding the replacement of the Visigoths by a less oppressive ruler.[18]

The Arab-Berber presence in Spain – which was known in Arabic as Andalus (derived from '(V)andals', the predecessors of the Visigoths) – gained momentum when a prince of the Umayyad caliphate fled from Damascus after the establishment of the new caliphate of the Abbasids in 750 CE, and made it all the way to the Iberian Peninsula where he was put on the throne as a ruler. The prince had a land to rule, Andalus had its legitimate ruler, and together as the emirate (princedom) of Cordoba they embarked on an adventure that turned out to be of historical proportions. Although geographically and politically disconnected from the Islamic Empire with its capital in far-away Baghdad, the emirate was an indissoluble part of Islamic civilization.

The presence of Arab-Islamic rule in Andalus was to continue for almost eight centuries, from 711 to 1492 CE. The presence of a Muslim population was to last longer, as we will see in the third chapter. Already in the ninth century its economic and agricultural progress made Andalus "at least four centuries more advanced that Western Christendom."[19] The tenth century witnessed a true golden age, spurred on and influenced by the economic, cultural, scientific and social achievements that took place in the entire Islamic Empire. The emirate became a caliphate from 929 to 1031 CE, and the capital of Cordoba was by then the largest city of the European continent, with approximately 100,000 inhabitants, to be matched only by Constantinople in the east.[20] In addition to all this prosperity, the caliphate also initiated what became known as a green revolution by introducing new irrigation techniques and new crops such as rice, sugar-cane, cotton, oranges, lemons, bananas, spinach, artichokes and aubergines.[21]

The emirate – later caliphate – and its Frankish neighbours on the other side of the Pyrenees made regular raids and incursions into each other's territories. Another small neighbour within the Iberian Peninsula, however, was to prove the proverbial nail in the coffin of the Muslim reign in the peninsula. The Arab-Muslim conquest had not covered the entire peninsula, and in the north several small Christian kingdoms remained. The seat of power of the Muslim realm was way down in the south, first in Cordoba and later in Granada, and its rulers had little interest in the north. Just as in the case of Byzantium and the Islamic Empire, the frontier between the Christian north and Muslim south was a fluid affair, a zone for mutual raids and trade rather than a fixed and impregnable line. This more or less stable situation would continue for several centuries, but changed dramatically to the disadvantage of the emirate in the eleventh century, as we will see in the next chapter.

Sicily

The other part of geographical Europe where Muslims were to live together with Christians was Sicily. This island in the middle of the Mediterranean had been occupied or colonized by the main powers that had dominated the Mediterranean in the past: the Phoenicians from the Levant, Carthaginians from North Africa, Romans from Italy and the Byzantines from Asia Minor.

At the time of the Arab-Muslim conquests, Sicily was under Byzantine rule, with a population that was predominantly Christian and mostly Greek- or Latin-speaking. Due to the maritime dominance at the time of the Byzantines, Sicily remained untouched by the early Arab aggression that went over land. Only when the Arabs had firmly established themselves in Tunisia (called Ifriqiya or 'Africa' in Arabic) did they cast hungry eyes at the island that on clear days could be seen on the horizon. From the Tunisian coasts the Arab Muslims engaged in pirate raids across the sea into Sicily and beyond, to the coastal areas of southern France and western Italy.

Starting in 827 CE, more than a century after the Arab-Muslim conquest of the Iberian Peninsula and almost two centuries after the first Arab-Muslim conquests from Mecca had started, Tunisian piracy turned to conquest: in the following years cities in Sicily were taken and, after initial plundering, Arab-Berber Muslim colonists from North Africa moved in to settle there. In the following century, Muslim domination never encompassed the entire island, because of recurrent uprisings from the native (Christian) population. It is therefore impossible to suggest a date from when one can speak of 'Islamic Sicily'.[22]

The political heart of Muslim power was located in the city of Palermo, which became a thriving centre of Arab-Islamic culture and gave Arab Sicily the name 'the little sister of al-Andalus'. The many religious jurists and scholars, grammarians, scientists and poets of great repute quickly earned Sicily intellectual and academic fame.[23] Like Andalus, Sicily also benefited from the agricultural innovations imported from North Africa, creating a second green revolution. Muslim domination of Sicily remained for over a century and a half, until it was ended in the late tenth century by the Normans.

2. Living with the Unbeliever

Both Islam and Christianity are monotheistic religions with a claim to universality. However, the urgency of spreading the word has manifested itself quite differently in the early Muslim and European worlds: European Christian conquerors, and especially Charlemagne, waged an aggressive policy of forced conversions, while Muslim conquerors did not. Also, given the chronological emergence of Judaism, Christianity and Islam, there was quite a difference between the two religions in their recognition of the other two religions: Islam recognizes Judaism and Christianity as its precursors, but Christianity recognizes neither (not Judaism because its adherents had betrayed Jesus, and not Islam because it was unknown at the time of emerging Christianity). Apart from these theological viewpoints, it is important to note that the worlds encountered by Islam and Christianity in their early days were very different: Christianity manifested itself in early medieval Europe, while Islam encountered the highly sophisticated civilizations of the Byzantines and Sassanides. All these differences had their effect on the coexistence of Muslims and Christians. In the period under discussion here, this coexistence at first took place predominantly under Islamic rule, and only later – especially since the late tenth century – also under Christian rule.

The Issue of Conversion

As has already been mentioned, conversion – whether voluntary or forced – took place in quite different ways under Christianity and Islam. In the European setting, early Christianity had spread gradually and sporadically, mostly by the efforts of missionaries. Conversion was not a personal choice for a new faith but rather the adoption of a new set of forms of worship, and therefore often a communal rather than an individual affair.[24] The conversion of a king would usually imply the conversion of his entire people. Later, under the Carolingian kings, in particular Charlemagne, conquests were accompanied by forced conversion. This coercion to convert, whether by missionary or forced means, was not exerted, however, on the Jews nor, later, on the Muslims who lived in Europe (except in Spain in the late fifteenth century, as we will discuss at length in the third chapter).

The situation in the Islamic realm was quite different from that of Christianity. Whereas Christianity first spread gradually through missionary activities and then was established by conquest, the Islamic situation was the reverse: first an empire was established by conquest and then, gradually, Islam spread within that empire.

Another distinct difference between the Christian and Islamic realms was that the peoples subdued by the Muslim armies were not pagan tribal peoples, as was the case in Europe, but established religious communities and civilizations – mainly Jews, Christians and Zoroastrians – that were much more advanced than the tribal Arab-Muslims who subdued them. But the most striking feature of Muslim conquest was that the conquering Muslim armies as a general rule did not impose on their non-Muslim subjects a compulsory conversion to Islam, nor was there any Muslim missionary activity among the non-believers.

Why did the conquering Muslim armies not convert all subjected peoples to Islam? Various reasons have been advanced by historians to explain this curious – from a Christian perspective, that is – position. First there is a theological answer: Islam does not allow forced conversion, as it is explicitly prohibited by the Quran.[25] Also, the Quran specifically mentions Jews and Christians as people to be recognized as predecessors to Islam and who need to be respected in their faiths. The second answer is of a military and political nature: the small bands of Arab-Muslim warriors would not have been able to impose and maintain the forced conversion of the entire population of such a vast conquered area. The third answer is related to ethnic superiority: although Islam claims universality, the Muslims of the Arab Peninsula who rode out to conquer the world were Arabs, and this first generation of Muslims considered Islam to be exclusively meant for Arabs, and for a long time non-Arabs could adopt Islam only if they were sponsored by an Arab.[26] It took a revolt by converted Persians to alter this ethnic exclusivity. The fourth answer that explains the lack of conversion zeal among the Muslim conquerors is financial, and according to most historians was probably the decisive reason not to convert the conquered peoples to Islam: the non-Muslims of the Islamic empire had to pay a poll tax that was not obligatory for Muslims. Conversion meant that the poll tax was no longer obligatory, and massive conversion would therefore lead to a lack of income for the Muslim conquerors who very much needed these taxes to build the empire and finance new campaigns.[27]

The Muslim reticence in converting the conquered unbelievers created the paradoxical situation of an Islamic empire being ruled by a Muslim minority. This was also the situation at first in Spain and Sicily. To call these powers and civilizations 'Islamic' is therefore, correctly speaking, in reference to the religion and culture of those in power, and does not refer to the majority population. Nevertheless, conversion to Islam by the native population, and the consequential change of an increasing Muslim population in the Islamic empire, eventually did take place, but was a gradual process. The speed of this process differed according to region, but it definitely took a long time, sometimes centuries, before Muslims became a majority in the various parts of the Islamic Empire.[28]

The reasons for conversion to Islam are generally assumed to be material, namely to get rid of the special poll tax for non-Muslims and to gain access to positions of authority and power, which were reserved for Muslims only. Another and perhaps even more compelling reason to convert to Islam was that in societies where religion was more a communal identity than an individual faith, converting to the religion of the ruler was the means to express one's acceptance of the dominant order. In the case of Al-Andalus, it has been argued that conversion by native Christians to Islam was mainly prompted by their wish or need to fully participate in the culture and society of al-Andalus which was, at least theoretically, restricted to Muslims.[29] We will see later, with the progress of the Islamic-Christian history in Europe, that this was a recurring phenomenon among Christians under Muslim rule. Interestingly, the reverse was hardly the case: very few Muslims under Christian rule would convert to Christianity. But this situation – i.e., of Muslims living under Christian rule – would only take place much later, and we will leave that to the next chapter. In the period under discussion here, that is between 700 and 1000 CE, very few Muslims in Europe were subjects under Christian rule.

Religious Rule

We must start with a remark on terminology that is to be borne in mind when reading this and the following chapters. When we speak of 'rule' this is not to be understood as the rule of a majority over minorities. As we have just seen, such majority rule was not always the case: in many instances the Muslim rulers constituted the minority in the society where they lived. 'Islam' ruled, but the Muslims for a long time constituted a minority in their own empire. This was to repeat itself under Islamic rule in Spain and in the European domains of the Ottoman Empire. The correct manner of describing the power arrangement within a realm is therefore more often to speak of ruler and subject instead of majority and minority.

Christian and Islamic rulers all claimed to have established God's rule and to uphold God's law. But what did this say about the treatment of non-believers? Should they be converted, or subjected to God's rule as upheld by the rulers, or be left to their own religious law? Here also we see another distinct difference between Christianity and Islam. Let us start with Christianity. From a theological point of view, Christianity in the period between the seventh and eleventh centuries considered all non-Christians to be pagans who had to be converted to Christianity, by force if need be. However, Christian rulers made an exception for Jews and later, when Muslims became subject to Christian rule, also for them. This exception should not be construed as recognition, but was merely the result of circumstances. Given the very few non-Christians in early medieval Europe, at least in those parts of Europe that were under Christian rule, no formal position was developed as regards such communities. The freedom of the Jews to practise their religion was limited to what the Christians believed to be the correct interpretation of the Old Testament, the Pope being the ultimate judge of what constituted correct Jewish doctrine.[30] This marginal toleration of the Jews, often combined with forms of social discrimination (they were excluded from several occupations, for example, and from membership of guilds), would turn quite ugly after the eleventh century.

The only Christian realm in Europe where Muslim subjects lived under Christian rule during the period between 700 and 1000 CE was the Byzantine capital Constantinople. These Muslims were an amalgamation of different backgrounds and origins. Most Muslims in Constantinople lived there on a temporary basis: merchants and prisoners of war waiting to be ransomed. They probably inhabited the Muslim quarter of Constantinople. Here also resided the 'permanent' Muslim residents: the Arabs, Persians and Kurds who had voluntarily offered their military services – an Arab chronicler in 943 CE mentioned 1,200 Arab cavalrymen in the Byzantine army.[31] This was not a typical Arab phenomenon: the opposite also happened, with Christians crossing the Arab-Byzantine frontier and seeking refuge in or offering their services to Arab rulers. Other Muslim permanent residents in Constantinople were prisoners of war who had accepted the offer of their Byzantine capturers to merge into Byzantine society by settling on plots of land.[32]

In addition to the presence of Muslim sojourners and residents in Constantinople, Arab chronicles speak of a mosque in Constantinople as early as the eighth century. It is said that it was built by, or at the request of, general Maslama, after whom the mosque was named. He had led the legendary expedition against Byzantium in 717 CE, and the mosque as well as the prison built for the Muslim prisoners of war was possibly part of his conditions for lifting the siege. The exact location of the Maslama mosque, as it became known, has never been found, however: it was destroyed around 1200 and, according to Arab chroniclers, rebuilt by the Byzantines in 1263, although this reconstruction could have been confused with the alleged construction of another mosque at the time by the Byzantine emperor to please the Mamluks who then ruled the Levant and who were in the process of mopping up the last remnants of the Crusaders' presence.[33]

The situation as regards non-believers was quite different in the Muslim realm, in terms both of Islamic law and the practice of Islamic rule. Islamic religious doctrine formally recognizes the so-called religions 'of the book', that is Judaism and Christianity, and this recognition was extended to Zoroastrianism and in practice also to Hinduism, creating in the Muslim realm multi-religious societies with Islam as dominating religion. Islamic law developed a legal status for these non-Muslim communities as 'protected people' (dhimmi), which formally meant that they enjoyed full religious freedom and legal autonomy in religious affairs within their religious community in exchange for a poll tax and recognition of the Muslims' sovereignty.

Of course theory and practice were not always in concordance. Legally, the status of the dhimmis provided both advantages and disadvantages.[34] An important advantage was that non-Muslims were allowed religious freedom and autonomy in religious affairs, including religious family law, which they were allowed to apply within their community. Religious freedom meant that these non-Muslims were exempted from several rules of Islamic law that were considered applicable only to Muslims. These exemptions were the rules of marriage and divorce (some Muslim scholars included inheritance and custody law as well), the consumption of and trade in pork and alcohol and, according to a majority of Muslim scholars, the rules of Islamic penal law as specifically determined by the Quran. These rules would officially not apply to non-Muslims.

The disadvantage of Islamic law, on the other hand, was that it granted non-Muslims a second-class status: non-Muslims were not allowed to take on a position of authority (for that would grant a non-Muslim authority over a Muslim), had to pay a separate poll tax, and were subjected to all kinds of rules devaluating the legal status of a non-Muslim to half of that of a Muslim, and discriminatory rules intended to emphasize the difference between Muslims and non-Muslims, like the prohibition on wearing certain types of cloth or riding certain animals.

As said, legal theory was not always the same as social practice. The situation of non-Muslim subjects could be better but also worse than their legal status. First and foremost, dhimmi status was usually granted only to cities that surrendered: resistance often led to pillaging the town and its inhabitants being sold into slavery (this was not typical of Muslim conquests but the general code of war at that time, as we will see later). But even when the pact of dhimmitude had been established with non-Muslim communities, practice could differ from the letter of the law. For instance, Jews and Christians held high positions at the Islamic courts of Baghdad, Palermo and Cordoba in the tenth century, a status which was formally not allowed by Islamic law. In other instances, non-Muslims were worse off than their official status, for instance when, contrary to Islamic law, they were subjected to discriminatory rules or even incidental persecution.

Tolerance and Social Tensions

The rules and practices of Islam as regards non-Muslim minorities as described above are largely reflected in the two European territories where Muslim rule was established in the early middle ages: the Iberian Peninsula and Sicily. When the splendour of military glory and the excitement of booty had worn off, the two realms were seen by the Muslim conquerors as dominions where they would settle and rule. There was no agenda of conversion: the native inhabitants were allowed to continue their ways as long as they recognized the new rulers and paid the special poll tax.

This situation has prompted observers to describe it in terms of tolerance.[35] Some nuance is required here, however. Insofar as historians can gain insight into the everyday life of those times, it has been shown that these Muslims and non-Muslims lived separate lives, perhaps only meeting in the market place or, in the case of conflict, in law courts.[36] Toleration in this respect does not mean a pluralistic community, but a pragmatic live and let live, based mainly on indifference and segregation. This could be different at the palace courts, the centres of power where enlightened rulers would allow non-Muslim intellectuals and artists to participate in government, science, arts and intellectual debates. These people would produce the writings that are preserved in history, and therefore these episodes are best known, while outside the palaces the treatment of commoners could be much worse.

For instance, during the period of Muslim rule in Sicily, the initial treatment of the native Christian population – including shipping them off into slavery to North Africa – apparently was such that they had little reason to welcome the new rulers, and there are various accounts of native Christians rising in revolt or migrating to Italy.[37] With many Christian communities, however, the Muslims concluded the so-called dhimmi pacts that granted them religious freedom and a certain degree of autonomy in exchange for their allegiance and payment of a poll tax. But the combination of depopulation by migrating Christians, repopulation by Muslim settlers from North Africa, and the remaining Christians' gradual conversion to Islam caused the Sicilian population to become a Muslim majority.[38]

While the conquest of Sicily was part of, or the result of plunder raids that had been taking place for decades, the conquerors of the Iberian Peninsula were much more indulgent with the native population. Muslim rule as established in Andalus in the centuries to come even gained a reputation for its religious tolerance. Given the circumstances of the time and the comparison with Europe of that time, this admiration is definitely justified. But one must keep in mind that Islam, however tolerant of other religions, remained the authoritative code of morality and behaviour. Islam was to be recognized as the dominating religion, and to be respected as such. Blasphemy and insults to Islam were not acceptable, nor apostasy from Islam. The reverse, on the other hand, was not considered an affront to public order: although apostasy from Christianity or Judaism was also forbidden by these religions, it was allowed by Islam as it meant conversion to Islam. And since Islam had supremacy, that was to be the rule.

This situation was challenged in the ninth century by the so-called martyrs of Cordoba.[39] In the period between 851 and 859 CE, a succession of, in total, forty-eight Christians were decapitated for publicly denouncing the prophet Muhammad and disparaging Islam. Most of these 'martyrs' – that is the title that Christian posterity gave them – were ascetic monks, but among them were also descendants from mixed Christian-Muslim marriages. The latter case proved particular serious, because even though these people considered themselves Christian, according to Islamic law they were Muslim since they were the offspring of a marriage between a Muslim man and a Christian woman, and their children consequently follow the religion of the father.* In these particular cases, however, the children persisted publicly in the religion of their mother and were therefore, from the Islamic point of view, Muslims guilty of the capital crime of apostasy from Islam. For these people there was little mercy. The monks, on the other hand, who publicly denounced Mohammed as a false prophet were treated leniently at first, being arrested and then sent away with a warning or a beating. Only when they persisted in returning to the public squares declaring the vileness of Islam and its prophet did the Muslim rulers apply the capital punishment.

Several reasons have been advanced for this curious trend of deliberately seeking martyrdom: was it the defiance of Muslim rule, a reaction to provocation by Muslims or, in the case of Christians with Muslim fathers, the challenge of parental authority? Any of these reasons seem plausible, but none of them explain why these events took place in this particular moment. A compelling reason is that this period of time witnessed the shifting balance in society in favour of Arab Muslim culture, which created unrest among the Christian population and led to the public denunciation

---

* That is also the reason that the opposite – a marriage between a Muslim woman and a Jewish or Christian man – is not allowed under Islamic law because that would make the children follow their father's Judaism or Christianity.

of that culture.[40] In particular native Christians who were adopting various aspects of the increasingly dominating culture of the Arab-Berber Muslim rulers, were a source of discontent among their fellow native Christians.[41] While the Muslims in Andalus were initially a tiny minority among a Christian majority, their number is estimated to have risen to 20–30 per cent by 850 CE, the period of the martyrs of Cordoba.[42] This percentage was to rise to 50 per cent in the next century, indicating a steady increase in conversions as well as influx of settlers from North Africa. This development had two consequences. On the one hand, there are recorded incidents of Muslims who abused their status of dominance by publicly defying Christians. On the other hand, it brought many Christians under Muslim rule to accommodate to Muslim dominance, among others by switching to speaking Arabic (hence their name *mozarabs*, which means 'those who are Arabized'). These developments incited some Christians to defend their religion, culture and way of life from being appropriated by the dominating Muslim culture.

The resulting stand-off by the martyrs of Cordoba can therefore be interpreted as a criticism not only of Muslims but also of fellow-Christians who were accused of giving up their Christian identity. The Muslim authorities responded with increasing severity towards the martyrs, but also towards the Christian community in general by enforcing a separate dress code and closing palace functions to Christians – rules that were already part of Islamic law but apparently had not been strictly applied before. The Christian community also responded with criticism of these acts of martyrdom, probably because they feared that their social and legal position in Andalus was put at risk.

This argument – avoiding criticism of Islam or Islamic rule in order not to jeopardize the delicate social position of the Christian community under Islamic rule – recurred a century later, with the visit of a delegation from King Otto I to the court in Cordoba in 954 CE.[43] At that time, caliph Abd ar-Rahman III of Andalus (ruled 912–961 CE) and King Otto, the first Holy Roman Emperor (ruled 936–973 CE) were the two most mighty rulers in Europe, and on several occasions they had exchanged delegates to negotiate certain issues. During Abd ar-Rahman's rule Andalus enjoyed the golden age for which it is renown. The martyrs of Cordoba were an incident of the past and non-Muslims were restored to favour, for they were again allowed to hold high positions at court. This was shown by the delegation of King Otto being received first by the caliph's personal physician, who was a Jew, and then by the bishop of Cordoba. The bishop, however, was sneered at by the head of Otto's delegation, abbot John of Gorze, for being too submissive to the rule of a religion inferior to Christianity. The abbot's disdain for the bishop only increased with the bishop's rising panic about the abbot's resolve publicly to denounce Islam once the caliph had received his delegation. This never came to pass, however, probably because the bishop made sure the delegation was sent back home without meeting the caliph.

3. Other Relations and Contacts

The general picture of relations between European Christians and Arab Muslims in the period between the eighth and eleventh centuries is that both sides mostly kept to themselves and met only on the battlefield. Indeed, the political, economic and cultural developments within the two realms took place in relative isolation from each other. However, the image of two isolated warring blocks that are predominantly characterized by their religious identity does not do justice to the complexity of everyday life, for there existed an intricate interaction of warfare and raids alternating with diplomacy and trade.

An important aspect we must keep in mind when viewing this period is that these two realms were not stable and singular unities: borders were fluid and under constant threat, and even within each of the realms there was the continuous peril of disintegration into political and warring factions, with warlords on both sides of the Mediterranean carving out their private fiefdoms. To preserve their power, lords on both sides would occasionally turn to each other for military assistance against a common foe. In the meantime, hostilities did not hinder commerce between the two sides, albeit on a very limited scale. Here we will pay closer attention to the nature of the belligerency, trade and diplomacy between the two realms in this period.

Wars and Raids

The armed conflicts that characterized relations between European Christians and Arab Muslims in this period were of two kinds: wars of conquest and raids. In the wars of conquest the Arab Muslims had the upper hand. Granted, the Carolingians in Europe also undertook wars of conquest, but these were directed northwards and eastwards rather than southwards, and therefore did not lead to military confrontations with Arab Muslims. So if we are to look at wars of conquest wherein Arabs and Europeans met on the battlefield, the Arabs were in almost all instances the aggressor, and we see hardly any organized European campaigns to fight the Muslim invaders or, once the Muslims had settled in European territory, to evict them. Europe simply lacked the centralized power to initiate such organized defence. The only exception was the Byzantine Empire, but its defence was futile against the agile and fast-moving Arab Muslim warrior bands. The other European power, the Carolingians, was established after the Muslim conquests were more or less complete, and even then it undertook hardly any action against the Saracens, despite what the Song of Roland or other European legends may have us believe.

Apart from the Arab-Muslim and Carolingian wars waged for the purpose of conquest, most wars in these times were actually raids aimed primarily at raising slaves, booty and tribute from border areas that served as "hunting grounds".[44] The purpose of these military confrontations was the maintenance of the border areas, resulting in the re-taking of the strips of land usurped by the opponent and the plunder of his lands. This feature of armed conflict was omnipresent, including in the frontier areas that divided the Muslim and Christian realms. Every year, Baghdad and Constantinople would dispatch an army to the frontier they shared, not as forces of conquest but to plunder the lands of the other and to defend their own land against the raiding enemy. In Baghdad the raids on the Muslim-Byzantine border took on almost ritualistic forms as they were scheduled bi-annually by court officials.[45] These raids took place in the frontier zone in present-day Turkey, but were extended to Byzantine dominions in Greece and Italy once the Muslims learned to build ships and sail them, extending the conflict zone into the Mediterranean with repeated acts of piracy against the European coasts.[46] Sicily was one of the Mediterranean islands that fell victim to these raids before it was turned from 'hunting ground' into Muslim territory.

The raiders and pirates did not always pick the infidel as victim: the Muslims in Crete became notorious for piracy against Muslims and Christians alike, just as the Christian Slavs who raided up and down the Adriatic and the Venetians were not too scrupulous in their religious selection of an occasional prey to piracy.[47] When the raiding of one side became too regular, it prompted counter measures from the other side, and sometimes such punitive actions resulted in conquest. For instance, it has been suggested that the Arab occupation of Italian ports was brought about by Italian piracy against Arab shipping.[48]

The other Muslim-Christian zone of confrontation was between the Western Europeans – the Carolingians, but also Frankish, German and Italian rulers and warlords residing along the western Mediterranean coastline – and the 'Saracens' and 'Moors' in Andalus and North Africa. According to European collective memory, the advance of the Muslims across the Pyrenees was stopped at Poitiers in southern France, as we will discuss in more detail below. But for centuries, the Pyrenees and the French Mediterranean coast were the zone of mutual raiding between Arabs and Europeans. Attacks in this zone were initiated not only by the craving for spoils, but also upon request of local rulers who used the enemy to fight another adversary. An illustrative example is the three Moorish governors of Barcelona, Zaragoza and Huesca who in 777–778 CE sent a delegation across the Pyrenees to France, offering Charlemagne parts of northern Spain in exchange for a guarantee of autonomy for their respective small governorates.[49] The reason for this overture was that the three governors felt their autonomous rule threatened by the growing power of their over-lord, the caliphate in Cordoba. Charlemagne was most willing to be of assistance, not only for strategic reasons but also because it fitted into his worldview of spread-ing Christianity by conquest. His army marched into Spain that same year but the campaign ended in a humiliating failure because no Muslim cities were conquered. Moreover, upon his retreat to France in 778 CE, Charlemagne's baggage train was at-tacked by Basques when crossing the Pyrenees. The military embarrassment seemed complete but was glossed over in the chronicles of that time, and three centuries later even transformed into a victory of mythical proportions in the Song of Roland. In this song the (Christian) Basques are replaced by the Saracens, and count Roland repre-sents the archetype of the gallant Christian knight suffering martyrdom while fight-ing the overwhelming forces of Islam.[50] The Song can be considered the European ur-text for embedding the Islamic threat "deep in the memory banks of the West."[51]

Another example of combined raiding, conquest and military alliances is pro-vided by the Arab presence in the late ninth and early tenth centuries along what is nowadays called the Cote d'Azur, the French and Italian coasts of the Mediterra-nean.[52] Already this area had suffered from Arab piracy, mostly initiated from the North African coast, with the sacking of Rome in 846 CE being only one of the many raids. But around 890 CE the Arabs established a land base in southern France by building a fortress near what is now Saint-Tropez. For a period of eighty years they raided from this stronghold the western Mediterranean seas but also the hinterland as far as south-eastern France and southern Switzerland. There, in the high Alps, the Arab raiders assaulted the many pilgrims on their way to Rome. Finally, the regional lord Hugo mounted a full-scale expedition against the Arab fortress with the help of the Byzantine fleet. Hugo was quite successful, but just when he was about to de-liver the final blow, he unexpectedly entered into an accord with the Arabs in 941 CE, granting them the Alpine passes as well as the territories already occupied by them. The reason for this sudden change of heart is speculative but most probably dictated by pragmatism: the Arabs in the Alps could act as a buffer against Hugo's French and German adversaries further north who felt threatened by Hugo's successes. And, in addition, Hugo did not want to jeopardize the good relations he had just established with the caliph of Cordoba by entering into a peace accord that also allowed for free commerce with Andalus. The raids by the Arabs in southern France therefore continued, this time legitimized by their accord with Hugo. Their forces were regularly supplied with Christian deserters from the surrounding lords – a phenomenon that was to remain quite common well into the eighteenth century, with Christian sailors and pirates joining the ranks of the Muslim Barbary corsairs (of whom we will come to speak in more detail in chapter three). The Arab presence on the French coast was ended in 973 CE by King Otto (the same who had sent the abovementioned embassy to the court of the Cordoban caliphate), who was eager to re-establish free passage across the Alps for pilgrims on their way to Rome, and in exchange receive papal blessing as a true Christian king.

Religious War?

Were the conquests and wars conducted by Arabs and Berbers (or Saracens and Moors, as Europeans called them) in this early stage of Muslim-Christian history religious in nature? In other words, are we to speak of conquerors who happened to be adherents to Islam, or can we point at Islam as the instigator for Muslims to undertake their conquests? This question is not easy to answer. First there is the problem of the notion of war itself. Are we to consider centuries of raids, skirmishes and wars of conquest as separate acts of belligerency conducted for different motives by different people, or are they all to be amassed in a single-purposed and continuous endeavour by Islamic military forces to conquer as much as they could whenever they could? The latter is implied by maps one can find nowadays on the Internet with all Muslim conquests and incursions shown in images set consecutively so that one sees centuries of warfare passing by within seconds.[53] On the other hand, Muslims and Christians were not very different in their belligerency and their lust for spoils and conquest: it was an integral part of the life of any warlord, prince, caliph or emperor; his reason for existing and the means to prolong that existence. Admittedly, however, the Muslims did a much better job of this than the Europeans during the last three centuries of the first millennium.

We must also take into consideration that, as a general rule, wars were not to be conducted within one's own realm, against one's brothers; wars were to be waged against others. This Otherness could be based on ethnicity, tribal affiliations, political allegiances or, as was increasingly the case in the era we are discussing here, religious affiliation. One was not to fight one's co-religionist, and therefore war was allowed only against the non-believer, not necessarily because the enemy was an unbeliever, but because his unbelief justified the hostilities against him. This kind of reasoning and rhetoric was shared by Muslims and Christians alike.

Such justification of war has also been suggested as an explanation for the swift and ever-expanding conquests of the Muslims in the seventh century. According to this argument, the root of Muslim belligerency must be sought in the culture of Arabs in the Arab Peninsula of conducting tribal feuds and organized plunder (ghaz-zas) of each other's encampments and caravans. However, Islam prohibited fighting and plundering among Muslims, so that the pent-up energy of the warriors was directed outwards, into lands where there was no Islam and where, in consequence, conquest and plunder were allowed.[54] This would also explain the continuous warfare of the Muslims, because with every territory they added to the Islamic empire they forfeited the right to continue fighting within that new territory and had to venture further for war and spoils.

If we follow this line of reasoning, then Islamic scripture did not provide Muslims with their marching orders, but rather provided them with a powerful new identity that gave them strength and an enormous self-confidence, prompting them to go to the end of the world (indeed, it is told that the Muslim general who spurred his warriors westward across North Africa, when reaching the Atlantic drove his horse into the sea and then is said to have called: "O Lord, if the sea did not stop me, I would go through the lands like Alexander the Great"[55]).

We will never know the exact motivations of these early Muslim warriors, however, because the history of early Muslim conquests was not recorded by the victors themselves but by Arab chroniclers decades or even centuries later. It is very possible that these chroniclers would retrospectively imbue the conquests with a religious purpose and justification. But this lack of precise information has fuelled speculation among modern historians. Some of them see mostly plunder and conquest in the early Arab Muslim wars, and very little religion or holy fervour (which would justify calling them 'Arab' wars).[56] Other historians, however, stress religious zeal as the most important motivator for Arab Muslim belligerency. Some take this argument further by invoking unsubstantiated images of fearless Muslim warriors craving for death in order to reach paradise, making them "the most terrifying of enemies, eager for death, like the kamikaze pilots during World War II".[57] Some of these historians find the evidence for such religiously motivated wars in Islamic holy scripture, an approach that has become very popular since 9/11, yielding dozens of books and articles on Islam's alleged call for religious (holy) war.[58] Other modern scholars argue that the notion of jihad is not to be understood as incessant warfare to expand the abode of Islam, nor as a duty on Muslims to engage in perpetual war against the infidel; they point out that, after the initial Muslim conquests, *jihad* was defined by most canonical sources as a defensive war to be undertaken when the world of Islam was under threat.[59]

Rather than trying to read the early Muslim mind by means of scripture or chronicles, it may perhaps be more telling to see what the early Muslim conquerors *did*. For instance, while the wars of conquest may have been waged in the name of Islam, conversion of the conquered peoples was not the aim, as we have seen above. The non-Muslim enemy was given the choice whether to fight or to surrender under two conditions: to pay a poll tax and to be subjugated to Muslim rule. This might serve as an argument that the Muslim wars were ordinary conquests rather than religious wars. Indeed, the Arab sources widely cite not conversion to Islam as a reason for fighting, but pride in being Arab and a tribesman.[60] On the other hand, while the Muslims did not spread Islam by means of forced conversion, they did force Islamic rules on their non-Muslim subjects. This is not typical of Islam, however: in the era we are discussing (and long afterwards, as we will see), Christian rulers also forced religiously inspired laws onto their subjects. But was this in itself the purpose of the wars of conquest conducted by Muslims and Christians in these times? The Arab and Carolingian wars seem to confirm that to be the case, although it is very possible that this aim came second to the primary goal of martial prowess, conquest and plunder. If there was indeed something like a religious war, it is not typical for Islam or Muslims, but a typical phenomenon of that time: religion determined who belonged to Us and Them, and was the prime inspiration and explanation for everything in life, including war.

The Battle of Poitiers

We need to pay attention to one specific battle that is very much present in European collective memory because, according to many European historians, it was decisive in terms of the Muslim presence in Europe. In 732 CE, twenty years after the Muslims had conquered the Iberian Peninsula, they suffered a defeat at the battle near the French town of Poitiers. This battle has gained mythical fame in Europe as the moment that the Muslim advance into Europe was finally halted and, according to some historians, was decisive for Europe's history:[61] "[i]t decided that Christians, and not Moslems, should be the ruling power in Europe."[62] The famous eighteenth century historian Edward Gibbon paints a futuristic picture if events had turned out differently at Poitiers: "[a] victorious line of march had been prolonged above a thousand miles from the rock of Gibraltar to the banks of the Loire; the repetition of an equal space would have carried the Saracens to the confines of Poland and the Highlands of Scotland; the Rhine is not more impassable than the Nile or Euphrates, and the Arabian fleet might have sailed without a naval combat into the mouth of the Thames. Perhaps the interpretation of the Quran would now be taught in the schools of Oxford, and her pulpits might demonstrate to a circumcised people the sanctity and truth of the revelation of Mahomet."[63]

Modern historians differ on the impact of this battle, however. Since historical evidence is hard to come by, it is difficult to establish the true intentions of the Muslims at the time. But one thing is clear: the Moorish raid into France was not a continuation of the invasion and conquest of the Iberian Peninsula, which had already taken place twenty years earlier. We do know that since then both the Muslims south of the Pyrenees and the Franks north of this mountain range had conducted raids into each other's territory. These raids were not aimed at conquest, but spoils and plunder. Was this then a Muslim raid that went wrong and ended in disaster?[64] The military historian Hugh Kennedy, however, argues that one should not dismiss the notion of a Muslim invasion of Europe on the ground that it was 'only' a raiding party: "[a]s the people of Central Asia were finding out at exactly the same time, Arab raids could be a prelude to more lasting conquest."[65] This battle could therefore indeed be considered a turning point, says Kennedy, not because a Muslim invasion army was stopped, but because it ended the routine of Muslim plunder raids into France. Kennedy's argument is not entirely correct, however, because the Moorish plunder raids from Spain did continue for another sixty years, although mainly confined to the area around Narbonne, east of the Pyrenees, the last one taking place in 793 CE.[66] In addition, as we have seen above, Poitiers did not end the Arab presence in the French region, because less than a century later the Arabs established a stronghold near Saint Tropez from where they dominated a large area for another eighty years.

Another approach to the battle of Poitiers is that it may not in fact have been of decisive importance but was deliberately given this mythical status by the rulers of that time, the Carolingian Franks, for the benefit of their own public image as saviours of Europe.[67] The victorious Frankish king Charles Martel, the founder of the Carolingian dynasty that was to conquer and rule large parts of Europe, created a mystique of himself as "leader of a special tribe, [that] had saved Christian civilization, which could mean nothing less than that he and they must be vessels through which God worked His wonders."[68] The mythologization of the Franks' victory in this battle would explain why another battle several years earlier has not received a similar prominent place in Europe's collective memory. The one-year-long siege of

Constantinople in 717 CE was a true battle, with a huge Muslim army amassed to conquer the city and thereby gain access to the European hinterland. If it had succeeded, the large Muslim army that – unlike the raiding party at Poitiers – was equipped and sent for the explicit purpose of conquest would definitely have continued its way into Europe. The scant attention paid by Arab chroniclers to the battle of Poitiers as opposed to their avid attention to the Muslim defeat at Constantinople a few years earlier would argue in favour of this interpretation of Muslim intentions. But from the Frankish point of view, this threat against Constantinople was primarily aimed at the Byzantines, their arch-enemy, and therefore not relevant to receiving attention (centuries later we will see a similar French indifference towards the Ottoman siege of Vienna in 1683). To establish their credentials as the defenders of Europe, the Carolingians embarked on a successful 'spin' avant-la-lettre of the battle at Poitiers.

We will probably never know the true intentions of the eighth-century Muslims with regard to an accidental or deliberate conquest of Europe. It is noticeable, however, that 'Poitiers' is engrained in the European collective memory, and has shown itself again as a throbbing nerve with the arrival of Muslim migrants in twentieth century Europe. We will discuss this in more detail in the final chapter. But the question that remains unanswered is: if the Muslims had conquered large parts of Europe, what would that have meant for Europeans and European civilization? The image depicted by Gibbon is one confined to religion, assuming that the majority of Europeans would have converted to Islam. We have seen that, just like other areas of Muslim conquest, such conversion would not be forced but be the choice of the Europeans themselves. Another, rather provocative image is that Europe could have shared the golden age of the Islamic empire there and then, rather than having to wait for several centuries: "[w]e [Europeans] would have gained 267 years ... We might have been spared the wars of religion".[69] In a similar vein, economic historian Gene Heck argues that Poitiers may have saved Europe from "Islamic political subjugation", but by consequence condemned Western Europe to its "economic subjugation in the Dark Ages".[70]

Diplomacy and Trade

In the previous paragraphs we saw several examples of Muslim Arabs and Christian European rulers exchanging delegates. These 'embassies' were of a temporary nature, sent with a specific task of negotiating a military or commercial alliance, although often they would stay at the court of the other party for longer periods of time, sometimes even years.

Extensive communications by exchange of letters took place between the Byzantine Emperor and the Caliphs in Bagdad, Cairo and Cordoba, and Emirs in the Middle East, and these letters were mostly delivered by embassies.[71] On both sides, the ambassadors received full diplomatic immunity. Arab delegates to Constantinople were also allowed to make trips into the area surrounding the capital. The difference in status between Western European Christians and Arab Muslims was reflected in the court etiquette that granted Muslim 'friends' a seat at the imperial table that was higher than that of 'Frankish friends'.[72] The same etiquette made sure that care was taken not to serve the 'Muslim friends' food prohibited by Islam.[73] The preference for Muslim rulers and delegates added to the Frankish antipathy towards the Byzantines, whose lifestyle – which was very close to that of the Arabs! – was already a source of Frankish mockery and disgust: they envied the Byzantine opulence and lavish lifestyle, they frowned on the use of the fork and eating habits like garlic and leek cooked in olive oil, and considered the dress code of robes instead of pants effeminate, just like the wearing of silk instead of wool and the use of eunuchs in court protocol.[74]

Arab-Byzantine communications concerned a number of issues, such as the ceasefire for the annual and sometimes bi-annual skirmishes at the border between the two realms and payment for, and the release of prisoners of war on both sides.[75] Sometimes the letters discussed issues of art and culture, and the caliph in Baghdad would occasionally engage in religious polemics in order to convince the Emperor of the primacy of Islam.[76] Commerce was also a source of intense negotiation and the signing of treaties, since the Byzantine Empire was an important supplier of slaves and an important trading partner at the far western end of the silk route that ran through Islamic territory. Muslim merchants would not venture into Europe, but they would easily and in great numbers enter Constantinople.[77] Trade was usually not direct, however, but operated through a chain of intermediaries in frontier areas, where the inhabitants themselves were mostly bilingual and of mixed Arab-Greek origin.[78] From the Levantine coastal ports – mostly in the hands of the Islamic Empire, except for a brief period in the second half of the tenth century when the Byzantine Empire ruled these areas – goods were shipped to Europe by merchants from Genoa, Venice and Pisa.

In the eighth and ninth centuries, the Byzantine and Islamic Empires were in an almost permanent state of war, but commerce between the two realms flourished as well. By the tenth century, almost three centuries after the Byzantine Empire had lost vast parts of its realm to the Arab Muslim armies, the Byzantines had re-established themselves within their confined empire as a commercial and military power in the region, thanks also to a collapsing power structure within the Islamic empire. This shift in the power balance may explain the magnanimity of Byzantine court protocol with its cordial reception formulas for ambassadors from Baghdad and Cairo. These two cities were by the tenth century the capitals of two rival Islamic realms: the old, but ever crumbling Islamic Empire under the caliph in Baghdad, and the newly arisen Fatimid Empire in the Middle East and North Africa. The Byzantine court cunningly played into the rivalry between these two Muslim empires that competed for supremacy over the Muslim community. Asylum was granted to Muslim notables seeking refuge in the Byzantine Empire to escape legal or political persecution in their own lands, and sometimes asylum was granted to an entire tribe that put itself under Byzantine command and suzerainty.[79] The extensive and often cordial relations between the Byzantine and Arab-Muslim rulers did not mean that there was mutual understanding or friendship. On the contrary, the abundant literature of those times shows that there was an overriding mutual disdain, even hate, "an instinctive hate and a profound contempt".[80]

Similarly to the Byzantine situation in eastern Europe, the Carolingians in France maintained a relationship with Cordoba that combined trade and war. While there were regular skirmishes and raids in the frontier areas, trade did indeed take place between the two realms, although on a limited scale and with Carolingian exports limited to weaponry, timber and, most prominently, slaves, who were exported through the Iberian peninsula and then further eastwards into the Islamic empire.[81]

Slavery was perhaps the main trading commodity between Europe and the Muslim world.[82] It was an established practice throughout the Mediterranean basin, and slaves were the main form of booty in raids, whether by Christian or Muslim pirates on the Mediterranean coasts, by the Moors in France, the Franks in northern Europe, or the Byzantines in the Black Sea region.[83] Since the Muslim side of the Mediterranean was prospering economically, as opposed to the European side, the Muslims had a much higher demand for slaves, and the slave trade undertaken by Franks, Venetians, Jews and Byzantines was mostly directed towards North Africa.[84] The role of Jewish slave traders operating from the Rhone region gave rise to accusations of Jews stealing Christian children and selling them off into slavery, one of the stories that, together with the story of Jews eating Christian children, would soon lead to the violent reactions against Jews in Western Europe during the First Crusade.[85]

Enslaving people is typically something that was done in enemy territory, and as a result slavery was conducive to forced migration of people.[86] For instance, in the ninth century during the Golden Age of Andalus, the caliphate of Cordoba imported nearly 14,000 white slaves from the Balkans whom they called *Saqaliba* ('Slavs'), who were to occupy sensitive positions in the army and government. They adopted the religion, language and customs of their masters and upheld the caliphal culture as intermediaries between the rulers and their subjects.[87] This situation was quite exceptional, however. Most slaves worked as domestic servants in households or as labourers on farms, while the less fortunate were confined to hard labour in mines.[88]

The slave trade from Frankish to Muslim lands was not as voluminous as that of the Byzantines. Nor did Carolingians have regular diplomatic contacts with their Moorish neighbours like the Byzantines had with their Arab neighbours in the Middle East. Diplomatic envoys were exchanged on an incidental basis with Cordoba, but on several occasions also extended as far as Baghdad. King Pepin 'the Short' reportedly sent a sizeable delegation to the court of the Abbasid caliph Mansour in Baghdad in 765 CE, while an Abbasid delegation visited France three years later.[89] The exchange of delegations in the period 797–801 CE between Charlemagne and caliph Haroun al-Rashid is well known.[90] These encounters-by-proxy between the two mythical leaders of the great empires of the time have triggered the imagination of many, but nothing is known of what was discussed or agreed, nor seem there to have been any practical outcomes.[91]

In the case of the Franks, their choice to make overtures to Baghdad was aimed not only at material gains, but probably more to establish strategic alliances against mutual enemies honouring the motto 'the enemy of my enemy is my friend.'[92] To the Franks their main enemy was not the far-away Islamic Empire, but the nearby Byzantine Empire. The Byzantines, in turn, had maintained a belligerent peace with Baghdad for over a century. But the hostile atmosphere between the Carolingian and Byzantine empires was of a more religious nature, with Constantinople vying with Rome for supremacy over Christianity. In the case of Frankish diplomatic overtures to the Cordoban emirate, the situation was similar but reversed: here Baghdad's bone of contention with Cordoba was its unwillingness to recognize the Baghdadi caliphate, while the Carolingians were engaged in a semi-permanent state of belligerent peace with Cordoba. The Franks and the Arabs therefore had their own reasons for reaching out to each other. Although the endeavour to establish alliances came to nought, it does illustrate that the religious divide between Christian and Islamic dominions was not strictly adhered to.

III. Virtual Islam

In addition to the physical contacts and interactions between Muslim Arabs and Christian Europeans, such as war, trade, diplomacy and coexistence, there were also what we have called the virtual encounters, that is the encounters of Europeans with Muslims or Islam in an intellectual, cultural, mythological or otherwise non-physical sense. In the period between the eighth and the eleventh centuries, however, Europeans had little, if any, religious or intellectual interest in Muslims or their religion, and maintained crude forms of imagery about them.*

Myths, Legends and Ignorance

This imagery must be considered in the light of the events of that time. Europe in the late seventh and early eighth centuries was confronted with Islam, a religion that no one had ever heard of, but that was militarily successful and expanding with alarming speed. This confrontation was primarily felt and experienced in the Byzantine Empire and the Iberian Peninsula, but news and images of it also found their way to the European mainland. The European reaction was mostly one of reconciliation, sometimes refutation and hardly any resistance.[93]

To start with the last: as we have seen, actual resistance against the Muslims was scant and mostly defensive. Charlemagne, the descendent of the victor of the battle of Poitiers, had donned the mantle of the great defender and champion of Christendom and is remembered by posterity for his battles against the Saracens in Spain through the Song of Roland (which dates from more than two centuries later). We have seen, however, that these fights were mostly raids into Arab lands or the repelling of raids by Arabs, and that Charlemagne did not mind an alliance with some Saracen Arabs against others. But with the feverish excitement of the First Crusade more than

---

* In the Islamic empire under the Abbasids, on the other hand, it was not uncommon for courts to organize theological debates between representatives of various religions (obviously with the aim of proving the superiority of Islam): see, e.g., Mun'im A. Sirry, 'Early Muslim–Christian dialogue: a closer look at major themes of the theological encounter,' Islam and Christian–Muslim Relations, 2005 (Vol. 16, No. 4), pp. 361–376; Jacques Waardenburg, Muslims and Others. Relations in Context, Berlin/New York: Walter de Gruyter, 2003, p. 110 ff.

two centuries later, Charlemagne would feature in popular imagination as having risen from the dead to lead this crusade against the infidel Saracens once again.[94] Part of this legend was that Charlemagne's army into Moorish Spain in 777–778 CE – retroactively proclaimed the first crusade against the Muslim infidel – had marched victoriously behind the *oriflamme*, the three-pointed red banner with golden flames that according to legend was brought by Charlemagne to the Holy Land to wait for the knight who would wield it in the final victory against the Saracen.

But this eleventh and twelfth century European mythology was ante-dated. At the time of the Muslim conquests, the medieval European Christian interpreted the Islamic victories mostly in religious terms, as a tribulation brought by God upon His faithful or, worse, as the coming of the Antichrist that was going to deliver the last blow to Christendom.[95] The Arab-Muslim conquests were not interpreted as military failures on the European side, but as a lack of faith that was to be punished by infidel victories – implying that infidel barbarians could never win on their own accord, but their victory was merely an instrument of God to punish Christians for neglecting their faith. The Other was used not in its own right, but as a function in the existence and self-image of the European. Later, long after the Muslim conquests had taken place, the image and the concept of the 'Saracen Other' were used to justify and glorify the violence of the European warrior class, reinforcing the ideology of Christian knighthood.[96] Yet another view of these events was that the new victorious religion of Islam was apparently better than Christianity, and since Christianity was on the losing side, Islam had to be reconciled with or even converted to. This last and radical conclusion, however, was not drawn by early medieval Christians within Europe, but only by Christians under Muslim rule.[97]

Whatever reaction medieval European Christians had to Islam, they had no urge or curiosity whatsoever to understand this new religion. According to Norman Daniel, who has written one of the authoritative studies on medieval imagery and studies of Islam, this was only natural in the circumstances where the Christian Church exercised pressure on its flock not to engage in any interaction or communication, whether commercial or otherwise, with Muslims. "The way was nowhere open to an ordinary Christian to know Islam better"[98] – assuming, of course, that these ordinary Christians in early medieval Europe *wanted* to know anything about Islam.

For lack of knowledge, medieval Europe gave Islam "a place in the three traditions of European thought and sentiment, those of Biblical history, apocalyptical vision, and popular imagination."[99] The net result was negative, combining feelings of fear, mistrust and downright hatred.[100] Saracens were considered pagan idolaters who worshipped combinations of several deities, mostly listed as Apollo, Jupiter, Lucifer (also known as Mahound, a convenient wordplay on Mohammed or Mahomet as he was known in medieval Europe), and an unknown deity called Tervagent. The European study of the Islamic sources would have to wait for another four hundred (!) years after the Byzantines first faced the Muslim armies.

CHAPTER TWO

Crusading Europe
(1000–1500 CE)

I. Setting the Stage

The turn of the millennium was also a turning of tables: the Islamic Empire was fragmenting with alarming speed, and with the fading of its unity gradually lost its political, cultural and military splendour, while Europe reached a stage of religious-cultural homogeneity and gained economic and military momentum. Indeed, the eleventh century was the period when Western European Christian civilization started to take shape and Latin Christendom expanded its ecclesiastic and worldly power as far as Spain and the Baltic. The Eastern European civilization of the Byzantine Empire, on the other hand, through the eleventh until the sixteenth centuries underwent a steady decline, ending finally in 1453 when the Ottomans took Constantinople.

The turn of the millennium was a time of relative peace for Europe: the periods of terrifying and devastating raids by the Vikings in the west, Arabs in the south and Huns in the east were past; the Magyars who had ravaged the interior of Europe had settled in present-day Hungary and converted to Christianity. European societal order took shape in the three-tier structure of knights and nobility, citizens and merchants, and clergy. This era of relative security on the continent put the knights out of work, but gave ample opportunity for citizens and traders to prosper. At the same time, Europe experienced an increasing religiosity that we would nowadays call fundamentalism. One of the most important events of this epoch, the Crusades, was an almost logic consequence of all these developments, as we will discuss in further detail below.

Compared with the previous period, a distinct shift took place in the form and nature of warfare. While wars in the earlier periods were aimed primarily at raising slaves, booty and tribute from border areas, with the turn of the millennium onwards wars were aimed at conquest and the permanent appropriation of territory.[1] This transformation in the goals of warfare coincided with the religious fervour of those times, so that conquests quickly acquired the quality of 'holy wars' and the conquered subjects were perceived in terms of their religion and treated accordingly.

1. Economic Revival

Historians offer different reasons for the millennium change in Europe. Was it the influence of the Arab-Islamic civilization that finally seeped through, or was it the technological innovations of European origin, especially in agriculture, or was it the upward mobility of the European middle class that stimulated commerce?[2] The last was definitely an important factor, for by the millennial year Mediterranean Europe had experienced a trade revival, especially in southern Italy, followed in the next centuries by a "great period of commercial and industrial expansion" that gradually included all of Europe.[3] This was the beginning of an economic reversal of fortunes of the Islamic Empire which in the previous centuries had been the highly economically developed and commercially advanced trading partner of the underdeveloped and industrially less sophisticated Western Europeans.[4] From this period onwards, Western Europe expanded its exports with dazzling speed, both in volume and in the variety of commodities traded.

Economic historians argue that the important impetus for the European economic revival was the interplay of the fracturing of the Islamic empire, on the one hand, and the Crusades into Muslim lands, on the other, resulting in the adoption of advanced Muslim business models. This interplay of factors contributed to – or even caused – the economic boom of Europe that started with the eleventh century.[5] This argument is expounded as follows. First, the fragmentation of the Islamic Empire created new commercial opportunities for the Europeans. While the Islamic Empire was officially still one, ruled by a caliph from Baghdad, the facts on the ground were different: in Egypt, the Shi'ite Fatimids had established a counter-caliphate in 909 CE with Cairo as its capital, followed by the caliphate of Cordoba in 929, and the Middle East was divided into independent and competing fiefdoms of generals and warlords (emirates). Internal competition and wars disrupted the trade within the Muslim realm that had once enjoyed the security of the Pax Islamica. Long-distance trade became impossible, and the Muslim powers bordering the Mediterranean that had previously relied on trade from Asia now turned to closer-by Europe for supplies. This meant more business for the Italian commercial city-states that had already monopolized Mediterranean trade.

The increase in trade across the Mediterranean coincided with the second factor, the Crusades. These military adventures were unprecedented (that is, for European standards of that time) long-distance enterprises into enemy territory, and maintaining and financing the far-stretched supply line posed a challenge. Until then, Europeans had had no experience with long distance trade and investment. Italian commercial enterprises, however, in their contacts with Muslims had come across new business tools and models that exactly fitted that purpose. Indeed, the Muslims had vast experience with long distance trade and their religion did not pose any impediments to entrepreneurship (contrary to Christian doctrine), as we will discuss in more detail below.[6] The ensuing business institutions that were adopted and further developed by Italian businessmen were to revolutionize mainland Christian Europe that was still enveloped in the throes of feudalistic economic stagnation.

2. Religious Revival

With the turn of the millennium, Europe experienced an increase in religious zeal. Christianity was an integral part of the European's identity and world vision, shaping what became known as Christian civilization[7] and determining Europeans' hopes and fears, the patterns of daily life, and views on business and war.[8] Outsiders like Vikings, Magyars or Saracens were pagans at best, or tools of God's punishment at worst.[9] The millennium brought an extra dimension to this religious outlook, causing much anxiety among Europeans: was this the end of times, was the Antichrist to appear in the wake of the Riders of the Apocalypse?

The transition into the next millennium turned out not to be catastrophic, however, which perhaps contributed to the growing optimism and self-consciousness of the medieval European. This disposition also showed in religious matters, for the layman increasingly set out his own terms for a religious life. He was enticed to do so, no doubt, by the not so religious examples set by some of the clergy. But it was not only the commoner who took the daring steps of religious self-assertion; kings also engaged in power games with the papacy to justify the divine ordinance of their rule.[10]

The Church in Rome saw these developments as a threat to its sovereignty, and quickly took action. Pope Gregory VII (Pope from 1073 until 1085 CE) implemented radical Church reforms and re-affirmed papal authority over the worldly rulers.[11] The Church also re-affirmed its authority in determining orthodoxy by branding all deviant Christian movements and sects as heretical. This confrontational attitude was effectuated in 1215 CE when the Church, during the Fourth Lateran Council, ordered the secular authorities to exterminate the heretic. The ensuing Inquisition, a quasi-independent ecclesiastical court, took an active role in persecuting alleged heretics and apostates, and would in the following centuries issue tens of thousands of death sentences that were mostly carried out by burning at the stake.[12] European society verily became a 'persecuting society'.[13]

The self-assertion of European Christendom was definitely Roman-Latin in character, which led to a continued confrontation with the Orthodox Church of the Byzantine Empire. The two churches excommunicated each other in the eleventh century, creating a fissure in the political European landscape and forcing the worldly rulers to choose between the Roman and Greek rites. This emphasized not only a political Latin-Greek divide in Europe, but also a strong identification on both sides with their respective rites as well as their culture and politics.[14]

Finally, the turn of the century also brought change to monasticism. Monasteries were spread all over Europe, and in addition to their original spiritual function as places of asceticism and worship they had also become centres of wealth and knowledge. In the Middle Ages, the Church owned vast areas of land that encompassed an estimated one-third of European territory. The clergy's worldly power brought them out of their isolation and propelled them into the world of commerce, politics and theological discourse. The monastery of Cluny, for instance, was important in developing the concept of a just war, which was to serve the cause of the coming crusades. And it was one of Cluny's abbots who undertook the first translation of the Quran into Latin, as we will see below.

3. The Crusades

The First Crusade was the product of the combination of religious zeal, commercial industry and the pent-up 'chivalry' energies of eleventh century Europe.[15] Many more crusades were to follow, but the first was the most successful: starting in 1096 CE, it succeeded against all odds in conquering Jerusalem four years later, in 1099 CE. The city was to remain in Christian hands for a century, and its loss in 1187 CE prompted several other crusades to recapture it, but none of these was successful (except for a brief tenure in 1229–1244, when Emperor Fredrick II, as leader of the Sixth Crusade, managed through negotiations with the Muslims to obtain control of Jerusalem for a period of fifteen years).

The reasons and enthusiasm for the First Crusade are still a matter of debate among historians.[16] The mere argument of recapturing the Holy Land and the city of Jerusalem does not suffice to explain this sudden passion, because these lands had already been under Islamic rule for over four centuries without any European clamour for reconquest. For the same reason (the long time span between the Muslim conquests in the Levant and the European crusade) it is inadequate to speak of the crusades as "counter attacks".[17] The reasons for the First Crusade are to be sought not in Muslim actions, but in European circumstances of that time. Three factors are suggested to have played major roles in the success of the call for a crusade. First, there was the Church that wanted to strengthen its papal authority and power. To call knights as well as commoners to a holy war gave the Church not only the power to command armies, but also to determine what was sacred. Of course, this could only work with Europeans who were genuinely devout, and the fear of one's soul and salvation has been suggested as a second, powerful factor in this "profound spiritual era".[18] Finally, the call for a crusade tapped into the early medieval violent and martial energies that needed new challenges now that the European borders were being secured and internal conflicts had subsided. These pent-up energies were given direction (East), purpose (holy war) and blessing (the promise of the absolution of all sins).

In order for the Church to champion these wars, an adjustment was needed to the basically pacifist Christian doctrine. The concept of a just war was already known in Christian theology, and it had become commonplace for the clergy to bless weapons or even to participate in wars of conversion, as conducted by Charlemagne. The Carolingian kings were also the ones who championed the notion of a Christian empire (*imperium Christianum*) that was to be inhabited exclusively by Christians (*populus Christianus*). Fighting an enemy therefore by default meant fighting non-Christians. These practices and acceptance of violence and warfare by Christian doctrine gradually developed into the concepts of holy war and sacred violence.[19]

The First Crusade of 1096 CE ended in the taking of Jerusalem in 1099, but it was again lost to the Muslims less than a century later, in 1187 CE. After that, eight more crusades were undertaken in the Middle East to recapture the city. While these crusades dominate European imagination, many more crusades were conducted within Europe. By this time, most military actions against pagans, heretics or infidels received papal blessing and hence merited the name crusade. Some of these crusades resulted in the acquisition of land, particularly in Scandinavia and the Baltic region; others were primarily aimed at the eradication of heretic movements, as in southern France, Germany, Denmark and Bohemia. Crusades against Muslims on the European continent were few. The best known of these crusades was the Reconquista in the Iberian Peninsula. The Christian kingdoms in the north of Spain had already been engaged in a tug-of-war with the southern Moorish states, but in conjunction with the religious frenzy of the First Crusade this belligerent peace turned into a full-blown crusade. Later, in the fourteenth century, crusades were also launched against the Muslim Ottomans in the Balkans, the Muslim Tartars near Lithuania, and against Muslim pirates operating from northern Africa, but the success rate of those crusades was very low.

II. Physical Islam

The period discussed in this chapter witnessed the expansion of Christian rule into territories that were previously under Muslim rule: Spain, Sicily, the Levant. By the twelfth century more Muslims lived under Christian rule than ever before. In the three following centuries, however, the political and demographical map changed radically. On the one hand, in the west the Arabs were evicted from Sicily in 1250 CE and the remnant of Moorish rule in Spain was brought to a final end with the fall of the emirate of Granada in 1492 CE. On the other hand, in the east Christian Franks were ousted from the Levant during the thirteenth century, and the Byzantine Empire came to its demise with the fall of Constantinople in 1453 CE. By the end of the fifteenth century, the Muslim 'threat' to Europe that traditionally came from the West ('Moors') had shifted to the East ('Turks').

Before we take a closer look at the relations between the Muslims and Christians who inhabited these southern territories, let us first briefly review each of them separately. Three of these territories we already know – Spain, Sicily and Byzantium – but the frontier zone was expanded with two more territories during this period: the Latin Kingdoms and Tataristan.

1. The Realm of Interaction

Al-Andalus: Reconquista and Convivencia

At the turn of the millennium, the Moors were still ruling most of the Iberian Peninsula, although the golden age of the Cordoba caliphate had by now come to an end, and its realm became fragmented into fiefdoms of feuding warlords. In the twelfth and thirteenth centuries, two Berber dynasties from Morocco, the Almoravids and the Almohads, both with intolerant fundamentalist traits quite unlike those of the Cordovan rulers, incorporated Al-Andalus into their Moroccan realms.

During this period of internal strife (known as the Ta'ifa-wars), the Moorish and Christian rulers fought each other, or among themselves, sometimes even joining forces against others. The legendary El Cid, who has become one of the mythical knights of Christendom fighting the Saracens, was in fact a successful warlord who fought for the highest bidder, including the Moors. In the Christian north, however, the belligerency of the kings and knights became infused with religious zeal, gradually transforming their wars for spoils into a crusade aimed at conquest. The northern kings, who preferred to call themselves 'Catholic kings', were successful in this endeavour and pushed the front line between the Christian north and the Moorish south rapidly southwards. In 1085 CE, the city of Toledo in central Spain was taken by the Catholic kings, and by 1250 CE the Moorish empire was reduced to the emirate of Granada on the coastal strip in the south of Spain. There the northern conquest came to a halt. A relative peace was maintained between the two sides for the next two and a half centuries, during which the emirate of Granada reached new epochs of splendour before it finally succumbed to the Catholic King Ferdinand in 1492 CE.

When we speak of 'Moorish Spain' we must bear in mind that there are two stories: that of its population, and that of its rulers. While the division between Moorish and Christian rule was quite clear-cut, the population throughout the Peninsula was an ethnic, religious and linguistic mixture. Religiously, there were Muslims, Christians and Jews. Ethnically, the Muslims were Arab or Berber or, in the case of converts, of native origin. In the case of Christians, most were of native origin, often maintaining religious rites and laws dating from Visigoth times, but many in the north were also Frankish immigrants who had crossed the Pyrenees into the Peninsula. Christians who had lived for generations under Moorish rule had adapted their ways and customs to those of their Muslim environment and rulers, as we saw in the previous chapter, adopting Arabic as their (second) language. For that reason they were known as *mozarabs* ('Arabized ones'), which became the name for a distinct ethnic identity. The languages spoken in the peninsula were those of the religions – Arabic, Hebrew and Latin – but also Frankish and the local Romance languages (of which *Ladino* and *Aljamia* were the Romance dialects used by the Jews and Muslims, respectively).

The literature yields various estimates of the total population of Spain and its number of Muslims. The tax registers are one of the few documents that modern historians can rely on, although colonization by the victors, emigration or expulsion of the population, and conversion all contribute to the complexity of the calculations. Harvey, after discussing the various calculations and figures provided by others, indicates a considerable decrease in the Muslim population in the period of 1000–1500 CE.[20] In the early eleventh century, that is in the aftermath of the golden period of the Cordoba Caliphate, Muslims constituted the majority in the peninsula – some argue even 75 per cent[21] – with the estimated number of Muslims set by some as high as 5.6 million.[22] By the fourteenth century these figures had dropped dramatically: the whole peninsula had a population of approximately 6 million souls, of whom only an estimated 1 million were Muslim.[23] The decrease in the number of Muslims is attributed to the armed conflicts of the extended civil war and the Reconquista, and the discrimination and riots by the Christian population against them, resulting in the Muslims migrating to northern Africa.

Keeping these shifting numbers in mind, we now turn to the impact of changing rulers. With the conquest of Moorish land by the Catholic kings, the Christian *mozarabs* inhabitants formally lost their centuries-old status as non-Muslim *dhimmis*. Interestingly, the cultural and religious customs of the *mozarab* Christians were so different from their Christian brethren in the north that their treatment as a minority was often continued under Christian rule. And the native Muslim population of the newly conquered territories now became subjects of Christian rule, acquiring an inferior status known as *mudéjar* which was the mirror-image of the *dhimmi*.

The period we are discussing now – from the eleventh to the end of the fifteenth century – is mostly described as *convivencia*, that is the harmonious coexistence of Muslims, Jews and Christians under Christian rule prior to the first expulsion of religious minorities (the Jews) in 1492 CE. Modern historians have disputed this notion of a 'golden age' of religious tolerance, pointing to the numerous forms and instances of discrimination and persecution of these minorities; we will discuss this in more detail later in this chapter. What is of importance to us now is to realize that during this period two mirror situations co-existed: Muslims under Christian rule (*mudéjars*) in the north and Christians under Muslim rule (*mozarabs*) in the south. Nevertheless, historians usually pay more attention to the *convivencia* and the position of the *mudéjars*, firstly because Christian rule dominated the largest territorial part of the Iberian Peninsula in this period, but also because there is more documentation and therefore more knowledge available on the *mudéjars* than on the *mozarabs*.

Sharing the religion of the ruler was of course a major advantage, and definitely had a positive impact on one's living conditions, as we will see below. But the Iberian Peninsula never was 'Christian' or 'Muslim' in the sense of religious homogeneity. Never, that is, until 1527 CE, when Islam was officially banned from the entire peninsula. The choice between conversion and emigration had already been given to Spanish Jews in 1492 CE, and then again to the Spanish Muslims during the period between 1499 and 1527 CE. The reasons for this grand project of religious cleansing were a mixture of religious intolerance by Christian ecclesiastic rule, deteriorating living conditions, and issues of security, as we will further discuss below in paragraph 2.

Sicily: Expulsion of Muslims

The only other case of massive expulsion of Muslims from Christian lands comparable to that of Andalus in 1499–1527 had already taken place in Sicily, two and a half centuries earlier, in 1250 CE. This was a rather sudden end to a community that was part of a society renowned for its tolerance and intellectual and cultural splendour – first under Arab Muslim rule, and then under the Normans who conquered Sicily during the period from 1060 to 1090 CE. These Normans had come a long way: they were the descendants of the Vikings who had established themselves in Normandy (France), and who had ventured forth to Italy from where they had launched their invasion of Sicily. They were known as devout Christians, and their conquest was backed, if not instigated, by Rome which for both religious and security reasons wanted to get rid of this Arab menace on its doorstep.

The Normans were not religious zealots, however, and established what became known as the Arab-Norman civilization which embraced social as well as cultural diversity, employing the intellectual and artistic backgrounds of the Greek, Phoenician, Italian, Arab and Norman inhabitants of the island. As in Spain, the Christian rulers continued the dhimmi status, but now applied it to those communities that did not belong to the Christian Norman class: legal autonomy was granted to Muslims, Jews and Greeks, and Muslim magistrates were appointed by the Norman kings.[24] King Roger II (1095–1154 CE) was the epitome of this tolerant and civilized culture, a philosopher-soldier and patron of the arts who spoke several languages (including Arabic) and assembled scholars and artists at his court, including Muslims. More than a century after the Norman conquest, the Norman kingdom of Sicily became part of the Holy Roman Empire through marriage and again produced a ruler who was renowned for his enlightened spirit: Frederick II (1194–1250 CE) was king of Sicily and Holy Roman Emperor, an Arabophile known as the 'Wonder of the World' (stupor mundi) because of his vast knowledge and wide erudition. Remarkably, it was this same ruler who decreed the expulsion of the Muslims from Sicily in 1250.

How had it come to this dramatic episode? What had happened to the utopian society of cultural diversity and social tolerance? As we mentioned earlier in the case of the Iberian Peninsula, the issue of tolerance and diversity was not as clear-cut as the modern observer might think it to be. The artistic and cultural splendour, as well as the tolerant attitude towards Muslims, were restricted to the enlightened Norman court and the so-called 'palace saracens' who resided there. This is the 'Golden Age' of twelfth and thirteenth century Sicily that has been recorded and transmitted through history. But this situation stood in stark contrast to the oppression and bound servitude of the Muslim population in the countryside in this period.[25] The situation must have been really bad if we look at the numbers of Muslims who emigrated: of the estimated 250,000 Muslims on Sicily in 1090 CE, approximately 25,000 were left in 1250 CE.[26] Their deplorable state caused them to rise up against their rulers in several revolts, which in turn justified the drastic ultimum remedium of deportation of the entire Muslim population to the Italian mainland in 1250 CE.

Byzantium: The Loss of an Empire

If we move further east, we come to the region with the longest experience of interaction with the Muslim world, the Byzantine Empire. At the turn of the millennium, almost four centuries after the loss of most of their territory to the Muslims, the Byzantines had reasserted themselves as an economic, military and diplomatic power to be reckoned with. No one would have predicted at the time the utter ruin that would befall this empire and its great capital city. But several developments, some of which had been emerging for decades or even centuries, would prove detrimental to the Byzantine Empire.

The balance of economic power in the region shifted considerably with the crusades and the establishment of the crusaders' kingdoms along the eastern Mediterranean coast. The crusades stimulated Mediterranean trade between Europeans (mainly Venetians and Genoese) and Byzantines as well as the various Islamic empires, and this became serious competition for the longstanding Byzantine-Arab trade.[27] Although the Byzantines, Franks and Italians shared a European and Christian identity, they were entangled in continuous and often fierce competition for political, religious and economic power. The Venetians in particular were crafty in maintaining their commercial interests with the Franks and Byzantines as well as the Muslims in Egypt.[28]

The lack of Christian unity or solidarity between the Latin and Orthodox Churches manifested itself with the military confrontations between the Byzantines and the crusaders. The age-old antagonism between the Western Latin and Eastern Orthodox Europeans had already resulted in mutual excommunication in the eleventh century, but erupted when the crusaders of the Fourth Crusade, shipped by the Venetians to the Holy Land, changed course and landed at Constantinople where they laid siege to the city. When they took the city in 1204 CE, they ransacked it with a vengeance, and then installed Roman Catholic rule that lasted until 1261 CE.

If this was not bad enough, new and aggressive powers arose in the east. In the early thirteenth century, the Mongols came westwards from the steppes of northern China with a speed reminiscent of the Arab-Muslim warrior bands six centuries earlier. The difference was that the Mongols were utterly destructive, destroying everything on their path. In 1258 CE, they took the capital of the Islamic empire, Baghdad, and razed it to the ground. The Byzantine Empire, located in what is now western Turkey, would have been overrun by the Mongols if they had not been stopped from reaching the Mediterranean by the Mamluks who, from their capital Cairo, successfully defended their Middle Eastern domains against the Mongols.

However, in the wake of the destruction wrought by the Mongols a new power entered the stage: Turkish tribes from Central Asia united under their progenitor Osman, and would become known in the centuries to follow as the Osmans or Ottomans. By piecemeal conquest they carved out a territory for themselves, even bypassing the impregnable city of Constantinople and venturing into the Byzantine territories on the European continent. During the fourteenth century, the Ottomans conquered most of Byzantine territory and beyond, including present day Greece, Bulgaria and Serbia. It was as two communicating vessels: what was won by Christians in the west was lost in the east (or, vice versa: what was lost by Muslims in the west was won in the east). By the late fourteenth century the Byzantine territories were taken by the Ottomans and Constantinople was left isolated, a grand capital without a territory, until it fell to the Ottomans in 1453 CE.

Latin Kingdoms: A Short-Lived Dream

Strictly speaking, the Latin kingdoms established by the crusaders next to the Mediterranean and Black Seas are not on the European continent and therefore outside the scope of our story about Islam in Europe. However, their presence was so interwoven with the European homelands and had such an impact on European imagination – even now, more than nine centuries later – that they need to be incorporated into our narrative of Islam in Europe.

As was the case with the Catholic kings in Spain, the Frankish and German Crusaders encountered a population of mixed religion and ethnicity that had been there for centuries. The Levant was the cradle of the Jewish and Christian faiths, and each community had produced numerous sects, speaking and writing in a variety of Semitic languages. The Byzantine Empire had imposed Orthodoxy as the state religion and Greek as the administrative and ecclesiastic language, and the Muslim Arabs did the same with Islam and Arabic. The large Christian and Jewish communities in Muslim ruled lands had adopted the Arabic language, reserving their specific languages for liturgical matters. In their capacity as *dhimmis* they enjoyed religious freedom, but were ultimately subjected to Muslim rule. They had little in common with the Crusaders, not even their religion because most Arab Christians were Orthodox. And the Crusaders acted in such brutal ways that there was no reason whatsoever for Arab Christians to see them as liberators.

The Christian-European enclave in the Islamic empire lasted two centuries in total: the first kingdom was created in 1096 CE, with the First Crusade, and the last Frankish stronghold of Acre was taken by the Muslims in 1297 CE. Jerusalem had already been lost (or re-taken, depending on one's point of view) in 1087 CE, less than a century after it had been taken by the Crusaders. During this period, however, successive Muslim armies had been gradually taking Frankish cities and fortresses. On the historical scale of events, therefore, the relatively short time span of the Frankish presence would appear as a mere link in the long chain of the region's history. But while the impact of the Latin kingdoms on the region may have been marginal, their effect on the European homeland was to be of great importance, reverberating well into the twenty-first century. But this effect was mostly on European imagination and collective memory, and much less in terms of a material impact.

Tataristan and Lipka-Tatars

Finally, to complete our round of European territory where Muslims ruled or lived, we must turn east, to the long frontier area that is now the steppes of Ukraine and Belarus, east of Hungary, Romania and Poland. In the period between 1236 and 1240 CE a Turkish-Mongol tribal federation known as the Tatars split off from the Mongol Golden Horde that had swept through Asia and turned northwards, conquering the western part of what is now Russia. Shortly after entering these territories they adopted Islam.

After their conquests and plunder raids, the Muslim Tatars established a steppe empire of which not much is known, mostly because little of this history is documented or, if it was, has not been preserved.[29] Also, they are a people that has raised little interest among Western scholars, although the few Tatar, Polish and Russian scholars in this field are gradually also publishing in English.[30] More is known of the so-called Lipka ('Lithuanian') Tatars, the Tatar mercenaries who in 1397 had been invited to settle in the Grand Duchy of Lithuania, in the Baltics. Lithuania had formally adopted Christianity ten years earlier, and was successful in the military expansion of its realm. To fight as well as protect these new territories, they called upon the Muslim Tatars who were roaming the steppes. The Lithuanian rulers encouraged them to settle in the Lithuanian realm, among others by allowing them to maintain their Islamic faith, to intermarry with the indigenous population and to raise the offspring of such unions in the faith of the father.[31] The Tatars accepted and would become a society within a society that was to last to this day. It apparently also worked out well in the early stage of their settlement in Lithuania, because during the next hundred odd years internal strife among the Mongols in the Black Sea area would often result in Tatar tribes splitting off and seeking – and receiving – refuge in the Lithuanian Duchy.

It is unclear why this coexistence worked so well, as opposed to similar mixed societies in other frontier states. For the Lithuanians (and later Poles) the answer might be sought in the fact that no action was ever undertaken to convert the Tatars, as the neighbouring Orthodox Russians forcefully did with their Muslim Cossacks or the Catholic Spaniards with their Muslim mudéjars after 1499 CE. For the Tatars the answer perhaps lies in the fact that they were for a long time a proud martial people, and in that capacity fulfilled a specific and indispensable role in Lithuanian (and later also Polish) society.

But they were more than mercenaries; they were also inhabitants of the Duchy of Lithuania. As such they proved to be staunch allies, in particular in the battles that the Duchy fought with the German Teutonic Knights who conducted crusades against what they considered pagan Lithuanians (which was peculiar given the fact that the Lithuanians were Christians, but they were probably considered not Christian enough in Teutonic eyes, or refused to submit to Teutonic rule). The Tatars demonstrated their loyalty to the Duchy of Lithuania time and time again by protecting their new homeland with their lives. In 1410 CE, when the Duchy defeated the Knights, an estimated 30,000 Tatars are said to have taken part in that decisive battle.[32] Ever afterwards, the Tatars had their separate units in the Polish army and were often raised to the ranks of the nobility for their deeds.[33]

2. Living with the Unbeliever: Muslims under Christian Rule

All these geographical changes on the political map of Europe's frontier areas created social challenges and tensions among the population of those areas. Robert Bartlett convincingly argues that the active expansion of Christendom in this period was a form of colonization, because a minority occupation force conquered and entered a new territory where they came to dominate the native majority population that was alien in language, culture, social structure and, often, religion.[34] There was a distinct difference, however, between the northern and southern European frontier areas in the exercise of this minority rule. This difference can be attributed mainly to the factor of religion. In the entire northern zone of Europe, which stretched from England to the Baltics, Christian missionaries had been active as early as in the eighth century in converting the pagan population. Later, with incursions by Christian neighbouring kings and crusader orders, this population was forcibly Christianized either because they were not yet converted or because they were but then allegedly had relapsed in their heathen ways.

In the Mediterranean frontier zone, on the other hand, there had been no missionary activity and the confrontation with and subjection to Christian rule came suddenly, and always by military defeat. In these regions, forced conversion was not an aim or option at the time of conquest, although religion was a determining factor in distinguishing between the ruler and his subjects. This situation meant that Christian Europeans had to deal with a fourth category of people: in addition to the Christians themselves, heretics (Christians who had strayed from the true teachings of Christianity as determined by the Church and who had to be returned to the true faith, by force if need be, or else had to be burned in order to cleanse the world from contamination by their polluted ways), and pagans (people who were said to have no religion and had to be forcibly converted to Christianity), there were the Muslim and Jewish unbelievers under Christian rule who were allowed to maintain their faith. While active campaigns of conversion were waged against the pagans on the northern borders of Europe, such was not the case against the Muslims and Jews.

In the south, the conquered Muslim peoples of Spain, Sicily and the Latin Kingdoms were allowed to keep their Islamic faith and modes of coexistence were employed. Conversion to Christianity was almost nil, and no conversion policies were employed by the Christian rulers.[35] Nevertheless, the lack of a clear status for Muslims and Jews – unlike under Islam, which had developed the religious notion of 'people of the book' and the legal status of the dhimmi – had resulted in Europe in a mixture of tolerance and discrimination, as we saw in the previous chapter. How different the treatment of heretics and unbelievers could be was exemplified by the Holy Roman Emperor Frederick II (1215–1250) who spoke fluent Arabic and was fond of Arabic culture, but who with all his tolerance towards his Arab-Muslim subjects was one of the first secular emperors in Christianity to codify the burning of Christian heretics.[36]

The distinction between heretic and unbeliever that had worked out in favour of the latter changed with the increase in religious zeal and crusading spirit. This volatile cocktail was first unleashed against the Jews. The masses that marched with the First Crusade in 1096 CE went on the rampage against Jews in several European cities. Persecution and pogroms continued to take place, and in the course of the twelfth to fifteenth centuries Jews were even expelled from most European countries. These exile orders were often revoked, although sometimes only after centuries. But by then many Jews stayed in the safe havens to which they had migrated: the Dutch Republic, Poland and Lithuania, the caliphate of Cordoba, and the North African states of Morocco and Tunisia, Egypt and, by the end of the fifteenth century, particularly the Ottoman Empire (the cities of Thessalonica and Alexandria, for instance, were known for their large Jewish communities). From these new homes the Jews would maintain important positions in the international commerce between the Muslim and Christian realms.

Conquering the Lands of the Infidel

The period between the eleventh and late fifteenth centuries witnessed a territorial expansion of Christian rule causing Muslim domination in these regions to recede. The territories with religiously mixed societies under Muslim rule within Europe shrank considerably, and remained in only two regions. The first is Muslim Spain which in the course of two centuries was reduced to the small territory of the Granada emirate; apart from the fact that Muslim Spain experienced a period of religious intolerance under the Almoravid and Almohad rulers in the twelfth and thirteenth centuries, there are not many details to be added to what has already been told in the previous chapter. The second territory with religiously mixed societies under Muslim rule within Europe is the Ottoman domains in south-eastern Europe, which we will discuss at length in the next chapter. In what follows we will focus on the newly arisen situation of Muslims under Christian rule.

In doing so, we need to make a distinction between the newly conquered territories in Catholic Spain, Norman Sicily and the Latin kingdoms of the Levant, on the one hand, and the Byzantine Empire on the other. The Byzantine Empire is the only part of Europe where Christian rule over Muslims was not established by conquest; the Empire already existed before Islam, and small numbers of Muslims had migrated into its realm, in particular into Constantinople. In the course of centuries the Byzantines had developed a delicate balance with their Muslim subjects, as well as with their Muslim neighbours.

From this perspective the Byzantine Empire was the *eminence grise* of the European Christian realms that had Muslim subjects. This was a position that was at least recognized by the Muslim rulers in the Mediterranean region, and they had granted the Byzantine Empire the role of protector of the Christians under Muslim rule.[37] In that function Byzantine officials were allowed to visit Christian communities in the Muslim realm. This unique position was not shared by the other Christian rulers of that time. And the Byzantines indeed took great interest in Christian life in the Muslim world (which, after all, used to be part of the Byzantine Empire), as shown in the Byzantine presence recorded in Cairo and Alexandria as early as the twelfth century: some were merchants, others appear to be mere rich sojourners who resided in these cities for short periods, visiting churches, Christian slaves and local Christian communities.[38]

In those parts of Europe where Christians through conquest had become rulers over Muslim and Jewish subjects, they often lacked standard policies for these people. These were devised on the spot by means of treaties, terms of surrender, or laws that had been applied to Jews in the Christian rulers' homelands.[39] In general, the Muslim subjects were allowed to keep their Muslim faith, and modes of coexistence were employed. With the exception of Spain and Russia in the late fifteenth century, Christian rulers did not employ policies of forced conversion. Instead, they found different ways to regulate the religious and ethnic plurality within their realms.

This situation of regulating coexistence arose only after the conquests were completed, however. Before that moment, lands had to be conquered and cities to be taken. Interestingly, just like the Muslim conquerors in previous centuries, the Christian victors resorted to similar ways of treating conquered populations: a city's population that resisted so that the city had to be taken by assault was usually slaughtered or enslaved, while its surrender mostly resulted in either its exile or its subjection to Christian rule.[40] Subjection meant that treaties were concluded between the victor and the population of the surrendering city, often allowing the inhabitants to keep their properties and their religious customs in exchange for tribute and recognition of the victor as their new overlord. In most instances the religious buildings and institutions remained intact, although often the main church or mosque was transformed into the holy site of the victor's religion. An exception to this general pattern of behaviour was the Crusaders, in particular those participating in the First Crusade. Their massacres of the local population were unusually ferocious, "probably because most Crusaders – unlike many Spaniards – had never before encountered Muslims, or because of the frenzy inherent in holy warfare".[41] Also unique was the Crusaders' decision to forbid 'infidels' – Muslims and Jews – to reside in Jerusalem.

Once the devastation and horrors of war had passed, the conqueror had to rule the newly appropriated territories and peoples. As said, in general there was no forced conversion or expulsion of the local population in the new lands under Christian rule. This is not to say that there was universal tolerance in these areas. The treatment of non-Christian subjects varied in time and place, and the same diversity can be seen in their living conditions: sometimes these subjects suffered oppression, sometimes they enjoyed peaceful and mutually beneficial relations with their Christian neighbours, and sometimes Muslim and Christian peasants had more in common with each other than with their Christian overlords.[42] Moreover, even if the ruling religion allowed for a subject religion to exist and to be practised – which to modern standards often seems to be the main criterion for viewing this period as tolerant – intolerances of a social and legal nature gradually increased.

Christian rule over religiously mixed communities in the European southern frontier areas usually started off in ways reminiscent of the Islamic *dhimmitude*, but gradually became less tolerant. In an admittedly simple manner we can characterize Christian rule as evolving in three fluid phases during the period between the eleventh and the end of the fifteenth centuries: tolerant segregation, strict discrimination and finally forced assimilation.[43]

From Tolerant Segregation to Forced Assimilation

The first phase of 'tolerant segregation' allowed for the different populations to keep their separate ways, whereby the Christian community enjoyed a favoured position as regards the other communities that had to endure various forms of legal and social discrimination. This practice was, intentionally or not, a continuation of the *dhimmi* practice established previously by the Muslim rulers in these areas. In the case of Spain, for instance, Christian rule was almost identical to Islamic rule in its regulation of the position of the non-believer: in exchange for fealty to their Christian rulers and payment of a poll tax, Muslims (known as *mudéjars*) were granted 'protection', that is relative autonomy with regard to their religious affairs and family laws, but their social-legal position was less than that of a Christian (for instance, their evidence in court was worth less than that of a Christian, sexual relations with Christians were punishable by death, they were not to wear certain styles or colours of clothes).[44] In addition, conversion by the *mudéjar* to Christianity was welcomed, but the opposite, conversion by a Christian to Islam, was deemed apostasy and punishable by death.[45] Tolerance in this respect should not be interpreted in terms of acceptance or equality; it merely meant that different religions and their practices were allowed, including the autonomy for the religious communities to regulate such practices.

An illustration of such tolerance was the charter of King Alphonso VI after the capture of Toledo in 1085 CE, which was later to be copied in other charters for Moorish cities that had surrendered. This charter granted in matters of religious and family law autonomy, with its own laws and magistrates, to Muslims and Jews, as well as to three (!) different groups of Christians: *mozarabs*, Castilians, and Franks, each community speaking its own language. Mosques and synagogues were to be maintained, and the non-Catholic Christians were allowed to preserve their own rituals.[46] This charter is often presented as the ultimate example of the celebrated tolerance of Catholic rule in Spain. This is undeniably the case, but the charter should not be taken to represent all places in Spain, and definitely not the entire period of the *convivencia*, as Catholic rule over Muslims and Jews during this period became known. As we have seen before, laws do not always reflect the realities of life, nor can they always dictate the realities.

On the one hand, as late as the fifteenth century, there were many cultural cross-overs between the religious communities, which showed mainly in cultural appearances like dress, food and dancing style. There are also recordings of friendly interactions, like attendance at each other's religious ceremonies and festivities, and apprenticeship in other communities.[47] On the other hand, segregation seemed to be the norm: there were many differences in lifestyle and language between the religious communities that mostly lived in separate quarters, and their religious leaders often instructed them not to mingle with the other communities.[48] Also, the attitudes expressed by Muslims and Christians about each other were definitely hostile,[49] and there is plenty of evidence that suggests that Muslims under Christian rule suffered discrimination.[50] And even in the most tolerant of times, when members of the Jewish, Christian and Muslim communities interacted as drinking and gambling companions, business associates, military buddies, visitors to each other's celebrations, the absolute red line between the religious communities was that of sexual relations: the protection of a community's integrity was formulated in terms of prohibiting the community's women from sexual relations with male members of other religious communities.[51]

The second phase of coexistence, which we suggested calling 'strict discrimination', can be characterized as a strict upholding of the segregation between religious communities. Allowing for exceptions to discriminatory rules, which was the hallmark of tolerance practised earlier, was replaced by strict adherence to the rules. This phase started in the thirteenth century and gradually developed into a trend of oppression: where under the terms of surrender in the twelfth and thirteenth centuries the minorities could maintain their property and mosques, as well as autonomy in most legal and religious matters, these privileges were gradually granted less often or even revoked.[52]

The Catholic Church was instrumental in the enforcement of this segregation. The Church had two aims: conversion of the non-Christians and preventing the faithful from 'contamination' by interaction with their infidel co-citizens.[53] In the Latin Kingdoms, dress codes that had been institutionalized a century earlier were now enforced.[54] In Spain, where the Reconquista had brought large numbers of Muslims under Christian rule, the clergy continuously complained about the religious freedoms granted to those Muslim subjects by the Christian rulers. This, in turn, incited the Christian lower classes to violence, riots and disturbances against Muslims.[55]

But the Church also developed its own, restrictive legislation vis-à-vis the infidel under Christian rule. At the Third Lateran Council of 1179 CE, for instance, Muslims and Jews were prohibited from testifying against Christians or otherwise holding offices that would put them in a position of authority over a Christian, and Jews and Muslims were prohibited from keeping Christian servants or slaves (Canon 26). The Fourth Lateran Council of 1215 CE took the separation between the communities a step further by ordering 'Jews and Saracens' to wear clothes that would distinguish them clearly from Christians in order to prevent confusion of identity that, in turn, might lead to the possibility of prohibited sexual intercourse between members of those religions (Canon 68).[56] In the case of Jews, this led to the requirement to wear a distinctive badge, but it is not clear whether this requirement was also made for Muslims.[57]

It should be noted that, however repulsive these measures may seem to the modern observer, they were quite common in both the Muslim and Christian polities of that era. Religious rule in both cases may have tolerated the non-believer, but always on the premise that one's own religion ruled supreme, that one's faithful could not be put in a position of subjugation vis-à-vis the others, and that there was not too much intermingling between believers and non-believers. Tolerance at that time was therefore interpreted as allowing the unbeliever to go his own way, according to his own rules, in the isolation of his own community, but separated from the community that shared the religion of those in power.

What may have prompted the strict enforcement of segregation rules, as Powel argues, was that tolerance as practised in the first phase failed to maintain the intended segregation, putting the Christian community at risk of being contaminated by non-Christian elements.[58] The Church took it upon itself to re-erect the social boundaries and to keep them firmly in place.[59] The actions by the Church can partly be explained by the epoch of Christian zeal combined with the Church's need for self-assertion as a power in everyday life. But, on the other hand, social tensions among the religious communities seem to have been real, calling for intervention by the rulers.[60] This led to the next phase: of complete and enforced assimilation: instead of strict separation and emphasis of the distinctions between the communities: everyone now had to conform to one single religious, cultural and political polity.

This trend of assimilation was a gradual process, as was clearest in Catholic Spain: first came the denial of judicial privileges, then restrictions on religious freedom, finally followed by the choice for Muslims between expulsion or forced conversion in 1499 CE in Granada and afterwards in all of Spain. And even those Muslims who chose conversion – the so-called Moriscos – were continuously pressed to conform to the dominant culture: they were not allowed to speak Arabic, to wear Moorish dress or the veil, or to use Moorish names. It is not surprising, then, that on several occasions they arose in protest and revolts which, in turn, confirmed the fears of the Christian community and its rulers that these minorities were not to be trusted, let alone to be allowed to pursue their own religious, societal and cultural ways. We will discuss the predicament of the Spanish Moriscos in more detail in the next chapter.

3. Social Tensions

In the Mediterranean frontier areas that were under Christian rule the practice of religious and ethnic plurality (first phase) was gradually replaced by a single polity of a definite Christian character (second and third phase). This development coincided with a growing tendency towards racial and religious discrimination, resulting in intensifying hostility towards non-Christian subjects. The historian Bartlett attributes these sentiments of religious exclusivity mixed with ethnic superiority to an increasing emphasis on the "natural hatred" that already existed between ethnic and religious communities.[61] The medievalist Powel, on the other hand, finds the cause of these tensions not in the natural disposition of people but in the circumstances of their social environment, calling the Mediterranean frontier societies "societies in stress, sometimes in agony".[62] The factors contributing to this 'agony', Powell argues, were of a social and economic nature, but also caused by demographic changes, in particular the immigration of Christian colonists into the newly conquered territories, creating pressure on the Muslims who had remained and who were reduced to an inferior legal status.[63]

Powel points out that the measures taken to curb contacts between Muslims and Christians were not necessarily anti-Muslim, but were primarily meant to protect the Christian community and faith. This community, living outside the Christian polity, was now exposed to ideas by, and to social (and perhaps even sexual) interaction with Muslims, and that was the kind of contamination that had to be prevented in order to preserve the Christian identity.[64] In times when the rise of heresy posed an internal threat for the church, the intermingling of Christians and non-Christians in frontier territories was perceived as an additional, external threat. The solution for heresy was one of severe persecution. The solution for the negative influence – whether real or perceived – caused by interaction with non-Christian subjects was less clear and depended on local authorities.

However, the obsession with religious 'contamination' seems more a whim of medieval imagination than related to reality, because the various communities already lived quite segregated lives. We argued earlier that one can hardly speak of toleration in those times, given the fact that communities lived in such isolation from each other: toleration would then equal ignorance, indifference and neglect of one another.[65] This situation of factual segregation continued well into the sixteenth century.[66] For this reason Powel dismisses the term *convivencia* – the term denoting the tolerant 'living together' under the Catholic kings of Spain – as a misnomer.[67]

The interactions that medieval Christians were worried about from a religious perspective, therefore, had not so much to do with social or intellectual interactions – which were negligible – but were often of a more legal nature. For instance, under Muslim rule, marriage between a Muslim man and a Christian or Jewish woman was allowed, and their offspring would by birth be Muslim.[68] When these societies passed under Christian rule, the dominating perspective became Christian, which disagreed with the situation that Christian mothers had to live in an Islamic family environment and were not allowed to raise their children in the Christian faith. However, since the family was designated as 'Muslim' and Christian rule allowed Muslims to maintain their ways, this situation was allowed to continue.

Another legal issue of mixed relations that led to religious 'contamination' was in the workplace. Slaves, servants and functionaries usually did not share the religion of their masters or superiors. Hierarchy was based on religious categories, with the religion of those in power always on top. Under Muslim rule, for instance, Christians could have their own local authorities or judges, but these were not allowed to rule over Muslims as masters, judges or functionaries. Consequently, the Christian's testimony against the Muslim was considered of a lesser value or even invalid or only under strict conditions, and a Christian man was not allowed to marry a Muslim woman. The same applied, *vice versa*, to Muslims under Christian rule.

Problems arose when one religious rule was replaced by another. Under Muslim rule, many Muslims employed Christian slaves, servants and functionaries. The coming of Christian rule demanded a reversed situation: the Muslims could not keep their Christian slaves and servants, their Christian neighbours would finally go to court over the contested plot of land because their testimony was no longer considered inferior to a Muslim's, and the children of a Muslim father and Christian mother could openly express their Christianity without fear of being persecuted as apostates. However, reality dictated that this new legal situation could not be put into practice immediately. Christian slaves and servant remained with their Muslim masters, but this situation was illegal under the new rule and had to be altered, as we will see below when we discuss slavery. Also, Muslim functionaries remained in court, but not in a position that was superior to Christian colleagues.

These forms of 'contamination' in work and family life could perhaps be contained, but became complex and unruly in the case of conversion.

4. Conversion

Both Christianity and Islam share the basic rule that conversion *from* another religion to one's own is applauded, while conversion *to* another religion is tantamount to the crime of apostasy. In consequence, the religion in power determined what was conversion and what apostasy: under Muslim rule all conversions to Islam were welcomed, while Christian subjects lacked the power to resist such acts of apostasy, just as under Christian rule all conversions to Christianity were hailed while Muslims could only look on in horror at such acts of apostasy. One can imagine what distortion in religious worldview was caused by a change of religious rule: the apostates under the previous rule became the newly welcomed converts under the next rule, while the converts became the new apostates.

In this religious-political sensitivity lies the explanation for the causes that led to the brutal choice given to the Granada Muslims in 1499 CE between conversion and banishment.[69] Seven years earlier, in 1492 CE, with the fall of Granada, the Catholic king had granted the most tolerant terms of surrender to the Granadians. However, the newly installed bishop of Granada took offence at the presence of Muslims in the city who had converted from Christianity to Islam – some only years ago, other generations ago – and who retained their Islamic faith even after Christian rule had been imposed in the city. According to the bishop, these Muslims were originally Christians and they therefore had to be invited – by force, if necessary – to return to the true faith. This was against the terms of Granada's surrender that expressly granted freedom of religion for all those who were Muslims at the time of surrender. The bishop nevertheless persevered in his zealous actions and the king, although in disagreement, did not dare to interfere lest it would cost him his credentials as upholder of the Catholic faith. The bishop's meddling caused unrest among the Granadian Muslims, leading to full-blown uprisings that, in turn, brought the king to the drastic measure of 1499 CE.[70] By then, the tide could not be turned, and the choice between forced conversions and expulsion was also offered to the Muslims in Castile in 1502, Navarre in 1512, and Aragon between 1520 and 1526 CE: by 1527 CE, Islam had officially ceased to exist in Spain.

The other massive expulsion of Muslims which comes to mind was two and a half centuries earlier, in Sicily in 1250 CE. Here the reason for taking such a drastic measure was similar to that of the Spanish kings: the Muslims had repeatedly risen in revolt against the authority and since the uprisings could not be quelled militarily, expulsion (or in the case of Spain: forced conversion) was the alternative solution. That is where the similarity ends, however. The reasons for the uprisings were quite different: in Sicily, the uprisings were a reaction to social-economical oppression, while in Spain the oppression and discrimination of Muslims was predominantly of a religious nature. Also, the means of expulsion were different: the Sicilian Muslims were deported with all their families and belongings and resettled in Lucera in southern Italy,[71] while the Spanish Muslims were given the choice between conversion to Catholicism and leaving the country – the latter often under impossible conditions such as payment of a departure fee, abandonment of homes and properties, and sometimes even leaving one's children behind.

In the lands with Muslim populations under Christian rule, few instances are known of voluntary conversion by Muslims to Christianity. This is a striking contrast with the massive scale of voluntary conversion among the pagans in the northern frontier zone of Europe, and also with the – much less massive, but still significant – voluntary conversion of Christian subjects under Muslim rule to Islam (whether for reasons of faith or of expediency). The utter lack of success in converting Muslims to Christianity then and in all the centuries to come has been a major source of frustration for missionaries. Reasons can only be speculated upon, but it has been argued that the main difference between the northern European pagans who converted to Islam and the southern European Christians who converted to Islam, on the one hand, and Muslims, on the other hand, was that the latter were much more embedded in a well-developed and highly sophisticated civilization and theology that had shaped an identity that was not to be shaken or altered easily.[72]

There was one exception to this Muslim unwillingness to convert: Muslim slaves in Christian ruled lands were prone to convert to Christianity, for that would release them from slavery (as was reconfirmed by papal decree of 1237 CE). Such conversions were of course very undesirable from an economic point of view. Although the Christian church and the Christian rulers formally welcomed conversion to Christianity, this particular case raised a lot of resistance in Spain and the Latin Kingdoms where slavery was a major source of labour.[73] In both realms, Christian masters – ecclesiastical as well as worldly – were concerned about the loss of human capital, and the rule was not applied in full everywhere. In Catalonia, for instance, laws made it far easier for a Muslim slave owned by a Jew, rather than by a Christian, to become free upon conversion.[74]

While conversion to Christianity was hardly a factor of demographic significance in these frontier areas under Christian rule, migration definitely was. The migration was of two kinds that were mutually reinforcing: Muslims would move out, and Christians would move in. In Sicily, for instance, the Muslim population by 1090 CE – when Norman rule was definitely established – was approximately 250,000, but had dwindled by 1250 CE, the year that they were being deported to Italy, to 25,000.[75] In the Latin Kingdoms, the Franks lived mostly in towns where the Muslim populations were either killed or driven into exile, while the countryside was predominantly inhabited by the native people since there were no Frankish settlers to colonize the lands.[76] In Catholic Spain, many Muslims stayed on as *mudéjars* under Christian rule if they were allowed under the terms of surrender to keep their lands and property; but when the convert-or-emigrate decrees became effective, the majority chose conversion, although an unknown number migrated to North Africa and the Ottoman Empire.[77] In the following chapter we will see that, although there were officially no longer any Muslims in Spain, those Muslims who had opted for conversion to Christianity were still suspected – and often with reason – of being crypto-Muslims, which made them apostates or heretics in the eyes of the Church and the Inquisition.

5. Other Relations and Contacts

Commerce and Trade

We have seen that warfare in the period between 1000 and 1500 CE had changed in character compared to the previous centuries, aiming at conquest rather than spoils and tribute, and often being inspired by religious zeal. What had not changed, however, was that war, in addition to creating havoc and destruction, also created ample business opportunities. The Crusades were no exception. On the contrary: they are considered by many scholars to have been the driving force behind the economic resurrection of Europe. The grand scale of the Crusades – sending large numbers of men and supplies thousands of miles away into enemy territory – demanded innovative thinking on logistics, maintaining supply lines, foraging, and long term investments. The First Crusade met most of these challenges on the way: the crusading army more or less haphazardly organized itself while moving through Europe towards Saracen lands, and mostly provided for its needs on the way, leaving in its wake a trail of devastation and ruin. No wonder that many European cities kept their gates shut, only bringing out food in the hope that this armed and fanatical rubble would move on.

This became different once the Crusaders had settled in the Latin Kingdoms and later, when new crusades were being organized. The overland route had proven to be too dangerous, and supplies and men were now shipped over sea. The only people capable of doing so were the Italian sailors and traders from the city-states of Venice, Genoa and Pisa. The Mediterranean shipping trade was entirely in their hands. The Crusades created immense business opportunities that the Italian merchants took on with enthusiasm and great commercial cunning. Soon, these city states were booming: warehouses were stocked to the roof and had to be expanded, shipyards were working round the clock, bankers and investors devised new financial models to accommodate the newly developing international enterprises. In this case, relations with the Muslim lands proved essential. Prior to the millennium, European commercial and financial institutions were almost non-existent. One of the reasons was the Church's adverse view of commercial enterprise, as shown in the strict prohibition of interest in canonical law.[78] Moneylenders in this period therefore were depending on Jewish financers and an occasional ecclesiastical lender who was willing to bend Christian rules. Islam's rules on commerce as well as Muslim economic experience were instrumental in Europe's revolutionary transformation to a vibrant economy.

The influence of Islam in this respect was not only the Islamic Empire's four centuries of experience with long-distance commerce but also Islam's theological approval thereof. The fact that Islam's prophet Mohammed was by profession an experienced merchant definitely contributed to the religious endorsement of capitalistic venture in the Islamic Empire. Getting rich is not a problem in Islamic eyes, but the ways one goes about it may be. Islam allows for business, as long as one does not unjustly enrich oneself, or misuse one's position to the detriment of others, and does not engage in speculative or other risky forms of business. As long as one adhered to these rules that were enshrined in religious doctrine, one was free to become a wealthy businessman – and the economic boom of the early Islamic empire showed that many did so.

In addition to theological justifications for commerce, Islamic law also provided the legal instruments that facilitated commerce without violating the tenets of Islamic religious doctrine. These were the practices Italian investors turned to in order to cope with the challenge of investing in a huge enterprise like the Crusades. From their Muslim counterparts they copied financial instruments and institutions that not only made the Italians the first bankers in Europe, but also propelled Europe into an economic and commercial renaissance. The most important problem faced by the Italian investors was how to get the funds safely to their lenders hundreds or thousands of miles away, and vice versa. The Arab Muslims, experienced in long distance trade, had developed for this purpose the *shakk* ('cheque') and *hawala* ('aval' or the guarantee of a bill) as a means to avoid carrying cash during the long journeys of the trade caravans. Similarly, the newly established Italian banks would issue 'cheques' to kings and rulers to be cashed in partner banks at the location in Europe where armies and supplies had to be raised, or even in the Middle East where they were deployed.[79]

More fundamental, perhaps, was the European transformation from a barter economy into a monetary economy. The Islamic empire already had a well-functioning monetary economy and its currency remained dominant in determining the monetary standard in the Mediterranean. The newly emerging commercial interaction between the two worlds, in particular in the Latin Kingdoms, arguably played a material role in the reappearance of a monetary economy in Europe: 'not only in creating a need for a new coinage to support commerce, but by concurrently undermining the Muslim coinage then in circulation.'[80] This undermining of Muslim currency started with European counterfeiting of Muslim currency, resulting in coins like those found in the Latin Kingdom bearing both Arabic inscriptions and a Christian cross.[81] Mediterranean alternatives that were introduced proved more lasting:

the first gold coin since the Carolingian monarchs was minted by the Sicilian King Roger in 1151 CE and was known as the *ducat*, followed by the *florin* minted in Florence.

Not everyone was pleased with these commercial and economic transformations. The Byzantine Empire had traditionally dominated trade between its Muslim neighbours and the Italian city-states. Very little trade was conducted directly between the Italians and the Arab Muslims. With the Crusades, however, the volume of trade between the Latin and the Arab-Muslim parts of the Mediterranean increased explosively, shifting the trade monopoly in the region from Byzantium to the Italian city-states.[82] In the resulting competition, Byzantium proved a master in playing out the city states against each other, by granting the merchants of one Italian city certain commercial privileges and the right of residence in Constantinople, while denying it to the other, and vice versa.[83] At the same time, both the Byzantine Empire and the Italian city-states concluded commercial treaties with the Fatimid, Syrian and Andalusian rulers.[84] The Italians were exclusively focused on trade, and the Arab rulers assigned to Venice, Genoa and Pisa each its own *caravanserai* or *fondacos* (*funduq* in Arabic), buildings that combined lodging and warehouse.[85] The Byzantines, on the other hand, already had long-standing diplomatic relations with Muslim rulers, in which commercial activities were included.

Even though Muslim demand for European commodities increased, the trading initiative remained one-sided: Byzantine and Italian merchants went to the Muslims' lands, not the other way round. This had already been the case in the preceding centuries, which at the time was understandable because there was no need for Muslims to come to Europe for it had little to offer to them. But now this pattern of European commercial initiative was to persist in the centuries to come.

Slavery

While the presence of Muslim population in Europe decreased considerably in the course of fourteenth and fifteenth centuries, there was one commercial commodity that enlarged Muslim presence in Europe: slavery. Slaves were primarily used in the Mediterranean basin, and less so on the continent itself. Slavery took place on both sides of the Mediterranean basin, and several cities in Italy (Genoa, Naples, Palermo) and France (Marseilles, Montpellier) were important slave markets where both Muslim and Christian slaves were traded.[86] The slaves used by Europeans were sometimes black Africans,[87] but mostly Muslims from North Africa who were enslaved through raids and in wars. They were put to work as domestic servants, as galley rowers and on plantations and mines in Spain and Italy, in particular in the Venetian colonies of Crete and Cyprus.[88]

Since the millennium, most wars had been increasingly fought along religious fault lines, and a captive was almost axiomatically a slave of his religious enemy.[89] This, in turn, gave rise to a new commercial enterprise, that of raiding for the purpose of selling the captives for ransom. This practice was not new, but while in previous times the ransom was reserved for the rich nobles, it became customary in European lands to ransom as many Christians as possible, and Christian organizations were established that made it their goal to ransom Christian captives.[90] To this end, town councils in the frontier zones of Spain made use of those Christian and Muslim merchants who maintained the flow of trade across the frontier, and officials were appointed in charge of arranging the ransoms, while from the twelfth century onwards the Church rallied the faithful to pay alms for these ransom sums.[91] This development in turn incited the Muslim corsairs to increase their raids on Christian coasts and ships, because the European willingness and infrastructure to ransom the captives made it a profitable venture.

III. Virtual Islam

Before the turn of the millennium, the European Christian perception of the Saracen or Moor was that of a victorious and fearsome warrior, not unlike the Viking, Hun or Maygar. In the period between 1000 and 1500 CE, Saracens or Moors were increasingly perceived as non-Christian, albeit not as the pagan peoples in the north who were easily converted by missionaries or by force, but as a people that was self-assured in their religion and civilization. The impossibility of Christian Europe to assimilate them into the religion, culture and language of the Christian commonwealth, as was done with all the other pagan peoples, and the refusal on the Arab Muslim side to do so created a divide between the two. This divide was similar to that between the realms of the Latin Catholic Western Europeans and the Greek Orthodox Byzantines in eastern Europe. There, too, religion, culture, prosperity and language were a source of differentiation. However, the Byzantines never acquired the position of the European Other, which became reserved for the Muslims. This can be partly explained by the fact that the Byzantines did not conduct raids or wars of conquest into Europe, as Arab Muslims had done. Another explanation may be the different views that the Western European held of the two: the Byzantines were regarded with animosity towards their heretical religion and loathing of their lifestyle, while the Arab Muslims were viewed with fear and awe of their power, combined with a disdain for their infidel religion.

After the millennium, Islam gradually became embedded in the European imagination as a source of knowledge, but also as the European Other. The Crusades played an important role in this respect, because even though they were of little historical or military consequence, they contributed to an increasing sense of solidarity and cohesiveness of European Christendom. This self-image was reinforced by being pitted against what European Christendom was *not*: the Muslim. This gave rise to an interest in the Muslim's religion, but the resulting study primarily aimed at maintaining the self-image of the European Christian. Islam served not as a matter of study in its own right, but as the photo negative of the European Christian. Even the physical interaction with Muslims and their religion that was brought about by the Crusades, both in Spain and the Latin Kingdoms, did not improve European knowledge about Islam. In European texts of that period the image of the Muslim as polytheist idolater remained dominant, as we will see below.[92]

1. The Study and Legends of Islam

With the twelfth century the European-Christian view of the religion of the Moors and Saracens altered, and Islam gradually "began to be treated seriously",[93] resulting in a considerable volume of literature on Islam by the end of the thirteenth century that had become quite widespread throughout Europe in the fourteenth century. The person known for the first European attempt to understand Islam by its own sources was Peter the Venerable, abbot of the famous monastery of Cluny. He commissioned Robert Ketton to translate the Quran and in 1143 CE, more than five hundred years after the Muslim conquest of the Byzantine Empire, and more than four hundred years after the Muslim conquest of Spain, the first Latin translation of the Quran was produced, quickly followed by a biography of the prophet (which was not based on the official Islamic biography, but on an obscure Arabic source). In the following centuries more translations of the Quran would be published, but Robert Ketton's translation remained the 'standard version' of the translated Quran until the eighteenth century.[94]

Peter the Venerable wrote a commentary on Islam, based on these translations.[95] His point of departure was – not unlike the present day's – the Islamic texts and how he read them, and not how the Muslim theologians read them. The textual and historical facts were therefore often correct, but the conclusions on what the tenets of Islam were supposed to be did not always concur with what Islamic doctrine stated. This is not so surprising: the mind-set of the medieval Christian, even one with as good intentions as the abbot of Cluny, was dominated by Christianity, and this would remain for many centuries the viewpoint when studying the Quran.

While the new study of Islam elevated this religion from its former status of an abject form of paganism to the belief system of a powerful infidel nation, it was not to be recognized as a religion in its own right. Christianity remained the frame of reference, and the many Christian elements of Islam, as well as Mohammed's acquaintance with Jews and several Christians, were reason enough to conclude that Islam was a heretical offshoot of the true faith. Islam was listed as one of the great Christian heresies, together with Nestorianism and Arianism.[96]

The Christian theologians were primarily focused on the Muslim prophet Mohammed. They regarded him as a renegade Christian missionary who had started his own sect, and consequently blamed him for corrupting the Christian message of which he was supposedly well aware, and for deliberately teaching falsehood and heresies, leading the poor Arab desert dwellers astray with tricks and magic. Popular legends also abounded with the theme of the impostor posing as a prophet.[97]

One of these stories was that Mohammed put a pea in his ear that was picked out of there by a trained pigeon – his way of tricking his audience into believing that he communicated directly with God. It is an interesting combination of Islamic and Christian elements: Islam holds that God conveyed His message to Mohammed by means of the messenger angel Gabriel, while the pigeon as a symbol of the Holy Spirit is typical for Christianity. A similar story is that of a trained bull showing up while Mohammed was addressing the crowd, holding a book on its horns, representing the Quran sent to God's prophet.

The image of the false prophet also brought Mohammed a place in Dante's *Divine Comedy* (1321), where he was positioned in Hell as a 'schismatic' on the ninth level in the eight circle ('fraud'). Mohammed shared this place with his cousin and son-in-law Ali. Other Muslims were much better of: Saladin was not in Hell nor in Heaven, but in Limbo, where virtuous non-Christians and unbaptized infants ended up, together with the philosophers Avicenna (Ibn Sina) and Averroes (Ibn Rushd).

Other medieval European stories about Mohammed have more mundane themes. The story of Mohammed drinking with his good friend, the monk Sergius, was famous (again a mixture of Islamic and Christian elements: according to the Islamic biography of Mohammed he had met a monk named Bihai during his travels as a merchant into Syria, while Christian folklore holds that an apostate priest named Sergius had run off to Arabia to spread falsehood). When the two companions fell asleep in a drunken stupor a soldier passed by who killed the sleeping monk and placed his sword in Mohammed's hands. When he awoke and the soldier told him that he had killed his companion in his sleep, Mohammed foreswore wine for the rest of his life. The Islamic prohibition of alcohol and pork greatly intrigued the medieval European, and recur in many stories, possibly because they represented the elementary food supply for the average European (we should keep in mind that beer and wine in many medieval European cities replaced water that was often too polluted to drink).

Medieval Europeans were particularly fascinated by several aspects of Islam that still capture the imagination and indignation of the modern Westerner: the violent nature of Islam, the sexual licentiousness of Muslims and Islam's Paradise, and the position of the Muslim woman.[98] To the Christian European, for whom marriage meant an indissoluble and monogamous bond, the Islamic notions of bigamy and divorce were shocking, and contributed to the notion of the ever lustful Muslim man. The oppression of the Muslim woman was explained by the fact that she did not enjoy the same rights as her husband – an argument that may sound odd given the social position of women in European medieval life, but made sense from a formal legal perspective: the medieval Christian woman indeed had exactly the same options as the man, namely a monogamous marriage, and no divorce.

2. Polemics

The scholars who had made the first serious attempt to come to an understanding of this Islam were limited in means as well as in aims. The limited means were reflected in the lack of Arabic sources that were available to them, and the European scholars' knowledge of the Arabic language and specific Islamic theological terminology was questionable. An exception was the Dominican monk Riccoldo da Monte di Croce (1243–1320 CE), who spent a decade studying Arabic in Bagdad and then devoted the remaining years of his life in Florence studying Islam.[99] His work, however, fitted in with the limited aim shared by all scholars of that time: their intention was not to understand Islam itself, but to refute it.

Medieval European scholars did so by engaging in polemics and disputations, using newly developed methods of logic based on theological and rational arguments to 'prove' that the faith of the Muslim infidel was wrong.[100] The result was a large production of polemics pointing at the contradictions within the Quran, and the contradictions between the (alleged) behaviour of Muslims and what the Quran ordained, and at the contradictions between the tenets of Islam and Christianity. The contradictions themselves were already sufficient proof that Islam was false, since Christianity was held to represent the truth. For instance, the fact that Islam recognized Jesus Christ as a prophet was not a reason for rapprochement between the two religions but, to the contrary, it constituted 'proof' that Islam was false because it refused to recognize Christ as the son of God.

The ostensible purpose of these polemics was to convince the Muslim of his wrong beliefs and, since Islam was considered a heresy of Christianity, to make him return to the fold of the true religion by means of reasoning. However, the aim of convincing the Muslim of his errors was mostly an academic exercise, because Christian theologians never even met a Muslim, let alone engaged the Muslim in a polemic debate. These polemic tracts were mostly written in European lands far away from societies where Muslims lived. The polemics were therefore not intended for Muslims but for a Christian readership as a scholarly proof of the rightfulness and truth of Christianity.

By the eleventh century, Christian Europeans considered the Muslim a person who, once shown the wrongfulness of his beliefs, would repent and embrace the true faith. This reveals a new view of the Muslim: the assumption that he would be susceptible to reasoning implied that in the eyes of the medieval theologian he was not a pagan barbarian but a human being gifted with reason. Abbot Peter the Venerable describes this effort as follows: "[b]ut I do not attack you, as some of us often do, by arms, but by words, not by force, but by reason; not in hatred, but in love".[101] This celebration of rationality was illustrated by stories of theological debates at faraway Muslim courts between Muslims, Christians and Jews that were – of course – won by the Christians. These stories were fictional but based on historical fact, for such encounters had indeed taken place, mainly at the invitation of Muslim rulers who occasionally invited representatives of the three monotheistic faiths to theological debates at court (no doubt to prove the truth of Islam). William of Rubruck's participation in the disputation at the Mongol court of Möngke Khan in 1254 CE involving Muslims and Buddhists was famous.[102] In his *Itinerarium* Rubruck describes how he outsmarted the Buddhists by asking them whether all their gods [sic] were omnipotent, to which they had to answer that no god was. The Muslims did not contradict the Christians but also did not convert: "[w]e concede that your law is true and that the Gospel is true: we have no wish to dispute with you". According to Rubruck's description, the debate ended with loud singing by the Christians and the Muslims, and copious drinking by all.

Another polemic disputation that acquired mythical status is that before the khan of the Khazars, a people near the Black Sea. The khan thought it time for him and his people to adopt a proper religion, and invited a rabbi, priest and imam to convince him of what was the best of religions. In the aftermath of this polemic battle, all three faiths claimed victory (although correspondence in the tenth century between the Andalusian foreign secretary and the khan of the Khazars indicates that Judaism emerged triumphant).[103]

Given the presumption of the truth of Christianity and the rationality of mankind, medieval Europeans therefore had high hopes for the Mongols. They were the new great power in Asia and the Near East, and by the thirteenth century had conquered most of the Islamic empire. They were pagans, but among them were Nestorians, a Christian sect that was persecuted as heretic by the Byzantine Empire and had moved eastwards where it settled in Central Asia. There were Nestorian priests among the Mongols, and quite a few Mongol rulers had married Nestorian women. The Mongol commander who conquered Damascus in 1260 CE was a Nestorian Christian, who rode into the city flanked by two other Christian princes, one Armenian and one a Frankish Crusader. Even though European Christianity condemned the Nestorians as a Christian sect, the marital and clerical presence of Christianity among the Mongols raised European hopes for their conversion to Christianity, and several missionary delegates had visited the Mongol courts for that purpose. Great therefore was the shock in Europe when the Mongols rulers – and, consequently, their people, including the Tatar tribes – in the course of the thirteenth and fourteenth centuries converted to Islam. So great was the disappointment among Christian Europeans that from that moment on they abandoned the idea of Muslims' rationality. From the fourteenth century onwards the use of force and coercion was permitted to bring Muslims to the right path, "as it was permitted with children or animals".[104]

Still, missionary orders like the Dominicans and Franciscans kept going into Muslim lands to convince the infidel by rational means of his erroneous ways. They did so sometimes on their own initiative, but mostly as emissaries sent by European kings or the Vatican to courts of Muslim (mainly Mongol) rulers.[105] The number of missionaries was very limited, however, and their success rate in converting Muslims was nil. An offshoot of medieval Christian missionary activity in Muslim lands was the missionaries who actively sought martyrdom by going into Muslim lands and publicly denouncing Islam and proclaiming the falseness of its prophet.[106] We saw such behaviour taking place several centuries earlier, with the so-called 'martyrs of Cordoba' in the period between 850 and 860 CE. In the thirteenth century there was a renewed pursuit of martyrdom at the infidel's hand, with preachers going into Muslim lands as far as Tatary to denounce the supposed wicked and false ways of Islam and its prophet. The response by the Muslim rulers was similar to that of their predecessors four centuries earlier: bewildered amusement turning into irritation when the missionaries persisted, even after they had been admonished or banned, and often ending with the death penalty – hence fulfilling the martyrdom the missionaries had craved for. These acts of martyrdom gained great prestige in Europe.

The most prestigious act of self-righteous defiance was that by Francis of Assisi who in 1219 CE, during the Fifth Crusade in Egypt, crossed enemy lines and was admitted to the tent of Egyptian sultan Al-Kamil where he was apparently allowed to speak to the sultan for a while before he was escorted back to the Crusaders' camp.[107] We will never know whether Francis of Assisi was intent on martyrdom or on the conversion of the great sultan, and whether he was disappointed in obtaining neither of these goals. It is an interesting twist of European history, however, that in the twentieth century this bold action of mission and zealous crusading was turned into a symbol of 'dialogue' with Islam: somehow the image was retained through all these centuries of one of Christianity's famous saints engaging with the leader of Muslim faithful in civilized conversation with the purpose of understanding each other.[108]

3. Culture and Technology

The eleventh century was the moment when Europeans became aware of, and started to take an interest in, the knowledge possessed by the Muslim Arabs on a wide array of subjects ranging from agricultural, financial and architectural techniques to the sciences of philosophy, mathematics, astrology, chemistry, medicine, and the like. Much of this knowledge was passed on into Europe by means of the translation of the Arabic works into Latin, an activity that took place predominantly in Toledo in the eleventh century, after its capture in 1085 CE. (The image of Baghdad's House of Wisdom comes to mind, but the translation activities in Toledo were not as organized and on a much smaller scale.) Techniques, on the other hand, were often copied by repeating what one had seen, and this took place in most areas where Muslims and Christians interacted. The mechanisms of financing are one example.

There has always been a modest interest among modern Western scholars in these transmissions of knowledge and in the Arab influences on medieval European scientific, artistic and intellectual developments. But after 9/11 the publications on this topic became prolific.[109] Apparently there was an urge to disprove the clash of civilization theory by demonstrating the strong links between the European-Christian and Arab-Islamic civilizations. The question then arises, however, whether a link or similarity between European and Arab thinking or techniques may bring us to conclude that these elements of the European-Christian civilization were influenced by or even directly taken from Arab-Islamic civilization. Since the Arabs had come up with many insights, discoveries and inventions long before the Europeans did, it would be fair to say that the Europeans were influenced by, or even had copied, what the Arabs had produced earlier. But this conclusion has its critics.

First, there is the problem of qualifying the influence itself: does a mere similarity between practices in different times and places justify the suggestion that the latter is influenced by the first? Or can it be that people thought of the same thing independently of each other? Was the emergence of educational colleges in European cities like Paris and Bologna directly influenced by those in the Muslim world, as some scholars have argued,[110] or was this a coincidental parallel development? Has Islamic law influenced European law?[111] And is there a causal connection between the first use of rib-vaulting in Italian and English churches and the capture of Toledo in 1085 CE, where Europeans could now come to see these techniques for themselves, or was it coincidental?[112] The same ambiguity with regard to the source applies to the guitar and the lute: while the word lute is etymologically derived from the Arabic al-ʿud, similar stringed instruments can be found in most cultures of the time.[113] In such cases it is hard to discern who had original intellectual ownership. On the other hand, research has demonstrated that Copernicus, in his calculations that demonstrated that the sun and not the earth was the centre of the planetary system, made use of models already developed by Arab and Persian mathematicians.[114]

Also, is the availability of Latin translations of Arabic books on a large number of scientific topics in itself proof that they actually influenced European thinking and practices? In some instances we know this to have been the case. Arab Muslim philosophers like Ibn Rushd and Ibn Sina have become part of the European canon of philosophy, known under their Latinized names of, respectively, Averroes and Avicenna.[115] Averroes, who applied the philosophical thinking of Aristotle to theological questions, was a major source of inspiration to Thomas Aquinas who referred to him merely as 'the Philosopher'.[116] Being an admirer of Averroes was also reason for being expelled from more religiously orthodox European universities – not because Averroes was a Muslim, which was not generally known, but because his Aristotelian ideas were considered too radical at the time.

The discussions on who influenced whom and who was first are not mere scholarly debates: they touch on the very essence of European identity, namely on the question whether Europe has invented itself, or whether European civilization is indebted to the Arabs for escaping from the Middle Ages and entering the Renaissance. Is it thanks to the Arabs that Europeans conceived of the concept of a library, hospital or university, that Copernicus discovered the workings of the solar system, that Thomas Aquinas introduced logic into theological thinking, that sailors can navigate with a compass and that new forms of irrigation and agriculture were developed? Or have Europeans made these discoveries on their own, merely assisted by Greek philosophers and Indian mathematicians whose works the Arabs passed on to them? It is one thing to represent 'Islam' as a 'carrier civilization' that had "little of [its] own to offer" but merely reproduced knowledge of Greek, Indian and Chinese origin that was of great use to Europeans.[117] But it is quite another matter to argue that the Islamic civilization has actually been at the cradle of pre-modern Europe and that it kick-started Europe into its Renaissance[118] and perhaps even introduced Europe to the notion of humanism[119] or modern science.[120]

I would argue that these debates on 'ownership' of knowledge presuppose an exchange of knowledge between civilizations as if these were closed boxes, and deny that science and knowledge are not owned by people, but used, developed and passed on from generation to generation by those who are capable of handling such knowledge. The legacy of the Arabs is not only the translation into Arabic of original works from the Greeks, Indians and Chinese, but also their elaboration of those works that brought them to the next stages of innovation and scholarship. Science and knowledge was thus passed on and further developed by those who had the ability to do so: first the Chinese and Indians, then the Greeks, then the Arabs, followed by the Europeans. Each period and community of scholars can be proud of its own achievements, but these are to be seen as a phase in a long history of scientific and scholarly development. However, the sensitivity of these debates illustrates how the perception of the Arab-Muslim Other provides an obstacle to such considerations: many Europeans prefer to hold on to the self-image of Europe that raised itself as a Baron von Munchhausen from the Middle Ages, without any help or influence from the outside world, let alone from those whom Europe came to see as its opposite Other.

CHAPTER THREE

Divided Europe
(1500–1700 CE)

I. Setting the Stage

By the late fifteenth century, the Muslim presence in Europe shifted from the western to the eastern Mediterranean. In the west, Spain had officially eradicated Islam from its Catholic territory and society by 1527 CE, and during the following century also expelled the remaining Muslims who were coerced to convert to Christianity, the so-called Moriscos. This expulsion of the entire Muslim population had already been accomplished in Sicily, several centuries earlier. In the east, on the other hand, it was the Christian presence in the form of the Byzantine Empire and Crusader states that had come to an end, and was replaced by the new Muslim power of the Ottoman Empire. As a result, Islam entered Europe in the Balkans by means of Muslim sovereignty, conversion to Islam, and Muslim colonists.

Perhaps the main characteristic of this period was the religious, political and national divisions that were cutting through the European continent in continuous shifting alliances. The Catholic Church's domination over the entire continent was challenged by the Reformation and powerful kings. The Ottoman Empire, the only Muslim power that was physically present on the European continent, was to become an intricate part of these divisions and power plays.

1. Europe: Reformation and National Self-Assertion

In the period under discussion in this chapter, the notion of Christian Europe as "a single commonwealth and a single body"[1] was an ideal claimed by many but pursued by few. Nations had become aware of their own and unique identity, and asserted themselves accordingly. Even religion became 'nationalized' as shown in the maxim *cuius regio eius religio* (to each region its own religion): European countries identified themselves either with Catholicism or with various forms of 'Protestantism' like the Anglican, Lutheran, Calvinist, Anabaptist, Hussite, Presbyterian or other denominations. At the same time, the overall endeavour of each king was to emerge as the champion of the Christian realm: Francis I of France bore the title 'the most Christian of Kings', Charles V of the Habsburg Empire in central Europe was called the 'Holy Roman Emperor', and Henry VIII of England used the title 'Defender of the Faith.'

The religious and political squabbles that dominated Europe in the sixteenth and seventeenth centuries rendered the image of a perpetual conflict of Christianity with the Muslim infidel mostly imaginary, although it remained appealing. The repeated calls for crusades that used to be so inflammatory in previous centuries now went unheeded or led to naught. National and petty concerns outweighed common interests, even when these were religious. The Italian political thinker Machiavelli, when exhorting against the "barbarians", meant not the Ottomans, but Spain and France.[2]

The Reformation created a religious north-south divide, with the Catholic south being caught between the hammer of Protestantism in the north-west and the anvil of Islam in the south-east. But there was also a political west-east divide, with the powerful Holy Roman Empire being squeezed between France in the west and the Ottoman Empire in the south-east. Within this political-religious matrix there was a continuous shifting of alliances between nations that all served one purpose only: preserving one's interests. If one of the European states acquired a power much greater than that of the other states, then those states would set aside any differences they might have and join forces against the other. In this intense and continuous struggle the Ottoman Empire might still be branded as the infidel Other, but actually was one of the competing European states – and a very powerful one, for that matter.

2. Rise of the Ottoman Empire

The late fifteenth century witnessed the emergence of the Ottoman Empire as the sole heir to the Byzantine Empire and later also to the Islamic empires of the Middle East. Its emergence had been gradual, dating back to the fourteenth century when a Turkish tribe moved from Central Asia into Anatolia where it had established its power base. They soon became known as the Osmans or Ottomans, after the progenitor of their tribe.

Long before the fall of Constantinople in 1453 CE, the Ottoman forces had already conquered most of the Byzantine Empire which included large parts of the Balkans and Anatolia (present-day western Turkey). The Ottomans' first foothold in the European continent dates from 1352 CE, when they came to the call of the Genoese colony of Galata, opposite Constantinople, in one of their military struggles against the Venetians and Byzantines. The Ottomans moved their capital to this new stronghold in Edirne, on the most eastern tip of the European continent, and from there gradually took over the adjacent territories in the Balkan hinterlands, taking advantage of internal struggles among the local warlords. On several occasions the Ottoman incursions were welcomed by the local population who hoped to be liberated from these hated overlords.[3]

The expansion of the Ottoman Empire usually followed the same pattern: first alliances were established with local rulers, then this relationship turned into vassalage with the rulers pledging allegiance and paying tribute to the Ottoman sultan, and in a later stage these territories were often annexed into the empire as provinces.[4] This was not a calculated strategy, but mostly prompted by the financial logic of conquest: the war machine had to be paid with the spoils of new conquests, and the income from new lands was highest if they were annexed because then the Ottomans could allot plots of land to their military commanders (the so-called *timar* lands).[5]

The capture of Constantinople in 1453 CE brought twelve centuries of Byzantine Empire to an end. This historical event was not without symbolic significance: for the Ottomans it meant the final usurpation of the Byzantine legacy to which they claimed to be the only heirs; for the Greeks it was the final demise of the Eastern Roman Empire; for the Russians it meant that the rightful seat of Orthodoxy was transferred to Moscow; and for the Western Europeans it signified that Western Christendom had now become the trustee of ancient Greek culture which, by that time, was conceived as the cradle of European culture.[6]

After 1453 CE, the Ottomans chose Constantinople – now renamed Istanbul[*] – as their new capital, where the Sultan established his court known as the 'High Porte' (from the Ottoman 'High Gate' or entrance to the court). A century later, the Ottoman Empire was at the zenith of its power and its realm reached as far west as Tunisia, as far east as Iraq and as far north as Hungary (basically the territory of the Byzantine Empire at the height of its power seven centuries earlier). The army as well as the administration of the empire was efficiently structured, securing a continuous flow of revenue that, together with the economic revival within the realm, made the empire's wealth and power the envy as well as concern of all European countries of that time. Moreover, Ottoman power was not established just on land, but also at sea. Thanks to their large fleet of galleys the Ottomans dominated the Mediterranean, making Italy, France and Spain vulnerable to possible attacks from the sea.[7] Invasions of these lands by sea did not come to pass, but the anxiety caused by Ottoman raids on their coasts was to have far-reaching consequences, as we will see later.

---

[*] 'Istanbul' was the combination of Greek 'stin-poli' ('in the city') and Ottoman-Turkish 'Islambol' (Ottoman for 'abounding with Islam'). The Ottomans referred to both Constantinople ('Konstaniniyye') and Istanbul, which became the official name of the city only in 1930. (Caroline Finkel, *Osman's Dream. The History of the Ottoman Empire*, New York, Basic Books, 2005, p. 57.)

The period that we will discuss in this chapter roughly matches the golden age of the Ottoman Empire. The two landmark events, at least from a European perspective, during this period are the fall of Constantinople in 1453 CE and the second siege of Vienna in 1683 CE which became the first major defeat of the hitherto invincible Ottoman army. After this period, the economic, social, political and military decline set in that led to dismemberment and final dissolution of the Ottoman Empire in 1914 CE, of which we will speak in the next chapter.

In what follows, we limit our discussion to the European provinces of the Ottoman Empire (called 'Rumeli' by the Ottomans). These provinces were central to the Empire, because they provided the largest portion of state revenues,[8] and most state dignitaries and the military elite came from this region. At the height of the Ottoman power, halfway through the sixteenth century, the most northerly boundaries of its European provinces ran across Romania ('Transylvania'), Hungary and Slovenia to the Adriatic Sea. The city-state of Dubrovnik (or Ragusia, in present-day Croatia) was allowed to maintain its independence,[9] as were most Venetian colonies along the Balkan coast, to serve as the economic link between the Ottoman Empire and Western Europe.

The Ottoman Empire had several European neighbours that we will briefly introduce here in order to obtain some background to the developments and events that we are to discuss later. The city-state of Venice was at the centre of a network of merchant colonies dotted along the Adriatic, Greek and Byzantine coastline. So powerful was this small state that the Ottomans at first left most of these colonies untouched. Only later were these commercial bases gradually usurped by the Ottomans, culminating in their conquest of Cyprus in 1571 CE, which had been under Venetian rule during the previous century. From the Venetian perspective, the Ottomans merely replaced the Byzantines as the Venetians' most powerful partner and rival in the region.[10] The Republic of Venice played an intricate and dangerous game of diplomacy that continuously sought a balance between France, the Habsburgs and the Ottomans, playing one power off against another.

The other and most lasting adversary of the Ottoman Empire was the Holy Roman Empire of the Habsburg dynasty, which straddled what is now Germany, the Czech Republic, Slovakia, Austria, Slovenia and northern Italy. While Venice was a power without territory, aimed only at commercial gain, the Habsburgs formed a power very similar to the Ottomans, with distinct territorial and universal claims. Indeed, both laid claim to be the rightful heir to the Byzantine Empire, the Habsburgs from a religious perspective and the Ottomans from a territorial and cultural perspective.[11] These two power blocks were permanently in conflict, the border territories of Transylvania and Hungary serving as the main bones of contention. Rather than assisting the Habsburgs in their plight, other European powers often took advantage of the Habsburg military preoccupation with the Ottomans. The most prominent example is France, as we will discuss at length below. The others were the German Protestants who, when engaged in the devastating civil war within the Catholic Habsburg Empire (known as the Thirty Years War: 1618–1648 CE), took advantage of Ottoman pressure on the Habsburg borders to consolidate and expand their position.[12]

Of the Ottoman neighbours, the Venetians and Habsburgs posed most problems for the Porte in Istanbul. There were two other immediate European neighbours of the Empire, but they were initially much less of a threat to the Ottomans. The first was the Polish-Lithuanian Commonwealth, an enormous empire established in 1569 CE and encompassing what is now Poland, Lithuania, Belarus and the Ukraine. During the two hundred years of its existence it was one of largest and most populous countries in Europe. The parts of its territory that bordered the Ottoman Empire were predominantly populated by nomadic tribes and ruled by several sedentary khanats, most of which were Muslim with whom the Ottomans maintained friendly relations. Relations between the Commonwealth and the Ottoman Empire were cordial, prospering from profitable trade in slaves and furs, and with a regular exchange of emissaries.[13] The main source of continuous antagonism between the two powers was the Commonwealth's use of the unruly and nomadic Cossacks as a mercenary defence force that regularly made incursions into Ottoman territories.

Cordial relations also existed between the Ottoman Empire and its other neighbour, the Grand Duchy of Muscovy, which in 1498 CE was granted the right to trade freely in the Ottoman Empire. This balance was disrupted in 1547 CE when Ivan, the Duke of Muscovy, embarked on the building of an empire by crowning himself tsar and subsequently annexing the Muslim khanates between Muscovy and the Ottoman Empire and forcing all their Muslim inhabitants to convert to the Russian Orthodox faith.[14] This was threatening to the Ottoman Empire, but more so was the Russian claim of custodianship over the Orthodox population in the Ottoman domains, which the Russian Empire was to use repeatedly in the eighteenth and nineteenth centuries as a justification for military interventions.

II.   Physical Islam

1.   Living with the Unbeliever

The European continent contained three states with mixed Muslim and non-Muslim societies: the Polish-Lithuanian Commonwealth in the east, the Ottoman Empire in the south-east and Spain in the south-west. Of these three realms, the Ottoman Empire was the only one with Islamic rule. Spain is an exceptional case, since Islam had officially been eradicated from the Peninsula since 1527 CE; however, the Catholic rulers spent the following century persecuting the Muslim converts who allegedly persisted in their Islamic ways. The ways in which the religious communities coexisted in these realms and how the ruler interacted with its subjects of another faith were so different that they need to be discussed separately.

1.1.   Lipka Tatars in the Christian Polish-Lithuanian Commonwealth

The eastern frontier zone of Europe consisted of the vast area between the Baltic in the north and the Black Sea in the south. Nations on the western side of this zone were, from north to south, Poland and Lithuania, the Holy Roman Empire of the Habsburgs, and the Ottoman Empire. On the eastern side of this zone was the Duchy of Moscovy, which from the sixteenth century onwards was to expand its territories and become the Russian Empire. The vast steppe of the frontier zone itself was dominated by two tribal nations: the Tatars and the Cossacks.[15] The Cossacks had embraced Christianity and their allegiance was primarily to the Russians. The Tatars,[16] on the other hand, were Muslim, so that the Tatars in the Crimea were vassals of the Ottomans, while the Tatars in the north had entered into allegiance with the (Christian) Duchy of Lithuania, as we saw in the previous chapter, and since then had been known as the Lipka ('Lithuanian') Tatars. They were allowed to maintain their cultural, linguistic and religious ways as Muslims and were even allowed to intermarry with the indigenous population, a remarkable privilege for those times, especially when this was accompanied by the right to raise the children of such mixed marriages in the faith of the father, that is Islam.

The Tatars' status as Muslim warriors loyal to the Duchy was continued when the Duchy merged into the Polish-Lithuanian Commonwealth in 1569 CE. The number of Tatars living in the Commonwealth during this period is subject to speculation. Numbers as high as 200,000 are mentioned for the entire Commonwealth, while in the sixteenth century the number of Tatars in the Lithuanian Duchy is estimated at between 20,000 and 25,000[17] and an estimated 100,000 are said to have migrated into Poland at the time of the Commonwealth.[18] With a total population of an estimated 11 million inhabitants in the late seventeenth century,[19] the Tatars constituted between 1 and 2 per cent of the entire population.

As early as during the fifteenth century, the Lipka Tatars voluntarily and "with startling rapidity" assimilated into their new living environment.[20] By the mid-sixteenth century the majority of the Tatars spoke only Byelorussian or Polish, and while the rank and file of the Tatar soldiers took up trade and manual labour and lived as communities in separate quarters of villages, the richer members of the community lived among their Christian social equals.[21] Compared to other Muslims in European frontier realms, this process of assimilation is exceptional. The reason that has been suggested for this voluntary and successful assimilation of the Lipka Tatars is their geographical and linguistic isolation: they had no connection with mainstream Islam or any Muslim country, and Polish or Byelorussian was not spoken in the Muslim world.[22]

The only part of Tatar identity that did not assimilate was religion: the Tatars lost the culture, customs and languages they had brought with them in earlier times, but they remained Muslim throughout the centuries. They built mosques, albeit in an architectural style similar to that of the local churches in the region, and maintained the Islamic rites of birth, circumcision, marriage, death and burial, all performed by or in the presence of imams and qadis (learned men who also acted as judges).[23] On the other hand, the Islamic rules of polygamy, veils for women, and the ban on alcohol were not adhered to.[24] The mixed identity of the Lipka Tatars is perhaps best illustrated by their religious texts, which were in either Polish or Byelorussian but written in Arabic script.[25]

The Ottomans had a keen interest in these Muslims. They made several diplomatic interventions during the early seventeenth century when the religious freedoms of the Tatars were being restricted under a growing Catholicism in the Commonwealth. The rise of the Ottoman Empire combined with religious intolerance in the Commonwealth culminated in the Tatar rebellion of 1672 CE, with many Lipka Tatars defecting to the Ottomans. What followed was quite remarkable, especially for those times, because the Polish king and nobles quickly restored the ancient privileges of the Tatars and invited the Tatars who had defected or migrated to the Ottoman Empire to return to the Commonwealth. A special role in this process of rehabilitation was played by King Jan Sobieski, known as the liberator of Vienna in 1683 CE, who on several occasions, when Polish forces were to meet Tatars serving in the Ottoman army, struck deals whereby the Tatars were allowed to return and even to be awarded privileges they did not have before, like exemption from all taxes and permission to settle on Crown estates. Many Tatars answered this call from the Polish king, but quite a few remained within the Ottoman realm. The reasons for this Polish indulgence must be sought in the Tatars' standing as a military caste, their defection causing a serious destabilization of the Commonwealth's military might.

1.2. Ottoman Europe

Settlement and Conversion

The census of 1520–1530 CE conducted in the Ottoman Empire records slightly more than 1 million households in the European provinces, of which 18.8 per cent were Muslim. With Jews being a tiny minority (0.5 per cent), Christians made up the dominant majority of 80.7 per cent in the European provinces of the Ottoman Empire. In most areas, however, Christians numbered even more, because the Muslims were concentrated mostly in towns. In the large towns, Muslims even constituted a majority, except in Christian-dominated cities like Athens, Nicopolis and Trikala, and in Saloniki where the Jews constituted a majority of 54 per cent.[26] Islam and Ottoman culture, therefore, were restricted to the urban centres, while the countryside remained the domain of the indigenous inhabitants who were mostly Orthodox.[27]

Let us now take a closer look at the Muslims in the European provinces of the Ottoman Empire. The census of 1520–1530 CE indicated that one third were estimated to be settlers (most of whom lived in large cities), and the remaining two thirds converts.[28] Both settlement and conversion need further elaboration.

Resettlement was a well-known policy of the Ottomans, which they applied often by means of incentives, but sometimes also by force. This policy, known as *sürgün*, was used from the early Ottoman conquests of Balkan territory to repopulate newly conquered areas, either as an outlet for overpopulation in Ottoman territories, but mostly to fill the voids left by the indigenous non-Muslim population in European territories that had fled the Ottoman advance.[29] An interesting example in this respect is Constantinople after its conquest in 1453. Sultan Mehmet II wanted to rebuild and repopulate the devastated and abandoned city in order to make it the new capital of the empire.[30] Although the Ottoman Empire was distinctively Islamic, Sultan Mehmet II wanted to restore the capital to its original grandeur, not least in the economic sense, and therefore ordered its re-population with people of mixed religions and ethnicity. These new inhabitants were attracted by favourable taxes and land prices and, if unwilling, whole communities (Muslims, Armenians, Greeks, Jews and Latin Christians) were forcibly resettled into the city.[31] While the population of 150,000 inhabitants prior to 1453 had diminished to several thousand after the city was taken by the Ottomans, the – mostly forced – resettlement policy of Sultan Murad paid off: thirty years later, according to the 1478 census, Istanbul had 70.000 inhabitants, of whom 58 per cent was Muslim, 32 per cent Christian, and 10 per cent Jewish.[32] The city by then had probably enough prestige to attract new citizens, and a century later, by 1600, it had an estimated population of over 250,000 inhabitants, making it the largest capital in Europe – compare Paris (220,000 inhabitants), London (200,000), Rome (105,000), Madrid (50,000), Vienna (50,000).[33]

The other segment of the Muslim population in the European provinces of the Empire was indigenous people who had converted to Islam. We saw that in 1530 CE they made up two thirds of the Muslims in the provinces. Research indicates that conversion to Islam was a gradual process,[34] but that it quickened in the seventeenth century (the Balkan 'age of conversions')[35] and then halted in the eighteenth century. No census was conducted in the seventeenth and eighteenth centuries, but modern historians mostly refer to an estimated 20 per cent of Muslims in the Balkans, although it has also been argued that the total Muslim population there had by the late eighteenth century increased to 40 per cent.[36] The percentage differed region by region, with Albania and Bosnia being Muslim majority regions (although Bosnia lost this majority position in the nineteenth century).[37]

Who, then, were these converts, and what made them convert to Islam? Extensive research has been conducted on this issue.[38] The Ottomans, upon their conquests of non-Muslim peoples, like their Arab predecessors in the seventh century, did not force or otherwise require conversion to Islam. The reasons were the same as with the Arab conquerors, namely an amalgam of theological, military and financial motivations, of which the last seems to have dominated: the non-Muslim subjects had to pay a mandatory poll tax (cizye in Ottoman) as required under Islamic law, which was a source of income to the Ottoman state. It has been calculated that in 1528 CE the poll tax from the European provinces made up 8 per cent of the total revenue of the Empire.[39]

A combination of three motives may explain conversion to Islam in the Balkans. First and foremost, conversion exempted the new Muslims from paying the poll tax compulsory for all non-Muslims. Also, the worldly and military successes of Islam seemed a sign of God's favour and, conversely, of the spiritual and institutional weakness of Christianity in this part of Europe.[40] Belonging to Islam was therefore belonging to the new order of power, which was a motivation not unlike the conversions that took place in the centuries after the first conquests of the Muslim Arabs. In the case of the Ottoman Europe, however, an additional role was played by the Islamic ascetic and mystical or *dervish* orders that were very active in establishing lodges in newly occupied areas and whose sufi Islam disseminated by travelling holy men (*babas*) was close to the local folk religion of the Balkans.[41] In addition, they operated as guilds, bringing material benefits and fraternization in addition to spiritual bonding.[42]

Conversion was not exclusively directed towards Islam, however. Among the many Christian dominations and sects there were those who chose to convert not to Islam but to Orthodox Christianity. The reason may have been expediency in the particular context of Ottoman rule: the Orthodox Church enjoyed more exemptions from taxes and more allowances on church building than other non-Muslim religions, and the location of the seat of its Patriarch in Istanbul facilitated quick access to the sources of power if the interests of the community needed empirical favour.[43]

A major exception to the voluntarism of conversion to Islam was the typical Ottoman practice of boy levy (*devşirme*): sons of non-Muslim peasants were rounded up as a government levy and taken to Istanbul where they were raised as Muslims and trained to fill the ranks of the Janissary military elite corps or the government apparatus. This levy focused specifically on Christian boys in the Balkans[44] and was imposed irregularly for approximately two centuries between the fifteenth and late seventeenth centuries, resulting in an estimated total of 200,000 boys being taken from their homes.[45]

The practice of recruiting slave soldiers and slave government functionaries was not new, as it already existed under the Romans, Arabs and Seljuks. We saw it in the caliphate of Cordoba (the *Saqaliba*, or Slavs) and at the time when the Ottomans instituted the *devşirme*, Egypt was ruled by the Mamluks ('slaves'), the military caste recruited from slaves imported from the Black Sea region. But what made the case of the Ottoman *devşirme* exceptional was its enslavement of boys by means of a levy among its subjects, and their obligatory conversion to Islam. The system of *devşirme* served the purpose of creating a military and governmental elite with absolute loyalty to the Ottoman rulers and their religion. It was taken so far that a significant portion of the military and state apparatus of the Ottoman Empire had become staffed with cadres recruited through the boy levy. The elite corps of the Janissary, which was the backbone of the Ottoman army, was entirely made up of men who were recruited through *devşirme*. Many of the boys recruited through the youth levy rose to high status, as is exemplified by the famous Ottoman vizir Köprülü Mehmet (from Albania), who was appointed grand vizier in 1656 CE, and whose family members and protégés would dominate Ottoman politics for the next half century. The *devşirme* therefore resulted in the peculiar situation that the Ottoman Empire for two centuries was ruled by people who were staunch Ottoman Muslims but of Balkan Slav-Christian origin.[46] As a result, Turkish elites resented the domination of Ottoman political life by people of Balkan origin, not for ethical considerations but because they felt threatened in their own positions of power.[47]

Although the boy levy was dreaded by many, the prospects of a better life would in some cases prompt Christian Balkan families to insist on having their boys taken to Istanbul.[48] The advantage was not only to the boys themselves; often they would not forget their origins and return favours to the land of their birth land and their families. Famous examples in this respect are the grand viziers Ibrahim Pasha and Mehmed Süküllü, who under the *devşirme* had been taken away as boys, were raised and trained in Istanbul, had risen to the highest echelons of power at the Porte, and in that position had lavishly spent on bridges and buildings in their Christian birth towns in Bosnia.[49] However, the boy levy was overall perceived as a humiliating and arbitrary act of the ruling class against its non-Muslim subjects which may have contributed to the gradually evolving resentment against Ottoman rule that was to explode in the nineteenth century.[50]

Religious Rule
While the Ottomans did not force their non-Muslim subjects to convert to Islam (except in the case of the boy levy) they did establish a form of government that we might call Islamic rule. This manifested itself in terms of political-legal constructs as well as a general identity.

The most renowned Ottoman political-legal construct vis-à-vis non-Muslim subjects was the *millet* system, which was a continuation of the *dhimmi* status described in the first chapter: the non-Muslim communities enjoyed relative autonomy in handling their religious affairs, with their own courts applying their religious laws, in exchange for a second-class social and legal position and the obligation to pay a poll tax.[51] While maintaining the *dhimmi* status of relative freedom of religion on the one hand, and second-class citizenship on the other, the *millet* system was a set of arrangements developed over time that made the non-Muslim communities part of the state apparatus by creating ties between the community leadership and the sultanate.[52] It was one of the strategies for managing an Islamic empire whose non-Muslim subjects might have been considered a minority from a political and legal point of view, but who *de facto* constituted the religious majority under Ottoman rule. For the Ottomans, allowing for religious freedom and the internal self-regulation of the communities was therefore a matter not only of Islamic law, but also of political expediency, because they did not want to antagonize their non-Muslim subjects, not least because they provided a substantial portion of the state revenues through the poll tax.[53]

During their conquests in the Balkans, the Ottomans had made *dhimmi* arrangements with the non-Muslim communities they conquered. These arrangements were often tailor-made to the needs of each community or region. With the conquest of Constantinople in 1453 CE, however, the Byzantine Empire came to its final end and the Ottomans were now formally in charge of the three non-Muslim communities in their realm: the Orthodox, who had a Church institution and a Patriarch as communal leader with a seat in Constantinople; the Jews, who had no institutional organization but had chief rabbis as communal leaders; the Armenians, who lived mostly in Anatolia and who had their spiritual capital and demographic centre outside Ottoman territory.[54] Ottoman rule was definitely to the advantage of the Orthodox patriarchate: under the Byzantine political structure the Emperor was head of the Church, but under Ottoman rule this position was delegated to the Patriarch. The power that the Orthodox Church exerted over the Orthodox inhabitants of south-eastern Europe not only continued under Ottoman rule, but was augmented and institutionalized by the Ottomans.

The arrangements that Ottoman conquerors had concluded with local communities in the two centuries prior to the fall of Constantinople remained intact, but communication with Ottoman authorities gradually became more centralized, transforming into an arrangement that later became known under the name of the *millet* system. This transformation was initiated on both sides: the communities needed access to the central authorities to defend and safeguard their interests, while the Ottomans needed direct contact with those communities through a representative body in order to communicate their desires or orders. A hierarchical structure developed, whereby the three religious communities, which were ethnically and linguistically pluriform, were subdivided into many local administrative units that were often mono-ethnic or mono-linguistic.[55] In the next chapter we will see that this was one of the factors that contributed to a development of nationalist sentiments.

The other manifestation of Islamic rule in the Ottoman Empire was the Ottoman-Islamic identity. The Ottoman rulers identified their state strongly with Islam, and the conqueror of Constantinople, Sultan Mehmet II, was the first to claim the additional title of caliph: 'sultan' denotes worldly power over a territory, while 'caliph' denotes authority over all Muslims, including those beyond the caliph's territorial power.

The Islamic identity further showed in the physical dominance of mosques over churches. Christians were allowed to maintain their churches, but their bell towers had to be removed or lowered, and restoration of churches was prohibited without the sultan's approval.[56] And rather than building new mosques, the Ottomans would commonly convert one or more of the largest churches of a newly conquered city into mosques.[57] The Haga Sophia in Constantinople, one of six churches converted after the city's fall in 1453 CE, is an interesting example. It retained its name, pronounced in Ottoman as Ayasofia and its transformation into a mosque was effected by the replacement of the altar, crosses and bells by the pulpit, prayer niche and the addition of minarets. Frescos and mosaics with representations of Christianity were at first kept, even those in plain view of the main prayer hall, like the paintings in the main dome. The paintings most visible to the public were painted over 150 years later, around 1600, during a period of intolerance towards figurative representation, while those not visible from the main prayer space were painted over only in the early eighteenth century.[58]

Quite contested – because contrary to Islamic doctrine – was the sale of monasteries and churches in the European provinces to fund the costly campaign against Cyprus in 1571 CE. This was reminiscent of Henry VIII's dismantling of Catholic monasteries and churches and sale of their properties thirty years earlier, but while the English king's ultimate aim was to get absolute control over the Catholic Church in England, the Ottoman's additional motive was not to subjugate the Orthodox church but to downsize the substantial land holdings of the Orthodox Church and mainstream them with that of the Ottoman state.[59]

Islamic identity was also expressed in the legal and social superiority of Muslims over non-Muslims. Christian and Jewish commoners were on a daily basis reminded of their inferior status as non-Muslims; they had to wear brightly coloured clothing, were not allowed to carry arms, or to ride horses or camels (or, if they were allowed to do so, had to dismount when encountering a Muslim riding a horse), and could be chastised or fined for not showing enough respect for Muslims "and for an almost endless number of other 'breaches of etiquette'".[60] In cities, Christians and Jews would keep off the streets during Ramadan, and stay away from Janissaries who might molest them with impunity: "Constantinople was a dangerous place for non-Muslims until the nineteenth century."[61] These discriminatory regulations and treatments did not necessarily apply to Christians and Jews in high positions. But all Christians and Jews, regardless of their social and economic position, were confronted with the poll tax, with inferior status in court in cases against Muslims, and the prohibition on marrying Muslim women. Christians were often not allowed high church towers, or to ring their bells, or to have their churches repaired.

No wonder, then, that non-Muslims did not identify with the Ottoman Empire. But neither did many of the Muslim Ottomans. While the Ottoman Empire identified itself with Islam, its subjects did not share a sense of national belonging. Compared to, for instance, the Roman Empire, where loyalty and belonging to the empire were expressed by the notion of citizenship which in turn was defined as a set of rights and duties, the Ottoman Empire was a conglomerate of fiefdoms intended to serve the emperor, its subjects identifying mostly with their religious or ethnic communities. The term 'Ottoman' designated a member of the ruling class, while the remaining population was referred to as 'flock' (re'aya) irrespective of its faith or ethnicity.[62] This population, on the other hand, would refer to itself exclusively in religious and ethnic terms. There were 'Muslims from Crete', 'Saloniki Jews', 'Catholics from Dubrovnik', and until the late nineteenth century, the Orthodox Christians, whether Greeks or Slavs, referred to themselves as Romans ('Romaioi' or 'Rum') or simply as Christians.[63]

The combination of this societal order and its religious-legal framework brought about a complex and delicate social infrastructure. It was, for instance, possible for a Christian or Jew to have a high position at court (although much less so than a Muslim, and certainly not the highest positions[64]), which would make him socially superior to Muslim commoners.[65] But in general, this system contributed to an institutionalized form of religious discrimination. Nevertheless, compared to the practices in Europe of that time, the Ottoman Empire was relatively tolerant towards its non-Muslim communities, attracting not only the admiration of Protestants in northern Europe, as we will see later, but also a substantial migration of Jews fleeing Spanish intolerance in the period between 1492 and 1527 CE, as well as religious refugees from Europe, like the Huguenots, Anglicans, Quakers, Anabaptists.[66] The number of Spanish Jews was substantial, and they received a warm welcome; most of them were directed towards Saloniki (present-day Thessaloniki) where they soon constituted the majority of its population.[67]

So while the Ottoman Empire was religiously tolerant in the sense that it allowed for different religious communities within its realm, it was definitely intolerant towards any defiance of, or sign of dominance towards, the Islamic order. This order, as we have seen, included certain discriminatory rules. But apart from that, Ottoman society was a religiously pluralist society. An interesting aspect of this coexistence was that there appeared to have been little religious segregation in terms of residence or profession: the three religions were represented in all trades and professions and exclusively Christian, Jewish or Muslim neighbourhoods were rare. "This urban topography suggests that employment and economic level may have been even more important than religion in Ottoman subjects' personal identity."[68] The non-Muslims were also known to 'shop' between their own religious courts and the Ottoman sharia courts to get the ruling that suited their interests best, even though this infuriated their community leaders who imposed bans trying to stop this practice.[69]

Nevertheless, the relative tolerance in the Ottoman Empire towards its non-Muslim subjects had its fluctuations. The early seventeenth century, for instance, witnessed a period of Islamic puritanism, missionary zeal and intolerance (possibly because of the Islamic millennium in the year 1591 CE). The intolerance manifested itself towards Muslims as well as non-Muslims.[70] Muslims faced an increase in charges of heresy, especially relating to allegations of shi'ite sympathies (so-called Kizilbas), which can partly be explained by the emergence of the neighbouring shi'ite Safavid Empire in present-day Iran. The non-Muslims, on the other hand, were subjected to a strict application of existing discriminatory regulations that until then had been relatively dormant. There was a sudden wave of churches being converted into mosques, and their figurative frescos and mosaics were covered up (including those depictions in church-turned-mosques that had been tolerated for decades). Envy of non-Muslims' wealth – in particular Jews, who were prosperous traders, tax farmers and bankers – and suspicion of their close links with foreign merchants led to an increase in discrimination and intolerance. The Jews of Istanbul, for instance, were blamed in 1660 CE for the fire that devastated much of Istanbul, leading to their expropriation and banishment.

This period of intolerance was not helpful in cementing a relationship of trust between the Ottoman state and its non-Muslim subjects in the following times that proved to be testing to the Empire.[71] Neither was the increasing regulation and bureaucratization of all aspects of life during the sixteenth century, which merely over-emphasized the social distinctions and dhimmi status of non-Muslims. And if there was any reason to be loyal to authority, then the millet system ensured that this loyalty was directed towards the communities themselves, rather than to the Ottoman rulers who were not interested in their non-Muslim subjects as long as they kept their place. So when by the eighteenth century the Ottoman state began to face social and economic hardship, there was little solidarity among its subjects whose cooperation was needed to overcome these problems, as we will see in the next chapter.

1.3. Moriscos in Catholic Spain

We have seen that the Ottoman Empire identified itself strongly with Islam but felt no need to impose this on its non-Muslim subjects, just as the Polish-Lithuanian state strongly identified with Catholicism but felt no need to impose that on its Muslim subjects. Catholic Spain, by contrast, since the late fifteenth century had pursued a policy of imposing its Catholic identity on all its inhabitants, even to the extent that everyone had to be Catholic. While Spain was unique in the scale of this task, the relentlessness in its urge to religiously cleanse its lands of all non-believers was typical of many European countries of that time, with Jews being expelled from France, England, Germany, Italy; Huguenots massacred and expelled from France; Catholics being persecuted in England, and Protestants and Catholics plunging into the terrors of the Thirty Years War of religion in eastern Europe. While we may now look back with horror at the plight of Muslims in Spain, the Catholic Spaniards themselves had no doubts about their actions: "[o]n the contrary, they possessed a profound conviction that they were carrying out a pious duty."[72]

Let us go back to where we left off in the previous chapter. By the end of the fifteenth century, the Reconquista in Spain was complete in territorial terms – the last Moorish stronghold of Granada was taken in 1492 CE – but then this struggle continued in human terms. In 1492, the Jews in Spain were given the choice between emigration and conversion to Catholicism. A similar fate befell the Muslims, although in a much more protracted way, over the period between 1499 and 1527 CE. By 1527, there were officially no more Muslims in Spain. The Muslims who had opted for conversion to Christianity were called 'new Christians' to distinguish them from the indigenous 'old' Christians, but became known as Moriscos (although the many among them who had converted without conviction kept referring to themselves as Muslims and maintained their faith in secret[73]). Around 1600 CE, a century after the conversions had taken place, an estimated 275,000–330,000 Moriscos lived in Spain, mostly concentrated in the eastern regions of Granada, Valencia and Aragon; that is 2.5 to 3.5 per cent of an estimated total population of 8 to 9 million.[74]

The forced conversion did not automatically lead to the desired religious unity, because the Moriscos were suspected – often correctly so – of secretly maintaining their Islamic faith. Nor did the conversion lead to the desired aim of assimilation, because most of the Moriscos maintained their customs, different clothing and Arabic language. Even more so were Moriscos perceived as racially different from the 'old' Christians, who claimed descent from the Germanic (Visi)Goths as opposed to the allegedly semitic Arab descent of the Moriscos. Even if such differences actually existed – which seems unlikely after eight centuries of coexistence,[75] but could have been the case because Christians and Muslims always lived quite segregated lives – it seems very unlikely that it showed in physical appearance: if it had not been for difference in dress or the circumcised males, the Moriscos of the sixteenth century could not be distinguished from the old Christians.[76] However, these differences do not explain why, in the period between 1499 and 1604 CE the Moriscos were persecuted and finally expelled. Four other reasons have been put forward that seem more plausible: the psychological state of mind of the Reconquista, religious fervour, demographic fears, and security dangers.[77]

Regarding the psychological state of mind, it has been suggested that Spain, with a long-fought Reconquista war coming abruptly to a halt, was in need of another enemy to channel its aggressive energies.[78] "It appears that in this age the Spaniards had a permanent need of an enemy, real or imagined, to confront as a nation."[79] This enemy was first found in the Jews, then the Muslims, followed by the Moriscos and from 1556 CE onwards the Protestants ('Lutherans').

The second reason to explain the persecution was religious zeal and the desire for a new and unified Spain that was entirely and exclusively Catholic, not only in name but also in devotion. As mentioned, this was not an ideal typical for Spain at that time, but the Spanish clergy were pursuing such religious unity with an aggressive missionary policy. They were assisted therein by the special and enthusiastic support of the papacy in Rome. Spain was one of the few countries in Europe where the Catholic Church gained unmitigated influence. The main instrument for doing so was the Inquisition, founded in Spain by papal bull in 1478 CE. This court operated independently of the secular courts, persecuting Christians for any infraction of Catholic doctrine. In the case of Spain, its main victims were Protestants and *conversos*, that is Jews and Muslims who had voluntarily or forcibly converted to Christianity.

The Moriscos appeared on the Inquisition's radar only in the late sixteenth century, nearly a century after the establishment of the Inquisition in Spain. In fact, the Moriscos of Granada had managed to buy off the Inquisition's scrutiny of Moriscos for a period of forty years, but when this period came to an end in 1560 CE, the Inquisition renewed its interest in Moriscos and started its trials and executions. Some Moriscos were sincere Christians, while others kept practising their Islamic faith in secret, but in both cases they maintained a distinct Moorish culture that set them apart from other Spaniards. But even the Moriscos willing to embrace Christianity experienced the problem of knowing little or nothing about Christianity, and instances are known of Moriscos pleading in vain with the authorities to be taught Christian doctrines.[80] The Inquisition had little consideration for these specific circumstances and the court would often base its verdict on circumstantial evidence that the accused were secretly practising Islamic rituals. These alleged 'Islamic' practices could take many different forms: the failure to observe holidays or to go to mass or confession; the use of Arab names in addition to the Christian names given at baptism; the refusal to have representations of saints in their homes; the refusal to drink wine or eat pork; the habit of regularly washing (an indication that one might prepare for Islamic prayer).[81] And if the evidence was insufficient, confessions were extracted by means of torture.[82] The Inquisition was to unleash a reign of terror that was to remain in Spain for three hundred years.

The third reason that Moriscos were eyed with anxious suspicion was the size of an unassimilated community that was perceived as not authentically Hispanic.[83] The Catholic Spaniards felt in danger of being demographically outnumbered by the Moriscos, who were said to have great reproductive powers. This anxiety was compounded by the fact that a decrease in the growth of the Spanish population was caused by the Catholic tradition of that time of sending daughters to monasteries and having at least one of the sons become a member of the clergy.[84] These fears, which were also mentioned in official reports,[85] did not correspond to the facts, however, because the Moriscos were not only a relatively small community (we mentioned 2.5–3.5 per cent) but also a community long in decline.[86]

In addition to the fear of the Moriscos as an internal enemy, there was the even greater fear of Moriscos acting as a fifth column for external enemies. One enemy was the corsairs from North Africa who repeatedly raided the coasts of Spain. Although the corsairs abducted both Christians and Moriscos as slaves, the Moriscos were accused of inviting the corsairs to conduct these raids so that they could be rescued from their Spanish bondage.[87] This accusation was not entirely unfounded, however, because it was known that some of the Muslims who had been expelled from Spain between 1499 and 1527 CE had joined the ranks of these corsairs.[88] A greater threat was posed by the Ottoman Empire which had obtained footholds in North Africa during the sixteenth century and whose fleet ruled the Mediterranean. The encroaching Ottoman power fuelled fears in Spain that it might invade the Peninsula, and the Moriscos were suspected of welcoming or even inviting such Ottoman invasion. This suspicion was not groundless, because Moriscos circulated prophecies of imminent assistance by the Ottomans.[89] And for his part, the Ottoman governor of Algeria had supported the Morisco revolt of 1570 CE with weapons and ammunition, and the Ottoman sultan as well as his vizier had written letters of support to the Moriscos, the sultan suggesting that they join forces with the Dutch rebellion against Spanish rule.[90] The latter was to become Spain's third enemy after the Barbary corsairs and the

Ottoman Empire: the Dutch Republic had risen in revolt against Spanish suzerainty in 1566 CE, followed by England entering the conflict on the side of the Dutch. While this conflict took place far away from Spain, it was feared that not only the Moriscos but also the few Lutherans in Spain might act as agents, possibly assisted by French Huguenots.[91]

Although the four concerns about Moriscos – their racial difference and consequent lack of assimilation, undermining Christian unity by secretly remaining Muslim, posing a demographic threat, and acting as a fifth column – are each of a different nature; together they convinced the Spaniards more and more that the Moriscos were a serious threat to Spanish unity and security. These concerns were compounded by a growing number of state reports in Spain warning of imminent danger from all sides.[92] Together they made for an atmosphere of panic and a siege mentality, and a fear of an internal fifth column. Consequently, most Lutherans and Moriscos who were executed during the second half of the sixteenth century had been accused of conspiracies and plots.[93] The kings of Spain who ruled during the Morisco-period – Ferdinand II (1479–1516), Charles V (1516–1554) and Phillip II (1554–1598) – attempted to pursue a policy of moderation, but were under continual pressure from the papacy in Rome and the Inquisition and clergy in Spain that produced a relentless barrage of accusations and complaints against Moriscos.[94] In several instances, measures were taken to assimilate the Moriscos by force. In 1524 CE, an edict prohibited the Arabic language, traditional Morisco clothing, amulets and jewels, and the practice of circumcision, ritual slaughtering and Islamic marriage – measures that were paraphrased by historian Green as: "these foreigners within the national body would have to learn to speak like 'us', behave like 'us', and become like 'us'."[95]

The edict was bought off by the Morisco community with a great amount of money, but did not fail to antagonize other Moriscos who rose up in revolt in 1526. This, in turn, led to the proclamation of a new edict in 1567 CE that reiterated the prohibitions of the edict of 1524 CE but went further by calling for the destruction of all public baths (which were suspected of being used for the ritual washing before Islamic prayer), and the requirement for Moriscos to leave their front doors open, women to unveil and the prohibition on dancing the traditional *zambra* or singing. This time there was no opportunity to have the edict rescinded in exchange for money, and again the Moriscos rose in a savage revolt that was put down with even more brutality.[96]

The culmination of events ultimately led to the final and desperate measure in 1609 CE of expelling all Moriscos from Spain, a project that was undertaken in phases that lasted until 1614 CE. The majority of Moriscos left in 1609 CE, after being given three days' notice to sell their goods, of which a set portion was already allotted to their feudal lords as compensation for the loss of their workforce. In total an estimated 275,000–330,000 Moriscos were deported from Spain,[97] most leaving for North Africa where they received a hostile reception as suspected renegade Christians, and often suffered misery and poverty.

The total elimination of 'new Christians' – converted Jews and Muslims – was a horrific catastrophe for the victims themselves, but also caused a significant disruption of Spanish society. The process leading up to the final expulsions had created an atmosphere of intense suspicion and fear, in which family squabbles and disputes with neighbours could end dramatically with accusations being made to the Inquisition. But the disappearance of the two communities was particularly detrimental to the social-economic fabric of Spanish society. In the case of the Moriscos, their sudden departure had left entire villages depopulated, agricultural lands and irrigation derelict, and Christian landlords without labourers.[98]

2. Other Relations and Contacts

We now move from coexistence to other forms of interaction. In the sixteenth and seventeenth centuries, these were both belligerent, like wars and raids, as well as cooperative, such as an increasing diplomacy and trade. Most of this interaction took place between Ottoman and European states, and had as a conspicuous characteristic that it was mostly one-sided: wars were mostly initiated by the Ottomans in their continual urge for conquest, while the cooperative interactions – trade, diplomacy, alliances – were mostly initiated by Europeans. The Europeans were too weak to engage in war with the powerful Ottomans (and were too tangled up in their own conflicts), while the Ottomans had very little need for the Europeans in terms of commerce or diplomacy (a position they were forced to reconsider in the eighteenth century, as we will see in the next chapter). The exception to this one-sidedness was raiding and piracy, which were undertaken by both Muslims and Christians.

The question that will continuously hover over the following paragraphs is: what is the role of religion in all this? We have seen in the previous paragraphs that religion was the main measuring stick by which societies were organized and ruled. In the next paragraphs we will see that religion is much less of a determining factor in other forms of interaction between Muslims and Christians. Two exceptions stand out, however. One is European states acting as protectors of religious minorities in the Ottoman Empire. The other is religion as the main indicator for selecting victims in raiding: pirates and raiders in the frontier areas of eastern Europe and the Mediterranean targeted the 'infidel', just as only the infidel could be taken into slavery. As we will see, this worked both ways, Muslims and Christians alike.

2.1. Wars and Raids

Holy Wars Revisited?

Many armed confrontations took place in sixteenth and seventeenth century Europe, between Christian states as well as between Christian and Muslim states. The question that concerns us here is to what extent the wars between Christian and Muslim nations were motivated by religion. The Ottomans often named their military campaigns 'jihad' and the Holy Roman Emperor, in particular Charles V, was glorified for his 'crusades' against the Turks.

By the sixteenth century, however, the numerous calls on the Christian side for a crusade or some form of 'holy' alliance against the Turk more often than not led to nothing, indicating that religious fervour did not rank highly on the list of motives for war. This does not mean that religion itself had lost its importance in general, or in visualizing 'the Turk'. The concept of holy war in Europe retained a "lingering popular legitimacy"[99] but was generally overridden by economic motivations and political rivalries.

Nevertheless, the notion of holy war maintained its appeal in frontier areas: the Barbary corsairs of Algiers, Tunis and Tripoli sailed with the patronage of the Ottoman sultan under the banner of jihad; the Catholic Uskoks from Croatia raided the northern Adriatic with the patronage of the Habsburgs and occasionally Rome under the banner of holy crusade; the Knights of St John, after their eviction from the Holy Land and later from Rhodes continued their holy war from the island of Malta; the Cossack bands raided the steppes of Ukraine and the Crimea, often with the Christian patronage of Polish-Lithuania or Muscovy princes.[100] It remains disputed to what extent their call for holy war was out of genuine conviction or merely justified their raids against merchants, soldiers and villagers of the opposing faith. We will speak of this more below.

Let us now take a closer look at the Ottoman intentions in terms of warfare, because their alleged desire to conquer all of Europe as a matter of religious duty is still a prevailing notion in modern European thought. Was Ottoman expansion motivated by jihad or holy war, or was it a warfare state aimed at expansion and riches? The Ottomans referred to their wars primarily as ghazza, and after the seventeenth century more as *jihad*. Both terms are commonly translated into English as 'holy war' without doing justice to the clear distinction between the two and what they meant in practice.[101] To appreciate this distinction we need to consider the chronological developments of Ottoman warfare.

During their early conquests in the fourteenth and fifteenth centuries, the Ottomans did not uphold any anti-Christian sentiments or ideology: "[t]he pervasive notion of permanent and irreconcilable division between the Muslim and Christian worlds at this time is a fiction".[102] Indeed, in this early period Christians made up a large part of the Ottoman army, in particular as part of the light and irregular cavalry that raided the frontier.[103] Rather than pursuing holy war, the Ottoman was a "predatory confederacy" comprising Muslim and Christian warriors alike, whose goal was booty, plunder and slaves, no matter the rhetoric used by their rulers.[104] Historians have made the same observation with regard to the Ottoman military of the sixteenth and seventeenth centuries: whereas they were perhaps motivated by religious zeal to fight the infidel, the main incentive to fight was "a well-calculated system of bonuses and promotions".[105] It therefore seems fit to translate *ghazza* as raiding aimed at conquest and booty.[106]

This does not mean that the ideology of holy war or *jihad* was not used – on the contrary, it was the term commonly used to announce a new war campaign. Moreover, this term was mostly reserved for wars against the Christian lands of the Balkans and Byzantine Empire, and not for wars against Muslim lands in the east and south.[107] This would suggest that *jihad* does indeed refer to war against the infidel and, more so, that it was not used in its canonical definition as a defensive war.[108] Before we draw our conclusions, however, we need to reflect on this particular form of Ottoman *jihad* in the light of the following observations.

First, Ottoman warfare was an annually recurring affair, almost ritualized with military campaigns starting every spring in order for the army to be back in time before winter. The need for this continuous war served several purposes, including booty as major source of state income, the acquisition of land to keep the military caste satisfied, and the need to keep the military occupied. Especially after the conquest of Constantinople we may attribute the Ottoman Empire with an "imperialist mentality, i.e. conquest for its own sake."[109] These conquests were not restricted to Christian lands: a larger part of the Ottoman territories comprised Muslim-dominated lands (Middle East, Gulf region, North Africa).

Second, there is the matter of Ottoman legitimization of its warfare. This is the part where religion comes into play. War against the infidel, or *jihad*, was by definition a legitimate reason to go into battle, regardless of the actual reasons. And if *jihad* was not declared, then a sultan would request the opinion of his religious scholars (a so-called *fatwa*) to legitimize war on other grounds. This Islamic justification was meant to make the war official, but was not necessarily the real reason for war.[110] Religious-military propaganda should not be taken at face value.[111]

A third consideration is that much of our information on the Ottoman conquests and the motivations therefore is based on what Ottoman chroniclers have recorded. Since they were writing in a time, and often in the service of, an imperial state that identified itself increasingly as distinctively Islamic (especially in the seventeenth century), we must take into account the possibility of political-religious correctness on their part. For instance, these chroniclers have omitted from their writings the many alliances with Byzantine and Christian rulers in early Ottoman times (including those by marriage), and they increasingly identified the battlegrounds in Europe as 'Christian' states.[112]

Based on these considerations we might conclude that the Ottoman conquests and military campaigns were not necessarily religiously motivated, but that religion played a role in their justification. How sincere that role was depended on the time, the personality of the sultan and on specific circumstances. When the Ottomans waged war against non-Muslims – who, in the geographic situation of the Ottoman Empire, were by default Europeans, since all other border areas where they engaged in military campaigns were inhabited by Muslims – they used the term 'jihad'. This notion did not mean a 'holy war' targeting non-Muslims for the reason that they were infidels, but merely indicated a war campaign for reasons of conquest against people who happened to be non-Muslims.

Vienna 1683

In the European collective memory, the Ottoman sieges of Vienna in 1529 and again in 1683 CE are the symbol of Ottoman expansionism in Europe, as Poitiers was the symbol of Arab-Muslim expansionism into Europe in the early eighth century. This historical event is still fresh, as shown in the remark of the EU commissioner Frits Bolkestein in 2004 that if Turkey were to be admitted to the European Union "the liberation of Vienna in 1683 would have been in vain."[113] Given its mythical proportions, the siege and battle of Vienna deserves closer scrutiny as to its historical circumstances and, in particular, the Ottoman intentions.

Starting with the latter, how far did the Ottomans want to go in their expansionism? Did they want to conquer Europe if they had the chance? The answer to this can only be based on circumstantial evidence. We have seen that Ottoman belligerency was of a permanent nature, causing its Empire to expand continuously. There is no reason or evidence to assume that the Ottoman Empire had specific aspirations to bring Christian Europe under 'Islamic' rule. Europe merely happened to be encapsulated into the ever-widening circle of Ottoman territorial gain. But that in itself meant that Europe's fears of this expansionist power were very well justified. These fears were further fuelled by the pervasive and persistent legend of the Turks being driven by a prophesy promising them the 'Red Apple', which was interpreted by Europeans to mean Rome which, in turn, symbolized the Christian commonwealth.[114]

Vienna, being the capital of the Holy Roman Empire, definitely was a great prize for any Ottoman general. But Vienna was also at the limits of Ottoman military reach. This has to do with the practical considerations of the weather (a war could not be sustained during the rainy autumn and cold winter seasons), the ever increasing distance to the front (a march of more than a month would severely shorten the time for actual battle), as well as the structure of the Ottoman military (the main body of cavalrymen or *sipahi* needed to return annually to their estates in the homeland to run their affairs and collect taxes).[115] The first siege of Vienna in 1529 CE appears to have been primarily to settle the Ottoman-Habsburg dispute over Hungary, the frontier zone between the two empires.[116] The siege of 1683 CE, more than a century and a half later, is said to have been motivated by the complex court politics in Istanbul demanding a spectacular victory.[117]

The exact reasons and motivations for the famous Ottoman attack on Vienna in 1683 CE are therefore speculative at best. What we do know is that Europe showed little unity in this perilous situation. The European powers were so divided among themselves that the possibility of rallying them to come to the Habsburgs' rescue was "infinitesimal."[118] This was illustrated in particular by the silence and indolence on the part of Habsburg's arch-enemy France, which had a secret agreement with the Ottomans and did not seem to care much if Vienna was taken. When the Ottomans were repulsed, an English pamphlet commemorating the Ottoman defeat and lauding the 'Illustrious Heroes' cynically mentioned that victory was one "without the help of the Most Christian monarch [i.e., the king of France] and against the Most Antichristian Monarch [i.e., the Ottoman sultan]." The relief force that ultimately came to the rescue was confined to those who knew they would be next if the Habsburgs fell: the princes from southern Germany and the Poles under King John III Sobieski (who was handsomely rewarded by the Pope).[119] They succeeded in dislodging the Ottoman siege, and Europe sighed with relief.

Looking back at this historical event as a 'European' effort to repel the Ottomans is therefore a retroactive mythification of events, just as the battle of Poitiers had been given a spin to accommodate the interests of the Carolingians. Similarly, the notion that Europe in 1683 CE was saved from Ottoman or Islamic rule is not justified by the facts and events of the time: while the Ottomans were unmistakably expanding their territory by means of conquest it seems unlikely that their taking of Vienna would have given them the stepping stone for the further conquest of all of Europe since Vienna was at the furthest edge of Ottoman military reach, just as Persia was in the east.

Raiding and Piracy

For centuries, the inhabitants of European frontier states and coastal areas lived with the threat of being raided, their goods and livestock being taken, their homes burnt, and the people themselves dragged off to be sold into slavery. The attackers could act on their own or as some state's proxy bandits hired to menace the realm of an enemy. Of the states engaging in such acts of raiding during the sixteenth and seventeenth centuries, the Ottomans were particularly known – probably because they were in more need of slaves than the Europeans – although many European states also hired pirates or raiding tribes, some even gaining national fame (the English pirate Sir Francis Drake and the Dutch pirate Piet Hein are still celebrated as national heroes).

We have already seen above that the eastern border of Europe was suffering from raids from the Muslim Tatar and Christian Cossack tribes. In the Mediterranean basin the main menace was the corsairs who pounced on their prey from small harbours. These corsairs were Muslim as well as Christian, but in the European collective memory these corsairs are commonly identified with the Barbary corsairs who operated from the North African coast. In addition to attacking merchant ships, which was the main line of business of these corsairs, they would occasionally raid European coasts, sometimes as far as England and Iceland, dragging entire populations of villages off into slavery in Northern Africa.[120] These raiders inflicted widespread fear in Europe, just like the Huns and Vikings had done centuries earlier, which explains why they are still remembered in Europe.

The daring of these raids so far away from their home base can be explained by the European origins of several of the most notorious corsairs. The Englishman John Ward, and the Dutchmen Dirk de Veenboer, Symen Danzeker ('Simon the Dancer') and Jan Janszoon were pirates who, after piracy services rendered to their own states, had become wanted criminals, and who sought and found new employment with the Barbary pirates – after having settled the practical matter of converting to Islam. The most notorious among these renegade pirates was the Dutchman Jan Janszoon from Haarlem who became known as Reis Murad, admiral of the pirates' fleet of Sale on the Atlantic coast of Morocco. He was the one who raided villages in Iceland in 1627 CE. Other famous corsairs were the Barbarossa brothers who established their base in Algiers in 1514 CE. So well known were the navigating skills of one of the brothers, Hayder Barbarossa, that the Ottoman sultan employed him as admiral of the Ottoman fleet. It was under the command of Barbarossa that the Ottoman navy gained dominance in the Mediterranean. But Barbarossa did not lose his pirate's plumage: he used that same fleet to pursue his old trade of raiding and piracy along the coasts of the enemies of the Ottoman Empire.[121]

The Berber corsairs were not the only pirates who made the Mediterranean seas and coasts unsafe. There were plenty of 'Christian' corsairs, such as the Uskoks in the Adriatic and Ionian Sea, the Knights of St John who operated from Malta, and various freelance pirates under English, French or Spanish flags. Such was their menace that it has been argued that 'Christian' piracy was worse in its impact than 'Muslim' piracy.[122]

A conspicuous aspect of these raiders and pirates was that they selected their victims on the basis of religion (hence our reference to them as 'Muslim' and 'Christian' pirates). The Muslim Barbary corsairs targeted the ships and coasts of Christian nations, and Muslim slaves found during these raids would mostly be set free. Christian pirates did the same in reverse, targeting only Muslim prey. The Christian Cossacks preferred to raid Muslim communities on the Black Sea coast as well as the booty-laden Tatars returning from their own raids,[123] while the Muslim Tatars from the Black Sea preferred to raid the Russian territories.[124]

But not every corsair was precise in the religious definition of his prey. The Uskoks used a strict Catholic definition when identifying their targets, which allowed them to rob not only the Muslim Turk, but also Ottoman Jews and even Orthodox Christians whom the Uskok Catholic considered heretics.[125] The Uskoks also raided (Catholic) Venetian merchant ships because they often shipped Ottoman cargo, as well as the (Catholic) republic of Dubrovnik and the (Catholic) Venetian domains along the Adriatic coast because, according to Uskok opinion, they had compromised themselves by entering into treaties with the Ottoman Empire.[126] Similarly, the Knights of St John in Malta at first attacked only Ottoman and Barbary vessels, but later also Christian ships under the pretext that they might be shipping infidel goods, or that they were not true Christians but schismatics like Orthodox or Maronites.[127]

2.2. Alliances

The overall characteristic of the sixteenth and seventeenth centuries was political scheming in order to find allies but also to abandon them as soon as they ceased to serve one's interests. This manoeuvring was accompanied by diplomatic envoys sent between the various powers (permanent embassies were to be established only in the eighteenth century).[128] The motto 'the enemy of my enemy is my friend' was widely applied, and Muslim-Christian boundaries were not sacrosanct, resulting in complex political scheming and diplomatic traffic. The myth of Christian unity was continuously upheld in speech, but very rarely in practice. There was no European bloc, nor a Christian commonwealth, versus the infidel Turk; on the contrary, the Ottoman Empire was one of the many players in the great game of power and changing alliances in Europe.[129] England and the Dutch Republic sought alliances with the sultans of Morocco as well as with the Ottoman Empire against their enemy Spain; Sweden needed Ottoman assistance against the Russians; France wanted the Ottomans as an ally against the Habsburgs; the Hungarian protestant princes were willing to become Ottoman vassals in exchange for an Ottoman attack on the Habsburg Empire. Later, in the eighteenth century, it was the turn of the Habsburgs to enter into an alliance with the Ottomans against their common enemy, the Russian Empire. Two of these examples will be elaborated below to illustrate the mechanisms of these processes: the relations between France and the Ottoman Empire, and between the Dutch Republic and the Moroccan sultanate.

France and the Ottomans

One of the most enduring rivalries in the period under discussion here was that between France and the Holy Roman Empire ruled by the Habsburg dynasty. The kings both vied for dominance in the European political arena, using all means including religion. The King of France, for instance, donned the epithet 'Most Christian King' in order to compete with the Habsburg emperor's official title of Holy Roman Emperor. But when the Habsburg emperor Charles V got the upper hand in this struggle for power, King Francis I of France made a move that astounded European Christendom: he entered into an alliance with the Ottomans. This alliance had a very profitable commercial dimension but was effectively also a military alliance directed against the Holy Roman Empire. Secret negotiations had started in 1526 CE, a year after the French had suffered a major defeat against the Habsburgs, and ten years later a treaty was concluded between France and the Ottoman Empire that was to last for two and a half centuries.[130]

The Franco-Ottoman alliance had its ups and downs, corresponding with the state of the relationship between France and the Holy Roman Empire, King Francis I being the ultimate Machiavellian: whenever relations with Charles V turned sour, he would revert to the Ottomans, and vice versa. The most controversial use of that alliance was the joint French-Ottoman military attacks against Habsburg territories. In 1528 CE, the French attacked the Habsburg Empire in the west, while the Ottomans marched in from the south and laid the first siege to Vienna in 1529 CE. In 1534 CE, upon the request of King Francis I, the Ottoman navy sailed out against Habsburg positions in the Adriatic, laying southern Italy to waste and carrying thousands of people off into slavery.[131] This joint French-Ottoman military campaign was repeated ten years later, in 1534–1544 CE, on a much larger scale. The Ottoman fleet of 110 ships commanded by the illustrious Barbarossa and again accompanied by the French ambassador, sailed from Constantinople to France, on its way pillaging all the coastal areas that were not indicated to be allies of Francis I (who, for all practical purposes, identified his enemy Rome and the papal territories as such allies).[132] The fleet moored in Marseilles, where the Ottoman admiral and his entourage received a festive welcome. It then sailed out again, this time together with French navy forces, to attack Nice. To overcome logistical problems that arose that winter, Francis I allowed the Ottoman fleet to spend the winter in the port city of Toulon, which was evacuated for that purpose and placed in the hands of Barbarossa and an estimated thirty thousand Ottoman troups. For several months, the city was Ottoman, with its own mosque (the cathedral was temporarily converted for that purpose) and slave market where they could sell the people they had enslaved during their pillaging raids (such as the entire population of Lipari, an island north of Sicily). But then, with the coming of a new year, the tables had turned: Francis I had now entered into a peace treaty with Charles V, and the Ottoman fleet returned to Constantinople in 1545 CE, but not until it had forcibly released all the Muslim galley slaves from the French fleet. The Franco-Ottoman alliance ebbed to a low point but was soon to be activated again: the French supplied material support for the Ottoman military campaigns against the Hungarians (1543–1544 CE) and the Safavid Persians (1547 CE). Francis' successor, Henry II, also availed himself of the alliance, and the French and Ottomans staged joint naval raids on Italian coasts during the period 1551–1559 CE, wherein the French captured Corsica and the Ottomans the Balearic Islands.

The military part of the alliance then became dormant for over a century, mainly because France and the Habsburgs had entered into a peace treaty. Ottoman-French commerce, on the other hand, the conditions of which were stipulated in the treaty, flourished. In the late seventeenth century, however, when relations between the

French and Habsburgs soured again, King Louis XIV thought it opportune to encourage the Ottomans on several occasions to initiate military campaigns against the Habsburg southern flanks. Indeed, as we have seen, when the Ottomans once more laid siege to Vienna, the French did not intervene and it was the Polish forces that came to the rescue. Five years after the Ottoman siege of Vienna had been repulsed, and the Habsburg army was still successfully pushing the Ottomans back, the French king Louis XIV attacked the Habsburg Empire, thereby relieving – whether intentionally or not is unclear – the Ottomans from Habsburg military pressure.

The Dutch Republic and the Moroccan Sultan

The reason that the Dutch Republic and Morocco got acquainted was their mutual enemy, Spain.[133] In the sixteenth century, Spain was entangled in a protracted rebellion in the Low Countries in which the Dutch Republic of the Seven Provinces declared independence from their Spanish sovereign in 1588 CE. When in 1604 CE the Dutch captured a Spanish ship at the North Sea with Turkish and North African galley slaves on board – for which the Dutch had no practical use, because they had no galleys nor were they engaged in the slave trade at that time – they decided to make a gesture of goodwill to the sultan of Morocco by returning the slaves to him. In doing so, they hoped to nudge the sultan into more belligerency towards Spain. The sultan, in need of European weaponry, responded positively.

In the ensuing diplomatic and commercial relations between the Dutch Republic and the Moroccan sultanate, Moriscos and Jews, both originally from Spain, became the most important middlemen, although The Hague also enjoyed the unusual sight of Arab-Berber envoys dispatched from the Moroccan court.[134] Negotiations resulted in a Dutch-Moroccan treaty in 1610 CE in which the Dutch committed themselves to the delivery of weapons and warships to the sultan, in exchange for a safe conduct from corsairs for Dutch trade vessels in the Mediterranean and the promise that no Dutch slaves would be traded in Morocco. The Dutch, being Protestant and fervently anti-Catholic at the time, were not deterred by the papal ban on any war goods to "Saracens, Turks and other enemies of the Christians" that had been in place since 1179 CE and was again renewed in the early 1450s.[135] Military alliances were not included in this ban, but were probably not foreseen at the time as being absurd and unimaginable.

From the Dutch perspective, a military alliance with the Moroccan sultan was not undesirable, but at the time of the treaty not considered possible since the Dutch Republic had by then entered into a truce with Spain. No objections existed against the sale of weapons, however, and several canons arrived safely in Morocco where they can still be admired, but of the three warships that were built for the sultan, two were sunk by the Spanish on their way to Morocco and the third returned to Holland in haste. Morocco actually had nothing to offer to the Dutch Republic, but eagerly imported Dutch cloth and weapons, a trade that continued until 1659 CE. The Moroccan-Dutch relationship ended with the English capture of Gibraltar in 1704 CE; from then on, trade with Morocco became an exclusively English affair.

2.3. Trade

Commerce between Europe and the Ottoman Empire was a one-way affair, prompted by a lack of Ottoman need for European commodities (except for slaves, as we will see below): compared to the total volume of trade within the Ottoman Empire, trade with Europe was a relatively marginal part of the Ottoman economy.[136] It was the Europeans who came to Ottoman lands to trade, not the other way round. The few Ottoman merchants that ventured into European ports were mostly Ottoman Jews, Greeks and Armenians.[137] This lack of interest on the Ottoman side was caused not only by economic motivations, but also by a fear of travelling into a Europe that was considered so intolerant towards non-believers that Ottomans thought they risked their lives if they were to venture there.[138] Venice was the only European city that tried to accommodate Ottoman traders by building a *fondaco* (from the Arabic *funduq* – that is a trading house that also functioned as a hostel), just as they themselves had been accommodated with *funduqs* in Syria and Egypt: Ottoman merchants now only had to sail into Venice, unload their goods straight from the canal into the *fondaco*, spend the night there if needed, and then leave, without having to venture into the city or having to get in touch with any Venetian.[139]

Insofar as the Ottoman merchants wanted to trade with Europe, they did so either through Ottoman Jewish, Greek and Armenian intermediaries, or through the city-states of Venice and Ragusa (present-day Dubrovnik at the Croatian coast), both of which had trading posts dotted along the Ottoman shores of the Adriatic and Aegean Seas. Most of these Venetian colonies were taken during the Ottoman-Venetia wars of 1570–1573 CE (resulting in the Ottoman conquest of Venice's most important outpost, Cyprus), but the city-state of Ragusa maintained its autonomous status within the Ottoman realm.[140]

From the sixteenth century onwards, the European states engaged in direct trade with the Ottoman Empire, a development that heralded the gradual decline of the traditional commercial dominance of the Italian mercantile city-states. Their position was now taken over by western European merchants and trading houses. These commercial activities were often secured by bilateral treaties at the state level, starting with France in 1569 CE,[141] followed by England (1580 CE), and the Netherlands (1612 CE) as a reward for having fought the Spaniards.[142] In the Dutch and English cases, these agreements were entered into by trading companies that had first secured trading monopolies from their own governments and subsequently from the Porte; the lack of any state interference in their commercial activities provided them with more acumen and agility than their counterparts in other countries.[143]

These trade agreements, known as 'capitulations', allowed both parties all kinds of commercial privileges, including free trade, tax exemptions, and the like. The European parties to these capitulations profited most from these agreements. France in particular saw an increase in the volume of its Mediterranean trade, and became a dominant commercial power when Venetian trade was brought to a near standstill after its loss of Cyprus and subsequent submission to Ottoman power in 1571 CE.[144] The capitulations also provided for consular assistance on Ottoman territory, and the European powers soon established consulates in one or more of the main Ottoman mercantile cities, such as Istanbul, Smyrna (Izmir), Aleppo, Sidon, Alexandria and Cairo. The capitulations also allowed for Ottoman consulates in European states, but the Porte did not see the need to capitalize on this possibility.

With the increase in volume of European trade with the Ottoman Empire, the foreign mercantile community within the Empire also expanded and, in consequence, increased the importance of the consul. With the regular extension of the capitulations – usually every five years – , the immunities of the consul and his staff were often augmented, even granting the consulate judicial powers in commercial matters. The development from occasional and individual permissions to trade in the tenth and eleventh centuries to the commercial treaties between states in the sixteenth century gradually resulted in the establishment of veritable European enclaves in Ottoman cities in the subsequent two centuries, as we will see in the next chapter.

2.4. Slavery

In the sixteenth and seventeenth centuries several European countries engaged in the slave trade between Africa and the Americas, but slavery became less practised in Europe except for a limited use as oarsmen in navy galleys or for hard labour in mines and agriculture in countries along the Mediterranean coast.[145] While the presence of Muslim slaves in Europe became less in comparison to the previous centuries, and the Western European states reserved the practice of slavery to most of their colonies, the practice of slavery increased in Muslim states in the Mediterranean basin, in particular the Ottoman Empire and the Barbary states on the North African coast in what is nowadays Morocco, Algeria and Tunisia.

This affected Europe since many of these slaves were Europeans captured in raids on European coasts or ships. The numbers of slaves in those times are of course hard to assess, but according to estimates a total of 1–1.25 million European Christians had been enslaved by the Barbary corsairs between 1530 and 1780 CE.[146] Some of these slaves were used to make money by means of ransom, many were sold to the Ottoman Empire, and the remainder were put to work to maintain the corsairs' harbours and fortresses or to build the immense palace of the megalomaniac sultan Moulay Ismail (1672–1727 CE) of Morocco.[147]

In Ottoman society, slaves were used for hard labour in mines and agriculture, but more so in domestic service and in economic and military domains.[148] By the seventeenth century, the Ottoman administration was entirely in the hands of slaves who were considered much more obedient and trustworthy to the sultan than the freeborn Turkish upper class, especially if they had converted to Islam.[149] Slaves were often allowed to earn their own income so that they would be capable of ransoming themselves, and Islam encouraged the manumission of slaves as an act of pious charity; the result, however, was a "constant erosion of the slave population" in Ottoman society that, in consequence, kept the demand for slaves high.[150] The need for new supplies of slaves also remained high because most slaves accepted the religion of their masters, and subsequently had to be set free.

Slavery in North Africa differed from that in Europe and the Ottoman Empire.[151] Slaves were primarily a source of income through the payment of ransom. This practice was reserved first for rich captives, but with the enormous rise of captives brought in by corsairs by the end of the seventeenth century, governments of European states started to send envoys to negotiate the ransom of larger groups of their countrymen. The rising number of slaves, combined with the work of charitable organizations working for the ransoming of Christian fellow men in captivity,[152] and the publication of narratives of ransomed and escaped slaves,[153] contributed to an increasing interest of the European public in the plight of Christian slaves in North Africa.

Already in the previous centuries slavery had become divided by religion: Christians would only use non-Christian slaves, and Muslims only non-Muslim slaves. On both sides, Christian and Muslim slaves had three ways to regain their freedom: ransom by their fellow countrymen, manumission by a friendly master or conversion to the religion of their master. The last was controversial, however, since losing a slave constituted a loss of income to the master.[154] In the case of the Barbary city-states, conversion combined with the joining of the ranks of corsairs was a way to escape slavery. The fact that so many did so was a source of scandal and unbelief in Europe, where it was widely believed that such conversion must have been the work of tireless efforts by the Muslim slave masters to turn their captives away from their Christian faith.[155] All those who converted to Islam and managed to escape or be ransomed, however, recounted that they converted not because of pressure by their masters to do so, but to escape the harsh conditions of slavery (although they often remained slaves after conversion).[156]

After the Barbary corsair states had been routed in the early nineteenth century, the practice of slavery continued in the Ottoman Empire until 1918.

III. Virtual Islam

1. The Image of the 'Turk'

During the sixteenth and seventeenth centuries, Europeans generally distinguished between Islam, which was an object of disdain and fear, and the 'Turk' who was an object of fascination. On the one hand, Ottoman victories were seen as a typical manifestation of Islam as a violent and aggressive religion, symbolized by the cruelties perpetrated especially by the elite corps of the Janissaries, and one had to pray for the undoing of this Islam.[157] On the other hand, the prominent presence of the Ottoman Empire on the European continent in the seventeenth century generated great popular interest in the 'Turk' and his customs and religion. Descriptions of Ottoman society were published as early as the late fifteenth century.[158] By the seventeenth century, however, an increasing stream of travel accounts, diaries and pamphlets with first-hand experiences and observations about Ottoman society appeared in Europe where "the Turks were filling the minds of nobles and peasants, seamen and intellectuals."[159] The authors were quite diverse: pilgrims travelling through the Ottoman realm on their way to Jerusalem, slaves who were liberated or had escaped, religious refugees from Europe who had found refuge in the Ottoman Empire, physicians hired by the Ottoman elite, European merchants and diplomats.[160] The merchants and diplomats also brought artists in their wake, so that pictorial images were added to the scriptural ones. These stories, in turn, greatly influenced plays, literature, folktales and apocalyptic literature of this period.[161] And they all reached a wide audience thanks to the newly functioning printing press.

This stream of information, combined with the new mindset of impending Enlightenment that invited the Europeans to exercise self-reflection and self-criticism, gradually transformed the image of the Turk as well as Islam. The Turk inherited from previous centuries the image of the negative or exclusionary Other, such as the fierce Saracen, the conquering Turk or the licentious Muslim, but also acquired the image of the positive Other, such as the tolerant Turk or the ally against a common enemy. The Turk was viewed negatively as someone exercising arbitrary power and unbridled lust and who disliked alcohol, but also positively as a person of honesty, sobriety, religious tolerance, with an administration of "swift, expeditious, inexpensive" justice.[162]

The European curiosity about the Turk stood in stark contrast to the near indifference of the Ottoman towards the European Christian. Apart from the keen
awareness of the Porte of the religious struggles in sixteenth century Europe of which
the Sultan tried to make political use,[163] Ottoman interest in European customs or
affairs was almost non-existent until the nineteenth century.

2. Dealing with the 'Turk'

While there was popular interest among Europeans in the Turk out of sheer curiosity and fascination, the European Christian states had great interest in the Ottoman
Empire for pragmatic reasons like political alliances and commercial treaties. From
1500 CE onwards, the Ottoman Empire became a power like any other European
power. Still, the 'Turk' remained an outsider, regardless of how much the European
Christian nations were engaged in internal bloody wars – especially the devastating
religious Thirty Years War (1618–1648 CE) – and regardless of all the diplomatic and
commercial overtures these nations made towards the Ottoman Empire. The European nations might be practising a considerable degree of Realpolitik as regards
the Ottoman Empire, but in their diplomatic exchanges among each other – even
with their bitter arch enemies – they maintained the jargon of a united Christian
commonwealth, admitting that their diplomacy with the infidel Turk was actually
inappropriate.[164]

The outsider's position of the Ottomans in the international European setting
became particularly apparent with the Reformation and the religious conflicts and
wars that followed in Europe. The debates on how to respond to the encroaching Ottoman military onslaught focused mainly on the infidel character of the
Ottomans, so that arguments were of a theological nature. The Catholics generally called for a general crusade against the Ottomans (the crusade being the term
for any war against non-Christians, not unlike the jihad as called for by the Ottomans when fighting non-Muslims). The Protestants, on the other hand, were
willing to lend their support only to a defensive war. There were of course pragmatic reasons for this position (the Roman Church was suspected of calling for a
crusade merely to reassert its authority), as well as political reasons (holding back
support might press the Catholic rulers to give in to Protestant demands).[165] But
the Protestants also raised various objections of a theological nature against participating in fighting the Ottomans. For one, the Protestants held a different concept of the notion of a just war. Such war could only be waged by secular offi-

cials and rulers in defence of the people and the land entrusted to them, not as an extension of their religious convictions. From this perspective, fighting the Ottomans might be justified, but not as a crusade.[166] Another argument was that the Turk might be fought as an aggressor, but not for the mere fact of being a Muslim, since all people, regardless of their religious differences, belonged to the same 'spiritual church' (geistliche kirche) from where they, ideally, should reach the true faith of Christianity; the Turk was therefore a 'potential brother' and not an infidel enemy. Finally, there were Protestants who saw the Ottoman onslaught as a punishment from God that had to be suffered as penitence; the more radical elements among the Protestants went even further and saw the conquests by the Ottomans either as the fulfilment of the Apocalypse and the coming of Judgment Day, or as a means of converting the Muslims once they had occupied all of Europe.[167]

Not all Protestants were so reluctant to withstand the Turk. There were also voices calling for Christian unity against the Turkish peril. Especially in England, authors and clergy called upon the Anglican faithful to stand shoulder to shoulder with the Catholics to withstand the Turkish onslaught.[168] But regardless of what argument was favoured, none of these arguments would have been made if the Ottoman Empire had been a Christian nation. The role that religion played in ordering societies by creating the dichotomy of us versus them and insider versus outsider also applied to the international arena: the 'Turk' was marked as an outsider by the mere fact of not being a Christian, and all additional stories and descriptions of the 'Turk' merely emphasized this difference. Even though so much more knowledge was available on Ottoman society and customs, the 'Turk' was set to follow the same fate as the Saracen and Muslim of being the European Other.

3. Islam: 'Better Turkish than Papish'

Knowledge of the religious tenets of Islam further increased in the seventeenth century with the establishment at various European universities of chairs dedicated to the study of Arabic and Islam. However, the attitude towards this religion remained polemic: it needed to be studied properly, but only with the purpose of proving it wrong and wicked. Arabic was not considered the key to a civilization, but the language needed to read Islamic scripture. While this was the situation in academic circles, the case of Islam was also taken up by religious intellectuals in the disputes between Catholicism and Protestantism.

Protestants in general looked favourably on the Ottoman relative tolerance towards their non-Muslim subjects as opposed to the Protestants' treatment at the hands of the Catholics. It did not go unnoticed that many religious refugees from Catholic Europe found shelter in the Ottoman Empire, like the Jews from Spain, Huguenots from France and some Anglicans and Quakers from England. From this observation stemmed the revolutionary slogan 'better Turkish than Papish' (Liever Turks dan paaps, meaning: better Muslim than Catholic) used by the Dutch (Calvinist) opposition against Spanish (Catholic) rule. But this battle cry had little to do with Islam itself, as one of the first professors of Arabic at Leiden University expounded in a lengthy lecture presented in 1648 CE: Islam itself was an evil heresy, but if ever offered the choice between Turkish and Catholic rule, a Protestant would prefer the first since the Turk allowed Protestants religious freedom, whereas the Catholic Church did not.[169]

Protestants detected quite some similarities with 'the Turk' and his religion. Were they not also against icons, clerical hierarchy, celibacy, alcohol and swearing and excessive religious architecture?[170] Indeed, the successes of the Ottoman army, as opposed to those of European armies, were explained by the prohibition of alcohol and the strict discipline in Ottoman ranks. The Ottomans were aware of these sentiments in northern Europe, and used them to their own political advantage, as shown in the letter from sultan Suleyman addressed to the 'Lutheran princes in the Low Countries' shortly after 1552 CE, offering them military help against the Pope and the Holy Roman Emperor, and writing that he saw them as standing close to him since they did not worship idols, believed in one God and fought against the Pope and Emperor.[171] Not much later, in 1574 CE, sultan Murad III wrote an open letter in a similar vein to the 'Members of the Lutheran sect in Flanders and Spain,' which is worth quoting: "[a]s you, for your part, do not worship idols, you have banished the idols and portraits and bells from churches, and declared your faith by stating that God Almighty is one and Holy Jesus is His Prophet and Servant, and now, with heart and soul, are seeking and desirous of the true faith; but the faithless one they call Papa [Pope – MB] does not recognize his Creator as One, ascribing divinity to Holy Jesus (upon him be peace!), and worshiping idols and pictures which he has made with his own hands, thus casting doubt upon the oneness of God and instigating how many servants to that path of error."[172] Of course, this religious overture to the Dutch merely served the Ottoman goal of forging alliances with these European countries against the common enemy, Spain.

Not all Protestants went so far as to prefer the Ottomans over Catholics. And those who did definitely did not go as far as the sultans to equate Islam with their protestant versions of Christianity. Islam remained to them an aberration or evil, and it was more common among Protestants to equate Islam with Catholicism, declaring them equally bad. For instance, a wall painting in the Gothem church on the Swedish island of Gotland depicts St Christopher carrying Jesus as a child safely across the water with, on either side, the Pope and Muhammad (with distinct Ottoman features) drowning, symbolizing their heresy and unbelief.[173] This imagery was also voiced by Martin Luther in whose Christian cosmology the Turks represented 'the Devil' who had come as 'the scourge of God' to punish the Christians for their sins, whereas the Pope and his clergy represented the 'Anti-Christ' because of their burning and persecution of "the innocent, the pious, the orthodox."[174] Still, he thought the Pope worse than the Turk, because the latter was at least tolerant towards other faiths.[175]

But even such a staunch theologian as Luther was influenced by the political realities of his time. In 1518 CE he wrote in his *Explanation of the Ninety-five Theses* that the Turk should not be fought since he represented God's punishment for the sins of European Christians, and this punishment should not be resisted but endured as a purification of these sins: "to fight against the Turk is the same thing as resisting God, who visits our sin upon us with this rod". But several years later, in 1529 CE, when the Ottomans were besieging Vienna for the first time, Luther strongly favoured fighting the Turk, albeit on "two fronts": one by penance and prayer, for in fighting "servants of the Devil" one first needs to beat the Devil before one can beat his servants; the other front was by war. This war against the Turk, however, should be a secular, not a holy war, because it was to be fought on the prince's command in his capacity as defender of his land and as protector of "our body and earthly life", and not in his capacity as protector of the Church.[176] But whatever Luther's thoughts on the role of 'the Turk', he had no sympathy whatsoever for Islam as a religion because, he said, it taught violence, deceit and disregard for marriage, denied Christ as a son of God, and had a prophet who had written "a foul and shameful book" full of lies.[177]

One might argue that equating Islam with Catholicism in terms of its evilness effectively elevated Islam from the shadowy world of heathendom to the level of a despised, but nevertheless Christian religion like Catholicism. This is twenty-first century logic, however, because the recognition of a plurality of equally valid religions was in the sixteenth and seventeenth centuries not part of the European mind-set. Only very few ventured actually to compare Islam and Christianity on an equal footing as religions. The French jurist and political philosopher Jean Bodin[178] (1530–1596 CE) in his *Colloquium heptaplomeres* ('Colloquium of the Seven about Secrets of the Sublime') described a fictional discussion among a philosopher of natural law, a Calvinist, a Muslim, a Roman Catholic, a Lutheran, a Jew, and a sceptic, ending with a call for mutual tolerance. Similarly, Guillaume Postel in his *Republique des Turcs* (1560 CE) argued that Muslims, Jews and Christians held many beliefs in common. Later, Jean de Savigny in his *Discours sur les choses torques* (1606 CE) would go even further by stating that Turks are "for the most part, half-Christians and possibly closer to true Christianity than many among us".[179] What is interesting here is not so much the favourable attitude towards Islam, but the fact that Islam was seen as a religion comparable to that of Christianity, which was a break with the centuries-old theological position that held Christianity as the only religious truth, condemning all other claims to similar truths as falsehoods and paganisms. This development was to continue but only became generally accepted in the late nineteenth century.

CHAPTER FOUR

Powerful Europe
(1700–1950 CE)

I. Setting the Stage

The period between 1700 and 1950 witnessed the demise of the Ottoman Empire and the formal ending of this last Muslim stronghold in Europe in 1923. Communities of Muslims continued to live in the former Ottoman provinces in Europe and beyond, however. The same European powers that had actively engaged in bringing the Ottoman Empire down had also expanded their own territories beyond Europe, and through these colonial projects acquired new subjects, many of whom were Muslims. So while the European continent for the first time was devoid of Muslim rulers and the Muslim population in Europe had reached an all-time low through migration and killings during the second half of the nineteenth century, European powers ruled foreign lands with vast Muslim populations.

European military, economic and political prowess, together with the successes of European imperialism all added up to a position of superiority and condescension vis-à-vis Islam and Muslims. At the same time, two new concepts gained popularity that were to prove a powerful source of dissent and even revolt among the Muslim communities both inside and outside Europe: nationalism and minorities. In the case of the Ottoman Empire, they played an important role in inciting non-Muslim communities to rebel against their Muslim overlords. The resulting break-up of the centuries-old Ottoman social, political and legal structures that were based on religion was to be very violent and brutal, and the volatile combination of ethnic, national and religious identities made the conflicts all the more complex.

1. Colonialism and Imperialism

The eighteenth century was the heyday of European colonialism: Spain, France, England, and the Dutch Republic established chains of trading posts on the shores of the American, Asian and African continents. Colonialism evolved during the nineteenth century into imperialism when the European countries also imposed their rule on these territories and their hinterlands and, as a final step, incorporated these realms into their sovereign domains. Consequently, the states with the largest Muslim populations in the world were not the Ottoman Empire or Iran, but the Netherlands (which ruled the Indonesian archipelago) and Great Britain (which ruled what are now India, Pakistan and Bangladesh). The nineteenth century witnessed the combination of exploration of unknown territories (for profit, but often also as part of genuine scientific interest) and frantic competition among the imperialist states to expand their empires with these territories outside Europe.

Muslim lands and peoples were completely overtaken by this European hunger for conquest and knowledge. The three great Muslim empires at the time were the Ottomans in the Mediterranean and Middle East, the Safavids in Iran and the Moghuls in what is now Pakistan and northern India. They could not withstand the military prowess of the Europeans – in particular the British, Dutch, French and Russians – and had to succumb, as the smaller Muslim sultanates and emirates in other parts of the world had already done. Resistance to the European powers was scanty and unity among Muslims almost entirely lacking. Even the Ottoman sultan, who was officially the caliph and hence the sole spiritual leader of all Muslims, did not function as a rallying point of resistance to European imperialism, nor did he act as such – perhaps because the Ottoman Empire was itself an imperialist power.

Between 1700 and 1950 CE Europeans did not speak of the Islamic world or Muslims, as is common nowadays, but mostly referred to the generic terms 'Orient' and 'Mohammedans'. The term Near Orient was often reserved for the region stretching from Morocco to Iran, while the 'Far Orient' referred exclusively to the region of East Asia. This terminology reflects the worldview of the nineteenth century European of a division between the civilized Christian West and the exotic but backward East. By the early twentieth century nearly all territories in the Orient inhabited by Muslims were either subjected to European rule or made part of an alliance that was dominated by the European partner.

Interestingly, the imperial endeavours of the European nations did not radiate outward, but rather from the outside inward. The first colonies were in far away places, and the territories close to Europe became of interest only at a later stage. By the time Napoleon made the first inroad of European imperialism into the Arab Mediterranean region by invading Egypt in 1798 CE, the Dutch had already established themselves in Indonesia and the British in India. Napoleon's military action has attained mythological properties in European history, but from a military and imperialistic point of view it was an utter disaster (Napoleon eventually abandoned his disease-ridden army in Egypt to return to France and embark on the conquest of Europe). It took another century before France and England acquired an imperialistic taste for North Africa and the Middle East: France because it considered North Africa part of its backyard and realized that it was one of the last territories left to secure during the late nineteenth century colonial scramble for land; England because the Middle East – especially after the opening of the Suez Canal in 1869 CE – was considered important in protecting its lifeline to British India. Oil, which was found at the time in Iran and in the Caspian Sea, became of importance only in the early twentieth century, especially when the British navy in 1910 CE switched from coal to oil (the Arab Gulf oilfields were discovered in the late 1930s and became of geo-strategic importance after the Second World War).

The period under discussion here, from 1700 to 1950, sets our topic of 'Islam in Europe' in a peculiar light, because almost all territories in the world inhabited by Muslims became part of European colonial domains. But, apart from the Ottoman Empire, none of these territories were located in Europe. And Europeans in this period encountered more Muslims than in the previous centuries, and Islam was never studied as much now as in the preceding epochs, but Islam and Muslims had never been so far removed from the European continent as in this period. With the gradual loss by the Ottoman Empire of its domains in the Balkans, the early twentieth century was the first period in European history since the advent of Islam in which no Muslim power had a foothold on that continent, and so few Muslims resided there. By the early twentieth century, Muslims and Islam were therefore no longer an issue of proximate danger, or of neighbourly relations, but had become the exclusive domain of colonial and foreign politics.

2. The Demise of the Ottoman Empire

The demise of the Ottoman Empire set in with the turn of the eighteenth century, and was reflected in a collapse of its military power, economic prosperity and social order.

Militarily, the Empire never recovered from its defeat at the walls of Vienna in 1683 CE, and it was the Empire's luck that the Habsburgs did not press their advantage to the full but settled for peace. The resulting Ottoman-Habsburg treaty of Karlowitz in 1699 CE marked a turning point. From then on, any battle fought by the Ottomans – mostly against the Habsburg Empire and tsarist Russia – would cause them only to lose territory, and other European powers like Prussia, France and Great Britain quickly moved in to share the spoils and to tip the balance in their favour. The Ottomans tried to recover, but the eradication of the insubordinate Janissaries in 1826 CE and a modernizing overhaul of its army in the late nineteenth century with the help of German and French instructors, came too late and was of little avail. The shortcomings of the military showed not only in the loss of territory, but also in the inability to maintain internal order. The uprisings of the nineteenth century in the Balkans could not be stemmed, resulting in an internal fragmentation of the Empire.

The economic situation was also worsening in this period, for a variety of reasons. First and foremost, the Empire had no industries and was not a trading nation, but relied almost entirely on its domestic agriculture. For its import and export it depended on its Armenian, Greek and Jewish inhabitants, but even they hardly moved outside the Ottoman realm. The transport of goods from and into the Empire was therefore dominated by European merchants who became increasingly intrusive, as we will see below. The Ottoman lack of interest in (and even disdain for) trade also made the Empire literally miss the boat in a rapidly developing global economy. By the early nineteenth century, the Empire was debt-ridden and engulfed in a major financial crisis. Its solutions were short-sighted and insufficient to solve the problems the Empire was facing: the issuance of promissory notes to raise cash added to inflation, and taking out foreign loans to pay off debts increased both the national debt and dependence on foreign powers.

And finally, the social order collapsed. This is perhaps the most complicated development of this period because a number of factors interacted. One was the breakdown of the millet system. This special religious system of the Ottoman Empire that had successfully existed for centuries had become dysfunctional. Another factor was the declining fealty of Ottoman landlords and governors in the provinces to the rulers in the far-away Porte. These two factors merged with the new sentiment of the nineteenth century, namely nationalism, and this proved a volatile cocktail that created series of uprisings by Ottoman subjects. And to complicate matters, Russia, Austria, France, England and other foreign powers exploited these uprisings to pursue their own interests vis-à-vis the Ottoman Empire.

These military, economic and social developments had their impact on the presence of Muslims and Muslim rule in the south-eastern part of the European continent, which became known as the Balkans. Ottoman rule rapidly receded from this region, its European provinces becoming independent or acquired by the Austro-Hungarian monarchy. The wars and many insurgencies in the Balkan region during the nineteenth century led to an unprecedented flow of migrants, settlers, refugees and forced expulsions of communities of all nationalities, ethnicities and religions, causing a dramatic shift in population composition in the Balkans. In 1923 CE, the territory of the Ottoman Empire on continental Europe was reduced to the furthest south-eastern tip of the continent, round the city of Edirne.

The Ottoman Empire finally left the European stage with one last and dramatic action: it entered the First World War by choosing to side with the German axis. The choice would prove disastrous, but was not illogical at the time. The Allied axis of Great Britain, France and Russia represented everything that the Ottomans had come to resent as European imperialism in the past century. The Prussian and German empires, on the other hand, were much admired by the Ottomans for their organizational and military skills (and probably also for the manner in which these empires defied the Ottoman arch-enemy, the Austro-Hungarian monarchy). In its modernization efforts during the nineteenth century, the Ottoman Empire had maintained close relations with them, and Prussian military advisors had come to restructure and train the Ottoman army according to the newest techniques.

The German defeat in 1918 CE signalled the final destruction of the Ottoman Empire by the victors in the Versailles talks of 1919–1920. The remnants of the Ottoman Empire in the Middle East were parcelled out among the French and English, and discussion was under way on what to do with the Ottoman rump state in Anatolia (present day Turkey). The Greeks, however, were not willing to wait for the outcome of these protracted negotiations and decided to put their idea of a Greater Greece (known as the Megali Idea) into practice: Greek forces invaded the western Turkish shores in 1919 and moved inland to repossess those areas that were ostensibly part of the historical Greek heritage. They were finally repelled in 1922 CE by the Turkish nationalist army under Ataturk. In 1923 CE, the Ottoman Empire officially ended and was replaced by the Republic of Turkey. A year later, the last remnant of this last Islamic Empire was cleared away with the abolition of the caliphate.

II. Physical Islam

1. Living with the Unbeliever

Estimates of the population of the Ottoman provinces in Europe during the eighteenth century are not available, but at the outset of the nineteenth century these provinces held the major part of the population of the entire Empire with about 10 million people, of whom approximately one third were Muslim and two thirds non-Muslim.[1] With the increasing territorial losses during the nineteenth century, compounded by the relocation of Muslim refugees into the shrinking Ottoman territory, the *number* of Muslims in Europe rapidly declined, but the *percentage* of Muslims in the remaining Ottoman provinces gradually rose to 48 per cent by the end of the century.[2]

These estimates, however, give only an impression of the population composition within the entire Ottoman Empire. We, on the other hand, are interested in the Empire's provinces in Europe. These figures are hard to come by, but one estimate is that the Muslim population in the Balkans had reduced from 2.3 million in 1911 CE to an estimated 1 million in 1923 CE, predominantly living in Bosnia, Bulgaria and Albania (the last being the only Muslim-majority country in the region and in the whole of Europe, for that matter).[3] The one place that during these decades of religious and ethnic turmoil remained a place of continued Muslim-Christian coexistence was Istanbul: during the entire nineteenth century its population remained, on average, half Muslim and half non-Muslim, and only by 1914 CE was the number of non-Muslims slightly reduced.[4]

What was it, then, that caused this sudden and violent break-up of the Ottoman society that had lived in relative harmony for centuries? As mentioned, the causes were a combination of loss of power by the Porte, economic crises and changes, a dysfunctional *millet* system, declining fealty of local lords, emerging nationalism and the increasing influence of foreign powers. We will discuss these factors in more detail below.

As we saw in the previous chapter, the social order of Ottoman society consisted of a legal and political classification of the population based on religion (the *millet* system), while an informal classification existed on the basis of one's social-economic situation. We have also seen that the Muslims primarily inhabited the urban areas of the European provinces of the Empire. Muslims and non-Muslims often lived separately, but not segregated. The often held view of "Ottoman subjects living in sharply divided, mutually impenetrable, religious communities called *millets* ... is incorrect."[5]

But with the beginning of the eighteenth century we can discern the developments that were later identified as factors contributing to the fracturing of the social order. One of these developments was the emergence of a political autonomy in the provinces. Muslim landlords started to act more independently, their loyalty shifting from the Porte in Istanbul to their own lands in the remote places of the Empire.[6] These landlords were of two kinds: descendants of officials who were appointed by the Porte and over time had become rooted in the area, and families of local notables whose status and power had been recognized by the Ottoman Porte, as was the case in Bosnia. Both kinds of local rulers were usually Muslim by religion, but not always Turkish by ethnicity. By the end of the eighteenth century, the central state had started to re-establish its power over these local elites and to claim its right to collect taxes directly from them, but after strong opposition had to settle for a compromise: the local notables recognized the political supremacy of the Porte but retained substantial power and wealth.[7]

The local, mostly Christian, population in the European provinces was also changing during this period, showing signs of a gradually emerging civil society. The middle class, in particular merchants and craftsmen, organized themselves into guilds. Empowerment of these guilds and organizations came from an unexpected source: the Janissaries. The boy levy had been abolished in 1703 CE and the ban on soldiers marrying had not been enforced for a while, so that this elite infantry had become hereditary. Moreover, the lack of annual campaigns meant that the Janissaries found other sources of income. Since their garrisons were in the towns, they became part of urban economic life, either as mafia-style chieftains or as members of the business community. They maintained their position of political power, enabling them to make and unmake rulers. In that capacity they became the new urban elite that acted as the voice and the sword of the local population, often defending it against local rulers.[8] The power of the Janissaries became such, however, that in 1826 CE the sultan thought it necessary to have them annihilated. One of the results of the removal of the Janissaries from Ottoman society was that with them also disappeared the larger part of the Muslim merchant elite that had monopolized commerce, resulting in a new phase of economic liberalism from which the emerging non-Muslim business elite in particular profited.[9]

The non-Muslim merchant class was by then already profiting from economic change that created new wealth and possibilities and this, in turn, spurred on the non-Muslims' social mobility that was increasingly defined by wealth rather than social origins. This merchant class expanded its already existing commercial contacts with European countries, importing not only Western commercial interests but also Western ideas of liberty, equality and political representation.[10] These ideas were received with apprehension by the Muslims, however, since they were considered a threat to the traditional social order wherein non-Muslims were supposed to know their place. The response was similar to those of earlier times: a barrage of old regulations on behavioural and dress codes was being re-invoked to restore the old order, including the prohibition on non-Muslim merchants wearing fur or yellow shoes.[11] These were local initiatives: when the sultan in 1799 CE issued a liberal decree permitting Christians to carry arms, including the *yatagan*, the long, curved traditional Turkish knife, the Muslim population protested; in particular the Janisarries, who had always exhibited brutal behaviour towards local peasants, were now faced with the possibility of armed opposition from Christian peasants. Surprisingly, these peasants received support from their Muslim landlords who resented the Janissaries' ruthlessness as undermining the landlords' authority as well as their estates' income. Rather than caving in to mounting opposition among the Muslim population of the Empire against the rules abolishing the discrimination of non-Muslims, the sultan pressed ahead with his equality programme. In 1829 CE, the sultan overnight abolished all laws on dress codes, but also prohibited all turbans and robes of honour worn by Muslims and imposed a uniform – the fez and frock coat – for all state officials. In doing so, the sultan reversed a centuries-old practice of using clothing regulations to create or maintain social differences, and replaced it with visual uniformity.[12]

We will discuss the effects of this revolutionary move by the sultan against the wishes of most of his Muslim subjects in more detail below, but must now continue with our discussion of the factors that were at the root of the disintegration of the Ottoman Empire. In addition to the military, social and economic factors mentioned above, there was also the novel phenomenon of the local population of the European provinces of the Ottoman Empire increasingly asserting itself in terms of religious and ethnic identity. This may sound self-evident in a society that was already structured on the basis of *millets* dividing Ottoman society into the four religious communities of Muslims, Orthodox, Jews and Armenians. Two of these communities, however, the Muslim and the Orthodox, started to fracture from within along ethnic and linguistic fault lines. This situation demands a closer look into these ethnic, religious and linguistic differences to understand the complexity of the conflicts that were to erupt in the nineteenth century between – and within! – the privileged minority of

Muslims and the second-class majority of non-Muslims, who were predominantly Orthodox Christians.[13]

The Muslim *millet* included several ethnic and linguistic communities like Turks, who originated from Anatolia, and those who identified themselves as indigenous Muslims from the European provinces, such as Albanians, Bosniaks and Pomaks (Bulgarian speakers), but also small minorities of Muslim Greeks and even Muslim Jews (who identified ethnically as Jews but religiously as Muslims). Many of the Greeks on Crete were Muslims, for instance, as was a distinct group of Jews in Saloniki.[14] As such they belonged to the Muslim *millet*, although it depended on the local context whether their religious affiliation was more determining than their ethnic, or vice versa. By the same token, many Albanians, Bosnians and Bulgarians belonged to one of the Christian *millets*, in particular the Orthodox. We must therefore realize that religion and ethnicity were not always conflated.

Ethnic and linguistic commonalities often provided sources of cohesion that were as strong as, if not stronger than, religious commonalities, since most ethnic communities maintained and increasingly cherished their own specificities.[15] The Greeks, for instance, were a seafaring nation, dominating Ottoman trade as private entrepreneurs and comprising most of the Ottoman merchant and military navy personnel. Many tradesmen knew several languages, and as a community they were probably also the best-educated of Ottoman subjects, with Greek schools and books proliferating across the Ottoman Empire. The Serbs, on the other hand, were mostly peasants and relatively poor, but cherished a strongly celebrated cultural heritage. Other prominent communities in the Ottoman Balkans were those of the Albanians and Jews. Most Albanians were Muslim, and since they had been the main target of the boy levy many Albanians were part of the Ottoman establishment. The majority of Jews in the Empire were descendants of the Sephardim who had fled fifteenth-century Spain. They spoke their own language, Ladino, and remained aloof from the other *millets*. Many were deported to remote areas in the Empire to stimulate the local economy. A true 'Jewish' town was Saloniki (later Thessaloniki) where the Jews had for centuries constituted a majority, and formed the centre of an economic hub dominated by Jewish trade in the region.[16]

We are, therefore, looking at communities that were not clearly divided into Muslims and non-Muslims, since these communities themselves were fractured into ethnic and linguistic communities. To add to this complex situation, we must now introduce the foreigners and the role they played in the Ottoman Empire.

2. The Combustible Mix of Capitulations, Millets and Nationalism

In its contacts with non-Muslims, the Ottoman Empire made use of two different systems: the so-called capitulations to deal with foreigners, on the one hand, and the millets to deal with non-Muslim Ottoman subjects, on the other hand. To a modern observer, the two systems may seem entirely different. With regard to the capitulations, their subject-matter was foreign nationals, their goal was to grant privileges connected to commerce and the contracting parties were the Ottoman and foreign states. The millet system, on the other hand, had the Ottoman national as its subject; its goal was to establish a social-legal status and the contracting parties were the Ottoman state and its indigenous communities. More importantly, the determining factor identifying the parties in the case of the capitulations was nationality, while in the millet system it was religion.

From an Ottoman perspective, however, the two systems were merely two sides of the same coin. Both provided institutional means for dealing with non-Muslims, as they were adaptations of the system developed by Islamic law: the dhimmi status for non-Muslims residing within the realm of Islam (which allowed religious freedom and a restricted form of autonomy, but a second-class legal and social status) and the so-called musta'min status for non-Muslim outsiders who were visiting the realm of Islam (granting them temporary entry and a status of relative immunity). In both systems the non-Muslim was assumed to belong to another community or 'nation', whether this was indigenous (the Greek subjects of the Ottoman Empire were referred to as 'Rum' or Romans, derived from the Eastern Roman empire) or foreign (Western Europeans were often referred to as 'Franks').

From this perspective, it was not uncommon for foreign states to intervene on behalf of religious communities in other states. Already in the sixteenth century, the Ottomans had made diplomatic interventions in Russia and the Polish-Lithuanian Commonwealth to protest – sometimes successfully – against alleged ill treatment of the Muslim minorities in these realms. Conversely, French diplomats would do the same on behalf of the Catholics in the Ottoman Empire, and Russians on behalf of the Russian Orthodox. Intervention by a state on behalf of the religious communities was perhaps not appreciated by the state where these communities resided, but it was not interpreted as an infringement of national sovereignty. Communities with a religion different from that of the state were conceived as a foreign body by that state; and while their political allegiance was to be with their sovereign, it was considered natural that their religious allegiance lay elsewhere.

Here we see a distinct difference between the Ottoman and European approaches: whereas the Ottoman Empire was strict in its condition of political allegiance but accommodated a religious allegiance out of state, the European countries conflated the two and deemed any religion other than the state religion a potential source of disloyalty or treason. The European position had led to devastating religious wars aimed at creating religious homogeneity. Since religious cleansing could not be achieved in full, the European states ultimately settled for modalities of religious tolerance (which, as we saw in the Introduction, is a pragmatic rather than principled tolerance).

In the religiously pluralist Ottoman Empire the state, as a matter of Islamic law, had entrusted itself with the protection of its indigenous non-Muslim subjects. Protection in this respect meant that these non-Muslims should be able to practise their faith. But since the religious leadership of some of these religious communities was located outside the Ottoman realm, the Porte allowed these subjects also to be 'protected' by foreign powers. Such protection was often confirmed in treaties, such as the treaty of 1637 CE that recognized France as the sole protector of Catholics in the Ottoman realm, and the treaty of 1774 CE that recognized Russia as the sole protector of Orthodox Christians in the Empire.

While the Ottoman Empire might consider its dealings with its non-Muslim subjects and non-Muslim foreigners to follow a certain logic that, to the Empire's mind, had created a fair and just system that had lasted for centuries, the two communities developed their own dynamics. The millet and capitulations systems served their purposes independently of each other, but by the late eighteenth century they became more and more intertwined and turned out to be one of the nails in the Ottoman Empire's coffin.

Capitulations as a Political Tool

The capitulations developed from mere commercial privileges like tax exemptions and diplomatic status for the local consul and his assistant to a fully fledged legal immunity for an ever-increasing community of foreigners that included their families and local staff. That such large communities could reside within Ottoman territory with legal impunity, as if they were living in a bubble, was increasingly considered a violation of Ottoman sovereignty.[17] This issue became prominent when the millets became involved by means of the so-called dragomans. The dragoman ('translator') was an Ottoman local hired by the foreign consulate as an intermediary between the commercial outpost and the Ottoman merchants and authorities.[18] The dragoman was mostly recruited from one of the Christian millets, mainly because the mercantile families in these millets could provide a commercial network within and outside the Empire, but also because a Christian was considered more trustworthy to the European employer than a Muslim.

Under the capitulations that were re-negotiated during the nineteenth century, the immunity granted to foreigners was expanded to their dragomans. They could now also claim immunity from the Ottoman legal system in a number of situations. This privilege (the so-called bera't, or exemption) became a source of criticism among the Ottomans, because it had the effect of granting foreign nationality to an Ottoman subject. Even worse was that bera'ts were handed out as if they were passports, and themselves became objects of trade.[19]

From the Ottoman perspective foreigners were increasingly abusing their privileges under the capitulation agreements, and expanding them at the expense of Ottoman sovereignty. But why, then, would the Ottomans extend these privileges in the first place? In answering this question we must realize that capitulations had been granted since the sixteenth century, when the Ottoman Empire was at the height of its power, and had been re-negotiated with every extension since then. In the early stages of the capitulations, the Ottomans were not so concerned with the commercial incursions of foreign merchants because the goal of the Porte was to establish political rather than commercial contacts. Also, in the Islamic legal terminology of the capitulations, the Ottomans viewed the merchants as musta'mins who, if they were to reside in Ottoman territory for longer than one (or more) year, would come under Ottoman jurisdiction as dhimmis.[20] But practice was different and that had to do mostly with a shift in power in the late seventeenth century: since then, the Ottoman Empire had lost its military edge and was increasingly dependent on financial arrangements with Europeans through trade and loans. This gave Europeans the leverage to re-negotiate the capitulations to their own advantage. And so they did, to the full.

The drawing of the Ottoman millets into a foreign sphere of influence cannot be exclusively blamed on European strategies in this respect. The Ottomans themselves also contributed to this development. For instance, they considered their non-Muslim subjects more as foreigners than as nationals – it is telling in this respect that the Ottoman millets in the nineteenth century came under the Ottoman Ministry of Foreign Affairs, just like foreigners.[21] This was partly a result of the millet system, which had created a parallel infrastructure with the state representing the Muslim millet while all non-Muslim millets, although residing under the ultimate sovereignty of the state, retained a degree of autonomy.

The elements of the *millet* system that had obtained so much praise in the past from Europeans – relative religious freedom, autonomy, no interference from the state – were now becoming a source of criticism from the same Europeans because they lacked equal rights and complete freedom of religion. When the Porte tried to remedy this by abolishing the *millet* system and instituting Ottoman citizenship in the first half of the nineteenth century, it was already too late: the centuries-old division between a state by and for Muslims, on the one hand, and its non-Muslim subjects who only needed to pay tax and know their place but were otherwise to manage their own affairs, on the other hand, was not to be repaired by a single constitutional reform.

Nationalism

The notion of nationalism, that became so popular throughout Europe and beyond in the nineteenth century, provided the growing social and economic unrest in the European provinces of the Ottoman Empire with a direction. It must be remembered that much of the social and economic unrest was at first internal and not intended to discredit or challenge the authority of the Porte. On the contrary: the Porte was often implored by the Christian communities to step in and solve their social and economic conflicts with Muslim landlords, local authorities or the Janissaries. But the complex mixture of events, sentiments and situations was channelled into a na-tionalistic idiom, leading to national revolts and a gradual break-up of the Ottoman Empire. We will discuss these revolts in more detail below in the paragraph on wars and insurgencies.

Nationalism was not embraced exclusively by the non-Muslim subjects of the Ottoman Empire. Muslims also became infected by the bug of nationalism. In the latter case we need to distinguish between Muslims who were living within the Ottoman Empire and those who used to be Ottoman subjects but came under non-Muslim rule when the lands where they lived were conquered from the Ottoman Empire. The Bosnian Muslims ('Bosniaks') are a typical example. The formation of the Bosnian Muslim identity was unlike that of other nationalist revivals in the Balkans. Bulgarians, Greeks, Serbs and Albanians had their own histories and folklore that they could refer to, and their nationalist revival was preceded – if not prompted – by large-scale social and economic changes. Moreover, the Ortho-dox and Catholic populations could rely on the centuries-old organizational in-frastructure of their churches. The Muslims in Bosnia had none of these and so, when the Ottoman rule of which they had been part for four centuries was replaced by that of the Austro-Hungarian double monarchy in 1878 CE, they were at a loss. The disappearance of Istanbul as a point of authoritative orientation and the lack of will to refocus on Vienna forced the Bosniaks for the first time to develop their own, separate identity.[22] They did so by primarily focusing on religion, Islam. Austria facilitated this by allowing religious freedom for Muslims: they retained their own religious institutions, such as courts, schools and mosques, and were autonomous in their religious affairs (an inversed dhimmi situation that we have seen repeatedly being applied by Christian European powers in the past). One exception was conversion: the case of a Bosnian Muslim woman converting to Christianity caused a confrontation between Bosnian local authorities arresting her for apostasy and Austrian authorities releasing her with the argument that she was free to choose her religion.[23] These confrontations over conversion continued in Bosnia even after a settlement was reached with the Austrian Conversion Ordinance of 1891 CE.

We must realize that the Muslims in Bosnia did not view their predicament as eternal: they considered themselves Ottoman subjects under Austrian occupation, which was expected to be temporary. This situation changed, however, with the Austrian annexation of Bosnia in 1908 CE. The new Austrian province of Bosnia-Hercegovina was granted autonomy, and its constitution of 1910 CE mentioned Serbs, Croats and Muslims as native peoples. These three communities were also politically organized, for each had its representative political party in the Bosnian parliament. Whereas Bosniaks had been lords and authorities under Ottoman rule, they were now a constitutionally recognized minority in an autonomous province under the Austro-Hungarian double monarchy

With regard to the Muslims within the Ottoman Empire nationalism came late. Throughout most of the nineteenth century, Muslim intellectuals in Istanbul and other urban centres of the Empire were very much engaging in new and exciting concepts like westernization, secularism, and centralization.[24] Nationalism – that is, Turkish nationalism – joined the ranks only by the end of the nineteenth century. Until that time, the elites and especially the Porte itself tried very hard to introduce the modern ideas of secularism and equality in order to unite all subjects of the Empire. But the legal, economic and political reforms initiated by the Porte, known as the Tanzimat, were too late or not rigorous enough to stem the tide of religious, ethnic and national fragmentation of the Empire.

Reforms (Tanzimat)

We have already seen that the sultan was willing to introduce forms of equality among his subjects when in 1829 CE he abolished all laws on dress codes for non-Muslims and prohibited all turbans and robes of honour being worn by Muslims. This decree turned out to be a prelude to the more radical reforms of 1839 CE and, when confronted with a general refusal by local Muslim landlords to implement the decree, a repetition of the reforms by the decree of 1856 CE. The reforms concerned a number of issues, but those that are of interest to us here are the ones related to the non-Muslim subjects of the Ottoman Empire. These were primarily aimed at establishing equal citizenship. The decrees abolished the separate (*dhimmi*) status of the non-Muslim and the special poll tax to be paid by every non-Muslim, and introduced the concept of Ottoman citizenship. Consequently, non-Muslims were allowed to assume positions in the Ottoman government. However, non-Muslims were not eager to enter the military, neither were they readily admitted to the foreign ministry, but their presence "became most pronounced" in the civil bureaucracy.[25]

The reforms were met with a lot of opposition from the Muslim subjects of the Ottoman Empire. The establishment of equality between Muslims and non-Muslims was perceived by many as disruptive to the social fabric of society that had been in place for centuries. There was strong opposition and even vandalism against churches that were newly built in Ottoman provinces like Bosnia after building restrictions were lifted by the Tanzimat reforms.[26] But the opposition was also motivated by practical considerations: the abolition of the poll tax caused a serious loss of income for the tax-farmers who lived off collecting the tax. It was the main reason for the uprising of Bosnian Muslim landlords in 1830 CE. Many of these tax farmers therefore quickly devised ways to impose other forms of tax that replaced the abrogated poll tax, which in turn caused opposition from their non-Muslim tax-payers who appealed to the Porte for help.

Not only Muslims were dismayed by these reforms; many non-Muslims opposed them as well, for various reasons. The non-Muslims who worked closely with foreign consulates, or who had obtained a *bera't*, correctly assumed that the institution of Ottoman citizenship was meant to bring them back under Ottoman suzerainty.[27] Others who cherished their *millet* autonomy feared that their courts would be taken away from them, just as the *millet* authorities were anxious that they would lose power over their communities.[28] These fears were unfounded, however, because the Tanzimat abolished the *dhimmi* position and its poll tax, but not the *millet* system itself. The communities maintained their infrastructure and the right to live in accordance with their own family laws to be applied by their own millet courts. Moreover, and quite paradoxically, the Empire not only maintained the structure of the millet system, but by 1914 CE had increased the number of millets from three (Orthodox, Jewish, Armenian) to thirteen: Greek-Orthodox, Catholic, Syrian Catholic, Chaldean Catholic, Syrian Jacobites, Armenian Gregorians, Armenian Catholics, Protestants, Melkites, Jews, Bulgarian Catholics, Maronites, Nestorians.

The millet system as an institution that for centuries had functioned as the go-between between the Ottoman state and its non-Muslim communities was now formally replaced by the institution of citizenship that positioned the individual in a direct relation with the state, without millet intermediary.[29] But the millet remained intact as the rallying point for communal interests of the individuals, for had not the millet over the centuries preserved the community's culture, heritage, language, religion and laws? And since the Ottoman state was increasingly incapable or unwilling to safeguard these communal interests and differences, all millets made sure that they were under the protection of one of the great powers, France for Catholics, Great Britain for the Protestants and Russia for the Orthodox.

But, as we saw above, religious identities rapidly fractured along ethnic and linguistic fault lines. The Orthodox Greeks, Serbs, Albanians, Bulgars – to name but a few – re-discovered their cultural identity and their own language and felt empowered by their economic freedom to assert that identity.[30] This development took a dangerous turn when these communities became dissatisfied with the fact that they had no territory of their own – that they were 'nations' without 'states'. The fulfilment of this need resulted in atrocious episodes of ethnic and religious cleansing, which we will discuss in more detail below.

The process of identity and loyalty did not end with the establishment of nation-states, however. Once the ethnic-linguistic communities had broken away from their larger religious communities to establish their own states, it was religion that appeared to determine national loyalty. For instance, the Bulgarian-speaking Muslims (Pomaks) would feel more allegiance to Turkey than Bulgaria, Greek-speaking Muslim Turks from Crete felt little affiliation with the Greeks on the mainland and preferred to settle in Turkey, while the Turkish-speaking Orthodox Greeks were loyal to the newly established state of Greece.[31] And since none of the new states with Orthodox communities was prepared to acknowledge the Orthodox Church as a supra-nationalist religious authority, they all established their own Orthodox state churches: Serbia (1832), Greece (1833), Bulgaria (1860), Rumania (1885) and Albania (1929). An exception was Catholic-majority Croatia which remained loyal to the Church in Rome.

3. Wars and Insurgencies

The loss of territory in its European provinces through wars and insurgencies was a major blow to the Ottoman Empire, more so than the loss of its dominions in the Middle East, because the European provinces had always constituted the heartland of the Ottoman Empire. The wars and insurgencies that were waged upon and within the European provinces of the Ottoman Empire during the nineteenth and early twentieth centuries were many and present a kaleidoscopic image of events. At the risk of simplifying two centuries of armed struggle, we will first distinguish between inter-state conflicts on the one hand and domestic armed conflicts, on the other, and then continue by discussing the role of religion in these conflicts.

Inter-State Conflicts

The inter-state conflicts can be divided into two categories. On the one hand there were the conflicts between the Ottoman Empire and its direct neighbours, the Habsburgs (from 1804 CE onwards known as the Austrian Empire, and from 1867 until 1918 CE as the 'Austro-Hungarian Double Monarchy') and the Russian tsarist empire. On the other hand there were the conflicts with far-away countries like France and Great Britain. The Ottomans fought several wars with the Austrians and Russians, while the conflicts with Great Britain and France in the Balkan region were mostly by proxy, with the two European powers occasionally siding with the local insurgencies and revolts in the Ottoman realm. They were instrumental, for instance, in bringing the Greek revolt of 1821 CE to its successful end in an independent Greek state in 1830 CE.

Ever since the Ottoman defeat at the walls of Vienna in 1683 CE, Austria had pushed the Ottomans back and gradually conquered parts of neighbouring Ottoman territory: Hungary finally became part of the Austrian Empire which, in its pursuit of the Ottomans, took Slovenia, Croatia and Bosnia. Russia also wanted its share and, with the justification of protecting its Orthodox co-religionists, engaged in several wars with the Ottoman Empire, acquiring Moldavia and the territories north and east of the Black Sea. Such was the Russian encroachment into Ottoman territory that for once the French and British sided with the Ottomans against the Russian advance in the Crimean War (1853–1856 CE). The British nurse Florence Nightingale became known during this war for her efforts to raise hygiene standards in English lazars and Ottoman hospitals.

In terms of territorial appetite, however, France and Great Britain were more interested in the Arab dominions of the Ottoman Empire, most of which had already acquired a semi-autonomous status. This region, comprising North Africa, the Middle East and the Arab Peninsula, was once the cradle of the great Roman, Byzantine and Islamic civilizations, but by the sixteenth century it had lost its splendour and prosperity, having slumped back into poverty and backwardness. Napoleon's invasion of Egypt in 1798 CE was therefore merely a military and romantic adventure with no political, economic or strategic gains. Perhaps the only impact of this adventure was that it ended the two and a half centuries-old French-Ottoman military pact, and triggered the European romantic and religious interest that became known as Orientalism, of which we will speak below.

Imperial interest by European powers in this region came only a century after Napoleon's adventure: the western Ottoman domains, Algeria and Tunisia, were taken by France in 1830 and 1881 CE, respectively, while Egypt was occupied by Great Britain in 1882 CE. Great Britain's interest in Egypt and several Gulf emirates was purely strategic at first, for it was only meant to safeguard free passage to its imperial domains in British India through the recently opened Suez canal. In 1911 CE, Italy invaded the Ottoman province of Libya. When the Ottoman Empire sided with the German axis in the First World War (1914–1918) and subsequently lost, its remaining provinces in the Middle East and Gulf were divided between the British and French powers: France gained Syria and Lebanon, while Great Britain took Jordan, Palestine and Iraq.

Internal Conflicts

The Serbian revolt of 1804 CE was the first in a series of insurgencies of non-Muslim Ottoman subjects who identified themselves on national-religious grounds. This, and subsequent rebellious acts were considered the ultimate disruption of the Ottoman social order in which non-Muslims were supposed to know and keep their place, and the Ottoman response was extremely harsh, with punishments like impalement, stoning to death, rape and prisoners being roasted alive.[32] The Ottomans were not alone in so gruesomely restoring order: the Serbs who had participated in the same revolt on the Habsburg side of the border faced mass executions, concentration camps and deportation of their elites by the Habsburgs. These atrocities were to set the tone – on all sides – for the following revolts. The Greek uprising (1821–1830 CE) was the next revolt of non-Muslim Ottoman subjects who identified themselves as Greeks, that is a singular religious and ethnic nation united by language. Bosnians, Bulgarians, Albanians, Macedonians and others followed suit and, mostly with the aid of European powers, were able to obtain varying degrees of autonomy.

In 1878 CE, after the Ottoman defeat in its last war with Russia, the European powers came together in the Berlin Congress to reach a final solution for the Balkans by dividing the former Ottoman territories thus: Greece, Bulgaria, Romania, Montenegro and Serbia were granted independence; Albania, northern Greece and Macedonia remained part of the Ottoman Empire; Slovenia, Croatia, Bosnia (including Herzegovina) were incorporated into the Austro-Hungary double monarchy. But by now the genie of national and religious sentiments was out of the bottle and could not be pushed back in by granting independence and re-drawing national boundaries. The problem that remained after the division of territories in 1878 CE was that the peoples ('nations') and their territorial home ('state') did not always coincide, because lands were often still shared by mixed populations.

The Role of Religion in Internal and Inter-State Conflicts

The uprisings in the Ottoman European domains were not always non-Muslim subjects rising against Islamic rule. Often other factors were involved. Many revolts by (mostly Christian) peasantry against their (mostly Muslim) overlords were prompted by economic oppression, the Christian rebels often emphatically proclaiming their loyalty to the Ottoman Empire, and even imploring the Porte for assistance against the local Muslim overlord. And when help was given, this could then cause the local Muslim elite to rise against the Porte, as was the case with the Bosniak revolt in 1850 CE. Bosniaks were the ruling Muslim elite in Bosnia who by religion and fealty owed allegiance to the Ottoman Porte, but who for centuries had lived in Bosnia and spoke Serbo-Croat as opposed to Ottoman Turkish. When the Ottoman Porte introduced the first set of Tanzimat in 1839 CE that included the alleviation of fiscal hardship of the Christian subjects, the local Muslim elite protested and refused to implement these regulations. Their disobedience was answered by the Porte with military force, which in turn caused the Bosniak revolt. The indiscriminate punitive actions by the Ottoman military against the local Bosnian population that was both Christian and Muslim led to the devastation of Bosnia and left the Christian peasantry in more misery than they were already in and turned their original loyalty towards the Porte into antipathy or hatred.[33]

While the causes of the many uprisings in the Ottoman Balkans were complex and need to be considered in their local contexts, we may make the general observation that these uprisings were at first prompted by social and economic reasons – poverty and oppression being the main causes – but increasingly became struggles for autonomy and independence. This development was typical of all Europe at that time. In 1848 CE, popular revolts swept through Europe like wildfire, either toppling existing powers or forcing them to make concessions for more political participation by the populace. This development did not leave the Balkans untouched, and made the ethnic, national, linguistic and religious patchwork even more complicated to comprehend as revolts and wars broke out among peoples that for centuries had lived in relative political and economic stability.

The Greeks may serve as an example. They had been living in the eastern part of the Mediterranean for centuries and continued to do so as subjects of the Ottoman Empire. Their commonality was therefore language and religion, not territory. Their revolt against Ottoman rule in the nineteenth century was precipitated by the actions of the Friendly Society (Philiki Etairia), a Greek secret society established in 1814 CE throughout the Empire, with the aim to 'liberate the Motherland' although the geographical contours of this motherland were unclear.[34] A flurry of incidents, bolstered by the uprising of a local Ottoman lord against the Porte, culminated in a nationwide Greek uprising that became known as their independence war (1821–1830 CE). Most parts of the Ottoman Empire with Greek communities experienced eruptions of violence and massacres of the local population by both the Ottoman military and Greek insurgents. It is hard to make clear-cut divides between the sides that were killing each other: in Crete and the Peloponnesian peninsula, for instance, the majority of the population was Greek-speaking, but Greek minority communities were also Muslim, and that characteristic made them fall victim to the Greek Orthodox mobs.

Religion was therefore not a cause of these conflicts, but a factor with varying importance. Religion was also an instrument used by the European powers, either out of conviction or for political purposes. Wars and diplomatic meddling were at first mostly territorial and power-related, but gradually became religious, in that European powers asserted ecclesiastical sovereignty over Ottoman subjects: Russians over the Orthodox, English over Protestants, French over Catholics. We have seen that such religious 'protectorates' by a foreign nation were not uncommon and that they were regularly confirmed in treaties. For some European states this was out of genuine concern for the plight of specific Christian communities with whom intensive contacts had been established through the capitulations system. For others it was just another way to get a foothold in the Empire.

The Empire at that same time was struggling with the role of Islam, which was traditionally an intrinsic part of the Ottoman Empire. During the nineteenth century, many Turkish intellectuals and state officials debated whether the solution to the many problems of the Empire had to be found in less Islam, hence secularism, or more Islam. The state had opted for the first solution, but many of the secular reforms imposed by the state were considered too radical and failed to have their intended effect. With the continuing disintegration of the Empire and with the threat, whether perceived or real, from indigenous and foreign forces that identified themselves as Christian, Islam became the only remaining unifying and legitimizing factor.[35] This reaction among the Ottoman elites coincided with – or was it prompted by? – the notion of so-called pan-Islam that became popular throughout the Muslim world during that period.

It is in this light that the call for a *jihad* by the Ottoman sultan in 1914 CE against the European enemies of Germany stirred the anxiety of these European allies; they were worried that this call might be taken up by the Muslims in European colonies across the globe to rise up against their colonial powers. Moreover, it was assumed that this holy war was concocted by, or otherwise 'made in', Germany, with which the Ottomans had sided in the First World War.[36] With hindsight we may say that too much was made of this call for *jihad*.[37] Just as in previous centuries, the Ottoman rulers often reserved the term 'jihad' for war against an enemy that was non-Muslim. Between 1768 and 1922 CE, six official Ottoman *jihad* declarations were identified, in addition to numerous references that were made to *jihad*.[38] The call for *jihad* in 1914 CE followed a similar procedure to these other *jihads*: the sultan would ask the highest Muslim cleric, the *sheyk-ul-islam* for a legal opinion (*fatwa*, or 'fetve' in Ottoman) on the religious validity of the intended war, and would then formally declare the war when an affirmative ruling was given. What was of great concern to the Allied forces, however, was that the *fatwa* also implicitly called upon all Muslims in the European colonies to rise in *jihad*.[39] The Europeans were anxious that the position of the Ottoman sultan as caliph, that is ruler of all Muslims, might prompt the Muslims in European colonies to rise. The concern among the colonial powers was unwarranted, however, because the Islamic call to arms went completely unanswered among Muslims worldwide. They ostensibly saw the Ottoman involvement in the war as an exclusively Ottoman affair.

Religious-Ethnic Cleansing

In the previous section we saw that religion, whether Islam or Christianity, was merely one of the factors contributing to the emerging sense of national identity among the Ottoman subjects during the nineteenth century. From the 1870s onwards, however, the conflicts acquired nationalistic overtones in which religion was subsumed with nationality. The Ottoman state first tried to give in to the nationalist aspirations by granting the various communities autonomy within the Ottoman realm. The expansion of the number of millets was one of the ways of doing this. However, one of the characteristics of the millet is that it is not defined territorially. And this was precisely what the emerging religious-ethnic nationalism aspired to: the communities wanted their own territory or state. In the mixed population of the Balkan region where so many people for centuries had migrated, settled and mixed, this seemed impossible. If one were to achieve that dream, drastic measures were needed. And that is what happened from the second half of the nineteenth century onwards.

What became known as the 'process of nation-building' in the Balkans started with all parties using various methods to create a homogeneous national population in a newly established state with its own territory. Ethnic and religious 'homogeneity' is the key word in this endeavour, and there were no nice ways to reach that goal. Massacres and expulsion were one way to achieve homogeneity, forced conversion another. But they all achieved the same end: a religiously and ethnically cleansed homeland. In 1914, the independent commission established by the Carnegie Endowment for International Peace that had investigated the causes and conduct of the Balkan wars, stated: "The Turks were fleeing before the Christians, the Bulgarians before the Greeks and the Turks, the Greeks and the Turks before the Bulgarians, the Albanians before the Serbians. ... The means employed by the Greek against the Bulgarian, by the Turk against the Slav, by the Serbian against the Albanian, is no longer extermination or emigration; it is an indirect method which must, however, lead to the same end, that of conversion and assimilation."[40]

The Commission also observed that the worst atrocities were not committed by soldiers or the armed gangs known as bashi bazouk, but by the populations themselves, who were "mutually slaughtered and pursued with a ferocity heightened by mutual knowledge and the old hatred and resentments they cherished."[41] The contemporary Europeans watched in horror, but tended to highlight the atrocities committed by the Muslims. As an observer wrote in 1905, "When a Christian kills a Muslim, it is a righteous act; when a Christian kills a Christian it is an error of judgment better not talked about; it is only when a Muslim kills a Christian that we arrive at a full-blown atrocity."[42]

The cleansing did not pertain just to people: religious monuments and buildings were torn down and houses and entire villages were destroyed to eradicate traces of another life or culture. The massive scale on which this took place was unique, but not the destruction itself. A century earlier, Habsburg armies upon their conquest of Hungary and Croatia burned down many mosques, Islamic buildings like tombs, bathhouses and schools, as well as the houses of Muslims: in Sarajevo alone, the Habsburgs destroyed 60,000 houses and 160 mosques, and in Beograd left only one of the 30 mosques intact.[43]

But even when the ultimate goal of a cleansed homeland was reached, its appeal was still limited. The creation of independent Greece and Serbia did not prompt the Greeks and Serbs who were still residing in the Ottoman Empire to migrate to these new states: most remained subjects of the Sultan by choice, and some even migrated out of these states back to the Empire to avoid the tax demands and poor economic prospects of the newly established states. In the case of Greece, an estimated 800,000 inhabited the new kingdom, while 2 million Greeks remained Ottoman subjects.[44]

Several scholars have undertaken the task of attaching numbers to the people massacred, deported, converted, fleeing or migrating.[45] Suffice it here to say that these numbers are all in the hundreds of thousands and sometimes even millions for each ethnic or religious people, which merely illustrates the staggering scale of events. Every person in the Balkans at one time or another was affected by horror and atrocities.

Under these circumstances the situation of mixed populations within the states and newly established autonomous areas became so untenable that countries opted to exchange each other's populations. Such organized exchanges of populations were proposed as early as 1826 CE between Turks and Greeks in the Greek peninsula, and in 1878 CE between Turks and Bulgarians, but became common only in the twentieth century.[46] The most notorious of these exchanges was between Turks and Greeks in 1923 CE. The situation was that the Greeks had invaded Turkey after the Ottoman defeat in the First World War, but were repulsed. Both parties then sat down in Lausanne to negotiate a solution to their conflict. This was done in the tumultuous aftermath of the war with millions of Russian, Armenian, Turkish and Greek refugees in need of repatriation, diplomats discussing ways to establish national homogeneity in the Balkan region in order to prevent future conflict, and American president Wilson proclaiming that 'nations' – in its meaning as peoples – had the right to self-determination. Perhaps these circumstances and considerations were the reason that the Lausanne treaty of 1923 was considered a diplomatic and practical success at the time, although it would be unimaginable in a post-World War II Europe. The treaty decreed a huge population swap: all the 'Turkish nationals of Greek-Orthodox religion' in Turkey (except those in Istanbul) were to move to Greece, and all 'Greek nationals of Muslim religion' in Greece (except those in the province of Thrace) were to move to Turkey. An estimated 1.5 million Greeks were forced to leave Turkey (or, as refugees from the Turko-Greek war, were not allowed to return), and an estimated half million Turks were forced to leave Greece. As a result the percentage of non-Muslims in Turkey plummeted from roughly 20 per cent to less than 2 per cent.[47] The nationalistic-historical idea of the need for people to be restored to their native soil had complete disregard for the human misery of people being uprooted from a land and society where they had lived for generations, sometimes for many centuries.

With this dramatic episode, Ottoman (Muslim) sovereignty over the south-eastern parts of the European continent had formally ended (with the exception of the region around Edirne) and the Ottoman Empire was subsumed by the secular republic of Turkey. Between 1822 and 1922 CE an estimated 5 million Muslims were driven from their lands in the Ottoman Balkans and the Black Sea region, and an estimated 5 million were killed during that period.[48] However, an estimated 1 million still remained in the Balkan region, especially in Bosnia, Kosovo and Albania, and in the eastern Greek province of Thrace. What also remained was the Islamic infrastructure, insofar as it had not been destroyed in the wars, such as mosques, religious courts, educational institutions and institutionalized leadership such as imams, 'ulama and muftis. The millet system was somehow retained, albeit in a much more restricted form: as citizens the Muslims of the Balkan states enjoyed equal rights like all nationals, but were allowed autonomy in religious matters, such as religious education and family law. Even the millet structure was left intact: the central government would communicate with the religious communities through their representative bodies. We will discuss this in more detail in the next chapter.

4. Diplomatic Relations and Trade

After all this violence it seems a little peculiar to speak of diplomacy and trade. But these, also, were important aspects of this period. The space in this chapter spent on discussing the hostile encounters between Muslim and non-Muslim subjects in the Ottoman Empire, and between Ottoman and European states, should not be interpreted as being representative of all interaction that took place during this period. The emergence of trade and diplomatic relations in this period, especially the eighteenth century, was unprecedented in its scope and new developments.

By the end of the eighteenth century, the rise of modern states and the increase in political and commercial trans-border activities required a new approach to diplomacy. The personal envoys sent on behalf of the ruler did not suffice and were replaced by diplomatic services that were an integrated part of the governmental administration. The European powers had established permanent embassies at the Porte as early as in the sixteenth century, starting with the French ambassador who was sent in 1535 CE upon conclusion of the French-Ottoman alliance. The Ottomans, on the other hand, did not feel the need to reciprocate until the late 1790s when they established permanent embassies in London (1793),[49] Vienna (1794), Berlin (1795) and Paris (1796). These embassies and the many reconnaissance envoys that preceded them throughout the eighteenth century provided the Ottomans for the first time with the opportunity to come into contact with Europe, causing a "drastic change in Ottoman perceptions of the West."[50]

The late Ottoman entry into European diplomacy was not without reason. By the eighteenth century the power balances in Europe had shifted and the Ottomans had lost the upper hand. They were bypassed by European powers that had become much stronger economically as well as militarily. Politically, the Ottoman Empire now had to rely on diplomacy and allies to secure its position. Militarily and economically, it started to imitate the developments and technologies that were modernizing Europe and bringing it such power and prosperity. The turning point was the Habsburg-Ottoman peace of 1699 CE that ended the series of Ottoman defeats it had suffered after being routed before the walls of Vienna, and allowed diplomatic and commercial relations between the two realms to improve and increase.[51] The Ottomans did not rely entirely on the newly established relations with the Austrians, however, and also rekindled the dormant treaty with France by intensifying their commercial and diplomatic relations with the newly established French Republic. One of the aims of Ottoman diplomatic engagement with France, and later with Prussia, was to bring in French and Prussian military advisors to restructure the Ottoman army.[52]

But it was too late, and the Ottoman Empire was not to regain its previous prowess. The European shift in power was permanent, as could also be seen in the languages used in European diplomacy. French became the European language for political affairs, Italian for commercial affairs, but very few diplomats had knowledge of Ottoman politics, commerce or language. The apparent lack of need for this knowledge is illustrative of the position of the Ottoman Empire and the relative indifference of Europe towards this state that they had once feared and admired.[53] The Habsburgs were the only ones who felt the need to know their neighbour, and in 1754 CE established the Academy of Oriental Languages of Vienna with the explicit purpose of training young diplomats in the language, customs and political and commercial peculiarities of the Ottoman Empire.[54]

Just as the Ottomans found no need to establish permanent diplomatic contacts with European powers at first, they did not venture into Europe to engage in commercial activities. It is unclear whether this was a continuation of a centuries-old lack of interest by Ottoman merchants. But even if the Ottoman merchants themselves had been interested, they might have been deterred by the lack of support from their government in the Porte that made little effort to claim protection and privileges on behalf of its Ottoman subjects in treaties with European powers.[55] There were also practical obstacles. In the Mediterranean sea trade of the eighteenth and early nineteenth centuries there was the permanent menace of Christian corsairs – who outnumbered the Muslim corsairs, even in the eastern parts of the Mediterranean – so that Ottoman trading houses had their trade carried by foreign, especially French ships.[56] Trade overland into the European mainland also used to be no option because it had to pass through the unsafe frontier zones between the Ottoman and Habsburg Empires.

This situation was to change drastically once these frontier zones were taken and secured by the Habsburgs between 1683 and 1699 CE. The Habsburg-Ottoman treaty of 1739 CE, which included numerous privileges granted to Ottoman merchants, spurred tens of thousands of them to resettle in the former frontier areas and set up shop in Habsburg cities in Hungary, but also as far away as Vienna, Lvov (western Ukraine, near Poland) and Leipzig (eastern Germany).[57] These Ottomans were never Muslims, however, but Orthodox Serbs, Bulgars, Greeks and Macedonians (Jews and Armenians tended to go to Italy). When three decades later many of the trading privileges were revoked by the Habsburgs, most of these Ottoman merchants preferred to be naturalized and stay.[58]

These Ottoman Christian mercantile initiatives into Europe were an exception, however. In general it was European merchants who travelled into the Ottoman Empire rather than the other way round. Under the protection of the capitulations, Western European traders established themselves throughout the Ottoman Empire: in its European domains there was a strong Western European commercial presence in the cities of Edirne, Saloniki and Istanbul, but more so in the city of Izmir (west coast of Turkey), and in Syria and Egypt.[59] In the eighteenth century, the Austrians were second to the French as the main trading partners of the Ottoman Empire, with the Dutch taking third place and the English fourth.[60] An important part of the Austrian trade was the transport of African slaves to the Ottoman Empire.[61]

From the European perspective, however, the importance of the Ottoman Empire for European trade quickly lessened. Western European powers had much greater economic interests in their colonies, and during the nineteenth century the global economy expanded so rapidly that by the end of that century the Ottoman economy was reduced to that of any other 'Third World' country in the world at that time.[62]

5. Muslim Sojourners: Students, Nationalists and Conscripts

We have seen that during the history of Islam in Europe few, if any, Muslims ventured into Christian Europe, whether as merchants, travellers or diplomats. An exception is perhaps the many Muslim slaves, but that was limited to the Mediterranean basin and against their will. In the late nineteenth and early twentieth centuries, however, this reluctance on the part of Muslims altered. Students and intellectuals came to Europe from the Muslim lands that were colonized by European powers, followed by nationalists and political activists (or sometimes the two qualities of student and activist were combined in one person). And finally, the largest but mostly forgotten segment of Muslims venturing into Europe by the early twentieth century was the conscripts and auxiliary forces in the European wars.

Many of the Muslim sojourners came as students to the universities of their colonial overlords as part of training programmes to return and take positions as local administrators: Muslims from Indonesia, British India and North Africa flocked to the universities of Leiden, Oxford and Paris. Several of them travelled extensively in Europe, thrilled by the new ideas they encountered and even more excited about the prospect of putting those ideas to use in their native countries to modernize them and perhaps even to gain their independence. These young men were few in number, but their intellectual impact on their home countries was often significant. In effect, we might observe a reverse intellectual impact compared to several centuries earlier: while Christian Europeans in the twelfth and thirteenth centuries made grateful use of Arab Muslim intellectual achievements, Muslims from the Arab and Ottoman world six to seven centuries later came to Europe to get a taste of the latest Western intellectual fruits. They eagerly studied newly developed concepts like people's representation, rule of law, freedom and equality, and took home with them the ideas of modern institutions like a parliament, constitution and division of powers.[63]

European ideas also had their impact on Muslims' reformist thinking about Islam. Two scholars from one the most influential centres of Islamic theology, the Al-Azhar in Egypt, may serve as an example. Rifa'a al-Tahtawi studied for five years in Paris (1826–1831 CE) and we know his impressions from the journal he kept.[64] He praises the sciences, cleanliness, efficiency of transportation and postal system he witnesses in France, as well as the benefits of newspapers to educate the people, and is enthralled by the rationalist approach to science, but is completely mystified by those who through "extreme rationalist" reasoning come to atheism. Tahtawi's countryman Muhammed Abduh, one of the great reformers of Islam, also spent four years in Paris (1884–1888 CE), but as an exile from the British who had occupied Egypt in 1882. Just like Tahtawi, Abduh was impressed by the notions of freedom of opinion and rationalist thinking, and by the importance of education. He went so far as to equate the European achievements with what Islam should stand for, as shown in his succinct remark: "I went to the West and saw Islam, but no Muslims; I got back to the East and saw Muslims, but not Islam."[65]

Later, in the inter-bellum period of the 1920s and 1930s, Europe became the destiny for political adventurers and nationalist intellectuals from Muslim lands. They travelled throughout the continent, and met in Istanbul, Zurich, Berlin, London, Paris, Vienna where they discussed politics and the future of their colonized homelands.[66] Here, also, they were few in number, but quite influential in impact as they functioned as lynchpins between Europe, where they tried to advocate their ideas of Islamic nationalism and independence, and their home countries, where they introduced the European ideas and ideologies of liberalism, socialism, nationalism and fascism.

The pious among these Muslims were often the ones who established the first Islamic mosques and study circles in Western European countries. The governments of the main European powers were not unwilling to accommodate them, but felt the need more to make overtures towards their Muslim subjects abroad or – as was the case in Germany – to the Ottomans, by establishing mosques in their European capitals: London in 1904, Berlin in 1924 and Paris in 1922 CE. Before that, however, smaller mosques had been built to accommodate sailors (the 1860 mosque in Cardiff for Yemeni and Somali sailors) or soldiers (the 1887 mosque in Vienna for Muslim military personnel in the Austrian army), and in Germany for Muslim prisoners of war (Senegalese, Moroccans, Algerians, Indians, Tatars) taken during the First World War.[67] Compared to these initiatives it is quite conspicuous that the Netherlands, as colonizer of Indonesia, until 1949 the European country with the largest colonial Muslim population after Great Britain, did not build any mosque at all.[68]

Some of the Muslim nationalist sojourners in Europe established contacts with the European powers that, in turn, would make use of them to their own advantage. Nazi Germany, in particular, made good use of them in its Arabic and Persian propaganda broadcasts from Berlin during the 1930s aimed at inciting the peoples in the colonies of the Allied powers.[69] History would stigmatize these young nationalists for holding Nazi sympathies, while from their perspective they were often merely siding with one European power that was against other European powers that colonized their home countries.[70] Perhaps the most famous – or should we say infamous – of these Muslim nationalists in this respect is Amin Hussain, Mufti of Jerusalem. Palestine was an English Mandate, and the Mufti went to Berlin to seek help from the

Germans. Whether he actually held Nazi sympathies – particularly the antisemitic ideology – is still a matter of debate, but the picture of him sitting amicably with Hitler is to many sufficient proof.[71]

Of a completely different nature was the presence of hundreds of thousands of Muslim soldiers and armament industry labourers who were recruited to sustain the English and French war efforts. In France, Muslims from Senegal and Morocco were recruited into the army as early as the Crimean War in 1845 CE, and later also in the 1870 war against Germany. An estimated 200,000 Algerians were involved in the First World War, and many stayed afterwards.[72] About 80,000 Moroccan soldiers had participated in the Spanish Civil War, while 73,000 fought in the Second World War.[73] Many war cemeteries in France have separate sections where tombstones bear the sickle moon to indicate the Islamic creed of the fallen. Most of these recruits were from North Africa, but many also from Sub-Saharan Africa, India and Bosnia. Although their loyalty was primarily with their colonial master, the defeats suffered by these same masters caused a breach in their image of invincibility.[74]

III. Virtual Islam

The European perception of Muslims ('Turks' or 'Mohammedans') and Islam underwent a "drastic change" at the turn of the eighteenth and nineteenth centuries from a period of respect and even admiration for the Islamic civilization and religion to one of contempt.[75] This switch in perspective was not limited to the Ottomans, but also included India and China: the mysterious and fascinating Oriental became the uncivilized non-European. The main cause of this transformation was European colonialism that introduced Europe to the wider Muslim world in Africa and Asia and was accompanied by a strong sense of superiority over other cultures and civilizations. While eighteenth century European historians thought of Islam as a great albeit bygone civilization, the nineteenth century European merchants, travellers, administrators and military in the colonies saw Islam as the main source of the backwardness and poverty of the Muslim societies they encountered. The same perspective was taken on the Ottomans: until the late eighteenth century, the Ottoman Empire was still a power to be reckoned with culturally, politically and economically, but in the nineteenth century it rapidly unravelled into social and economic turmoil not unlike what Europeans witnessed in the many other Muslim societies in their colonial dominions.

The Ottoman of the eighteenth century still represented the Other, but he was 'one of us', the strange but fascinating neighbour at the end of the street. Europeans were perhaps a bit frightened but mainly fascinated about him, his customs, his religion. But while this Ottoman was what we might call the 'inclusive' Other, the Ottoman of the nineteenth century became the 'exclusive' Other who represented everything that Europeans abhorred. And even if the Europeans for the sake of political expediency allowed the Ottoman to be one of us, he definitely was not anyone like us. By the end of the nineteenth century, when colonial Europe had entrenched itself in most of the Muslim world, the notion of the exclusive Other, who was so unlike the civilized and rational European, was extended to Islam and the Muslim.

This transformation of perspective from the eighteenth into the nineteenth century became clear in the contemporary studies of Islam, as well as in the two successive trends of Turquerie and Orientalism, which we will discuss separately in the following paragraphs.

1. Eighteenth Century: Turquerie and Inclusive Othering

Turquerie

The sixteenth and seventeenth century fascination for the Turk as both the 'scourge of God' and the mysterious Oriental developed into a fashion that became known as Turquerie. Turquerie was the European fashion to imitate aspects of Ottoman culture, ranging from decorative motifs to fashion and coffee.[76] The first forms of Turquerie were observed in Venice which had always been in close contact with the Ottoman Empire. Ottoman influences could be seen in Venetian paintings and fashion. In 1630 CE, the first coffee house was opened in Venice, a novelty in European society, followed by coffee houses in Paris and London, and developing into a very coffee house culture in eighteenth century Europe. It has been argued that the coffee house where men (not women) could sit together and exchange ideas was one of the characteristics of the eighteenth century that, together with newspapers and clubs, created a public domain in which critical thoughts could be exchanged, thereby laying the ground work for later democracies.[77]

Turquerie is said to have been introduced into France by the doings of the first Ottoman ambassador to Paris, Muteferikka Suleyman Agha.[78] When he was to submit his credentials to King Louis XIV (the 'Sun King') in 1669 CE, he had been ordered by the sultan not to show too much deference for a king who, from the Ottoman point of view, was of much lower status than the sultan. The ambassador followed this instruction so well – he appeared in a wool coat, refused to bow to the king and apparently did not pay any attention to all the pomp and magnificence that was brought out to impress the sultan's envoy – that King Louis in his rage denied him further access to Versailles. In his residence in Paris the ambassador subsequently opened a salon in good Parisian custom, but did so in an Ottoman style with Turkish coffee, tobacco and pipes, draperies and sofas. The salon became very popular, and quite a few prominent Parisian ladies had their portraits painted while reclining on couches in Turkish robes and hair styles.

Turquerie was not the only fashion at the time; it was part of a larger demand for anything exotic from the Orient. We therefore also see in this period a similar interest in the Far East (the so-called 'Chinoiserie'). This longing for exoticism was a particular feature of the European bourgeoisie that by the late seventeenth century had developed into a very rich and independent middle class that was willing to spend money to show off its wealth and to have itself entertained. This sometimes took excessive forms, as was the case with so-called tulipomania in Holland.[79] The tulip was imported from Istanbul by a Dutch botanist to the Dutch Republic where it was successfully cultivated in many different varieties. During the prosperous seventeenth century the tulip became a fashion among the rich merchants in Holland who were willing to raise their bids on the onion-like bulbs speculating on the prospects of what flower they might yield. This form of speculation reached grotesque heights when payments amounted to more than a million euro – calculated in present day currency – for a single bulb, causing the collapse of the market in 1637 CE, taking many a merchant's wealth in its wake.

The Ottoman decorative style – or what was assumed to be so – found its way throughout Europe in tiles, carpets, pottery and the like. These, as well as the Ottoman fashion, were often reproduced in paintings, especially of Biblical scenes, such as those of Rubens and Rembrandt, but also in dresses like those worn by Frans Hals' *Girl with the Pearl Earring* or by Rembrandt himself in one of his latest self-portraits. Ottoman themes also featured in plays and operas, such as Molliere's *Le Bourgeois Gentilhomme* (1670) Rossini's *Il Turco in Italia* (1814) and Mozart's *Die Entführung aus dem Serail* (1782). Several composers also used the typical Ottoman military marching music in their compositions: Mozart's *Rondo alla Turca* and Beethoven's *Turkish March* are the well known examples.[80] Even European literature did not escape Turquerie. Goethe wrote twelve poetry collections inspired by Persian poets under the title *West-östlicher Divan* (*West-Eastern Diwan*), and Victor Hugo wrote the poem *Les Djinns* (which was later put to music by Fauré).

Studying Islam

The eighteenth century witnessed widespread interest in Islam as a civilization and as a religion in its own right. The approach taken by European scholars was quite different from that of their predecessors, however. Enlightenment demanded rationality and impartiality, and European explorers took to feverishly collecting all sorts of information and material from the new and exotic worlds in a manner that was to be objective and factual. The example was set by the 'army' of scholars that Napoleon had taken with him to Egypt in 1796 CE: they took measurements of pharaonic temples and Islamic mosques, made detailed drawings of the dress people wore as well as flora and fauna, and studied the wildlife and the customs of the people. The results were published in the voluminous *Description de l'Egypte*, a collection of exceptionally thorough and accurate studies published during the years 1809 to 1822. The study is still a delight to peruse, and is astonishingly relevant to the modern reader.

This approach was also taken to the study of religion. The earlier view of Christianity as the only true religion, reducing all other beliefs to either paganism or heresies, was replaced by a view of religious pluralism, with Christianity being one among other religions. Although many scholars would personally still deem Christianity to be the only and ultimate truth, they employed a secular philosophy in their study of other religions. Consequently, Islam was elevated from its status as an object of polemic discourse to a position of one of the world religions worthy of study. Studies came out that tried to provide objective and accurate descriptions of Islam's religious rites and dogmas.[81] Some of these studies were even sympathetic to Islam, especially several biographies of Mohammed, possibly as a counterweight to the malicious and derogatory descriptions of the prophet of Islam that were published in previous centuries. The problem with all these studies, however, was that, like their predecessors in previous centuries, they all relied, directly or indirectly, on a limited number of sources in the Arab language. Only with colonial presence in Muslim lands in the nineteenth century did European scholars gain access to the source material needed for the study of Islam.

The newly acquired knowledge encouraged academic and political correctness in terminology. While it was still common to use an ethnic adjective like 'Saracene' or 'Turkish' in combination with the word 'faith' or sometimes even 'religion,' scholars gradually started to refer to Islam (the medieval Dominican monk Riccoldo da Monte di Croce, mentioned in chapter Two, who had spend time learning Arabic in Baghdad was perhaps the first to use this term, but also one of the few who did so before the nineteenth century).[82] Nevertheless, even the most impartial academic did not use the name that Muslims call themselves – 'Muslim', that is 'he-who-submits' (to God) – but referred to 'Mohammedans', following the Christian emphasis on the position of Christ and naming his followers after him. Such perspective is an insult – intended or not – to Muslims, however, for their religion emphasizes that they worship God and not His prophet.

With all the shortcomings in the study of Islam and its prophet during the late seventeenth and eighteenth centuries, this study was no longer set in the context of Christian polemics. Neither were Muslims perceived as a hostile tribe but as carriers of a great civilization that was retroactively recognized as one of the great world civilizations. Prominent philosophers like Leibniz (1646–1716) and Voltaire (1694–1778) were quite sympathetic towards Islam and its civilization; the historian Edward Gibbon (1737–1794) devotes a large part of his *Decline and Fall of the Roman Empire* to it, and a scholar like the English historian Ockley (1678–1720) in his *History of the Saracens* even made the point of favouring the civilization of the Muslim East over that in the Christian Western world. In short, "the eighteenth century saw the Muslim East through fraternal and understanding eyes."[83]

2. Nineteenth Century: Orientalism and Exclusive Othering

Vision of the Turk and Orientalism

This perspective of admiration for a great Islamic civilization changed in the nineteenth century, however, and was replaced by a Western sense of superiority over other cultures and civilizations. The Christian superiority of previous centuries, supported by theological studies, was now succeeded by a civilizational superiority supported by scientific study. The evolutionary theory of Darwin was applied by academics to explain why Europeans had evolved to a social, economic, political and cultural status that was deemed so much better and higher than that of all other peoples in the world.[84] One of the sciences that was fashionable at that time was racial studies, which tried to determine the qualities of a race and, consequently, its level on the ladder of civilization.[85] Within these studies the question became pertinent whether the Ottomans or Turks could be considered 'Europeans.' The answer was mostly negative, for two reasons: Turks were considered descendants from Asian tribes and were therefore, firstly, racially different and, secondly, invaders who had colonized the Balkans.[86] From this perspective, the collapse of the Ottoman Empire was nothing more than the rightful final expulsion of an 'Asian' power from Europe.

According to nineteenth century Europeans, it was the Asian character of the Turk that made him prone to barbarism and brutality, and explained the atrocities he allegedly committed during the Balkan wars.[87] And it was the same character that, according to the nineteenth century historian Marriot, explained the "clash" between "the habits, ideas and preconceptions" of the West and East in south eastern Europe as an "immemorial antithesis" that had started with the contest between Persians and Greeks, and in the Middle Ages between "the forces of Islam and Christianity", and that "reached its climax, for the time being, in the great battle of Tours [Poitiers – MB] (732) and, again, with the battle of Vienna (1683)."[88]

The Ottomans did not hold similar views on their origins, however. On the contrary, not only did they have strong ties with Europe, but they also saw themselves as part of Europe's legacy.[89] From a ideological perspective, they considered the Ottoman Empire as the heir to and substitute for the Byzantine Empire (which also straddled the lands of south-eastern Europe and Asia Minor). From a pragmatic perspective, these were the areas that provided the main income of the Empire, as well as most of its functionaries.[90] These functionaries were mostly recruited through the system of *devşirme* or boy-levy, and of the forty-nine grand vizirs who served the Ottoman sultans between 1453 to 1632 CE, only five were of Turkish origin: eleven were Albanian, eleven Slav, six Greek, one Armenian, one Georgian, one Italian, and the rest were Christian-born of unknown nationality.[91] And finally, from a cultural and institutional perspective, the Ottomans since the fifteenth century had "drifted closer to European standards", and by the end of the seventeenth century were "as integrated into Europe as [they] would ever be".[92] In short, the Turks and their predecessors, the Ottomans, had for centuries were oriented westward rather than eastward.

But even if, for whatever reasons, one might consider the Ottoman Empire *de facto* part of Europe, in practice it was not accepted as such. European states, despite their internal differences, defined themselves as a 'Christian family of nations,' a grand narrative that in the nineteenth century had replaced its religious specificity with the notion of a common European civilization and culture that rose high above all the others in the world.[93] The Ottoman Empire was not considered a member of this family. This became manifest in its exclusion from the Congress of Vienna in 1815 CE, where the European countries re-arranged their political and geographical relations after the defeat of Napoleon. Only in 1856 CE, after the Crimean War in which European powers sided with the Ottomans against the Russians, did the victors decide that the independence and integrity of the Ottoman Empire was vital to the 'Peace of Europe,' and consequently allowed the Sublime Porte "to participate in the advantages of the Public Law and System of Europe."[94] In return, the European powers demanded from the Ottomans reforms on property, justice and rights of their Christian subjects, which the Porte granted by decree in that same year. This status was codified at the Hague Conference in 1899 CE, and again in the Treaty of Lausanne in 1923 CE. Nevertheless, these treaties could not deny that the Ottoman Empire, and its successor the secular Turkish Republic, in the eyes of Europeans remained an outsider, as became apparent when Turkey applied for membership of the European Union. We will come to speak of this in the next chapter.

The idea of Turks as the exclusive Other – as opposed to the civilized European – found its expression in the new trend of Orientalism. While Turquerie was an innocent fashion without preconceptions or judgmental predispositions, Orientalism definitely was not. Orientalism – not to be confused with the academic discipline, of which we come to speak below – was the representation of the image that Europeans had of the Orient, and in particular the Arab Muslim world.[95] This exotic world appealed to the rising trend of Romanticism. More prominently, however, Orientalism was a European discourse based on stereotypes and prejudices, whereby the Orient was a projection of the Other who embodied all the characteristics and qualities that were considered the opposite of those held by Europeans. The many paintings in the so-called Orientalist style show a whole range of these characteristics and qualities: sensual ladies, often nude and reclining (as opposed to the self-composed and virtuous European), malicious men at female slave auctions (as opposed to a European sense of gender equality), poverty and backwardness (as opposed to European modernity and prosperity), fatalistic believers (as opposed to European Christianity that inspires self-determination and self-development), and fanaticism (as opposed to European self-restraint based on rationalism).

The ideological construct called Orientalism reflected Europe's sense of cultural hegemony and self-righteousness towards the rest of the world that served as a justification for its colonial policies as a mission to bring civilization. This was mainly a feature of the late nineteenth and early twentieth centuries. Before that, the arrows of Enlightened critics were mostly pointed at Europe itself, and Islam was instrumental in that criticism: Islam's relative religious tolerance and its lack of a church structure that imposed religious doctrine were used as mirror for the rigidity of European Christianity of that time. By the nineteenth century, however, the Enlightenment was identified with the European mind-set, and was carried along with imperialist adventure into the world. The European vision of Islam acquired new impulses, the images of the well-structured, highly organized and relatively prosperous Ottoman Empire being replaced by the poor and backward societies of Africa and Asia. The critique of Islam that was commonly framed in religious polemics was now reformulated into the newly found secularized narrative framed in the Enlightenment philosophy: Islamic societies were portrayed as closed, rigid and lacking the freedom and the rational thought that would otherwise have brought them progress and prosperity.[96]

Studying Islam

By the nineteenth century, colonies were not mere sources of profitable trade or extortion, but had become vast lands ruled by colonial European powers. Many of the European colonies were Muslim majority countries. The Dutch in Indonesia, the British in India and Egypt, and the French in North Africa were for the first time in their history confronted with Muslim subjects, Islamic institutions like the religious scholarly clergy ('ulama) and Islamic courts, religious culture and traditions. Ruling these countries meant that Europeans had to have knowledge of them, and the existing European academic discipline of Arabic (a philological study that focused primarily on the study of Islamic theological texts) was geared in that direction and became known as Orientalism (a term that encapsulated all of Asia, including China and Japan, and was therefore not restricted to the Muslim world).[97]

Orientalist academics of the nineteenth and early twentieth centuries are not to be compared with modern scholars of Islamic or Middle Eastern studies. The Orientalist academics had a background of philology and philosophy. They were often not interested in the daily and contemporary situation of Muslim people, culture, religion and societies, but in disclosing the textual legacies of these cultures, and in theories that situated Islam in larger conceptual frameworks like history of religions or the anthropology of races or the genealogy of civilizations. With the exception of a few, these academics did not feel the need to be in physical contact with the peoples or societies they were studying, but devoted their time to the study of the legacy of their cultures and civilizations as documented in texts.

On the other hand, the policy makers of colonial rule in the European capitals, as well as the diplomats, merchants, travellers, military, administrators living within the colonies had a great interest in factual information about these places and peoples: agriculture, economics, politics, legal systems and customary law, social and cultural characteristics of the societies and peoples. These are what we would nowadays call the academic disciplines of anthropology, sociology, economics and political science – disciplines that were non-existent in the nineteenth century, or at best in their infancy. In the nineteenth century, the gathering and analysis of this kind of information, whether academically sound or not, was mostly instigated for pragmatic reasons, for it was to serve the purposes of colonial rule.[98]

The distinction made here between a philological ivory tower approach and a pragmatic policy-oriented approach does not mean that research undertaken by either was academically unsound or biased. On the contrary, quite a few scholars applied a rigid positivistic discipline in their scholarly activities and were the founders of the encyclopaedias and vast library collections that were to serve as the sources for future research (including research undertaken by modern scholars coming from the Muslim world to study in the West). Also, among the European travellers and explorers in the Muslim world were several scholars who were often recruited by their governments. The English archaeologist and Arabist T.E. Lawrence (1888–1935 CE) is the most famous, and he shared his dismay about what he considered European betrayal of the Arabs (they were not given the lands promised to them by the English in return for their revolt against the Ottoman Turk in World War I) with the French scholar Louis Massignon (1882–1962 CE) who had conducted research in Morocco, Algeria and Iraq. Another example is the Dutch scholar Snouck Hurgronje (1857–1936 CE), who was renowned for his research in Mecca, and acted as an advisor to the Dutch military command that was in charge of putting down the rebellious Muslim people of the Indonesian province Aceh.

When it came to Islam, the European of the nineteenth century had two approaches. On the one hand, there was a pragmatic approach employed by the colonial rulers who used their knowledge of Islamic clergy and Islamic law to facilitate their colonial administration. For instance, the French and English allowed the local *sharia* courts to continue their work and maintain their authority, but only insofar as they contributed to the general order of colonial rule.[99] On the other hand, Islam was often conceived as one, if not the main cause for the backwardness of the Muslim countries at that time. This idea was based on several theories that we briefly introduced above and that had become common knowledge for the average nineteenth century European. According to these theories, not only race but also religion was an intrinsic part of each civilization, and each civilization was unique in its own right and developed at its own pace. From this reasoning sprang the idea that European civilization of that time was attributed to Christianity, and that by consequence Islam was to be blamed for the deplorable state of Muslim societies. Why this was the case at this particular juncture (nine centuries earlier the situation between the Muslim and Christian worlds was reversed) was the main question that put many European academics to work. Some would argue that Islamic civilization had had its time, with the golden age of economic and intellectual prosperity in the tenth century, to be only briefly resuscitated by the Ottoman Empire in the sixteenth century. Others merely declared Christianity to be a religion of progress and Islam a religion of stagnation. And then there were those who shared the conclusion of many Muslim reformists that Islamic doctrine had become stagnant in the course of time and had to be revived if it was to cope with the demands of modern times.[100]

Regardless of the validity of the reasons put forward to explain the difference between the Western and Eastern worlds, the primal focus of attention was Islam. In consequence, the people living in these societies were regarded as *homo Islamicus*, a person who is shaped and guided by no other factors than his religion of Islam. This concept conflated racial and religious qualities, defining Islam as the only identity to the exclusion of all other identities. In this mindset, the position of women was attributed to Islam rather than to tradition or culture, revolts were the result of

Islamic fanaticism rather than political or economic factors, and anti-imperialism was a characteristic of pan-Islam rather than local social-political opposition.[101] The view of Islam as the single factor and motivation of Muslim lives remained a persistent concept, and enjoyed a second life in the late twentieth century, as we will see in the next chapter.

CHAPTER FIVE

Struggling Europe
(1950 CE–)

I. Setting the Stage

We now come to the last period of Islam in Europe, which has a relatively short timespan compared to the previous periods. But then this period is the start of new developments that have not yet ended. It is also a period characterized by several developments that have no precedent in Europe's history with Islam.

The first development is that after two devastating world wars Europe managed truly to unify itself, at least more so than in previous centuries. This unity was different from those of preceding centuries because it was based on economic cooperation and political-legal values like individual freedoms, rule of law and democracy.

The second development was the secularization of the European public domain. By this we mean the decreasing relevance of religion as personal piety or as a factor of societal importance. The authority of the churches and their clergy dwindled and Christian-Democratic political parties were religious only in name.

The third development was unique mainly to the western parts of Europe, and that is the settlement of large numbers of Muslims within European societies and, in consequence, Islam becoming a feature of the new Europe. The Muslim communities in Europe, and particularly the migrant communities in Western Europe, combined national, ethnic, religious and local identities which were disturbing to many in Europe since they challenged the strong sense of a single national identity. The challenge became a security threat when Muslim youth radicalized and some even committed terrorist attacks on European targets.

The fourth development that is significant to these times was globalization and transnationalism. Political and economic structures, but also cultural and religious identities, had become interwoven on a global scale. People identified and connected with causes and communities that were not only local but spread over the world. In the case of Muslims in Europe, one of the manifestations of this development was the notion of a single global community of believers (umma) that transcended local and national identities.

1. A New Europe

Why refer to Europe as 'struggling' if it managed to pull itself from the ashes of two world wars with such vigour and determination, and even established a European union? Notwithstanding the many achievements of this period, we may observe that

Europe is still going through a process of transformation. This transformation is multifaceted. On a historical – and perhaps psychological – level, Europe had to come to terms with the fact that it was not the world power it had been for centuries. After the 1950s and 1960s, when European colonies gained their independence, Europe lost most of its political power to the United States (and, until the 1980s, to the Soviet Union) and as of recent times seems to lose its economic power to Asian, South American and perhaps even African rising economies.

On the other hand, on an internal level, Europe was, and still is, in a process of political and economic unification. Whereas clerical or cultural unity of the past centuries was often more imagined than real, Europe since the 1950s has managed to create a true unity, first economically, then legally, and gradually also politically. This unification is a complex process with its crises and criticisms. However, while many may criticize the degree of integration of European states into the Union, or the role of the European Commission and European Court of Human Rights, few question the existence of these institutions. In that respect, many Europeans still share the notion of a European unity, regardless of the form it will ultimately take. Relevant to the topic of Islam, as we will see below, is the fact that this unity was also expressed in political-legal values, such as individual freedoms, democracy and the rule of law. Many of these values were enshrined in the European Convention on Human Rights of 1953, which applies to all member states of the Council of Europe which, in addition to all states in Europe, also includes states like Russia, Georgia, Azerbijan and Turkey.

Another important aspect of the transformation of Europe is religion. In the 1950s and 1960s, the authority of the clergy as well as that of religion itself reached an all-time low worldwide, a trend that was known as secularization. But the idea that religion had receded with the rise of modernity – the so-called secularization thesis – was challenged by the re-emergence of religion, both as personal piety and as a societal force, from the 1970s onwards. Christianity, Judaism, Islam, Hinduism, Buddhism and new forms of religion have again become important to many. The one region where this resurgence of religion was relatively limited was Europe. Here, secularization remained dominant in the public domain: religion was considered a private affair and public manifestations thereof – whether in politics, public celebrations, state functions, social behaviour or public morality – were limited. *Secularization* as described here is a cultural process rather than a political or legal one: religious manifestations were not prohibited (on the contrary, they were ensured by the freedom of religion), but merely 'not done', either because they had lost their meaning or because they were frowned upon as relics from times when they had merely caused conflict. *Secularism*, on the other hand, is a political-legal institution to separate state and clerical powers that had been established since the nineteenth century and remained unaltered in most European countries.

If we take these characteristics of the new Europe – unification as an economic power, unity in political-legal values, and secularization – it is surprising that during the first decade of the twenty-first century the presence of 'Islam' in Europe was experienced as a serious challenge to this very same unity. Some authors even warned that Europe might be on the brink of destruction.[1] This feeling of anxiety, more than anything else, warrants the characterization of a 'struggling' Europe – because if a relatively small group of Muslims can pose such a threat to the values and integrity of Europe, then surely something must be amiss with the stability and foundation of those values. On the other hand, we must bear in mind that the warnings against the 'Islamic threat' to Europe came predominantly from American authors. This is significant because, from the perspective of many of these American observers, Europe's main problem is its lack of religiosity combined with too much liberalism and political generosity (as opposed to the United States which, according to these authors, is more religious, patriotic and security-minded). These characteristics of Europe, American authors argue, allow the new religion of Islam to make quick and successful incursions into European life.

I agree with the American authors' observation that Europe is being challenged, but disagree with their diagnosis. Europe has reached a stage in its history where the political, legal and social balance of creed, coexistence and conflict have entered a new constellation. Also, the presence of Muslims and Islam is in many respects a new challenge for Europe. But, as I will argue in this chapter, it is not the existence of the new European constellation that is challenged, but the presumptions that uphold it. If there is a conflict between 'Europe' and 'Islam', it is not with the European political and legal values on which the constellation of the new Europe is based, but with the cultural values that are presumed to be its underpinnings.

2. Islam in the New Europe

From the previous chapters we know that the physical presence of Muslims in the geographical area of Europe is not new. Muslims ruled as empires in the Iberian Peninsula for nearly 800 years, in Greece for 500 years, in the Balkans for 300 years, and in Sicily for 100 years. As subjects under non-Muslim rule, Muslims stayed on even longer: they lived in Spain for 900 years, in Sicily for 400 years, and still live in Lithuania and Poland after more than 600 years, and in most Balkan countries after more than 500 years.

However, when we come to speak of Islam in Europe from 1950 onwards, a distinction needs to be made between Western and Eastern Europe with regard to the presence of Muslims. Since the late sixteenth century very few Muslims have resided in the European region west of the Warsaw-Vienna-Trieste line (a region that, for lack of a better term, I will refer to as 'Western Europe'). The arrival of large numbers of Muslim migrants in these lands from the 1970s was therefore a development that confronted the native Western Europeans with a situation that is a historical novelty. The presence of large numbers of Muslims and the visibility of Islam – mosques, women with headscarves, bearded men in *jalabas*, *halal* restaurants – was not only sudden, but also new for Western Europeans.[2]

The novel situation turned into a confrontation in two ways. On the one hand, the discussion arose to what extent these migrant Muslims needed to be social-economically or culturally part of Western European societies. The debate wavered between the need for those Muslims to adapt ('integration'), on the one hand, and society's obligation to accommodate differences ('multiculturalism'), on the other hand. The other confrontation was the radicalization of Muslim youth, with some of them resorting to violence. Europe was shaken up in bewilderment and terror by the bombings by Muslim extremists in New York (2001), followed by attacks on European cities: Madrid (2004), Amsterdam (2004), London (2005), Glasgow (2007), Toulouse (2012), Brussels (2014) and the occasional news that similar attacks had been thwarted in several European countries. These attacks not only prompted fear of Islam in the European mind, but also justified the idea that Muslims could not and did not want to be part of Western societies, especially when it became apparent that many of the perpetrators were young men who had been educated in Western European societies and done relatively well there.

The situation in Eastern Europe, on the other hand, is quite different from that in Western Europe (and we must remind ourselves that this geographical distinction is made for the purpose of this discussion only). First and foremost, Muslims and their Islamic cultural, institutional and architectural heritage have existed here for centuries. In addition, the Eastern European countries with established Muslim communities have been under a communist regime for over four decades – with the exception of Austria[3] and Greece. During that period, Islamic life was incorporated into the state system but was quite limited by virtue of the doctrinal secularism – sometimes amounting to state-sponsored atheism – of the communist regime. These regimes were dismantled in the 1990s, after the fall of the Berlin Wall in 1989. In Yugoslavia, this process was accompanied by a devastating civil war. Although the conflict was between (Orthodox) 'Serbs', (Catholic) 'Croats' and (Bosnian) 'Muslims' – note the interesting different use of adjectives and nouns in the reference to religion and ethnicity – the role of religion in this conflict still remains unclear, as we will see below. In the new Balkan states that emerged from the fall of the communist regimes and from the Yugoslavian civil war, Islam gradually re-established itself as an institutionalized part of society and the state. In addition, however – and here we may observe one of the few parallels with Western Europe – orthodox and even radical forms of Islam emerged among the younger generation.

3. Identity, Loyalty and Security

In Western as well as Eastern Europe there is a tendency among Muslims to emphasize their religious identity, and since the 1990s they do so mainly in conservative ways. This development is in parallel with – but mostly independent of – an emerging Islamism in most of the Muslim world. Many a European considers the emerging 'Islam', both within and outside Europe, as a phenomenon that is alien to everything that Europe stands for politically, socially, culturally and historically. The rise of this phenomenon therefore becomes a challenge at best and a threat at worst when these worlds inside and outside Europe become connected.[4]

Scholars have called this connectedness 'transnational Islam', a notion that in this book's terminology has both a physical and a virtual dimension. Physically, Muslims migrate and move across borders, whether as migrants or political refugees into Europe (including several radical Muslims who acquired asylum in Europe because they faced torture or the death penalty in their homelands) or as students outside Europe (many European Muslims study Islam in Turkey, Pakistan and the Middle East). In doing so they maintain economic, social and religious ties that cross national borders.[5] The virtual dimension is that pious Muslims keep Islam as their main frame of reference and identity, irrespective of national or cultural boundaries.[6] In doing so they identify with a global Muslim community (umma) rather than a homeland or national culture.[7] Transnational Islam, in brief, can be defined in terms of an ideological sense of belonging to a – real or imaginary – world-wide community of Muslims (the umma),[8] as well as through its ethnic and national diaspora networks, migrant organizations, educational and cultural links, the Internet and satellite television, etcetera. This transnational Islam is a development that is typical among the generation Muslims born since the late 1980s.[9]

Transnational Islam does not mean that European Muslims represent a unified or single community – on the contrary, they have multiple and shifting identities, resulting in varying loyalties:[10] Pakistanis in England may identify with England as well as with Pakistan, and for their religion may refer to the local imam in Birmingham, or to the Muslim customs of Lahore or Peshawar, or to any Muslim cleric on the Internet whom they deem authoritative. This English-Pakistani Muslim may feel loyal to England, but may cheer on the Pakistani cricket team, and he or she may feel affronted by English discourse on Islam but also by the Islamic fundamentalist tendencies in Pakistan.[11] Indeed, the loyalty of many Muslims to the umma does not exclude a similar national loyalty, for they show considerable commitment to and pride in their European country of settlement.[12] However, the consciousness of belonging to a global religious community definitely contributes to a sense of Muslim uniqueness,[13] and according to some observers this may lead to isolation or even radicalization.

These turbulent developments among Muslim communities within Europe are bewildering to many Europeans who are used to a single cultural identity and an ensuing single national loyalty. To many the emerging Islamic identities in Western and Eastern Europe are seen as alien and even threatening to 'Europe'. The loyalty of Muslims is being questioned – is it with their new home country, or with their country of origin, or with some imaginary Muslim community? – adding fuel to the already heated debates on integration. Citizens with more than one identity or nationality are suspected of having loyalties across the confines of national borders and therewith contribute to a fear of 'the insider enemy' or fifth column.[14] The sensation of threat was enhanced by the terrorist attacks by European Muslims, and the many reports of global networks of such extremists who were out to fight 'the West' in a jihad that was to be conducted from outside Europe as well as within. The combination of these factors has contributed to what has been called the 'securitization' of Islam in Europe, meaning that Muslims and their religion were perceived as a security threat to 'Europe'.[15] The 'in' of 'Islam in Europe' thus acquired another meaning when Islam became a global and transnational phenomenon.

II. Physical Islam

1. Living with the Unbeliever

Counting Muslims

How many Muslims are living in Europe at present? This may seem an innocent
statistical question, but has become for many – especially for those warning against
'Islamization' of Europe, or an impending 'Eurabia' – an issue of concern. Bernard
Lewis in 2004 warned that Europe would have "Muslim majorities by the end of
the twenty-first century,"[16] and downplayed this ominous prediction several years
later with his statement that "in the foreseeable future" Muslims would constitute
"significant majorities in at least some European cities or even countries."[17] Another
persistent 'fact' that circulates on the Internet is that Muslims will comprise "at least
20 per cent of Europe's population by 2050".[18]

Trying to answer the question about the number of Muslims in Europe is not
easy because it confronts us with two problems: quantifying Muslims and qualifying what is a Muslim.[19] Quantifying Muslims is problematic since most European
countries do not keep records of their population on the basis of their religious affiliation. This means that all figures relating to religion are based on estimates and must
therefore be taken broadly. Recalculations in Germany, for instance, conducted by
the government in 2009 raised the previously used estimates of 3.1–3.4 million Muslims to 3.8–4.3 million, an increase of almost thirty per cent.[20] On the other hand,
recalculations in the Netherlands in 2007 lowered the number of Muslims from
950.000 to 850.000, a decrease of more than 10 per cent.[21]

Another problem is the relative and absolute nature of these numbers and related percentages. For instance, the United Kingdom ranks third in all of Europe in
absolute numbers of Muslims (after France and Germany), but takes sixteenth place
(after Belgium and Sweden) in percentage.[22] Also, the picture can change dramatically depending on the view one takes. For instance, the percentage of Muslims is
close to 12 per cent in Bulgaria and 6–8.5 per cent in France, but less than 4 per cent
in the entire European Union.[23] Such differences apply in particular on a domestic
scale. While the overall percentage of Muslims in The Netherlands in 2010–2011 was
6 per cent, it was 28 per cent in the city of Amsterdam and 37 per cent in Rotterdam.[24]

Similar demographic differences between cities and countryside can be observed in most European countries.[25]

Taking all these caveats into consideration and using the available statistics, we may use the following estimates. The number of Muslims in 'Europe' is estimated to be 15–17 million (approximately 3 per cent) in Western Europe, 17–19 million (approximately 3.5–4 per cent) in the European Union and 24–26 million (approximately 4.5–5 per cent) in the entire European continent that borders on Russia, Belarus and the Ukraine.

However, these quantitative data bring us to the problem of qualification: on what basis do European statistics categorize people as Muslim – or, for that matter, a Catholic, Jew, or non-believer?[26] Most official European estimates are based on the assumption that people from Muslim-majority countries are Muslim. How this assumption may affect the statistical calculations was illustrated by the abovementioned 2007 recalculation of Muslims in the Netherlands, because it became clear that many Iraqis and Syrians were not Muslim but Christian, and that many Iranians and Alevite Turks did not consider themselves 'Muslim'.[27]

Once we start to qualify what 'Muslim' means, the figures may alter drastically, especially when people are being given the option to identify as Muslim – or not. In Germany, for instance, recent studies have indicated that only 7.5 per cent of Turks define themselves as "quite religious",[28] 40 per cent of Iranians consider themselves without religion, and more than 10 per cent declared themselves as Christians.[29] In France, 59 per cent of the North Africans and Turks identified themselves as "Muslim" and 20 per cent as "without religion".[30] In Sweden, only one third of Swedish Muslims indicate they are "practising".[31] Similarly, Albania is said to be the only European country with a Muslim majority population (70 per cent Muslim), but scholars have indicated that its population does not consist of a majority of Muslim *believers*.[32] The only exception, perhaps, is the Turkish Muslim community of Thrace in eastern Greece that identifies strongly with Islam, partly because it remained isolated from the secularization process in neighbouring Turkey, and partly because it felt the need to reassert itself vis-à-vis the dominant Orthodox culture.[33] Suffice it to conclude that the term 'Muslim' is highly complex.

Muslim Identity

What, then, makes a person in Europe a 'Muslim'? With the risk of oversimplifying, we may resort to the following categories. First we can make a division between cultural (or sociological) Muslims and religious (or devout) Muslims.[34] The main characteristic of the cultural Muslims is that religious dogma has no influence on their lives. They may be agnostic, indifferent or respectful, and many may observe certain rituals or practices such as circumcision, religious feasts or marriage. But they do identify as Muslims, sometimes in a manner that is reminiscent of Jews who may be non-religious or even atheist, but strongly identify as 'Jew'.

The other category of Muslims are those for whom religion plays an important part in their lives, whether as a strict scriptural doctrine or as spiritual guidance. Among these 'religious Muslims' we may make a further division based on generation: there is a veritable generation gap between the younger generation for whom religiousness is mostly associated with higher knowledge of Islamic doctrine, and their parents for whom religion is mainly rituals for which they refer to the interpretations of their local cleric.[35] This new generation of what I suggest calling 'puritan Muslims' (formerly also called 'fundamentalist', nowadays often referred to as 'salafi' in Western Europe and 'Wahhabi' in Eastern Europe) has an interest in the study of religious texts and the critical questioning thereof, and try to live their lives in accordance with the prescripts of these scriptures.[36] As a result, these Muslims, who are often highly educated, are turning away from traditional sources of leadership and develop an interpretation of Islam that, to their minds, reflects a 'pure' or 'universal' Islam.[37] This does not necessarily lead to interpretations that are very different from those of classical doctrine: often it is an exercise of the re-appropriation of religion by the individual believer – he or she had to reconfirm the doctrine for him- or herself rather than merely taking it for granted.

One consequence of this focus on religious doctrine is that Islam becomes more detached from ethnic or national identity, and is increasingly perceived as a personal choice.[38] In addition, these European Muslim puritans emphasize their religious-universal commonalities rather than religious-ethnic differences, so that differences among sects and juridical rites of Islam tend to diminish.[39] But overall, Islam to the puritan Muslim has become a way of life that encompasses all human activities,[40] including those which are otherwise quite secular, such as sports and rap music, which have become new forms of Islamic lifestyle.[41]

Why, then, this religious resurgence among younger Muslims in Europe? To answer this question we must distinguish between developments in Western and Eastern Europe. In Eastern Europe, Islam was already part of the identity of certain communities, as we saw in the previous chapter, and this identity resurfaced after the ending in the late 1980s of communist rule and the ensuing civil wars.[42] In Western Europe, on the other hand, the emergence of an Islamic identity happened in a context of migration. Scholars have pointed to the importance of both ethnicity and religion as identity markers for migrants in general, and Muslim migrants in Europe in particular.[43] However, since the 1990s European Muslims have undergone a gradual shift in identity marker from ethnicity to religion. For instance, the term 'Muslim' became common use only from the 1990s onwards in both Western and Eastern Europe. Before then, ethnic and national labels were used: Pakistanis and Moroccans, Berber and Kurds, Bosniaks and Pomaks. These names revealed the national, ethnic and linguistic patchwork of 'Muslims' in Europe. Most Moroccans, for instance, are Muslim but some are also Jewish, and most Arab-speaking Moroccans live in France while most Berber-speaking Moroccans live in Belgium and the Netherlands. The Bangladeshis and Pakistanis who live predominantly in the United Kingdom are mostly Muslim, but also Hindu, Buddhist, Sikh and Christian. And among the Bosnians we find Serbs and Croats as well as Christians and Muslims (the latter called 'Bosniaks'). The linguistic and ethnic differences also explain the differentiation between mosques on ethnic or national grounds – Albanian, Pakistani, Moroccan – each with its own religious doctrine, customs and organization. The new generation is gradually breaking with this trend and identifying mosques on religious grounds: liberal, conservative, *salafi* etcetera. Their choice of marriage partner is also increasingly determined by religion rather than ethnicity or nationality – a trend that is not uncommon in migrant communities when their faith has no tradition in the society of settlement.[44]

The emphasis on religion as an identity marker for the next generation of Muslims of foreign origin in Western Europe – who are often born and raised there – is not to mean that they are more religious *per se*. As indicated above, a religious identity can be cultural as well as pious. Why, then, would people identify with a religion if they were not religious? Here the notion of Othering offers an explanation. Since the late 1990s, Western public discourse has vilified Islam for reasons that sometimes might have been very justifiable, but the effect was that young people felt pushed into a corner because they were given no alternative of identification other than assimilation into the society of residence, while the other identity – the culture of the homeland of the parents – had lost its meaning to the generation born and raised in the West. As a reaction, they identified even more with that same Islam that was the source of criticism, whether out of defiance or for lack of an alternative. The main problem that Western society had with the Muslim Other, namely their social-religious identity, became precisely the rallying point for these Muslims.[45]

Conversion

As in previous centuries, not all Muslims in Europe were migrants; some of them were local converts. The number of native Western Europeans who have converted to Islam in the period since 1950 is not known; in 2004 it was estimated to be no more than one per cent of the Western European Muslim population,[46] but it appears to be steadily rising, with recent estimates of almost 7 per cent in the United Kingdom[47] and 2 to 6 per cent in France.[48]

While we have seen that in previous periods conversion to Islam took place mainly to get access to the cultural and political polity of the Muslim ruler, such considerations are not in play here. The literature on Western European converts to Islam has come up with a number of other motives.[49] One motive which has always existed is conversion for the sake of marriage, either to enable a non-Muslim man and Muslim woman to marry (Islam does not allow such marriage) or, the opposite, when a non-Muslim woman who married a Muslim man (which is allowed under Islamic law) felt the need to join her husband in his faith. This relational conversion has been overtaken, however, by a larger number of single adolescents who convert to Islam for other motives; some find in Islam the spirituality they seek, others a reasoned structuring of life and society, and yet others because it grants them the intimate membership of a close community. An interesting aspect of these conversions is that there seems to be a correlation between the rising criticism of Islam and the increase in conversions to Islam.

The general response of the environment to such conversions is generally one of puzzlement. Given the negative image that the larger European public opinion has of Islam, conversion to that religion is tantamount to an irrational act.[50] For that reason the voluntarism of the conversion is often questioned, in particular with regard to female converts – given the alleged bad reputation of Islam with regard to the position of women, how can a European woman in her right mind embrace such a religion?[51] An additional factor that contributes to the suspicion of the motives for conversion is the fact that converts – not only those converting to Islam, but converts in general – tend to be zealous in their new religion, and quite a few of the European Muslim extremists involved in terrorist acts were Muslim converts, just as many of these converts have travelled to countries like Chechnya and Syria to participate in the local civil wars as a matter of *jihad*. No wonder that conversion to Islam is eyed suspiciously by intelligence agencies as a potential security threat.[52]

In this respect we must make an addendum to the notion of conversion: much wider spread than 'ordinary' conversion to Islam by non-Muslims is the many young

Muslims who have 'found' their religious roots and become religious, often in a zealous or conservative manner. These conversions are similar to those of the so-called 'born-again' Christians in the United States, and are therefore often labelled with the same term: 'born-again Muslims.'[53] The difference with their Christian counterparts is the motivation for the return to religion: in case of the born-again Muslim, he has been described as "a Muslim who having adopted or absorbed many modern or foreign influences makes a show of discarding them in his search for personal identity and cultural authenticity."[54] But in both cases of conversion the voluntarism of the conversion is questioned and the cause of conversion is sought in factors outside the will of the person: for women this is usually said to be the oppressive role of men (fathers, husbands, brothers), while for men it is said to be the indoctrinating power of Islam itself or that of fanatical clergy. While these situations may very well be the case, the resulting image is that Muslims, and in particular Muslim women, are powerless, without will or agency.

So far we have discussed people turning to Islam. But the opposite also happens – strictly speaking this is also conversion, but from the perspective of Islam it is considered the prohibited act of apostasy. Apostasy is considered forbidden by most religions, but legally the act of apostasy is no longer a problem in Europe as freedom of religion includes the freedom to abandon one's religion, while culturally the act of apostasy is not frowned upon in Europe and in some social circles even welcomed. This poses a predicament for European Muslims: the more religious they have become, the more condemnable apostasy from Islam is to them, but at the same time they live in an environment where the opposite sentiment dominates. It has resulted in two conflicting situations. On the one hand, Muslims who want to change religion or abandon Islam have come under enormous pressure and even threats from their Muslim peers. On the other hand, there is the pressure from outside the Muslim community to modify or preferably give up one's Islam as the only way to integrate into European society.

Visibility of Islam

Speaking of 'Islam' in Europe implies, among others, that there is something recognizable as such. The manifestation of Islam can be observed either by architectural presence or by Muslims' behaviour or a visibility that is – rightly or wrongly – identifiable as Islamic. In the political-legal constellation of modern Europe, such visibility or behaviour is generally not problematic as it pertains to personal liberty in general and the freedom of religion in particular. Insofar as there is unease in European countries it is about Islam's visible presence through mosques, religious dress and behaviour.

In the case of mosques, Western Europe has witnessed an enormous increase in prayer rooms and Islamic centres where the faithful gather for prayer, but gradually also the construction of so-called purpose-built mosques usually with the visible architectural signs of a dome and one or more minarets. The latter has been considered by some scholars as a sign of final settlement and integration into European societies (why else would Muslims invest in such expensive and permanent projects?),[55] but the European public generally perceives the purpose-built mosques in Western Europe as 'out of place' or otherwise alien and therefore undesirable.[56] The use of traditional ('Oriental') architecture is interpreted by critics as questioning the norms and values of the host country or, as is the case with the minaret in particular, as a symbol of Muslim domination.[57] The Swiss 2009 referendum outcome prohibiting the building of minarets (not mosques) is quite telling in this respect, because Switzerland was at that time a country with only four minaret-bearing mosques.[58]

Critics of the architectural representation of mosques are not limited to non-Muslim Europeans. Some Muslim European architects reject what they call 'homesick mosques' and have proposed futuristic glass mosques to emphasize their transparency.[59] Similarly, many Muslims in south-eastern European countries consider their Ottoman-style mosques symbols of traditional and peaceful Islam, and are anxious about the construction of many new 'Arab' style mosques funded by the Gulf States that they perceive as the representation of a growing influence of so-called 'Wahhabism'.[60] In Western Europe, on the other hand, it is these 'Wahhabi' Muslims (better known as salafi Muslims) who joined the chorus of mosque critics, arguing that the typical mosque with dome and minaret is not Islamic at all, but representative of cultural additions to the originally simple structure of a walled and partly roofed courtyard. This has given rise to a curious paradox: the simple brick and concrete mosque structures used by these puritan Muslims may look quite 'integrated' into the Western European architectural landscape, but some of them are under the scrutiny of national intelligence services for potential radicalization tendencies among the young salafi congregations, while the ostentatious 'Oriental' mosques get all the public attention and criticism because of their Otherness, but their congregations are mostly traditional and otherwise pose no security risk in the eyes of the intelligence services.[61]

Religious dress is yet another manifestation of religious visibility. The opposition to Islamic dress, and in particular the headscarf, has been particularly passionate in Western Europe.[62] Muslim women may consider it a symbol of identity and piety, but to many native Europeans this is a symbol of growing conservative Islam in general, and women's oppression in particular. This view was shared by the European Court of Human Rights which in two controversial rulings argued that a headscarf had a negative impact on a secular environment, was a sign of proselytization, and was in general a symbol of intolerance and gender inequality.[63] While these debates took place in Western Europe, the headscarf and conservative Islamic dress have also become fashionable in south-eastern European countries. While the headscarf, or the turban and kaftan may be a normal sight in Bulgaria, Macedonia, Eastern Greece or Bosnia, many Muslims as well as non-Muslims in these countries considered the new conservative forms of religious dress contrary to the traditional form of Islam.[64] It is interesting to note, therefore, that the only two Muslim-majority countries in Europe, Kosovo and Albania, have banned the head-scarf from state institutions, including universities – a ban that is shared only by France.

The visibility of Islam in Europe further shows in behaviour that Muslims may consider typically Islamic. Such behaviour is predominantly related to religious ritu-als, and sometimes these clash with the practicalities and culture of the non-Muslim environment, in particular in Western Europe. Prayer and fasting, in particular, have occasionally resulted in problematic situations, either at work or in the public do-main. In particular Muslims who have taken or demanded space for their ritual 5-minute prayer have at times come into conflict with employers or colleagues who argue that such behaviour pertains to the private domain and should therefore not be allowed or accommodated at work. Dietary rules of halal food and the prohibition of alcohol can also be problematic – the latter especially has become an impediment for devout Muslims to socialize with colleagues or neighbours since, according to European custom, social events usually involve alcoholic beverages, and often take place at cafes or bars.

In addition to these known manifestations of Islam, new forms of behaviour have arisen in Europe that Muslims have attributed to Islam and that have caused conflicts within both Western and Eastern European societies. An example is the physical separation of men and women, which is practised in particular by young European Muslim puritans. The refusal by these Muslims to even have physical contact with the opposite sex not only causes dismay in European societies, but is also problematic in jobs where social interaction is considered vital,[65] or in the case of medical treatment.[66] An exponent of this segregation is the wearing of the full-face veil (also called burka or niqab). Reactions against such behaviour are vehement throughout Europe: in Western Europe because it is considered contrary to European values (of which we will come to speak below), and in Eastern Europe because it is considered contrary to Islam.

2. Secular and Religious Rule

The 'Muslims' – as we will continue to call them – who came as migrants and guest workers in the 1950s and 1960s, and later came on their own accord to find work in Western Europe, were until the 1980s treated as labour migrants who were bound to return. Later, many more economic and political refugees and migrants flocked towards Europe, targeting in particular the Mediterranean countries as the place of entry. Only when many of these labourers and refugees brought their families over – which they were entitled to as a right of family unification, as stipulated by the European Convention on Human Rights – did it dawn on the Western European societies and governments that a situation of permanence was taking place.

European countries had quite different attitudes in their shift from a policy of labour migration to one of incorporating large communities with foreign cultures into their societies. France for a long time maintained the strict differentiation between citizens (that is, those with French nationality) and non-citizens; it took Germany until 2000 to grant long-term citizens German nationality; the Netherlands and the United Kingdom championed 'multiculturalism' which allowed for far-reaching cultural and linguistic differences; and Greece maintained that Muslim-minority rights were only for Greek Muslims who live in the province of Thrace and not for the many Muslim migrants living in other parts of Greece.[67] But by the late 1990s most European countries felt a need to gear these approaches towards a policy aimed at 'integrating' the many communities of foreign origin into their new societies: in the case of France, for instance, allowances needed to be made for cultural differences, while in the Netherlands and United Kingdom the policy of multiculturalism had to be curbed in order to let people partake in the larger social-economical and cultural structure of society.

The European – and particularly Western Europe – policies of 'integration' focused on two domains: social-economical and cultural. To stimulate people of foreign origin to take part in society in terms of education and jobs, for instance, primary importance was attached to the need for proficiency in the national language of that society: first as an option, later as a condition. But with the second and third generations who were born and raised in Western European societies and who had gone through the educational systems of those societies, the discussion on integration shifted to the domain of culture: public and political opinion demanded from these young people that they adopt the norms, values and customs of the European societies where they lived. This demand focused most prominently on Muslims. Some advocates of this cultural integration argued that Muslims needed to adopt European political and constitutional values (assuming that the Muslims did not do so), while others went further by putting more emphasis on cultural and customary values that Muslims needed to embrace (which many Muslims resisted since that conflicted with their identity and was tantamount to assimilation).[68]

The issues of integration, acculturation and assimilation are typical for any migrant community at any time in history. Our interest here is the question what issues of European 'rule' were typical for Muslims and, therefore, Islam. This means that we need to take a closer look at policies and political-legal structures of European states that related to religion in general and Islam in particular. The most significant of these are secularism, freedom of religion and the impact of Islam-criticism.

European Secularism and Religious Freedom

We have distinguished before between 'secularization' as a process of decreasing religiosity among people and 'secularism' as a system that governs the relation between state and religion or religious institutions.[69] Almost all European countries adhere to more or less strict interpretations of secularism, meaning that the state is (officially, at least) neutral towards religion and will not favour one religion over another, nor deny the existence of certain religions. Not all countries will adhere to this principle and profess their preference for a national religion, as is the case in Greece, for instance. Within this framework of secularism, however, there are quite a few differences among the Europe countries, by the use of which we may distinguish between what I propose to call 'active' and 'passive' secularism. Active secularism is a state's policy to remove religion from the public domain as much as possible so that the domain is religiously neutral. An example is France where religious parties are not allowed in parliament and religious manifestations are prohibited in all public institutions, including public schools. Passive secularism, on the other hand, merely demands the state's neutrality in its dealings with religion, but leaves everyone free to manifest their religious preferences in the public and political domain. This is the case in most other European countries, albeit in many different forms.

So while in most European countries there is no separation between religion and politics (think of the many Christian Democrat parties), there is often a distinction between the state and the religious communities (or: 'church'). The separation of 'church and state' is in Europe commonly explained as non-interference by the state in matters of doctrine and organization of any religion. But here, also, there are different national traditions that stem from historical developments. Generally speaking, religious communities in Eastern European countries adhere to the legacy of the Ottoman *millet* system because religious communities maintain a form of autonomy as regards the state. In the case of the Muslims, their so-called 'Muslim Communities' are formally recognized in most Eastern European countries, and their spiritual leaders, or *muftis*, hold office in countries from Lithuania, Poland and Austria to Bulgaria and Greece. The state recognition of these Muslim communities implies that they are entitled to regulate matters like mosque maintenance, religious education, the appointment and payment of clerics. In most cases the representative bodies of these communities receive funds from the state to fulfil these duties to the community.[70]

In Western European countries, on the other hand, such a relationship is non-existent, with a few exceptions (in Belgium, for instance, clerics of recognized religious communities with proper representation receive their salaries from the state). Most states, however, maintain formal communication with most of the religious communities, just like the south-eastern European states do. This was only the case with established religious communities, however, like Protestants, Catholics, Jews, and not with the new religions like Islam or Hinduism that had been brought in by immigrants (not to speak of the many other new and exotic religions that flourish among Europeans). When Western European states wanted to establish a similar form of communication with their Muslim communities in order to discuss issues like integration, radicalization and terrorism, this turned out to be more difficult than anticipated. The national, ethnic, linguistic, generational and even religious differences among the Muslims were such that they did not manage – or were unwilling – to unite in a single organization that represented all Muslims of a country. In desperation, European governments like France, Germany and the Netherlands broke with the tradition of secularism, that is non-interference in religious affairs, and actively prompted their Muslim communities to organize themselves. This resulted in the emergence of national Muslim bodies in these countries. How representative they are of the entire Muslim national community in each country remains to be seen, because they mostly appear to represent the first generation.[71]

The constituent principle of secularism is religious freedom, which had become one of the most distinctive features of Europe in the period after the 1950s. The European Court of Human Rights has made it clear that this freedom means not only that the state should not interfere in matters of religion, but that it should also actively guarantee that the faithful can freely practise their religion.[72] This has prompted some European states to change laws on burial and slaughter in order to accommodate the religious needs of non-Christians, such as Jews, Muslims and Hindus. In other instances, European states make sure that the faithful who are hindered in the free practice of their religion due to their stay in government facilities such as prisons, army barracks or public hospitals are provided with access to clergy and prayer rooms and are given religious diets.[73]

Freedom of religion also means that religious communities are free to organize themselves and to regulate their own affairs in accordance with their own wishes, including their own religious laws. This will always, however, be under the scrutiny of the national law of the land. Here we see the fine line between, on the one hand, the principle of liberty, including the freedom of religion and, on the other hand, certain rules that need to be followed by all citizens. With regard to Muslims a point of friction in this respect is family law. Until the nineteenth century, religious communities were free to regulate their own family affairs. By the early nineteenth century, and particularly under Napoleon's rule, family law had become a state responsibility, resulting in the promulgation of national civil laws that applied to all citizens regardless of their religious beliefs. Couples were free to celebrate their religious unions according to their own traditions, but before the law only civil marriage counted. This situation created a parallel legal structure of civil and religious institutions that each adjudicate on the basis of their respective laws (but with the civil law being dominant). In most European countries the Protestant, Catholic, Orthodox and Jewish communities still maintain their own councils (also called 'religious courts'). In Eastern Europe, such councils also exist in the Muslim Communities.[74] At the time of writing, such Muslim advisory or judicial bodies ('Sharia councils') did not exist in a formal manner in Western European countries, except the United Kingdom.[75] There are two reasons for this omission: one is that Muslims cannot agree on a single set of Islamic rules, and the second is that the establishment of such Islamic bodies proved to be highly controversial.[76] We will discuss this issue of 'sharia courts' in Europe in more detail below.

In addition to the freedom to regulate the religious affairs of their communities, Muslims also have the right to pursue religion in politics, just like Christians have been doing in the past century. The only European country where this is not allowed is France. However, initiatives to establish Muslim or Islamic parties on a national or local (municipal) level are either non-existent or have met with little success.[77] The representation of Muslims in political positions, like municipal councils, parliaments or government, is therefore often not on a religious ticket as 'Muslim', but on a political ticket such as socialist, liberal and even Christian Democrat. Romania is the only European country where the constitution reserves one seat for every national minority, including Muslims, provided they are represented by a single organization.[78]

Romania is an exception, however, and its constitutional provision is based on minority rights rather than religious rights. It is typical of modern Europe that minority rights pertain to ethnic, national or linguistic minorities, but are not extended to religious minorities.[79] The reason for this omission is that the protection of this category of people is supposed to be achieved by the constructs of secularism and freedom of religion: states are not to interfere with the beliefs and internal regulations of religious communities. The question then arises whether Muslims, given their special position in Europe, should nevertheless demand specific minority rights. Among Muslims it is a matter of debate whether they are to perceive and organize themselves as a religious minority (as is argued by the prominent Muslim cleric shaykh Qaradawi[80]) or as European citizens with a distinctive Islamic identity (as is argued by the equally prominent Muslim intellectual Tariq Ramadan[81]). This debate seems mostly theoretical, however, as the Muslim communities in Europe – in particular Western Europe – are quite differentiated and dispersed. Moreover, it is not entirely clear from what kind of minority rights Muslims would benefit more than they already do under the freedom of religion.[82]

Tolerance: A Clash of Fundamental Rights

The feeling among Muslims in Europe, and in particular Western Europe, is that their Islamic identity is under a constant barrage of criticism and ridicule with impunity.[83] The combination of hostility towards Islam and fear or dislike of Muslims has become known as 'Islamophobia', which we will discuss in more detail below. This trend has also been a cause of concern for European governments. For one, this situation might cause young Muslims to radicalize since it emphasizes their alienation from the European societies in which they live. But governments have also been apprehensive that it might disrupt societal harmony and violate the Muslims' freedom of religion. The question therefore arose whether tolerance should be enforced and, if so, how?[84] This question was mostly phrased in terms of one of the fundamental rights embraced by the European states: equality and non-discrimination. Governments could – and they often did – take action in this field, especially in the labour market, although it was not always successful.

But most public attention was geared to the other aspect of toleration: respect and recognition. Regulating such basic forms of human behaviour and interaction proved extremely difficult, however, due to another fundamental right: freedom of opinion. Little could be done against the defamation and criticism of Islam since these expressions pertained to the freedom of opinion and speech. Of course, this freedom was not absolute, and insult, slander and hate speech are considered criminal offences in most European jurisdictions. The issue here, however, is a principal one: European laws protect people, not religions.[85] From this point of view religions, ideas, ideologies and all other abstractions remain subject to the freedom of opinion, including criticism. But how far can one go in expressing one's opinion with regard to a religion in the knowledge that this will offend and hurt the faithful? The European answer is: very far. The reason therefore is that the freedom of opinion and expression is considered a corner stone of European democracies: only by continuous critical debate can a democracy be sustained. This principle is enshrined in the European Convention on Human Rights which says that the freedom of opinion may be limited only when that is "necessary in a democratic society".[86] The European Court of Human Rights has interpreted this provision to mean that, in the interest of a functioning democracy, freedom of expression must be allowed to the extent that it may even "shock, disturb or offend".[87] In other words, the freedom of opinion and expression is so important that it may override good manners or decency.

This explains the reluctance of European states to intervene in public and political discourses about Islam that were sometimes indeed shocking and offensive. Criticizing or ridiculing religions, ideas or ideologies is not prohibited by law, even if it is offensive to the adherents to those religions, ideas or ideologies. Only people who are targeted are protected by the law. This distinction between protection of people and their convictions shows in the difference between anti-Semitism and Islamophobia. While in the case of anti-Semitism the criticism and abuse is directed against Jews rather than Judaism, in Islamophopbia it is generally directed against Islam rather than Muslims. Legally, this makes quite a difference, because persecution of those guilty of anti-Semitism is easier than persecuting those who direct their criticism, satire, abuse or hate speech against Islam.*

---

* The distinction between beliefs and believers is not always easy to make. In a case in the Netherlands where a banner was hung out of a building with the text "Stop the cancer called Islam. We won't

In addition to the two fundamental rights – non-discrimination and freedom of opinion – we need to add a third fundamental right to the equation: freedom of religion. While Muslims in Europe may have to endure disproportional criticism of their religion, they also experience more freedom of religion than they would have in most Muslim countries (this is perhaps more true in Western Europe than in Eastern Europe, where the boards of the Muslim Communities keep a check on Islamic doctrine). The freedom of religion in Europe allows Muslims to develop their own interpretations of Islam, whether liberal or conservative. Many Muslim 'puritans' in Western Europe, in consequence, are critical of their countries of origin that, in their opinion, are not 'Islamic' in a correct manner. Some of those countries would not tolerate such views and enforce a state doctrine of Islam. Muslims in Europe, on the other hand, enjoy the freedom of religion to live and manifest their religion in ways they see fit. But while they make use of that freedom, they must also suffer the consequences of another freedom that allows for criticism of that very same religion.

3. Wars and Terrorism

In the period under discussion here, Europe was confronted with two major violent conflicts in which Islam allegedly played a role: the Yugoslavian civil wars and the acts of terrorism by Muslim extremists. In the following we will briefly discuss these two conflicts with an emphasis on the question what role Muslims or Islam played in them.

The Yugoslavian Wars

Yugoslavia, the kingdom of several Balkan nations since 1918 CE, became a socialist federal state of six republics under Marshall Tito after World War II. After Tito's death in 1980 CE, the federal state of Yugoslavia began to unravel, and old grudges and aspirations that had been suppressed in the previous decades emerged: Serbs in Kosovo complained at the way they were treated by the Kosovan Albanians; Croatia

---

submit to Allah", the Supreme Court ruled that the offensive remarks were directed towards Islam, not Muslims, so that there was no criminal offence (Dutch Supreme Court: HR 10 maart 2009, LJN BF0655). But in a similar case in the United Kingdom, however, concerning a banner with the text "Islam out of Britain – Protect the British People", the English court ruled that the offence was clearly directed against Muslims (ECHR, Norwood vs UK, 16 Nov 2004).

and Slovenia resented the fact that their income through tourism was to be spent on the poor regions elsewhere in the federacy; Bosnian Muslims discussed autonomy on the basis of Islamic principles. In 1989 the new Yugoslavian president, Milosevic, first tried to revoke the autonomy of the federal nations but, realizing that he could not accomplish that, switched to the notion of Greater Serbia. A break-up of Yugoslavia would be allowed, he argued, as long as all territories where Serbs lived – including those outside the borders of the republic of Serbia – remained within a Greater Serbia. When Slovenia and Croatia declared independence in 1991, Serbia claimed the Serb territories in those lands and triggered a war that lasted from 1991 until 1995 CE.

The main theatre of war was the territories in and around Bosnia-Herzegovina where the three main populations, Orthodox Serbs, Catholic Croats and Muslim Bosnians ('Bosniaks'), had coexisted for centuries. The factions fought each other but also formed alliances against each other. Muslims and Serbs teamed up against Croats in Herzegovina, rival Muslim forces fought each other in north-west Bosnia, Croats and Serbs fought against Muslims in central Bosnia. But the overall aim of their respective armies and militias was to carve out a territory for each people ('nation') to the exclusion of others who were forcibly removed. The Bosnian Muslims were least successful in these ethnic-religious projects, and as a result constituted the largest group of refugees from former Yugoslavia into Europe. Finally, in 1995, the Daytona peace accord settled the conflict by creating a complex government structure in a carved up Bosnia-Herzegovina. In 1999, another war broke out between Serbia and the autonomous state of Kosovo over the conflicts between the Orthodox Serb and Muslim Albanian inhabitants of Kosovo. This conflict was settled with military force by NATO.

The horrors of the resulting ethnic-religious cleansing were a brutal reminder of those that had taken place in the late nineteenth and early twentieth centuries. The need for a religious and ethnically pure state was apparently still there, and four decades of strictly secular communist rule had not changed these aspirations. This was not only the case in Yugoslavia. In Bulgaria, for instance, a policy of Bulgarianism was adopted in the 1980s claiming that Bulgaria had always been a Christian state, resulting in suppression of religious freedom and forced assimilation of the Muslim communities to Slavic norms, including mandatory name change and a ban on certain clothes and on any language other than Bulgarian.[88] This policy drove 370,000 Turkish Bulgarians to move to Turkey in 1985.[89]

The origins and developments of the Yugoslavian wars have been sketched here in an admittedly simplistic manner since they merely serve as a general background to describe the role and position of Muslims in this part of Europe, but also to raise the question that we for the purpose of this book are interested in: what was the role of religion, and in particular Islam, in these conflicts? Many scholars and observers have tried to analyse the causes of these wars and different opinions exist on the importance of the role of religion therein. To Samuel Huntington, this conflict was an example to prove his point that religion plays a major role in conflicts between civilizations.[90] Some have compared the Yugoslavian war with the conflicts in Lebanon and Northern Ireland, in which "it is obvious that religion has not been a purely passive onlooker of the war, but has been actively involved and engaged in it."[91] But others argued that the main conflict was of an ethnic or nationalist nature and that religion was only an indirect aspect of that conflict[92] or that religion had been abused for political purposes.[93]

Given the fact that religion was of little importance in the daily lives of most Yugoslavians prior to 1990 CE, a depiction of the conflict as a collision of religious communities seems incorrect. However, the conflation of ethnicity and religion into a national identity proved a volatile cocktail.[94] And even if the secular elites had little affiliation with the religious part of their identity, the religious rhetoric that was being used greatly influenced the rank and file in the conflict.[95] Religion provided the different nationalisms with a religiously mystical aura: the Croation and Serbian warriors carried Catholic and Orthodox crosses, respectively, and the Bosnian Muslims would use the battle cry "Allahu akbar".[96] And all sides felt the need to accompany their acts of ethnic cleansing with the destruction of religious artefacts and buildings of their adversaries, as they were considered the main symbols of the opponent's identity.[97]

In the case of the Muslims, however, the conflation of religion and ethnicity was not as conspicuous as it was with others. The Serbs could clearly identify with Orthodoxy, and the Croats with Catholicism, but the 'Muslims' – as they became known – identified with various ethnic and national identities: Bosnian, Albanian, Bulgarian, Turkish. 'Muslim nationalism' therefore took on different forms: Islam played a larger role to the Bosnian Muslims, while ethnicity was more important to the (predominantly Muslim) Albanians.[98] Among the Bosnian Muslims there had since the late 1970s already been an Islamic revival or Islamic renaissance, and this trend intensified during the war.[99] The leader of the Bosnian Muslims during the wars, Izetbegovic, was one of the main proponents of that trend, and he had written extensively on the relationship between Islam and the state (writings which were interpreted by some as a call for an independent and Islamic Bosnia).[100]

Religion, therefore, including Islam, was a powerful factor in the Yugoslavian wars. However, it cannot be seen in isolation from other factors, such as ethnicity, nationalism, economics or politics. From this point of view one could indeed argue that the wars in Yugoslavia were neither civil, ethnic nor religious wars – they were all of them combined.[101] Nevertheless, religion remained strongly connected with nationalism, and the sentiment of a religious-ethnic 'pure' state has always been strong since the nineteenth century, and possibly will remain so in the future, although it may be pursued by different means. An example of such different means is the 'Millennium Cross' in Macedonia, a 66-metre high cross built between 2002 and 2008 CE on a mountain top overlooking the capital Skopje. The cross – the largest in the world – was funded by the Macedonian Orthodox Church and the government to celebrate two thousand years of Christianity. In a country with a third of the population being Muslim, it is not surprising that this construction is interpreted as a symbol to emphasize the Christian identity of the state[102] – just as Bulgaria had done thirty years earlier.

Extremism and Terrorism

The other form of violence that involved Islam and Muslims in Europe after 1950 CE is the attacks on civilians by Muslim extremists in the first decade of the twenty-first century. These attacks had shaken Europe's sense of confidence and safety and set in motion an unprecedented security effort. The focus in trying to understand this Muslim anger – "why do they hate us?" – was at first primarily pinpointing the religion of the perpetrators since that was how these people explained their actions.[103] Other researchers, however, argued that the radicalization of Muslim youth in the West was primarily rooted in external circumstances and that there were more reasons for Muslim anger beside innate Islamic anger or militancy itself.[104] It became clear that there were specific grievances among Muslim youth in Europe other than a general hatred for the West and Western lifestyles. The source of their resentment was not what the West *is*, but what the West *does*. The Western actions that caused resentment among European Muslims were, on the one hand, Western military interventions in Muslim-majority countries (or the lack of such intervention, as is the case in the Syrian civil war that started in 2011) but more so, on the other hand, the negative attitude of the European native population vis-à-vis the Muslims in Europe.

The fact that European governments could not – and often did not want to – act because the defamations and criticisms of Islam were considered part of the freedom of expression merely added to the general feeling among Muslims in Europe that they were left unprotected from public scorn and abuse. The other development that caused grievances among many of the Western European Muslims was their position at the lower end of the social-economical ladder.[105] They experienced higher unemployment rates, under-representation in higher jobs and offices, over-representation in prison. Discrimination – whether real or perceived – was experienced not only in education and employment, but also socially. Muslims in Europe, and in particular in Western Europe, felt 'under siege'.[106]

The combination of all these factors had led to feelings of alienation, exclusion and disenfranchisement among European Muslims. Whether this sensation was justified is not important – the perception was already enough to make it real.[107] This psychological factor is of critical importance in understanding the motives for terrorist acts by European Muslims, even those who were well educated and from middle class families.[108] Their sense of not belonging and exclusion arguably drove these youths into the ideology and acts of *jihadi* terrorism. Of course, these explanations merely provide the general contours of what is conducive for Muslims to radicalize, because in the end it is the particular psychology and choices of each individual Muslim that determines whether he or she will actually embark on that process.

The awareness of sources other than Islam feeding into Muslim anger brought about a change in policy among Western European governments:[109] in addition to security and judicial measures, the key word for the counter strategy became 'integration'. Radicalization of Muslim youth might be prevented, so ran the argument, if they were made part of European society to the extent that they actually *felt* a sense of belonging. The German intelligence service was most explicit in doing so when it defined its new strategy in the catch phrase "successful integration equals prevention of extremism and terrorism."[110] Hence a flurry of activities financed by security services, like social programmes for school dropouts, intellectual empowerment of those considered vulnerable to radical rhetoric, training of young cadres, and social reinforcement of neighbourhoods. Such initiatives were taking place mainly in countries like England, the Netherlands and Spain, and to a much lesser extent in Germany and France.[111] Often cooperation was sought with local mosques and Islamic organizations. In some instances municipal councils approached imams and scholars (in)directly in order to influence Islamic discourse among their Muslim constituencies.[112]

The fact that security agencies were actively engaging with domains that traditionally belonged to the civic and social realm also created confusion and suspicion among Muslims. Questions were raised about money made available by the ample funds of security agencies for social events or discussion seminars on issues like civil responsibility. While such involvement usually takes place behind the scenes, it took on more explicit forms, as when the German intelligence service established the 'Confidence Working Group' with the purpose of engaging in dialogue with representatives of Muslim organizations in Germany. As a young Dutch Moroccan once said in a public meeting about integration in 2008, "They may talk about our welfare, but that is only because we are a security concern."[113] This development has been called the 'securitization of Islam', meaning that Islam is considered a national security issue and as such affects all kinds of laws, policies and measures relating to immigration and integration.[114]

4. Europe and Its 'Neighbourhood'

In the previous chapters we discussed numerous forms of diplomatic interactions between European and Muslim sovereigns and states. Charlemagne sent envoys to Baghdad and plotted with Moorish governors against the caliph in Cordoba, Western European nations sent ambassadors to Istanbul to secure first economic and later also political interests. This process continued in the twentieth century, but on a different scale: it was not individual European states but the European Union which identified a Mediterranean and North African (MENA) 'neighbourhood' that it wanted to remain as stable as possible. At the same time, the European Union was involved in a seemingly endless negotiation with Turkey about its membership of the European Union.

Exporting Stability?

It was in the European interest to create a stable environment at its borders for a number of reasons: wars or unrest had to be prevented from infecting the European Union zone, economic refugees from Asia and Africa had to be stopped from illegally entering, and the European Union was to benefit from trade with its neighbours. A set of political and economic measures was developed to create stable 'neighbourhoods' in the former communist eastern European countries and in the Mediterranean and North African region.

In November 1995 CE, on the date exactly 900 years after Pope Urban II called for the first Crusade, a new phase of relations was heralded by the historic partnership between the 15 EU members states and 12 states from North Africa (Morocco, Algeria, Tunisia), the Middle East (Egypt, Jordan, Lebanon, Syria, the Palestinian Authority, Israel), as well as Turkey, Cyprus and Malta.[115] One of these measures was the so-called 'Association' agreements with individual countries in which economic advantages were promised in exchange for good governance. This so-called 'Europe-Mediterranean Partnership' was lopsided: while the North African and Middle Eastern countries had considerable economic interests in cooperation with the EU, the European side was predominantly concerned with the '3 Ds': the lack of democracy, the explosive demography, and the lagging development in these countries.

Islam played a very limited role in these interactions and contacts.[116] This is remarkable, given its role in social and political developments on both sides of the Mediterranean. Its absence is understandable from the European perspective, however, given the fact that the EU has no competence over religious affairs[117] and that Islam had become a highly sensitive issue that better remained untouched.[118] Even the formally established EU-Arab dialogue that was officially "to encourage understanding between cultures and exchanges between civil societies"[119] was of little use in this respect, because it gradually dissolved into a differentiation of policies and bilateral contacts between individual European and Arab states.[120] Nevertheless, practices and initiatives were developed on an informal level that foster dialogue 'with Islam' within the framework of intercultural and interfaith dialogue of the Euro-Mediterranean Partnership.[121]

Still, Islam, and in particular political Islam as it manifested itself in the Middle East and later also in Turkey, was a source of concern for Europe, firstly because the volatile mix of Islamic fundamentalism, terrorism and migration was considered a threat to Europe's security,[122] but also because of the anxiety about the direction in which the trend of political Islam was to go: would it develop into a political tradition similar to that of the Christian Democrats in Europe, or into a theocratic regime which might be hostile to Europe just like Iran's Khomeini had proclaimed America as the 'great Satan'? Even though Europe advocated democracy as the primary system of good governance, it was very weary of what might be called the Hitler syndrome: the possibility that the Islamists in Arab countries would participate in the democratic process in order to gain access to power and subsequently dismantle the democratic order and establish their own Islamic regime.

This concern made the European Union prefer to support undemocratic but stable regimes rather than pushing for a potentially unstable democracy. It has been argued that this position was detrimental to European credibility to those in the Middle East and North Africa who genuinely advocated democracy, and was the cause of the development of anti-Western sentiments. President George Bush was one of the first to admit this in 2003, in a statement that otherwise received little attention: "[s]ixty years of Western nations excusing and accommodating the lack of freedom in the Middle East did not make us safe ... because in the long run, stability can not be purchased at the expense of liberty. As long as the Middle East remains a place where freedom does not flourish, it will remain a place of stagnation, resentment, and violence ready for export."[123]

This recognition prompted American and European endeavours to promote democracy and freedom in the Middle Eastern region. In the eyes of many Muslims, that policy failed miserably with the violence that erupted in Iraq after the American-British invasion in 2003, and the Western refusal to recognize Hamas after its landslide victory in the 2004 Palestinian elections. In the Muslim world one points to double standards at work in Western foreign policies when promoting democracy for some while denying it to others.[124] As we have seen, this bitterness is shared by Western European Muslims with regard to the foreign policies of their national governments and the ensuing resentment among Muslims provided new recruiting ground for Islamic extremism.[125]

The Arab Spring revolts of 2011 finally brought about the situation that had for so long been dreaded by Europe: the toppling of dictators and the establishment of forms of popular rule that was by many heralded as 'democracy'. At the time of writing the outcome of these new political constellations is still unknown as only few appear to have maintained some kind of stability, while others have succumbed to the feared situation of chaos and violence. In Turkey, on the other hand, the Islamist AK Parti has had a huge majority since 2002, and has managed to implement a religiously motivated policy within the strict secular system of Turkey although opposition to the alleged autocratic rule of the AK Parti is growing. The eastern and southern Mediterranean region, therefore, has produced a distinctive Islamic political and social voice that Europe will have to deal with. So far, the European attitude has been one of acceptance and cautious involvement in the political processes in these countries.

Importing Extremism?

In the aftermath of 9/11, Europe felt threatened by 'Islam' from two sides: the (sometimes violently) anti-Western sentiments in the Muslim world, as well as the rising orthodoxy among Muslims within Europe, on the one hand, and the radicalism and terrorism among some of them, on the other hand. The connection between the Muslims inside and outside Europe became one of the main concerns of the European security agencies. However, severing any link between the two was an impossible task in a world dominated by globalism and transnationalism where Europe's Muslim population had access to ideas, people and organizations abroad by means of modern media.[126] Insofar as Muslims from outside tried to influence their sisters and brethren in Europe, such endeavors were not so much undertaken by governments of Muslim countries vis-à-vis their nationals in Europe,[127] but much more by foreign Muslim individuals and organizations. For instance, many mosques in Western Europe recruited imams from abroad, mainly because they did not have their own imams and lacked the ability to train their imams within Europe, and such recruitment was permitted as a matter of freedom of religion. The result of this arrangement was that Western European Muslim communities remained dependent on their countries of origin, and that they were often exposed to religious leaders who had little knowledge of the European context.[128]

Another situation that yielded unexpected results was the asylum granted to Muslim foreigners who were persecuted in their homeland for extremism and had fled to Europe, and who could often not be extradited if torture or the death penalty awaited them in their countries of origin. Such was the case, for instance, with members of the Muslim Brothers who had found refuge in Europe.[129] Many of them were conservative and politically opinionated, initiating discussions among European Muslim youth in support of Islamist opposition movements in the Middle East and of the various wars in Bosnia, Algeria, Chechnya and Afghanistan. They encouraged the viewpoint that European Muslim youths belong to the worldwide Muslim community or *umma*, and that it was their duty to defend this community, even with violence if need be. This vision drew the conflicts from outside into Europe. Western Europe became a target of Middle Eastern radical Islam with the spill-over of the Algerian civil war into France in 1994. The attacks of 11 September 2001 and the involvement of European nations in the 2003 war in Iraq further globalized the theatre of operations into EuropeEurope.[130]

The main influence on European Muslims appears to come from foreign Muslim organizations.[131] Many of these organizations see it as their duty to educate and inspire European Muslims in the 'true' spirit of Islam, not unlike the way Christian missionary organizations go out to help and support minority Christians in Muslim lands. While these organizations are mostly concerned with the spiritual wellbeing of Muslims in Europe, they sometimes also gear them towards an isolationist position vis-à-vis their European environment, or even towards radicalism. In the particular case of the Yugoslavian civil war of 1991–1995, the plight of the Bosnian Muslims made a great impact on Middle Eastern Muslims, prompting not only an influx of military volunteers during the war, but also after the war humanitarian support and strenuous efforts by Islamic organizations from Turkey, Saudi Arabia and Iran to 're-Islamize' the secularized Bosnian Muslims.[132] While their impact at first may have been small,[133] we have seen that concerns have been expressed about the increase in Middle Eastern-style mosques and garments, and Middle eastern-style orthodox views on gender and non-Muslims.[134]

But not all Islamic-political sentiments were imported. The new generation of European Muslims developed their own opinions and ideas. The Syrian civil war that erupted in 2011 and the establishment of a 'caliphate' in northern Iraq by the Islamic State organization (known as 'IS') in 2014 were illustrative for events that took place abroad but greatly enticed Muslim youth in Europe. It showed how much European Muslims are engaged with the political turbulences in the Middle East, and how these events reflect on their lives in Europe. All these foreign elements contributed to the complexity of and growing concerns about Islam in Europe. These concerns have been compounded with the new development since 2011 of hundreds of European Muslim youth joining the ranks of extremist Islamic militant organizations in their jihad against the Syrian regime, and some even taking part in the atrocious wars of conquest undertaken by the IS. The net result of all these developments was that they added fuel to the already existing concern that linked 'Islam' with 'security'.

Turkey and the European Union

Turkey was already a member of the Council of Europe (which also includes countries like Russia and Azerbaijan) and had applied for EU membership as early as 1959.[135] The main obstacle, however, was the Turkish human rights track record and lack of democracy. Turkey's prime-minister Tansu Çiller argued in 1995 that a delay in granting Turkey membership of the EU would not only be considered an insult to the Turks, but would also play into the hands of the Islamist Refah Parti (the predecessor to the AK Parti). According to Çiller, these Islamists would surely take Turkey away from Europe and further into the fold of the Middle East: "Now it's me versus them [the Turkish Islamists – MB]. I represent Westernization, secular government, liberalization, the link with Europe."[136] In 1999, the European governments offered Turkey the concrete prospect of full membership of the EU, and the two sides entered into protracted negotiations.

But then the political landscape in Turkey changed drastically: the Islamist AK Parti won landslide victories in the elections of 2002, 2007 and 2011. Çiller's dark forebodings did not come true, however, because the Turkish government under the AK Parti has, more than any of its secular predecessors, actively campaigned for Turkish membership of the European Union. This may seem remarkable, given the generally assumed friction between Islamic politics and 'the West.' But it has also been argued that the AK Parti aimed at linking up with European politics where secularism enjoyed a happy marriage with a strong tradition of Christian Democratic politics. This might have been very appealing to an Islamic party in a country where secularism was so strictly enforced that religiously motivated parties had been dismantled and outlawed.[137]

When Turkey under AK Parti leadership was indeed making progress in fulfilling the requirements for EU membership, a debate erupted among the European partners about Turkish membership. Proponents held that fulfilment of requirements should lead to membership since that was promised, and that Turkey would greatly contribute to the European economy, while opponents back-pedalled on the prospect of Turkish membership for three different reasons. One was political: admission to the EU would make Turkey with over 70 million inhabitants the largest of all the EU states and that would seriously change the balance of power within the EU. Another reason for opposition was concern about security because the admission of Turkey would extend the borders of the EU to Armenia, Azerbaijan, Iran and Syria and by consequence to a zone rife with conflict and instability. These opponents thought it wiser to keep Turkey as the buffer state between the EU and Asia Minor. An interesting aspect of these two arguments is that they neglect the fact that Turkey, as a member of NATO since 1952, has been co-responsible for the defence of Europe, and has been sharing military and national security details relating to Europe ever since.

The third reason for opposition to Turkey as an EU member state – even if it were to fulfil the formal conditions for membership – was of a cultural nature, arguing that Turkey was not 'European'.[138] We mentioned before the remark by a EU commissioner that the admittance of Turkey to the EU would render the liberation of Vienna in 1683 "in vain". This imagery was magnified with the concern that, once admitted to the EU, millions of Turks would enter the EU looking for work and, in consequence, raise Islam to the status of the largest religion in Europe. This was rebutted in 2002 by the European Commission's director general for enlargement, who pointed out that the EU "is not a club of Christian peoples" and that membership was based on political, not religious or cultural principles.[139] But the former president of France and then head of the convention working on the EU's constitution, Valerie Giscard d'Estaing, replied that Turkey was "not a European country" and that its admittance to the EU would mean "the end of the EU".[140]

The Turks themselves did not share these cultural arguments against their participation in the EU. For Turkey, Europe represented a political and economic cooperation, not a religious or cultural unity. The alleged 'Christian' identity of Europe was no cause for concern or debate in Turkey in that it might lose its Turkish or Muslim identity by joining the EU. Of the approximately 5 million Turks living in Europe, more than half perceived the EU as an economic integration project, and only 20 per cent believed that the EU is a "Christian club".[141] Only the AK Parti used a moderate Islamic discourse, but merely to present itself as a bridge between Christian Europe and Muslim Asia and Middle East.

International Actions against 'Defamation of Islam'

In parallel to these European endeavours that were directly related to its border areas, Europe also had to deal with the effects of globalized politics. European participation in military interventions in Muslim lands could have repercussions at home, just like incidents and politics at home in Europe might affect Muslim lands far away. These exchanges took place on numerous levels, ranging from the Internet to meeting rooms of the United Nations. Although Europe's image in the Muslim world was slightly better than that of the United States, several incidents (in particular the Rushdie affair in 1982, the Danish cartoons in 2006 and the Dutch film Fitna in 2008) were quite damaging. While the United States launched a new strategy of 'public diplomacy' after 9/11, the European Union tried to engage its Muslim neighbours in dialogue, as we have seen above.

But while Europe tried to mend the fences by improving its image, the Muslim perception of the West being anti-Islamic became so strong that Muslim countries, united in the Organization of Islamic Conference (OIC), initiated diplomatic pressure to stop what they considered Western Islamophobia. The OIC did so by actively campaigning for an international ban on the defamation of religion that would force European countries to re-introduce the blasphemy laws that they were in the process of gradually abolishing. This initiative started in 1999 when the OIC introduced a resolution in the United Nations Human Rights Commission[142] demanding that "defamation of Islam" had to be combatted. This resolution was passed, and although it had no legal effect (resolutions in international law are non-binding statements) it was definitely a diplomatic victory for the OIC. The resolution was then passed again every year, although its title changed from defamation of 'Islam' to defamation of 'religion.' This agenda was pushed ever more forcefully after 2001 and again after the 2002 report on European Islamophobia,[143] the Danish cartoons (in 2006) and the Dutch film *Fitna* (in 2008). From 2005 onwards, the resolution was also passed annually by the General Assembly of the United Nations.

The 'Western' nations – mainly represented by Europe, North America and Australia – did not budge, holding on to the freedom of opinion and expression, but the situation was diplomatically quite uncomfortable, especially when the levels of Islam-critique in the West acquired forms that the Western governments themselves disagreed with but had to allow as a matter of freedom of expression. Even though these instances were minor, and often the initiative of a single person (think of the Burn a Quran Day in 2010, and the Internet film about the prophet Muhammad in 2012), they received wide attention in the Muslim world, fuelling the image of an Islam-bashing West. In 2011, a diplomatic compromise was reached on the issue of defamation: the Muslim countries united in the OIC agreed that blasphemy laws were not needed in Europe to protect Islam, but that they would jointly combat intolerance, discrimination and violence that was based on religion.[144]

III. Virtual Islam

We started this book with the premise that in order to understand Islam in Europe, we need to understand the situation in Europe at each particular time, and how 'Europe' in that period was conceptualized by Europeans. With regard to Europe since the 1950s, it has been argued that Europeans have continued their construction of a common legacy or identity that has been called the "grand narrative of Europe".[145] According to Talal Asad, Europe "is ideologically constructed in such a way that Muslim immigrants can not be satisfactorily be represented in it."[146] What, then, is this construction, this grand narrative?

With the fall of the Berlin wall in 1989, the 'Question of Europe' emerged: the debate on European identity, sovereignty and loyalty within the setting of the larger Europe. The debate on the essentials of this 'Europeanness' focused primarily on political and judicial institutions, bypassing the cultural and religious dimensions of European societies.[147] Leading intellectuals in this debate, such as Jurgen Habermas, Charles Taylor, Alain Touraine and Will Kymlicka, who tried to eliminate differences and forms of 'otherness' with notions like multiculturalism and pluriformity, discussed these issues in terms of citizenship, group recognition and rights.[148]

While these debates were confined to the realm of political-legal discourse, a parallel debate took place within the domain of religious-cultural discourse. In these debates the notion of Europeanness as a common civilization or culture was introduced, often phrased in religious terms like 'Judeo-Christian civilization'. This idea was not new, but tapped into the nineteenth-century concept of 'Europe-as-Christendom' that was set within the key of 'Otherness': "the construction of the idea of Europe was defined by means of the 'Others' which it excludes, and *vice versa*."[149] An interesting aspect of this religious-cultural identity is that by the late twentieth century it had incorporated secularism as an integral part of that European civilization. Even though the European was identified on the basis of his Judeo-Christian heritage, secularism was conceived as a next progressive step in the European civilizational narrative. The Other was then identified as being not secular.[150]

In the following we will elaborate how this European self-perception reflected on Muslims in Europe. We will be discussing the mechanisms of Islam-criticism and of the negative image that Muslims generally have in Europe, but we must keep in mind that in doing so we are talking about images and perceptions. This does not necessarily reflect reality. Yes, European Muslims may suffer from discrimination, but they are not second-class citizens as was the case in previous centuries; they have access to education and are represented in high positions in the judiciary, politics and government and gradually also in business, the media and academe. Yes, the majority of European public opinion may have a negative impression of Islam, but the European Muslim enjoys a religious freedom that is unparalleled in most Muslim majority countries. Yes, many Europeans may have qualms about Muslims and their un-European cultures, but Europe has embraced parts of these same cultures in a manner that can be best described as neo-Turquerie: interior decoration items like lamps and furniture with Moroccan and Afghan designs became fashionable, just like the waterpipe cafes and certain forms of clothes like the baggy pants and embroidered long-sleeved shirts, and both pop and classic musicians use Arabic or Pakistani music or collaborate with musicians from Muslim lands.

1. Images of Islam and Muslims

Criticism and Islamophobia

We have seen that Islam and Muslims have been under heavy criticism since the 1990s, and in particular since 9/11. The sentiments, causes and justifications behind this criticism are complex and often intertwined.

First, criticism of Islam has a longstanding European tradition, as we have seen in the previous chapters. But from the nineteenth century onwards Europe developed a tradition of criticism of religion in general, and Christianity already had its fair share of criticism and abuse, first in the nineteenth century and then again in the 1960s and 1970s. In European majority public and political discourse, religion does not enjoy a status of prestige, as we have seen. The manifestation of Islam through dress, behaviour, and manners of speech as is manifested in Western, and to a lesser extent in Eastern Europe therefore runs counter to the dominant European notions of the position of religion in the public domain.

The criticism of Islam from this perspective is mostly in line with the earlier forms of criticism of religion that consider it backward, irrational and oppressive. Some critics of Islam are therefore not necessarily targeting Islam as such but are critical of religion in general, and they are concerned with the fact that in a quite secularized Europe a new community is manifesting itself with a distinct religious identity. Other critics of Islam can be found among the devout Christians who are continuing the centuries-old theological criticism of Islam as a 'wrong' religion. But while the secular Europeans may distrust Muslims for being violent and fanatical, religious Europeans are less inclined to think in that way about Muslims.[151]

Another source of criticism was related to social practices of European Muslims, for instance their high rate of involvement in crime or their alleged lack of integration in European society. While these issues in themselves were indeed reason for concern (crime rates among the youth of immigrant origin – not just Muslims – were disproportionately high, and people of immigrant origin – again, not just Muslims – tended to isolate themselves in communities that had poor socio-economic prospects), they were often linked to Islam. In the case of Moroccan or Pakistani young criminals, for instance, their behaviour was explained by the fact that they were Muslim and that Islam as a violent religion instigated this behaviour. This was a typical issue of the *homo Islamicus*: the actions of 'Muslims' were explained as being motivated by Islam. These arguments were generally dismissed by the academic and most of the political community, but were recurring themes in public discourse. Quite a few new political parties have arisen since the 1990s that have adopted this view by equating their opposition to further immigration in their countries with strong anti-Islam rhetoric.[152] Their popularity may be seen as a reflection of such beliefs among the population.

A third important reason for the criticism of Islam was the many acts of intolerance and violence that were committed by Muslims in the name of Islam within but even more so outside Europe during late twentieth and early twenty-first centuries: Islamic regimes like those of Pakistan, Iran and Saudi-Arabia, movements like the Taliban, Shabab or Boko Haram, the replacement of the secular PLO by the Islamic Hamas in Palestine, and the suicide attacks all over the world, including those in Europe. Islam, so it seemed to the European observer, once it becomes part of a political or societal discourse, is prone to becoming violent or oppressive. The manifestations in Europe of intolerance and violence in the name of Islam were being interpreted as dark forebodings of what was being witnessed in many parts of the Muslim world.

Criticism and anxiety about Islam and Muslims were therefore often rooted in practical and tangible issues that were of public concern – a resurgence of fundamentalism, immigration, terrorism, loss of national identity – but in many instances tended to be focused on Islam and Muslims. This focus reached such proportions in the late 1990s that a new word was coined for it: Islamophobia. The near impossibility of defining this term – is it racism, religious intolerance, an equivalent of anti-Semitism? – has put many scholars to work.[153] Suffice it here to say that some define Islamophobia in terms of a behavioural attitude (hostility toward Muslims), while others define it as an emotion (unreasonable fear of Islam and Muslims). Islamophobia is classed with xenophobia and anti-Semitism but, as we have seen, whereas the latter two target people (foreigners and Jews, respectively), Islamophobia combines anti-Muslim with anti-Islam sentiments, which makes legal action against this form of defamation difficult.

In addition to a dismissive or discriminatory attitude towards a Muslim for being somehow inferior (the centuries-old image of the irrational, fanatical Other), the late twentieth-century Islamophobia has added a second component: the fear of the compatriot Muslim as a potential threat (either because he cannot or refuses to integrate, or because he may pose a security threat). While the first attitude puts the Muslim in a very uncomfortable position shared by many minorities in Europe, the latter attitude puts the Muslim in a corner from which there is no escape but to disappear, either by leaving, or by dissolving (assimilating) into the native society. The call for assimilation shows itself in numerous ways: Muslims should not hold foreign nationality (in several instances impossible since some countries do not allow nationalities to be revoked by their citizens); should pledge their allegiance to their new state by a variety of means (including citizenship tests which, as an aside, are failed by most native citizens who have taken them for fun); and, most importantly, should not show their Muslim-ness (hence the fierce objections to the headscarf and the mosques with 'Oriental' architecture). The extreme consequence of these views on assimilation is that Muslims should give up their religion altogether – a liberal version of the forced conversion of former times, and although hardly expressed in those terms we see time and time again how Muslims who openly denounce Islam are embraced by the critics of Islam.[154]

The 'Third Wave'

While in previous centuries the Muslim as the European Other was often physically situated in a far-away place, that situation has altered dramatically for Western Europe since the 1970s. The coming of migrants who adhered to or identified with Islam was not merely a confrontation with the Other, but also reinvigorated the image of Islam as a religion that is out for conquest. According to scholars like Bernard Lewis and Bassam Tibi one needs to conceive the massive migration of Muslims to Europe as a "third wave" that may prove successful after the first two 'waves' were repulsed at the battles of Poitiers (732 CE) and Vienna (1683).[155] The imagery of the two 'waves' may be psychologically powerful but, as we have seen in previous chapters, is historically debatable. In the case of the battle of Poitiers in 732 CE, historians have pointed out that the defeated Muslims were not an invasion army out to conquer the heartland of Europe, but one of the many raiding armies that for decades had crossed the Pyrenees for loot and spoils – a practice they continued even after the defeat at Poitiers.[156] In the case of the siege of Vienna in 1683, we have seen that the 'Europe' as a representation of a Christian commonwealth that was saved from the Turk at the battle of Vienna in 1683 is a myth that was created retrospectively.[157]

The image of Islamic conquest is the source not only of fear for some Europeans, but also of hope for some devout Muslims. The famous Muslim scholar Yusuf Qaradawi remarked in 2007 in a televised interview: "Perhaps the next conquest [of Europe] will be the conquest of da'wa [preaching] and ideas. There is no need for conquest to be with the sword. We may conquer these countries without armies. We want armies of preachers and teachers."[158] From a missionary point of view, these remarks are understandable, but from the perspective of the current European situation, they merely confirm the notion of the Muslim's hunger for conquest. This fear was reinforced – or justified, according to some – by the Muslim extremist attacks of 9/11 in 2001, and the consecutive attacks in European cities. The notions of a 'third wave' and of an aggressive Islam that is out to 'take over' tap into the European collective memory of a perpetual conflict with Islam.

Although the notion of 'taking over' seems to reverberate through the centuries of European-Muslim relations, it has distinctly different meanings to the modern as opposed to the pre-modern European. To the pre-modern European 'taking over' meant the fear of actual conquest by Muslim armies. To the modern European, on the other hand, the notion of 'taking over' is much more nebulous. Military conquest is surely not a realistic option, but other forms of domination apparently are to be considered. To some, the notion of an Islam that 'takes over' is represented by the physical presence of Muslims in Europe and, consequently, the values they bring with them. As early as in 1995 the secretary general of the trans-Atlantic military coalition NATO argued that Islamic "fundamentalism" had replaced Communism as the new threat to European "civilization".[159] Many more such warnings and anxieties were to follow, whereby the allegedly anti-European tendencies among Muslims in Europe were often directly connected with similar sentiments in Muslim countries outside Europe. The threat was therefore not only from outside Europe, but also from within.

But what, then, is this threat? Since it cannot be the physical presence of Muslims since their numbers are so small – except in certain cities where they live in concentrated numbers – it must be what they stand for: Islam. We must therefore rephrase the question 'is Islam a threat to Europe' into: does the presence of Muslims in Europe represent a presence of Islamic values that contradict or even threaten European values? And, if so, do these values represent an impediment to integration or, worse, a set of values that Muslims want to impose on their environment? We have already seen that some authors warn that this is indeed the case.[160] European politicians have been elected on the basis of this view. The problem, however, is an assessment of these values – both the Islamic and European values: what exactly do we mean by them? We will discuss this in the next section.

A Conflict of Values

It would be too simplistic to reduce the values upheld by Muslims to the tenets of Islamic theology. We have seen in the previous sections that Muslims in Europe – and anywhere else, for that matter – are not necessarily believers. Neither is everything a Muslim does inspired by Islam or in accordance with Islamic orthodoxy, nor is everything that Islam prescribes adhered to by Muslims. On the other hand, there are Muslims in Europe who claim that they strictly adhere to precisely these tenets. But then again, they differ among each other on the correct interpretation of these tenets.[161] And what European Muslims actually hold to be Islamic rules or tenets may very well differ from those upheld by Islamic doctrine. It is therefore almost impossible to give definitions or general overviews of 'Islamic values' that may or may not conflict with European values.

Rather than trying to define the Islamic values that Muslims in Europe adhere to, we might ask ourselves what European values are allegedly violated by European Muslims in the name of Islam. In this approach it is helpful to make use of the two aforementioned sets of European values: political-legal, and religious-cultural. The political-legal values, such as democracy, liberty, equality, rule of law, are at the core of modern European legal and political systems. The religious-cultural values, on the other hand, are at the core of what is considered by many to be a European identity. Acknowledging that these two sets of values are not entirely clear in their definitions, they do provide clarity when discussing the confrontation with Islamic values, as we will do now.

European political-legal values are elaborated in political systems as well as in legal systems where they are enshrined in constitutions and in human rights treaties, in particular the European Convention on Human Rights. How do the many different Islamic theological values as practised by European Muslims relate to these European political values? On the one hand, we may observe numerous practices justified by Islam that are considered contrary to European values, such as gender segregation, the position of women, face covering, the attitude towards non-believers. At the same time, however, it is precisely a political-legal value like liberty that allows people to behave in accordance with their own wishes or rules, even if others find them reprehensible. This applies also to the notion of equality that grants every person the right to enjoy an equal position before the law, but does not determine what that person should *do* with that position. Equality and liberty allow people to put themselves in a position that may be considered unequal and illiberal. In short, European political-legal values, including the rule of law and the notion of equality, provide the freedom to be different.[162] It is therefore not surprising that European Muslims support European political-legal values.[163] Muslims may be angry about discrimination and Islamophobia, but they are in need of the basic freedoms and liberties provided by the European political-legal system in order to maintain their religious identity. It is the legal and political values of Europe that grant Muslims the freedom to be what they want to be: Muslims.

The anxiety about European values that may conflict with Islam should therefore not be sought in Muslims' alleged rejection of European political-legal values themselves, but their use (or abuse) of these values. An example is the notion of *sharia*. Based on what we know from research so far, we may tentatively assert that the devout and orthodox among European Muslims who want to live in accordance with the rules of Islam ('sharia') focus on four domains: religious rituals, family law, financial transactions, and interaction with the non-Muslim environment.[164] While most of these *sharia* rules as being practised by European Muslims are generally allowed within a European context of legal liberty, there is distinct opposition in Europe – mostly in Western Europe – to such practices. The reasons for this opposition are manifold. Some argue that a separate infrastructure of religious rules, in particular related to family relations, creates a segregation that is undesirable from a social as well as a legal perspective. Socially, such practices might be detrimental to Muslim women, because their community might deny them the liberties of European life by exerting considerable pressure on them to submit to the traditions and laws of Islam.[165] Legally, it is argued that a state's rule of law should not permit parallel legal structures. While all these arguments are valid by themselves, one may point to different experiences within Europe. In Eastern Europe, for instance, as we have seen above, the self-regulation of Muslims is much more institutionalized, and therefore strictly speaking 'segragated', mainly as the legacy of a centuries-old practice (although, of late, these practices have also come under criticism and scrutiny[166]). And in Western European countries there has been a long tradition of Catholic, Protestant and Jewish family courts operating parallel to the national civil courts.

The alleged infringement of 'Islam' on European values can also be surmised from the angle of religious-cultural values. While political-legal values are relatively easy to identify, the religious-cultural values are more ambiguous. They represent the European grand narrative mentioned above. The religious component of this narrative holds that Christianity, either as a religious value-system or as a religious tradition or civilization, is said to have shaped the identity and unity that we call Europe.[167] It is important to note that this religious dimension of European values is not exclusively embraced by devout Christians but also by the non-religious: to them, Christianity represents the cradle of modern European civilization rather the articles of faith of any of the Christian denominations.

The religious-cultural component of the European narrative is not only historical, but also very temporal. European values in this meaning represent values that are mostly enshrined not in laws but in customs, and are held as self-evident truths: 'the way we do things around here'. I contend that these values are central in the conflict between 'Europe' and 'Islam'. Apart from the terrorist attacks, most 'conflicts' between Islamic and European values that make headlines in European news relate to differences of social interaction. The European public generally considers not shaking hands with members of the other gender insulting, and the wearing of headscarves degrading, to name the most conspicuous examples. Interestingly, the European political-legal values allow for such behaviour, as no law prescribes how to greet or what to wear. It is precisely this difference between the two sets of European values that causes much of the confusion about what is acceptable and what not in a European society.

The two sets of values – political-legal and religious-cultural – together make up for the peculiar situation of European secularism which is to some the most typical confrontation with Islamic values. As we have discussed above, European societies have developed the customary practice of not publicly manifesting religion, even though that would be perfectly admissible by law. Religious dress in public has become rare, and even self-proclaimed Christian politicians will seldom refer to Scripture to make their point. Despite a strong tradition of Christian Democratic politics in many European countries, and regardless of references to the Christian identity of Europe, religion is mostly absent from the European political and public domains.

This is often referred to as secularism, and according to several observers this is the point where Islam clashes with European values.[168] I would argue, however, that the issue here is not secularism but a typical European cultural tradition of handling religion. In the United States, for instance, we observe a completely different tradition of secularism where religion plays a very prominent role in the public and political domain.[169] Manifestation of religion – whether Islam or any other religion – is therefore bound to clash with the European way of handling religion, but not with the American way. This clash is much less prominent, on the other hand, if secularism is defined as a political-legal institution of separating religion and the state. It is precisely this separation that is embraced by many European Muslims because it guarantees their freedom to practise their faith according to their own wishes and without state interference.[170]

The clash of values between 'Islam' and 'Europe' therefore is not that European Muslims adhere to values that are prohibited by law – on the contrary, the political-legal values allow for diversity and liberty – , but by the religious-cultural objection that 'this is not how we do things here'. The French law of 2011 banning the face veil illustrates this dilemma: on the one hand, the French State Council advised against such ban on the basis of the political-legal principle of personal autonomy which allows a woman freely to wear what she wishes;[171] and, on the other hand, the legislature deemed the face veil contrary to the cultural principle that open-faced encounters in public are a matter of 'social contract'.[172]

2. The Study of Islam

The study of Islam in Europe has changed considerably since the last decades of the twentieth century, on the one hand because the study of Islam gained popularity and European scholars have broadened this academic domain, and, on the other hand, because European Muslims have now also engaged in an intensive study of Islam for the purpose of knowing its foundations as well as of adopting these tenets in their every-day lives in European societies.

European Scholarship

European scholarship of Islam after the 1950s was mostly still confined to the philological discipline of Arabic studies, but soon became immerged in area studies (Asia, Middle East, Africa) where the disciplines of anthropology and political science dominated. In consequence, Muslims and Islam were to be studied not only as representations of texts that dated from the past, but as living entities of today.[173]

The European scholars of Islam and the Muslim world received a wake-up call with the publication of Edward Said's *Orientalism* in 1979.[174] He argued that the academic objectivity claimed by these scholars was false, since many were infatuated with preconceived notions of Orientalism (see the previous chapter) about their objects of study. This image was perpetuated by the colonial supremacy of European countries in the Muslim world, and was reinforced by scholars in their academic work, Said claimed. Although Said's accusations were too broad and not always sufficiently substantiated,[175] they did hit a nerve in the European academic world. The word 'orientalist' gained a pejorative meaning, and various academic disciplines set out to reconsider their academic premises and methodologies. (This self-reflexion, in turn, sometimes swung too far the other way with academics blaming European colonial domination for all kinds of shortcomings in the Muslim world.)

In addition, the arrival of Muslims in the West brought a new challenge to the European study of Islam. Until the 1980s, studying Islam meant a trip to the library or to some faraway exotic land. But now Islam was in Europe, and Muslims were fellow-citizens in European societies and fellow-students in European universities. European scholars had to become used to the fact that Muslims and Islam, as objects of study, were part of the shared habitat of researchers, and that they responded to lectures and studies about them.[176] The fact that the politically and socially charged atmosphere in (mainly Western) European societies had put Muslims in a permanent spotlight during the late 1990s and the first decade of the twenty-first century merely added to the complexity of this interaction.[177]

The attacks of 9/11 and subsequent attacks by Muslim extremists in European cities have yet again changed the research agenda of Islam in Europe. During the first decade of the twenty-first century, most of the research on Islam and Muslims in Europe became embedded in the overall theme of security. This situation was not necessarily by scholarly design, but often prompted by the practical circumstance that national research funds during this period tended to prefer research proposals that had relevance to practical needs of the time.[178]

Nevertheless, a steady stream of studies on Islam and Muslims both within and outside Europe emerged from universities, think tanks, and investigative journalists. Most studies tended to discuss the Muslim identity in ethnic and national minority terms rather than religious terms. As opposed to what was quite common in public and political discourse, very few of these studies referred to Islam as a source of Muslims' actions. On the contrary, importance in this respect was attached much more to culture, ethnicity and migration. Most scholars identified religion as a secondary motivator like faith or identity, which highlighted existing issues and conflicts rather than being their instigating factor.[179]

European Muslim Studies of Islam

While the theological approach was gradually removed from European academic studies of Islam, European Muslims expressed the need for precisely that: the study of Islam as theology. The purpose of that kind of study was different from what was conducted at most European universities, however: these Muslims were not studying their religious behaviour or texts, but their own faith. In some Eastern European countries, such studies could be pursued at Islamic theological institutions and seminars. In Western European countries, on the other hand, there was an absence of a tradition as well as an infrastructure for the theological study of Islam.[180] Moreover, the Muslim communities in these societies lacked religious authorities that could guide or instruct them in these studies. This posed a problem with the growing need since the 1990s among Muslims for knowledge of Islamic theology. Their response, generally speaking, was twofold: some actually went abroad to study, while others resorted to self-study.

For Western European Muslims in particular the self-study was not easy, for they had limited access to Islamic theological literature and, more problematically, were often unable to read it since they were losing the native language of their parents. And even if they had overcome these hurdles, they needed some guidance in navigating the voluminous body of Islamic literature. Most Muslim students tried to find their way by means of the Internet; others by connections they might have with religious insitutions abroad.[181] Private initiatives emerged: lecture series, classes in mosques and Islamic centres, and the establishment of private Islamic seminaries. The problem of finding instructors with sufficient theological background remained, however. This situation was quite different from that in Eastern Europe where Muslims might turn to their *muftis* or leaders, or might study at one of the few Islamic theological faculties or seminaries. But even in that case, quite a few of the Muslim youth in Eastern Europe preferred to study abroad, either in Turkey or in the Middle East.[182]

One particular feature of Islamic studies as pursued by European Muslims deserves further attention. This is the so-called 'minority *fiqh*', the scholarship of Islamic theology that proclaims adaptations of Islamic rules to the particular context of Muslims living in the West.[183] The underlying argument of this scholarship is that *sharia* serves the needs and interests of Muslims and should therefore accommodate them rather than make their lives more difficult. As a result, rules of *sharia* should be adapted to the circumstances if need be. For example, a strict interpretation of *sharia* rule would oblige a Muslim in Scandinavia to fast the long hours of summer, or prohibit him from working in restaurants or establishments where pork or alcohol is served, or from participating in elections or political processes in non-Muslim countries; 'minority *fiqh*', on the other hand, would provide solutions for Muslims in the West to somehow move forward on the social-economic scale by participating without neglecting the essential tenets of their faith.[184]

While it is unknown to what extent European Muslims actually follow the interpretations of minority *fiqh*, the development of this scholarship by several international Islamic organizations is an interesting example of globalizing Islam: Muslim scholars of different nationalities, and even of both sunni and shi'a origin, join in regular meetings to discuss questions sent by Muslims in the West and, after long deliberation, issue their decisions (*fatwas*).[185] This particular branch of applied Islamic theology therefore has become a truly global or at least transnational undertaking, whereby knowledge from abroad is fed into a local European setting of political-legal freedoms and religious-cultural rejection.[186]

Minority *fiqh* is not uncontested. The abovementioned procedure and its theological methodologies are advocated by Islamic theologians like Yusuf Qaradawi in Qatar and Taha Jabir Al-Alwani in the United States, but are criticized by their colleagues from both the conservative and liberal sides of the theological spectrum. Conservatives, predominantly from the Gulf region, reject the minority *fiqh* methodology with the argument that Muslims are to abide by *sharia* rather than the other way round. Liberals, on the other hand, reject the fact that Muslims in the West are considered minority or are given exceptional treatment within the Islamic theological framework; according to them, Islamic theology needs thorough revision in order to meet the needs of *all* Muslims in the modern world.[187]

Whether this cauldron will – or should – lead to a 'European Islam', as some observers argue, is too early to tell, but we will reflect on this question in the next, and last, chapter.

Epilogue

Islamization of Europe, or Europeanization of Islam?

What do thirteen centuries of Islam in Europe tell us? Does the story of this inter-action consist of a series of episodes and events that we have conveniently thrown together under the title 'Islam in Europe'? Or is it justified to speak of a single ex-perience or narrative that continues through the centuries? And if so, how can we characterize this experience? We have seen in the previous chapters that the Euro-pean interaction with physical as well as virtual Islam has been very diverse. Mus-lims have been enemies and allies, foreigners and compatriots, Us and Them. Their civilization has been feared as aggressive and expansionist, but also praised for its religious tolerance and its culture that has produced great and innovative artists, scientists and intellectuals to which Europe is indebted. On the other hand, Europe has consistently upheld the picture of the Muslim Other that embodied everything that the European was not. Still, some patterns do emerge, and here the distinction between physical and virtual Islam is helpful.

Historical Patterns

With regard to physical Islam, there are few, if any, patterns to be discerned in the European interactions with Islam until the late nineteenth century. Both sides have alternated in conquering each other's territories and, in consequence, created societies of religiously mixed populations. Both sides have for centuries more or less continuously been active in raiding and enslaving each other's populations. The same mutuality applies to the exchange of diplomatic missions. The only forms of interaction in which there was little initiative on the Muslim side were trade, adventurous exploration and the establishment of resident embassies or commercial outposts – throughout the centuries of interaction, these domains were dominated by the Europeans.

In all these interactions one cannot speak of two unified blocks facing each other; both the Muslim and Christian sides were fractured by internal differences and strife, and common interests often called for military alliances and commercial treaties across the religious divide. On the other hand, both sides always upheld a self-image that strongly identified with religion – if not in the sense of commonly held religious beliefs, then at least as a shared culture. Religion as an identity marker was a source of many frictions within the Christian and Muslim communities, but also served as a rallying point when confronted with the other community. Let us examine this mechanism of diversity-in-unity by examining two issues: conquest and coexistence.

Thirteen centuries of belligerent interaction between Islam and Europe is not one of perpetual Muslim aggression vis-à-vis Europe, "the great *jihad par excellence*".[1] Both the Islamic Arab and Christian European worlds were driven by intermitted periods of hunger for conquest, and it was geographical proximity that made the other a target, not religious fervour. Religion did play a role, however, as the additional driving force that vindicated war. It is presumptuous and even a form of European self-victimization to assume that Muslims, whether Moors in the eighth century or Ottomans in the sixteenth and seventeenth centuries, saw Europe as their main target. They did not. The Arab Muslim conquests in the seventh and eighth centuries were targeting North Africa (westward) and Western Asia (eastward), while Spain was a mere extension of North Africa. And the Ottomans did indeed engage in regular military campaigns in Eastern Europe, but also did so towards Persia; the European domains made up only a part – albeit an economically and culturally important part – of their vast empire that stretched from Tunisia to Iraq and from Yemen to Hungary.

Even if the conquests in Europe were sideshows in Arab and Ottoman large-scale military operations, let us be clear on the fact that Europe was part of these conquests and consequently these wars are part of European history. But is it then justified to speak of the Crusades, the Reconquista, or the Balkan Wars as acts of European self-defence against Muslim aggression, as some authoritative figures tell us? Pope Urban II wanted his audience to believe so when he made his call for the First Crusade: his argument was that Jerusalem had to be re-taken. However, that call was made more than four centuries after the city had been taken by the Arab-Muslim armies. Moreover, we have seen that the recruitment for the crusade was successful for reasons that were more of an internal European nature than of foreign belligerency. In a similar vein, the historian Bernard Lewis claims that Europeans, by fighting in Spain against the Moors and rising in the Balkans against the Turk, were "restoring homelands to Christendom."[2] This is an odd remark from a historian. In the case of Spain, for instance, the Catholic claim of Reconquista may have been a justifiable emotion for the Catholic Spaniards of that time, but in the light of Spain's history of seven centuries of Roman rule, followed by two centuries of Visigoth Christian rule, and then eight centuries of Moorish Muslim rule, the claim that Spain was originally a Christian homeland is spurious. And in the case of the Ottoman Empire we have seen that many of the revolts were not people's uprisings against the yoke of the Ottoman, but often motivated by other factors.

Lewis takes the argument of European defence against Muslim aggression further when stating that the "complex process of European expansion and empire" has its "roots in the clash between Islam and Christendom": in his view, European expansionism is a result of the "long and bitter struggle of the conquered peoples of Europe, in east and west, to restore their homelands to Christendom and expel the Muslim peoples who had invaded and subjugated them."[3] In this European re-conquest it was "hardly to be expected" that the vanquished Muslims would be merely left at the borders, and so "the victorious liberators, having reconquered their own home territories, pursued their former masters whence they had come". These sweeping statements are simply untrue. The Europeans who engaged in imperialist ventures in Muslim lands in Asia and Africa were not the Europeans who had been former subjects of Muslim rule: of these former Muslim subjects, the Spaniards and Portuguese were mainly active across the Atlantic, and the Balkan peoples have not engaged in any imperialist adventures at all. On the contrary, it was the European peoples that had *not* been affected by Moorish, Ottoman or any 'Islamic' domination, such as the English, French, Russians and Dutch, who were the colonists and imperialists in the African, Asian and Arab domains of the Muslim world. This can hardly be called a reaction to Muslim aggression.

Moreover, the imagery of European Christians rising against and expelling the dreaded Muslim occupier seems more a retroactive use of emotions and terminology that belonged to the American Revolution or the Second World War than substantiated by historical facts. The European-Christian "victorious liberators" (Lewis' terminology) in the Ottoman domains had to resort to carnage and conversion to create a "Christian homeland" that they had only recently invented. And the Catholic kings, when "liberating" Christian subjects from their Muslim rulers, did not take them into the fold of Christendom but recognized them as a separate community, first tolerated with their own religious courts and rites, just like the Muslims and the Jews, and later persecuted by the Inquisition.

I would argue that the wars and insurgencies against the two main Muslim powers in Europe – Ummayad ('Moorish') and Ottoman – were not Christian uprisings against centuries of bondage, but were part of a development on a much grander scale that took place between the fifteenth and twentieth centuries in Europe: the formation of nation-states where people with a single identity (cultural, ethnic, linguistic, religious) lived within a single territory under majority rule. Oppressive and violent means were often deployed to achieve this goal, starting with the expulsion and forced conversions of Muslims and Jews in Spain in the late fifteenth century (the Jews of Western Europe had already experienced extradition in the twelfth and thirteenth centuries), then religious wars in Europe in the sixteenth and seventeenth centuries, followed by the fragmentation of the Ottoman and Austro-Hungarian Empires and, most recently, the civil wars in Yugoslavia in the 1990s.

An interaction of an entirely different nature between Europe and physical Islam was the coexistence of religious communities as a result of conquests by one of the parties. It is not always clear to what extent the conqueror was welcomed; this seems to have been the case when the Arabs conquered Spain and in some instances of the early periods of Ottoman conquests in the Balkans; but such welcome seems to have been absent during the Crusades in the Middle East and the Reconquista in Spain. Nevertheless the reaction of subjugated peoples appears to have been more pragmatic than principled: if the conqueror provided security, a reasonable tax burden and a degree of religious and cultural freedom then he was acceptable to most people.

In the situation of religiously mixed societies religion played a prominent role in the regulation of social order. Religious identity was such that it provided not only a powerful self-identity, but also a social frame of reference. Social and political life in religiously mixed communities might be determined by a variety of factors, and piety among their peoples might differ from person to person, but the underlying structure was controlled by the dichotomy of believer and unbeliever. Religion was the most important identity marker that decided the demarcation lines between the communities in terms of believers versus unbelievers and accordingly set the rules of engagement between those communities. This order did not necessarily have to reflect everyday reality in the interaction among people, but was imposed from above: the ruling elite represented the believer and all other communities were categorized under the single title of unbelievers.

Such was the case in the Christian as well as Islamic realms in Europe until well into the nineteenth century. Religion was the measuring stick that maintained fixed boundaries between believers and unbelievers (heretics as third category had to be persecuted) that could at times perhaps be crossed socially and economically, but only within certain limits. Sexual relations, joining the military, being eligible for slavery or becoming part of the ruling elite were such limits, and crossing these lines required that one converted. Tensions and revolts in realms with religiously mixed societies in pre-modern Europe were often for social or economic reasons, but almost automatically acquired a religious dimension since that was the factor delineating the structural differences in such society.

If there is any pattern to be seen in the interaction between Europe and physical Islam, it is that they have interacted in a variety of ways like any other countries or communities at any given time. The main difference is that Europeans and Muslims did not *feel* that they were the same. This was the domain of the interaction between Europe and the Islam that we have called virtual Islam. Whereas we found few patterns in the case of physical Islam, the interaction with virtual Islam – that is all interaction involving ideas, images and knowledge about Islam – has been quite consistent through the centuries. This interaction can be summarized as conflict: in the studies, polemics and images of Islam, Europeans have mostly – not always – maintained a position of antagonism towards Islam. Even the Protestants who claimed preference for Turkish over Catholic rule still dismissed Islam as a heresy at best. Islam represented more than a mere religion; it was presented as the opposite of European Christian identity, and this otherness was discerned in many aspects, some of which have survived until now with remarkable tenacity: Islam is intolerant; Islam is degrading towards women; Islam incites violence; Islam is anti-intellectual; Islam prevents progress; Islam is against democracy and secularism – and to all of these we must add: unlike us, Europeans of Christian stock. These conceptions and views of Islam can easily be justified by historical facts. But we may equally easily find historical facts that will back up the opposite argument. The diversity of the interaction of Europe with physical Islam provides us with such a rich source of historical realities – intellectualism as well as ignorance, benevolent rule and despotism, religious tolerance and oppression of religion – that they can be used in any kind of argument. We have seen in the Introduction to what different conclusions two eminent historians like Bulliet and Lewis have come on the basis of the same history of European-Islamic relations.

The explanation for the negative image of Islam as the European Other must therefore be sought not in physical Islam, but in virtual Islam. Physical Islam represents the inclusive Other who is different and strange and perhaps even repulsive, but who at best is a source of fascination or admiration, and at worst is someone one has to put up with in order to conduct business or keep diplomatic ties or maintain neighbourly relations. Virtual Islam, on the other hand, is a representation of the exclusive Other who is truly different in a negative way.[4] Virtual Islam allowed the European to develop or maintain ideas about Islam without the need to check with reality. Much, if not most, of the image of Islam and its adherents has been developed, studied, cherished and passed on by the many Europeans who had never met a Muslim in their lives. Insofar as they received first-hand information from Ottoman lands and later also from Muslim societies in European Empires, this information was not provided to them by those who lived there, but by their compatriot Europeans who travelled or worked in those lands and returned with their personal experiences. Even in societies where Muslims and Christians lived together, as in the Balkans, the togetherness was mostly one of segregation: either they lived removed from each other, or they knew little of each other.

Patterns into the Present

The European initiatives to create nation-states that were ethnically, linguistically, culturally, and religiously homogeneous reached an apotheosis with the two great wars in the first half of the twentieth century. After that, Europe took a radically different course by implementing a system that had already been under construction for some time: a political and legal structure that allowed for diversity by guaranteeing fundamental rights and a rule of law. Religion as the main source of social and legal structuring was replaced by the notions of liberty and equality: each individual was to pursue his own lifestyle, voice his own opinion and practise his own religion, and in doing so all individuals were to be treated equally before the law regardless of their religion, gender, colour or political affiliation.

In Western Europe the sudden and numerous presence of Muslims since the 1970s has challenged this new political-legal constellation, not because Muslims were against it – on the contrary, it provided them with the freedom to maintain their identity – but because it revealed that the underlying infrastructure of national, cultural, linguistic, ethnic and religious unity was still in place, either in practice or as an assumed quality of society. It was a self-imposed predicament: Europeans cherished the new political-legal values that granted freedoms to everyone, but these same values demanded that Europeans allowed people to have and practise religious and cultural values and customs that were alien to them. The antipathy that some Western Europeans harboured against foreign migrants who came in large numbers from the 1970s onwards was therefore not only of a socio-economical nature –

they were accused of stealing jobs and undermining European society by purportedly refusing to integrate – but also of a cultural nature: allowing different values and customs that were allegedly not European was considered disruptive to European society. This applied in particular to Muslims, resulting in the particular form of anxiety called Islamophobia.

Nevertheless, Muslims in Western Europe were gradually entering all echelons of society. This is a dramatic change from all previous centuries of Muslim-Christian coexistence where religion dictated one's position in society. As mentioned, the new political-legal constellation in Europe had replaced this social order with one based on non-discrimination and personal liberty. These rights were arguably already in place in earlier times (one needs to just think of the American and French bills of rights of the late eighteenth century), but it took another century and a half to put these rights into practice: Jews, coloured, women and gays all had to fight prolonged battles to claim equal treatment. The European Muslims of today may be suffering similar forms of discrimination, but they definitely benefitted from the many minority struggles that preceded theirs. The rapid rise of some Muslims to positions of prominence in European politics and government, and their gradual formation into representative bodies and vocal lobby groups are mere examples of their relatively advantageous position in this respect. In the particular case of the Muslims, however, there are two factors that distinguish them from other minority communities: religion and historical ballast.

With regard to religion we have seen that modern Europe is distinctively secularized in two ways: religion is not important in the lives of the European majority, and that same majority does not appreciate the manifestation of religion in the public domain. This attitude has become incorporated into the European psyche and many Europeans therefore feel ill at ease when confronted with actions and behaviour that are of a distinct religious nature. We have seen that most modern scholars study such actions and behaviour with a focus on issues like ethnicity, culture and migration, with religion merely being an additional factor that may compound social and economic processes. Much of the political and public discourse, however, takes the other extreme by explaining Muslim behaviour in terms of religion only. The sale of Qurans in the Western world peaked after the attacks of 9/11, as did that of many other books on Islam. This is a continuation of the centuries-old European tradition of studying Muslims by means of Islamic scripture and texts. When I am invited by teachers' unions, police academies or medical schools to talk "about Islam", they never want to know about the prophet, the meaning of Ramadan or pilgrimage to Mecca, or the tenets of Islam: they want to know if there is anything special about these people that makes them different – because that is what they experience in their interactions with them at work – and assume that it is Islam.

Apparently religion has not disappeared from the social equation in Europe even though it has dissipated as an official form of ordering society and modern Europe has to a large extent secularized. Religion has stayed, but taken different forms. While secularization gradually removed religion from the public domain, the great European narrative of 'Christian Europe' is continued, albeit in a cultural manner. This religious anchoring of European identity by default excluded Jews and later also Muslims. Granted, it is fashionable to speak of 'Judeo-Christian civilization', but the 'Judeo' part is only a politically correct supplement that came into use after the horrors of the Holocaust. In addition to this cultural meaning, religion also plays a second, important role in modern Europe. In times when religion is of much less importance to a majority of the European population,[5] their understanding and consideration for those who are still religious have also become less. From the perspective of religious people, regardless of their religion, such environment can be considered unfriendly or even hostile. This staunchly secular or even anti-religious environment is not exclusively targeting devout Muslims, because it targets all religious believers, but it has definitely contributed to the Muslims' sense of alienation, a feeling multiplied by the fact that they are mostly of foreign origin.

The second factor that distinguishes Muslims from other minorities is the historical ballast of the old notion of the Muslim as the European Other. Here again we see an uninterrupted continuation of Othering that has taken place in the previous centuries: Muslims are not European, because they are not secular, not woman-friendly, intrinsically violent, primitive in their customs. An often-heard explanation of this different attitude inserts a time element into this process of Othering: the Muslim is placed in another, pre-modern time from that of the modern European, as if he is literally behind, so that the two live together but in parallel time frames.[6] Some add yet another element to the Muslim Other: he is not merely different, but a foreigner who does not belong here. We have seen this with regard to the Moors and the Ottoman Turk, and nowadays again in the reaction to Muslim radicals and terrorists. The European leftist radicals and terrorists of the 1970s were feared, frowned upon and sometimes prosecuted, but never was it suggested that they should be deported, as has been proposed with Muslim radicals and terrorists who were born and raised in Europe. In the former case, the Other was 'our' problem; in the latter case the Other was a problem imposed on 'us' from the outside. A large part of this sentiment has been attributed to the changing notion of borders;

whereas they used to keep people out, they were crossed by immigrants and have now been made permeable by globalism and transnationalism.[7]

That said, we must keep in mind that it does not hold for all Europeans; some do not see a problem at all, and many Europeans work hard and conscientiously to understand their Muslim patients, juvenile delinquents, students and neighbours so that they can more easily engage with them.

While the issues of religion and historical ballast may have made the position of the modern European Muslim different from that of other minorities, and while the main obstacle to the devout Muslim may be the secular nature of modern Europe (an obstacle the Muslim shares with devout Christians, Jews, Hindus and other faithful), the most pressing problem in current times to my mind is the issue of tolerance. I contend that tolerance has undergone a drastic transformation because of the modern notion of equality.

In earlier times, racial, religious and gender differences were regulated by hierarchical orders that gave everyone pre-fixed positions in the social order, whether divinely or imperially ordained: "[i]mperial rule is historically the most successful way of incorporating difference and facilitating (requiring is more accurate) peaceful existence."[8] Equality, on the other hand, demands an affirmative recognition of others and of each other's differences. Consequently, equality has drastically altered the notion of toleration. Before, the ruling community or majority indulged itself by allowing for certain differences in its subjects or the minority, respectively. From its position of power, it determined what the limits of acceptable differences were as practised by its subjects or minorities, and demanded full recognition of its own ways. This situation no longer holds. Equality has turned the power mechanism that was essential to tolerance into a reciprocal process: we will recognize you (and your differences) if you do the same to us.[9]

In the context of modern Europe, this change is a serious challenge to the perceived self-evidence of the culture of the majority. According to the principles of their own political-legal structure, native Europeans cannot claim a majority position demanding that their religious or cultural values are imposed on others. The notion of tolerance has changed accordingly and has acquired a new meaning: as recognition. One is to recognize the differences of the other – within the framework of the parameters set by the law, of course – but this has become subject to negotiation: the European Muslim is asked to acknowledge loyalty to his society, while the Muslim is prepared to do so only on the condition that he is recognized as Muslim, a notion of religious identity that many secular Europeans find difficult to deal with.

The transformation of the notion of tolerance lies at the heart of the European struggle with immigrants and, more particularly, Muslims. The European demand for cultural integration may contradict the immigrant's or Muslim's right to be different, and to be treated as an equal in that respect. According to Talal Asad, this is at the root of Europe's identity crisis. He argues that Europeans are not self-assuredly declaring who they are, but anxiously demanding that Others recognize who they, the Europeans, are: "(instead of) 'This is my name,' we now declare 'I need you to recognize me by that name'."[10]

... To Be Extrapolated into the Future?

From this evaluation of the present let us now look into the future. How will the interaction between Islam and Europe develop? Some observers speak hopefully of the emergence of a "European Islam"; others are worried about the trend of orthodoxy among European Muslims and fear an 'Islamization' of Europe. Have Europe and Islam indeed reached a juncture that will prove crucial to their future, so that we are facing a choice between either "Islamization of Europe" or "Europanization of Islam", as some would have us believe?[11]

From a European perspective the notion of "Islamization of Europe" is not a neutral observation indicating that Europe is experiencing more of the presence of Muslims – and hence Islam – than it had before; it is a notion of concern, possibly of fear. It is the anxiety about Europe losing its identity, irrevocably transforming into something that it should not. We have seen that it is hard to assess the exact numbers of Muslims in Europe, and that it is almost impossible to gauge their religiousness, but they are a tiny minority. Also, the fear that Islam by its nature drives Muslims to impose their values on their environment is not justified by the facts. Insofar as they claim space in the secular European domain to apply certain rules of Islam, it appears to be exclusively for their own use. Of course there are zealous Muslims in Europe calling for the spread of Islam and who welcome any convert to Islam, but they are not unlike the many Christian missionary movements active in Europe. But even if, for the sake of argument, we were to assume that Muslims have hidden agendas of domination, it is quite striking that Europeans demonstrate so little faith in the strength of their own values and structures to withstand the allegedly different Islamic values of a very small minority.

Just as the notion "Islamization of Europe" is biased because it reflects an anxiety, so is its mirror-notion "Europeanization of Islam" based on preconceptions because it reflects – from the perspective of many Europeans – an optimistic anticipation. It is the expectation that Muslims, under the influence of European liberalism and enlightenment, will transform their Islam into a moderate religion. It is therefore dumbfounding to many Europeans that the younger generation of Muslims in Europe in particular is more religiously orthodox than the previous generation: how can someone who is born and raised in a European secular, liberal society and education system adhere to religion even more strongly than his or her parents? The puzzlement about this alleged paradox is typical for Europeans; Americans, for example, will have fewer problems understanding this situation because they are much more accustomed to public intellectuals, scholars, scientists and politicians who are also devout believers and publicly declare themselves to be so.

If there is any Europeanization of Islam, it is that Muslims are living in Europe, and have adopted the European political-legal framework that provides them with opportunities to practise their religion in ways they want to – opportunities that they would not have in most Muslim-majority countries. At present many Muslims in Europe use their freedom of religion to pursue an orthodox interpretation of Islam, but this in itself does not justify the conclusion that such development is anathema to European values or identity, nor that it will continue with the next generations of European Muslims. What we are currently witnessing is Muslims of migrant origin who are coming to terms with their particular European environment as well as with an understanding of their identity, and consequently will have to negotiate ways to adapt to a European religious-cultural and political-legal environment and find ways to solve conflicts between that environment and their Islamic tenets and identities. This dialectic of critical engagement by European Muslims is not new: it is a process that began in the period between the two World Wars[12] and has regained its intensity from the 1990s onwards.[13] An interesting role in this respect is being played by Balkan Muslims who have a much longer and richer experience with Islam in Europe, and therefore deplore the fact that Western European Muslims, as relative newcomers to the European scene, have so little, if any, interest in their experiences.[14]

The two-choice question between Islamization of Europe and Europanization of Islam, therefore, is a misguided way of looking at the phenomenon of 'Islam in Europe'. If there ever was a choice with regard to the future of Islam and its role in Europe, it is a choice that Europe needs to make: will it adhere to its political-legal values, such as liberalism, equality, human rights and democracy, and by consequence allow for and recognize the many differences that new Europeans will bring, or will it block these differences by emphasizing a homogenuous set of – allegedly

'European' – religious-cultural values? The burka bans in Belgium and France are a typical sign of the latter: irrespective of whether one agrees or disagrees with those bans, they were essentially a legalization of cultural values, of 'this is how we do things here'. Although enshrining cultural values in legal statutes may reaffirm European cultural identities, such an approach carries the distinct risk that it denies other, fundamental values proclaimed by the European political-legal framework.

Notes

Introduction

1   See, e.g., Bruce Bawer, *While Europe Slept: How Radical Islam is Destroying Europe from Within* (New York: Doubleday, 2006); Claire Berlinski *Menace in Europe: Why the Continent's Crisis Is America's, Too* (New York: Crown Forum, 2006); Christopher Caldwell, *Reflections on the Revolution in Europe* (New York: Anchor, 2010); Walter Laqueur, *The Last Days of Europe: Epitaph for an Old Continent* (New York: St Martin's Griffin, 2009); Mark Steyn, *Lights Out: Islam, Free Speech And The Twilight Of Europe* (Montreal: Stockade Books, 2009); Bruce Thornton, *Decline & Fall: Europe's Slow Motion Suicide* (New York: Encounter Books, 2007); Bat Ye'or, *Eurabia: The Euro-Arab Axis* (Madison, NJ: Fairleigh Dickinson University Press, 2005).

2   See, e.g., Jonathan Lyons, *The House of Wisdom. How the Arabs Transformed Western Civilization* (New York: Bloomsbury Press, 2009); Mark Graham, *How Islam created the Modern World* (Beltsville (Mi): Amana Publications, 2006); George Makdisi. *The Rise of Humanism in Classical Islam and the Christian West*. Edinburgh: Edinburgh University Press 1991; George Saliba, *Islamic Science and the Making of the European Renaissance* (Boston: MIT Press, 2007); Jim Al-Khalili, *The House of Wisdom: How Arabic Science Saved Ancient Knowledge and Gave Us the Renaissance* (New York: The Penguin Group, 2011).

3   Richard Bulliet, *The Case for a Islamo-Christian Civilization*, Columbia University Press, 2006 and Bernard Lewis, *Europe and Islam*, Washington: The AEI Press, 2007.

4   Madeleine Heyward, 'What Constitutes Europe?: Religion, Law and Ideology in the Draft Constitution for the European Union', *Hanse Law Review*, 2005, pp. 227–235; Iordan Bărbulescu & Gabriel Andreescu, 'References to God and the Christian Tradition in the Treaty Establishing a Constitution for Europe: An Examination of the Background', *Journal for the Study of Religions and Ideologies*, 2009 (Vol. 8, Nr. 24), pp. 207–223.

5   See, e.g., Jan Assman, 'Collective Memory and Cultural Identity' in Jan Assman and Tonio Hölscher (eds.), *Kultur und Gedachtnis*, Frankfurt/Main: Suhrkamp, 1988, pp. 9–19 and Alon Confino, 'Collective Memory and Cultural History: Problems of Method', *The American Historical Review*, 1997 (Vol. 102, No. 5), pp. 1386–1403.

6   Tony Judt, 'The Past is Another Country: Myth and Memory in Postwar Europe', Dae-
     dalus, 1992 (Vol. 121, No. 4), pp. 83–118 (p. 84).

7   David Blanks & Michael Frassetto, Western views of Islam in medieval and early modern
     Europe: perceptions of the other, Basingstroke: Macmillan, 1999; Norman Daniel, Islam
     and the West. The Making of an Image, Edinburgh, Edinburgh University Press, 1960;
     John Tolan, Saracens. Islam in the Medieval European Imagination, New York, Columbia
     University Press, 2002, and Sons of Ishmael: Muslims through European eyes in the Middle
     Ages, Gainesville, University Press of Florida, 2008. See also: Franco Cardini, Europe
     and Islam, London: Wiley-Blackwell, 2001; Bernard Lewis, Islam in the West, New York/
     Oxford: Oxford University Press, 1993; Peter O'Brien, European Perceptions of Islam and
     America from Saladin to George W. Bush: Europe's Fragile Ego Uncovered, London: Palgrave
     Macmillan, 2009.

8   See Chapters 2 and 3.

9   See Chapter 3.

10   In doing so, this book may be considered a contribution to the recent thinking on
     transnational and transcultural history. That approach to history aims to get away
     from the conventional focus of the nation state, and to study those mechanisms and in-
     fluences that are not confined to boundaries or single peoples. Hence the emphasis on
     the importance of phenomena and processes like culture, migration, science, multi-
     nationals, ideologies. (See, e.g., Madeleine Herren et al., Transcultural History. Theories,
     Methods, Sources, Heidelberg/New York: Springer, 2012; Akira Iriye, Global and Transna-
     tional History, New York: Palgrave MacMillan, 2013).

11   See, for instance, Fransesco Gabrielli, Arab Historians of the Crusades, Los Angeles: Uni-
     versity of California Press, 1984; Bernard Lewis, The Muslim Discovery of Europe, New
     York/London: W.W. Norton, 1982; Nabil Matar, Europe through Arab Eyes, 1578–1727, New
     York, Columbia University Press, 2009; Robert Woltering, Occidentalisms in the Arab
     world: ideology and images of the West in the Egyptian media (Library of modern Middle East
     studies, 96), London: I.B. Tauris, 2011.

12   Marshall G.S. Hodgson. The Venture of Islam, Volume One: The Classical Age of Islam (Chi-
     cago: Chicago University Press, 1977), pp. 57–59.

13   See Chapter 5 for detailed discussion of this quote.

14   This conceptualization is largely based on Clifford Geertz, 'Religion as a Cultural Sys-
     tem' (in Anthropological Approaches to the Study of Religion, Michael Banton (ed.), ASA
     Monographs, 3. London: Tavistock Publications, 1966, pp. 1–46), and Talal Asad's ad-
     ditions thereto in 'The Construction of Religion as an Anthropological Category' (in
     his Genealogies of Religion; Discipline and Reasons of Power in Christianity and Islam, Balti-
     more MD: Johns Hopkins University Press, 1993 (1st ed. 1982), pp. 27–54).

15 Power was the element that Talal Asad argued was missing in Clifford Geertz' definition of religion (see previous footnote).

16 John Horton, (ed.), *Liberalism, Multiculturalism and Tolerance*, New York: St. Martin's Press, 1993, p. 3. See also Will Kymlicka, *A liberal theory of minority rights*, Oxford: Clarendon Press, 1995; Preston King, *Tolerance*, London: George Allen & Unwin Ltd, 1976; J. Raz, *Ethics in the public domain. Essays in the Morality of Law and Politics*, Oxford: Clarendon Pres, 1994.

17 Catriona McKinnon, *Tolerance. A Critical Introduction*, London: Routledge, 2006, pp. 3, 14–15.

18 Idem.

19 Wendy Brown describes tolerance mainly in terms of power (in: *Regulating Aversion. Tolerance in the Age of Identity and Empire*, Princeton University Press, 2006, pp. 25 ff.).

20 McKinnon, *Tolerance*, 2006, pp. 18 ff.; Aaron Tyler, *Islam, the West, and Tolerance*, London: Palgrave Macmillan, 2008, pp. 69 ff. Also: Michael Walzer, *On tolerance*, New Haven and London: Yale University Press, 1997.

21 A.J. Conyers, *The Long Truce: How Tolerance made the World Safer for Power and Profit*, Dallas: Spencer Publishing Company, 2001, pp. 7–8; George Carey, 'Tolerating religion' in Susan Mendus (ed.), *The Politics of Tolerance in Modern Life*, Durham: Duke University Press, 2000, pp. 45–66; McKinnon, *Tolerance*, 2006, pp. 22–23.

22 The aforementioned Bernard Lewis is one of those who supports that view.

23 See for a theoretical exposition on this issue: Rodney Stark & Roger Finke, *Acts of Faith. Explaining the Human Side of Religion*, Berkeley/London: University of California Press, 2000, pp. 141–146.

24 Francis Barker et. al. (eds.), *Europe and Its Others*, Colchester: University of Essex, 1985; Diez, Thomas, 'Europe's Others and the Return to Geopolitics' in *Cambridge Review of International Affairs*, 2004 (Vol. 17, No. 2), pp. 319–335; Neumann, Iver B., *Uses of the Other. 'The East' in European Identity Formation*, Minneapolis: University of Minnesota Press, 1999; Hall, Stuart, 'The West and the Rest: Discourse and Power' in Stuart Hall & Bram Gieben (eds.), *Formations of Modernity*. Polity Press, 1992; Inayatullah, Naeem and Davind L. Blaney, *International Relations and the Problem of Difference*, London/New York: Routledge, 2004.

25 Tony Judt, *A Grand Illusion. An Essay on Europe*, London: Penguin Books, 1997, p. 46.

26 Hall, Stuart, 'The West and the Rest: Discourse and Power' in Stuart Hall & Bram Gieben (eds.), *Formations of Modernity*. Polity Press, 1992, pp. 276–320.

27 Iver B. Neumann and Jennifer M. Welsch, 'The Other in European self-definition: an addendum to the literature on international society' in *Review of International Studies*, 1991 (Vol. 17), p. 330.

28   Stuart Hall, 'The West and the Rest', p. 314.

29   Mary Anne Perkins, *Christendom And European Identity: The Legacy of a Grand Narrative since 1789*, Berlin/New York: Walter de Gruyter, 2004, p. xi.

30   Idem.

31   Idem, p. 187.

32   Bernard Lewis, *Islam and the West*, New York/Oxford: Oxford University Press, 1993, p. 17.

1. Uncivilized Europe (700–1000 CE)

1   Jacques Le Goff, *La civilization de l' Occident Médiéval*, Paris, Editions Arthaud, 1984; Peter Heather, *Empires and Barbarians: The Fall of Rome and the Birth of Europe*, Oxford, Oxford University Press, 2010.

2   This is the so-called Pirenne Thesis, as suggested by Henri Pirenne in his *Mahomet et Charlemagne*, first published in 1937.

3   E.g., Gene W. Heck, *Charlemagne, Muhammad and the Arab roots of Capitalism*, Berlin, De Gruyter, 2006, p. 164; Eliyahu A. Ashtor, *A Social and Economical History of the Near East in the Middle Ages*, London, Collins, 1976.

4   Robert Latouche, *The Birth of Western Economy. Economic Aspects of the Dark Ages*, London, Methuen, 1967, p. 47.

5   David Lewis, *God's Crucible: Islam and the Making of Europe*, New York, Norton & Company, 2008, p. 286.

6   Conversion to Christianity was one of the pretexts for conquests, however, given the fact that most conquered peoples were already Christian; Diarmaid MacCulloch, *A history of Christianity: the first three thousand years*, London, Penguin Press, 2009, p. 349.

7   Diarmaid MacCulloch, *A history of Christianity: the first three thousand years*, London, Penguin Press, 2009, p. 349.

8   Marshal G.S. Hodgson, *The Venture of Islam, Volume 1: The Classical Age of Islam*, Chicago, University of Chicago Press, 1977; John J. Saunders, *A History of Medieval Islam*, London, Routledge, 1965.

9   Hodgson, *The Venture of Islam*; Saunders, *A History of Medieval Islam*.

10   Andrew M. Watson, *Agricultural Innovation in the Early Islamic World. The Diffusion of Crops and Farming Techniques, 700–1100*, Cambridge, Cambridge University Press, 1983.

11   Dimitri Gutas, *Greek Thought, Arabic Culture: The Graeco-Arabic Translation Movement in Baghdad and Early Abbasid Society*, London, Routledge, 1998; Hodgson, *Venture of Islam*; Jonathan Lyons, *The House of Wisdom: how the Arabs transformed Western civilization*, London, Bloomsbury, 2009; Jim Al-Khalili, *The House of Wisdom: How Arabic*

Science Saved Ancient Knowledge and Gave Us the Renaissance, London, Penguin Press, 2011.

12 E.g., Hugh Goddard, *A history of Christian-Muslim relations*, Edinburgh, Edinburgh University Press, 2000, pp. 36–37.

13 Walter E. Kaegi, *Muslim Expansion and Byzantine Collapse in North Africa*, Cambridge, Cambridge University Press, 2010.

14 Warren Treadgold, *A Concise History of Byzantium*, Basingstoke, Palgrave, 2001, p. 114.

15 Treadgold, *A Concise History of Byzantium*, p. 116.

16 Thomas Glick, *Islamic and Christian Spain in the Early Middle Ages*, Princeton: Princeton University Press, 1979, p. 165–193.

17 Kenneth Baxter Wolff, *Conquerors and Chroniclers of Early Medieval Spain*, Liverpool: Liverpool University Press, 1990.

18 "The state of affairs in Hispania [prior to the Muslim conquest] could best be described as tyranny restrained by anarchy" (Lewis, *God's Crucible*, p. 112); Also: Anwar G. Chejne, 'Islamization and Arabization in al-Andalus', in: Speros Vyronis Jr. (ed.), *Islam and Cultural Change in the Middle Ages*, Wiesbaden, Otto Harrassowitz, 1973, p. 66.

19 Lewis, *God's Crucible*, p. 286.

20 Richard Fletcher, *Moorish Spain*, London, Phoenix, 1992, p. 65.

21 E.g., Watson, *Agricultural Innovation in the Early Islamic World*.

22 Alex Metcalfe, *Muslims and Christians in Norman Sicily*, London, Routledge Curzon Taylor & Francis Group, 2003, pp. 22–23.

23 Ahmad Aziz, *A history of Islamic Sicily*, Edinburgh, Edinburgh University Press, 1975, pp. 18–21.

24 MacCulloch, *A History of Christianity*, pp. 342–343.

25 'No compulsion in religion': la ikrâh fî dîn (Quran 5:99).

26 Gerald R. Hawting, *The First Dynasty of Islam: The Ummayad Caliphate AD 661–750*, London, Routledge, 1986, pp. 1–10.

27 E.g., Daniel C. Dennett, *Conversion and the Poll Tax in Early Islam*, Cambridge MA, Harvard University Press, 1950; Lewis, *God's Crucible*, p. 175.

28 Youssef Courbage and Philippe Fargues, *Christians and Jews Under Islam*, London, Tauris, 1997; Richard W. Bulliet, *Conversion to Islam in the Medieval Period: An Essay in Quantitative History*, Cambridge MA: Harvard University Press, 1979; Alwyn Harrison, 'Behind the curve: Bulliet and Conversion to Islam in Al-Andalus Revisted,' in *Al-Masaq: Islam and the Medieval Mediterranean*, 2012 (Vol. 24, No. 1), pp. 35–51.

29 Mikel de Epalza, 'Mozarabs: An Emblematic Christian Minority in Islamic Al-Andalus' in Salma Khadra Jayyusi (ed.), *The Legacy of Muslim Spain*, Leiden: Brill, 1992, pp. 159–160.

30 James Muldoon, *Popes, Lawyers and Infidels*, Liverpool, Liverpool University Press, 1979, pp. 30–31.

31 Marius Canard, 'Les relations politiques et sociales entre Byzance et les Arabes', *Dumbartons Oaks Papers*, 1964 (Vol. 18), pp. 43–44. See also Canard's *Byzance et les musulmans du Proche Orient*, London: Variorum Reprints, 1973.

32 H. Gibb, 'Constantinople', *The Encyclopedia of Islam*, 1982 (Vol. 2, Part 2); Canard, 'Les relations politiques et sociales entre Byzance et les Arabes', p. 43.

33 Gibb, 'Constantinople', p. 534; Nadia El-Cheikh, *Byzantium viewed by the Arabs*, Cambridge MA, Harvard University Press, 2004, pp. 210–211.

34 Sami Abu-Shahlieh, *L'Impact de la religion sur l'ordre juridique: cas de l'Égypte: non-musulmans en pays d'Islam*, Fribourg, Éditions universitaires, 1979; Laurent and Annie Chabry, *Politique et minorités au Proche-Orient*, Paris, Maisonneuve & Larose, 1984; Kessmat Elgeddawy, *Relations entre systèmes confessionnels et laïque en Droit International Privé*, Paris, Dalloz, 1971; Antoine Fattal, *Le statut légal des non-musulmans en pays d'Islam*, Beirut, Imprimerie Catholique, 1958; Bat Ye'or, *The Dhimmī: Jews and Christians under Islam*, London/Toronto, Associated University Press, 1983.

35 E.g., Maria R. Menocal, *The Ornament of the World: How Muslims, Jews and Christians Created a Culture of Tolerance in Medieval Spain*, Boston, Little Brown, 2002.

36 Charles Dalli, 'From Islam to Christianity: the Case of Sicily', in: Carvallo Joaquim (ed.), *Religion, Ritual and Mythology: Aspects of Identity Formation in Europe*, Pisa, Pisa University Press, 2006; Fletcher, *Moorish Spain*; Vivian Mann and Thomas Glick (eds), *Convivencia: Jews, Muslims and Christians in Medieval Spain*, New York, George Braziller, 1992; James Powell, *Muslims under Latin Rule, 1100–1300*, Princeton, Princeton University Press, 1990.

37 Metcalfe, *Muslims and Christians in Norman Sicily*, pp. 13–14; Aziz, *A history of Islamic Sicily*, p. 15.

38 Metcalfe, *Muslims and Christians in Norman Sicily*, p. 17; Aziz, *A history of Islamic Sicily*, pp. 17–23.

39 Jessica A. Coope, *The Martyrs of Cordoba: Community and Family Conflict in an Age of Mass Conversion*, Lincoln, University of Nebraska, 1995; Kenneth B. Wolf, *Christian Martyrs in Muslim Spain*, Cambridge, Cambridge University Press, 1988.

40 Chejne, 'Islamization and Arabization in al-Andalus', pp. 69–70; Coope, *The Martyrs of Cordoba*.

41 Kenneth Baxter Wolf, 'Mohammed as Antichrist in Ninth-Century Cordoba' in Mark D. Meyerson & Edward D. English (eds.), *Christians, Muslims, and Jews in Medieval and Early Modern Spain. Interaction and Cultural Change*, Notre Dame (I.): University of Notre Dame Press, 2000, p. 5.

42 Coope, *The Martyrs of Cordoba*, referring to Bulliet (*Conversion to Islam*), pp. 124–128.

43 Hitchcock, *Mozarabs in Medieval and Early Modern Spain*, pp. 41–51.

44 Robert Bartlett, *The Making of Europe. Conquest, Colonization and Cultural Change, 950–1350*, London, Penguin Books, 1995, p. 305; El-Cheikh, *Byzantium viewed by the Arabs*, p. 83.

45 El-Cheikh, *Byzantium viewed by the Arabs*, p. 160.

46 Barbara Kreutz, 'Ships. Shipping, and the implications of change in the early medieval Mediterranean,' *Viator*, 1976 (Vol. 7).

47 Kreutz, 'Ships. Shipping, and the implications of change in the early medieval Mediterranean,' p. 88.

48 As reported by the Arab chronicler Ibn al-Athir; translated by Edmond Fagnan, *Annales du Maghreb et de l'Espagne*, Alger, 1898.

49 See for the alliance and following campaign: Richard Hodges and David Whitehouse, *Mohammed, Charlemagne and the Origins of Europe: archeology and the Pirenne thesis*, London, Duckworth, 1983, p. 120; Lewis, *God's Crucible*, p. 244 ff.; Barton Sholod, *Charlemagne in Spain: The Cultural Legacy of Roncesvalles*, Geneva, Droz, 1966.

50 See for a description of the Song of Roland, e.g., Robert Francis Cook, *The Sense of the Song of Roland*, New York, Ithaca Press, 1987; Lewis, *God's Crucible*, pp. 255–262.

51 Lewis, *God's Crucible*, p. 262.

52 The following is based on the detailed study by Kees Versteegh, 'The Arab presence in France and Switzerland in the 10th century', *Arabica*, 1990 (Vol. 37, Nr. 3), pp. 359–388.

53 See, e.g., 'A World Map History of Religion and Its Faith Based Wars' on www.mapsofwar.com; 'the Third jihad' on http://topdocumentaryfilms.com/third-jihad.

54 Maxime Rodinson, *Mohammad*, Pantheon Books, 1980, pp. 293–294.

55 Quoted in Hugh Kennedy, *The Great Arab Conquests: How the spread of Islam changed the world we live in*, London, Weidenfeld & Nicolson, 2007, p. 214.

56 Fletcher, *Moorish Spain*, pp. 76, 117; Kennedy, *The Great Arab Conquests*, p. 370.

57 Paul Fregosi, *Jihad in the West. Muslim Conquests from the 7th to the 21st Centuries*, New York, Prometheus Books, 1998, p. 67.

58 Cheich, *Byantium viewed by the Arabs*.

59 E.g., James T. Johnson and John Kelsay, *Just War and Jihad: Historical and Theoretical Perspectives on War and Peace in Western and Islamic Thought*, New York, Greenwood Pub Group, 1991; Rudolph Peters, *Jihad in Medieval and Modern Islam*, Leiden, Brill, 1977; Michael Bonner, *Jihad in Islamic History: Doctrines and Practice*, Princeton: Princeton University Press, 2006; Cook, David, *Understanding Jihad*, Berkeley: University of California Press, 2005.

60 Kennedy, *The great Arab conquests*, p. 63.

61   Edward S. Creasy, *Fifteen decisive battles of the world: from Marathon to Waterloo* (orig. 1851), repr. Da Capo Press, 1994.

62   John Haaren and Addison Poland, *Famous Men of the Middle Ages* (orig. 1904), repr. Yesterday's Classics, 2006.

63   Edward Gibbon, *The History of the Decline and Fall of the Roman Empire, Vol. IV*, New York, J&J Harper, 1829, repr. 1993 by Everyman's Library, p. 336.

64   E.g., Robert Cowley and Geoffrey Parker, *The Reader's Companion to Military History*, Boston, Houghton Mifflin, 2001, p. xiii; Franco Cardini, *Europe and Islam*, London, Wiley-Blackwell, 2001, p. 9.

65   Kennedy, *The great Arab conquests*, p. 320.

66   Joseph F. O'Callaghan, *A History of Medieval Spain*, Cornell, University Press, 1983, p. 106.

67   Lewis, *God's Crucible*, p. 178 & 183; Paul K. Davis, *100 Decisive Battles from Ancient Times to the Present: The World's Major Battles and How They shaped History*, Oxford, Oxford University Press, 1999, p. 3.

68   Lewis, *God's Crucible*, p. 183.

69   Jean-Henry Roy and Jean Deviosse, *La Bataille de Poitiers: Trente journées qui ont fait la France*, Paris, Gallimard, 1966, p. 85.

70   Heck, *Charlemagne, Muhammad and the Arab roots of Capitalism*, p. 17.

71   Canard, 'Les Relations Politiques et Sociales entre Byzance et les Arabes', pp. 35–39.

72   El-Cheikh, *Byzantium viewed by the Arabs*, p. 162.

73   Canard, 'Les Relations Politiques et Sociales entre Byzance et les Arabes', pp. 39–40.

74   Judith Herrin, *Byzantium. The surprising life of a medieval empire*, London, Penguin Books, 2007, p. 211.

75   Herrin, *Byzantium*, p. 211; Michael McCormick, *Origins of the European Economy: Communications and Commerce AD 300–900*, Cambridge, Cambridge University Press, 2002, p. 138.

76   Herrin, *Byzantium*, p. 211; McCormick, *Origins of the European Economy*, p. 138.

77   Gibb, 'Constantinople'; Herrin, *Byzantium*, p. 158, 244.

78   Canard, 'Les Relations Politiques et Sociales entre Byzance et les Arabes', p. 45; Herrin, *Byzantium*, p. 145; John Haldon, *Warfare, State and Society in the Byzantine World 565–1204*, London, Routledge, 1999, p. 234 ff.

79   Canard, 'Les Relations Politiques et Sociales entre Byzance et les Arabes', pp. 42–43.

80   Canard, 'Les Relations Politiques et Sociales entre Byanze et les Arabes', pp. 46–47.

81   Heck, *Charlemagne, Muhammad and the Arab roots of Capitalism*, p. 181–190; Bernard Lewis, *The Muslim Discovery of Europe*, New York/London, W.W. Norton, 1982, p. 188.

82   David Abulafia, *The Great Sea: a human history of the Mediterranean*, London, Allen Lane, 2011, pp. 246–247; McCormick, *Origins of the European Economy*, pp. 668, 675.

83 Charles Verlinden, *L'esclavage dans l'Europe médiévale*, Tome I: *Péninsule Ibérique-France*, Bruges, Persée, 1955, p. 189; Youval Rotman, *Byzantine slavery and the Mediterranean World*, Harvard, Harvard University Press, 2009.

84 Verlinden, *L'esclavage dans l'Europe médiévale*, Tome I; McCormick, *Origins of the European Economy*, pp. 252–253.

85 Ashtor, *A Social and Economic History of the Near East in the Middle Ages*, p. 245 ff.; Robert Lopez, 'The Trade of Medieval Europe: the South', in: Stephan Broadberry and Kevin O'Rourke, *Cambridge Economic History of Europe*, Cambridge, Cambridge University Press, 2010, p. 262.

86 Verlinden, *L'esclavage dans l'Europe médiévale*.

87 Chejne, 'Islamization and Arabization in al-Andalus', p. 73.

88 Verlinden, *L'esclavage dans l'Europe médiévale*.

89 Margaret Deanesly, *A History of Early Medieval Europe, from 476 to 911*, London, Taylor & Francis, 1963, p. 294.

90 Mariam Greenblatt, *Charlemagne and the Early Middle Ages*, New York, Benchmark Books, 2002, p. 29.

91 M. Khaduri, *Silat al-diblumatikiyya bayn Rashid wa Sharlaman*, Bagdad, 1939.

92 Heck, *Charlemagne, Muhammad and the Arab roots of Capitalism*, pp. 179–181; Nancy Bisaha, *Creating East and West: Renaissance humanists and the Ottoman Turks*, Philadelphia, University of Pennsylvania Press, 2004, p. 207.

93 John V. Tolan, *Saracens. Islam in the Medieval European Imagination*, New York, Columbia University Press, 2002, pp. xv–xvii.

94 Norman Cohn, *The Pursuit of the Millennium*, Oxford, Oxford University Press, (rev. and exp. ed.) 1970, p. 72.

95 Tolan, *Saracens*, pp. xv, 41–42, 276–278; Richard Southern, *Western views of Islam in the Middle Ages*, Cambridge, Harvard University Press, 1962, pp. 41–42.

96 John Tolan, *Sons of Ishmael: Muslims through European eyes in the Middle Ages*, Gainesville, University Press of Florida, 2008, p. 67.

97 Tolan, *Saracens*, pp. 45 ff.

98 Norman Daniel, *Islam and the West. The Making of an Image*, Edinburgh, Edinburgh University Press, 1960, p. 265.

99 Southern, *Western Views of Islam in the Middle Ages*, p. 33.

100 Daniel, *Islam and the West*, p. 265.

2. Crusading Europe (1000–1500 CE)

1   Robert Bartlett, *The Making of Europe. Conquest, Colonization and Cultural Change,* *950–1350,* London: Penguin Books, 1995, p. 305.

2   E.g., Margaret Deanesly, *A History of Early Medieval Europe, from 476 to 911,* London, Taylor & Francis, 1963; Gene W. Heck, *Charlemagne, Muhammad and the Arab roots of Capitalism,* Berlin, De Gruyter, 2006; Gerald Hodgett, *Social and Economical History of Medieval Europe,* London, Methuen, 1972.

3   Hodgett, *Social and Economical History of Medieval Europe,* p. 59.

4   Heck, *Charlemagne, Muhammad and the Arab roots of Capitalism,* p. 163.

5   Heck, *Charlemagne, Muhammad and the Arab roots of Capitalism,* pp. 162, 245–251; Hodgett, *A Social and Economical History of Medieval Europe,* pp. 59–66; Angeliki Laiou, 'Byzantine trade with Muslims and Crusaders', in: Angeliki E. Laiou and Roy Mottahedh (eds.), *The Crusades from the Perspective of Byzantium and the Muslim World,* Washington, Dumbarton Oaks, 2001, p. 180; Alfred Lieber, 'Eastern Business Practices and Medieval European Commerce', *Economic History Review,* Vol. 21, No. 2, 1968, pp. 230–243; Robert S. Lopez, *The Commercial Revolution of the Middle Ages: 950–1350,* Cambridge, Cambridge University Press, 1987; Robert Latouche, *The Birth of Western Economy. Economic Aspects of the Dark Ages,* London, Methuen, 1967, p. 47; Jairus Banaji, 'Islam, the Mediterranean and the rise of capitalism', *Journal of Historical Materialism,* Vol. 15, No. 1, 2007, pp. 47–74.

6   E.g., Heck, *Charlemagne, Muhammad and the Arab roots of Capitalism,* p. 7.

7   Jacques Le Goff, *La civilization de l'Occident Médiéval,* Paris, Editions Arthaud, 1984, p. 73; Robert Bartlett, *The Making of Europe. Conquest, Colonization and Cultural Change, 950– 1350,* London, Penguin Books, 1995, p. 313.

8   Norman Cohn, *The Pursuit of the Millennium,* Oxford, Oxford University Press, (rev. and exp. ed.) 1970.

9   John V. Tolan, *Saracens. Islam in the Medieval European Imagination,* New York, Columbia University Press, 2002, p. xvii.

10   E.g., Harold J. Berman, *Law and Revolution: The Formation of the Western Legal Tradition,* Cambridge/London, Harvard University Press, 1983.

11   Berman, *Law and Revolution;* Berman Harold, *Faith and Order: The Reconciliation of Law and Religion,* Cambridge, Scholars Press for Emory University, 1993.

12   Edward Peters, *Inquisition,* Berkeley, University of California Press, 1989.

13   Robert I. Moore, *The Formation of a Persecuting Society: Power and Deviance in Western Europe, 950–1250,* London, Wiley-Blackwell, 2001.

14   Bartlett, *The Making of Europe,* pp. 254–255.

15   Thomas Asbridge, *The First Crusade: A new History,* Oxford, Oxford University Press,

2004; Jonathan Riley-Smith, *The Oxford History of the Crusades*, Oxford, Oxford University Press, 2002.

16 Thomas Asbridge, *The Crusades. The War for the Holy Land*, London, Simon and Schuster, 2010; Vicente Cantarino, 'The Spanish Reconquest: A Cluniac Holy War against Islam?', in: Khalil Semaan (ed.), *Islam and the Medieval West. Aspects of Intercultural Relations*, Albany, State University of New York Press, 1980, pp. 82–83.

17 Bernard Lewis, *Islam and the West*, New York/Oxford: Oxford University Press, 1993, p. 12.

18 Asbridge, *The Crusades*, p. 11.

19 Asbridge, *The Crusades*, pp. 16–17.

20 Leonard P. Harvey, *Islamic Spain, 1250 to 1500*, Chicago, Chicago University Press, 1990, pp. 5–9.

21 Richard Fletcher, *Moorish Spain*, London, Phoenix, 1992, pp. 37–38; referring to Richard Bulliets findings in his *Conversion to Islam in the Medieval Period: An Essay in Quantitative History*, Cambridge MA, Harvard University Press, 1979.

22 Thomas F. Glick, *Islamic and Christian Spain in the Early Middle Ages*, Princeton, Princeton University Press, 1979; Harvey thinks that it must be much lower, arguing that, if the estimate of the fourteenth century is credible, a drop in population from 5.6 to approximately 1 million in two centuries is 'very unlikely'; Harvey, *Islamic Spain*, p. 8.

23 Harvey, *Islamic Spain*, pp. 8, 135.

24 Metcalfe, *Muslims and Christians in Norman Sicily*, 2003, pp. 37–38 Also: Jeremy Johns, *Arabic Administration in Norman Sicily: the Royal Diwan*, Cambridge: Cambridge University Press, 2002.

25 Abulafia David, 'Monarchs and Minorities in the Christian Western Mediterranean around 1300: Lucera and its Analogues', in: Scott Waugh and Peter Diehl (eds.), *Christendom and its Discontents: Exclusion, Persecution and Rebellion, 1000–1500*, Cambridge, Cambridge University Press, 1996; Houben, Hubert, *Roger II of Sicily: A ruler between East and West*, Cambridge, Cambridge University Press, 2002, p. 183; James Powell, 'Frederick II and the Rebellion of the Muslims of Sicily, 1220–1224', in *Uluslararasi Haçli Seferleri Sempozyumu: 23–25 June 1997*, Istanbul (pp. 13–22), p. 15; Charles Dalli, 'From Islam to Christianity: the Case of Sicily', in: Joaquim Carvallo (ed.), *Religion, Ritual and Mythology: Aspects of Identity Formation in Europe*, Pisa, Pisa University Press, 2006, p. 152.

26 Charles Dalli, 'From Islam to Christianity: the Case of Sicily'.

27 Angeliki Laiou, 'Byzantine trade with Muslims and Crusaders', in: Angeliki Laiou and Roy P. Mottahedh (eds.), *The Crusades from the Perspective of Byzantium and the Muslim World*, Washington, Dumbarton Oaks, 2001.

28 E.g. Donald M. Nicol, *Byzantium and Venice: A Study in Diplomatic and Cultural Relations*, Cambridge/New York, Cambridge University Press, 1988.

29 See for an elaborate analysis of one of the earliest historiographical documents from the seventeenth century: Allen Frank, *Islamic historiography and 'Bulghar' identity among the Tatars and Bashkirs of Russia*, Leiden, Brill, 1998.

30 E.g., Damir M. Iskhakov, 'The Tatar Ethnic Community', *Anthropology & Archeology of Eurasia*, 2004 (Vol. 43, No. 2), pp. 8–28.

31 Shirin Akiner, 'Oriental Borrowings in the Language of the Byelorussian Tatars', *Slavonic & East European Review*, 1978 (Vol. 56, No. 2), pp. 224–241; Marek M. Dziekan, 'History and Culture of Polish Tatars', in: Katarzyna Gorak-Sosnowska (ed.), *Muslims in Poland and Eastern Europe. Widening the European Discourse on Islam*, Warsaw, University of Warsaw, 2011 (also with many Polish references).

32 Akiner, 'Oriental Borrowings in the Language of the Byelorussian Tatars', p. 16.

33 Dziekan, 'History and Culture of Polish Tatars', p. 28.

34 Bartlett, *The Making of Europe*. e.g. p. 301.

35 Bartlett, *The Making of Europe*. e.g. p. 301.

36 Bernard Hamilton, *The Medieval Inquisition*, New York, Holmes & Meier Publishers, 1989, p. 17.

37 Laiou, 'Byzantine trade with Muslims and Crusaders', p. 187–188.

38 M. Canard, 'Les Relations Politiques et Sociales entre Byzance et les Arabes' *Dumbarton Oak Papers*, 1964 (Vol. 18), pp. 33–56; Judith Herrin, *Byzantium. The surprising life of a medieval empire*, London: Penguin Books, 2007, pp. 178 ff.

39 Powell, *Muslims under Latin Rule*, p. 7.

40 Benjamin Z. Kedar, 'The subjected Muslims of the Frankish Levant', in: James M. Powell (ed), *Muslims under Latin Rule (1100–1300)*, Princeton, Princeton University Press, 1990, p. 137. Elaborated in Benjamin Z. Kedar, *Crusade and Mission: European Approaches towards the Muslims*, Princeton, Princeton University Press, 1984.

41 Kedar, 'The subjected Muslims of the Frankish Levant', p. 147.

42 Powell, *Muslims under Latin Rule*, p. 8.

43 The terminology is the author's.

44 Fletcher, *Moorish Spain*, p. 138–139; Harvey, *Islamic Spain*, p. 104–106 & 133–136.

45 Fletcher, *Moorish Spain*, p. 139.

46 Bartlett, *The Making of Europe*, p. 207–208.

47 Fletcher, *Moorish Spain*, p. 14 & 138.

48 Fletcher, *Moorish Spain*, p. 94.

49 Fletcher, *Moorish Spain*, p. 135.

50 Fletcher, *Moorish Spain*, p.138.

51 David Nirenberg, 'Sexual Boundaries in the Medieval Crown of Aragon', in Salma Khadra Jayyusi (ed.), *The Legacy of Muslim Spain*, Leiden: Brill, 1992, pp. 141–160. For the situation of Jews see: James A. Brundage, 'Intermarriage Between Christians and Jews in Medieval Canon Law,' *Jewish History*, 1988 (Vol. 3, No. 1).

52 Bartlett, *The Making of Europe*, p. 240–241.

53 Harvey, *Islamic Spain*, p. 134.

54 James Brundage, 'Prostitution, Miscegenation, and Sexual Purity in the First Crusade' in Peter W. Edbury, *Crusade and Settlement*, Cardiff: University College Cardiff Press, 1985, pp. 60–61.

55 Harvey, *Islamic Spain*, p. 135.

56 Alan Cutler, 'Innocent III and the Distinctive Clothing of Jews and Muslims' *Studies in Medieval Culture*, 1970 (Vol. 3), pp. 92–116.

57 Powell, *Muslims under Latin Rule*, pp. 190–191.

58 Powell, *Muslims under Latin Rule*, pp. 206; Harvey, *Islamic Spain*, pp. 65–66.

59 Powell, *Muslims under Latin Rule*, pp. 206; Harvey, *Islamic Spain*, pp. 65–66.

60 Powell, *Muslims under Latin Rule*, p. 8.

61 Bartlett, *The Making of Europe*, pp. 236–239.

62 Powell, *Muslims under Latin Rule*, p. 8.

63 Powell, *Muslims under Latin Rule*, pp. 8–9.

64 Powell, *Muslims under Latin Rule*, p. 206.

65 Charles Dalli, 'From Islam to Christianity: the Case of Sicily'; Fletcher, *Moorish Spain*.

66 Louis Cardaillac (ed.), *Les Morisques et l'Inquisition*, Paris, Editions Publisud, 1990, pp. 15–16.

67 Powell, *Muslims under Latin Rule*, introduction.

68 The Islamic justification for his rule is that a child automatically follows the religion of the father: the child of a Muslim woman and a non-Muslim man would therefore be lost to Islam.

69 Harvey, *Islamic Spain*, pp. 324 ff.

70 Harvey, *Islamic Spain*, pp. 329–335; Andrew Hess, 'The Moriscos: An Ottoman Fifth Column in Sixteenth-Century Spain?', *The American Historical Review*, 1968 (Vol. 74, No. 1), p. 4.

71 David Abulafia, 'Monarchs and Minorities in the Christian Western Mediterranean'.

72 Bartlett, *The Making of Europe*, p. 296.

73 Kedar 'The subjected Muslims of the Frankish Levant', 1990, p. 152.

74 J.N. Hillgarth, *The Spanish Kingdoms, 1250–1516*, Oxford, Clarendon Press, 1976–1978, Vol. 1, p. 87.

75 Dalli Charles, 'From Islam to Christianity: the Case of Sicily'.

76 Kedar 'The subjected Muslims of the Frankish Levant', 1990, p. 173.

77 Harvey, *Muslims in Spain*; Matthew Carr, *Blood and Faith. The Purging of Muslim Spain*, New York/London, The New Press, 2009.

78 John T. Gilchrist, *The church and economic activity in the Middle Ages*, London, Macmillan, 1969; Hodgett, *Social and Economical History of Medieval*, pp. 59–66.

79 Heck, *Charlemagne, Muhammad and the Arab roots of Capitalism*, pp. 235–247, 251–252; Hodgett, *Social and Economical History of Medieval*, pp. 59–66.

80 Heck, *Charlemagne, Muhammad and the Arab roots of Capitalism*, p. 208.

81 Heck, *Charlemagne, Muhammad and the Arab roots of Capitalism*, pp. 207–208.

82 Laiou, 'Byzantine trade with Muslims and Crusaders', p. 187; Stefano Carboni, *Venice and the Islamic World 828–1797*, New Haven, Yale University Press, 2007; Eric R. Dursteler, *Venetians in Constantinople: Nation, Identity, and Coexistence in the Early Modern Mediterranean*, Boston, John Hopkins University Press, 2008.

83 Gerald W. Day, *Genoa's Response to Byzantium, 1155–1204: commercial expansion and factionalism in a medieval city*, Chicago, University of Illinois Press, 1988; Nicol, *Byzantium and Venice*.

84 Olivia R. Constable, 'Funduq, Fondaco, and Khan', in: Angeliki Laiou and Roy P. Mottahedh (eds.), *The Crusades from the Perspective of Byzantium and the Muslim World*, Washington, Dumbarton Oaks, 2001.

85 Constable, 'Funduq, Fondaco, and Khan', pp. 145–156.

86 Charles Verlinden, *L'esclavage dans l'Europe médiévale, Tome I: Péninsule Ibérique-France*, Bruges, Persée, 1955, p. 376.

87 T.F. Earle and K. Lowe (ed.), *Black Africans in Renaissance Europe*, Cambridge, Cambridge University Press, 2010.

88 E.g. Sally McKee, 'Domestic Slavery in Renaissance Italy', *Slavery & Abolition*, 2008 (Vol. 29, No. 3), pp. 305–326; P.S. Koningsveld, 'Muslim Slaves and Captives in Western Europe During the Late Middle Ages,' *Islam and Christian-Muslim Relations*, 1995 (Vol. 6. No. 1), pp. 5–23.

89 James W. Brodman, *Ransoming Captives in Crusader Spain: The Order of Merced on the Christian-Islamic Frontier*, Philadelphia, University of Pennsylvania Press, 1986, p. 2.

90 Brodman, *Ransoming Captives in Crusader Spain*, p. 2.

91 Brodman, *Ransoming Captives in Crusader Spain*, pp. 7–8, 10.

92 Housley, N, 'The crusades and Islam,' in *Medieval Encounters*, 2007 (Vol. 13, No. 2), pp. 189–208, p. 197.

93 Norman Daniel, *Islam and the West. The Making of an Image*, Edinburgh, Edinburgh University Press, 1960, p. 7.

94 Thomas Burman, 'Tafsiir and Translation: Traditional Arabic Qur'an Exegesis and

the Latin Qur'ans of Robert of Ketton and Mark of Toledo,' *Speculum* 1998 (Vol. 73), p. 705.

95 James Kritzeck, *Peter the Venerable and Islam*, Princeton, Princeton University Press, 1964.

96 Daniel, *Islam and the West*, pp. 83, 185 ff.

97 Daniel, *Islam and the West*, pp. 27–39.

98 Daniel, *Islam and the West*, pp. 135–152.

99 See Francisco, A.S., *Martin Luther and Islam. A Study in Sixteenth-Century Polemics and Apologetics*, Leiden: Brill, 2007, pp. 12–16 for brief overview and references.

100 John V. Tolan, *Sons of Ishmael: Muslims through European eyes in the Middle Ages*, Gainesville, University Press of Florida, 2008, p. 277. Daniel, *Islam and the West*, pp. 35–37.

101 Kritzeck, *Peter the Venerable*, p. 161.

102 Tolan, *Saracens*, p. 223–2244; Richard Southern, *Western views of Islam in the Middle Ages*, Cambridge, Harvard University Press, 1962, pp. 47–52.

103 Norman Golb and Omeljan Pritsak, *Khazarian Hebrew documents of the tenth century*, Ithaca/ London, Cornell University Press, 1982.

104 Tolan, *Sons of Ishmael*, p. 278.

105 Hugh Goddard, *A history of Christian-Muslim relations*, Edinburgh, Edinburgh University Press, 2000, pp. 116–117.

106 John V. Tolan, *Saint Francis and the Sultan: the curious history of a Christian-Muslim encounter*, Oxford, Oxford University Press, 2009, p. 7–12; Daniel, *Islam and the West*, p. 120–125; Goddard, *A history of Christian-Muslim relations*, pp. 116–117.

107 Tolan, *Saint Francis and the Sultan*.

108 Tolan, *Saint Francis and the Sultan*, pp. 3–4.

109 See the Introduction for a cursory list of these publications.

110 George Makdisi, 'On the Origin and Development of the College in Islam and the West', in: Khalil I. Semaan (ed.), *Islam and the Medieval West. Aspects of Intercultural Relations*, Albany, State University of New York Press, 1980, p. 26–49.

111 John Makdisi, 'The Islamic Origins of the Common Law', *North Carolina Law Review*, 1999 (Vol. 77, No. 5), pp. 1635–1739; Marcel Boisard, 'On the probable Influence of Islam on Western Public and International Law', *International Journal of Middle East Studies*, 1980 (Vol. 11, No. 4), pp. 429–450.

112 Robert Hillenbrand, *Islamic Art and Architecture*, London, Thames and Hudson Ltd., 1999, p. 182.

113 Henry George Farmer, *Historical Facts for the Arabian Musical Influence*, London: William Reeves, 1930.

114 George Saliba, *Islamic Science and the Making of the European Renaissance* (Boston: MIT Press, 2007), pp. 137 ff.

115   Charles E. Butterworth & Blake Andree Kessel (eds.), *The Introduction of Arabic Philosophy into Europe*, Leiden/New Jork, Köln: E.J. Brill, 1993.

116   Goddard, *A History of Christian-Muslim Relations*, pp. 97–98.

117   Trevor-Roper, *The Rise of Christian Europe*, p. 141.

118   Charles Burnett, *Islam and the Italian Renaissance*, London: The Warburg Institute, University of London, 1999.

119   George Makdisi. *The Rise of Humanism in Classical Islam and the Christian West*. Edinburgh: Edinburgh University Press, 1991.

120   Harold P. Nebelsick, *The Renaissance, The Reformation, and the Rise of Science*, Edinburgh: Edinburgh University Press, 1992, p. 9.

3. Divided Europe (1500–1700 CE)

1   The sixteenth century Spanish theologian and jurist Francisco de Vitoria in his *On Civil Power* (1528) in: A. Pagden and J. Lawrence (eds.), *Political Writings*, New York, Cambridge University Press, 1991, p. 31.

2   Niccolò Machiavelli, *The Prince*, London, Bantam Classics, 1984, (orig. 1513), chapter 26.

3   Caroline Finkel, *Osman's Dream. The History of the Ottoman Empire*, New York, Basic Books, 2005, p. 40; Robert J. Donia and John V.A. Fine, *Bosnia and Hercegovina. A Tradition Betrayed*, London, Hurst and Company, 1994, p. 34.

4   Donald Quataert, *The Ottoman Empire 1700–1922*, Cambridge, Cambridge University Press, 2005, p. 27.

5   Quataert, *The Ottoman Empire*, p. 29.

6   Arnold J. Toynbee, 'The Ottoman Empire in World History', *Proceedings of the American Philosophical Society*, 1955 (Vol. 99, No. 3), pp. 119–126.

7   Brummett, Palmira, *Ottoman Seapower and Levantine diplomacy in the age of discovery*, Albany: State University of New York Press, 1994.

8   In 1475, Rumeli provided 2/3 of state revenues (Halil Inalcik with Donald Quataert, *An Economic and Social History of the Ottoman Empire*, Vol. 1, 1300–1600, Cambridge, Cambridge University Press, 1994, p. 55).

9   Peter Sugar, *South-Eastern Europe under Ottoman Rule, 1354–1804*, Seattle/London, University of Washington Press, 1977, p. 168–183; Traian Stoianovich, 'The conquering Balkan Orthodox Merchants' *Journal of Economic History*, 1960 (Vol. 20, No. 2).

10   Eric R. Dursteler, *Venetians in Constantinople: Nation, Identity, and Coexistence in the Early Modern Mediterranean*, Boston, John Hopkins University Press, 2006, p. 3.

11   Sugar, *South-Eastern Europe under Ottoman Rule*.

12   Fisher-Galati, Stephen A., *Ottoman Imperialism and German Protestantism, 1521–1555*, Cambridge: Harvard University Press, 1959.

13   Dariusz Kolodziejczyk, *Ottoman-Polish diplomatic relations (15th–18th century): an annotated edition of ahdnames and other documents*, Leiden, Brill, 2000.

14   Finkel, *Osman's Dream*, p. 139 & 156; Michael Khodarkovsky, *Russia's steppe frontier: the making of a colonial empire, 1500–1800*, Bloomington, Indiana University Press, 2001, p. 40 & 103; Alan Fisher, *A Precarious Balance: Conflict, Trade and Diplomacy on the Russian-Ottoman Frontier*, Istanbul, Isis Press, 1999.

15   E.g. William H. McNeill, *Europe's Steppe Frontier 1500–1800*, Chicago/London, The University of Chicago Press, 1964.

16   See for an elaborate description of Tatar ethnicity: Damir M. Iskhakov, 'The Tatar Ethnic Community', *Anthropology & Archeology of Eurasia*, 2004 (Vol. 43, No. 2), pp. 8–28.

17   Shinin Akiner, 'Oriental Borrowings in the Language of the Byelorussian Tatars', *Slavonic & East European Review*, 1978 (Vol. 56, No. 2), p. 14.

18   Marek M. Dziekan, 'History and Culture of Polish Tatars', in: Katarzyna Gorak-Sosnowska (ed.), *Muslims in Poland and Eastern Europe. Widening the European Discourse on Islam*, Warsaw, University of Warsaw, 2011, p. 37.

19   Iwo C. Pogonowski, *Poland: a Historical Atlas*, New York, Hippocrene Books, 1987.

20   Akiner, 'Oriental Borrowings in the Language of the Byelorussian Tatars', p. 17.

21   Nalborczyk, Agata S., 'Islam in Poland: the past and the present,' *Islamochristiana*, 2006 (Vol. 32); Akiner, 'Oriental Borrowings in the Language of the Byelorussian Tatars', p. 17.

22   Akiner, 'Oriental Borrowings in the Language of the Byelorussian Tatars', p. 17; Dziekan, 'History and Culture of Polish Tatars', p. 37.

23   Dziekan, 'History and Culture of Polish Tatars', p. 33.

24   Dziekan, 'History and Culture of Polish Tatars', p. 35.

25   Akiner, 'Oriental Borrowings in the Language of the Byelorussian Tatars', pp. 18–19.

26   Omer L. Barkan, 'Essai sur les données statistiques des registers de recensement dans l'empire Ottoman au XVe et XVIe siècles', *Journal of the Economic and Social History of the Orient*, 1958 (Vol. 1, No. 1), pp. 9–36.

27   Inalcik with Quataert, *An Economic and Social History of the Ottoman Empire*, pp. 602–603.

28   Barkan, 'Essai sur les donnes statistiques des registers de recensement dans l'empire ottoman au XVe siecle'; Speros Vryonis, 'Religious Changes and Patterns in the Balkans: 14th–16th Centuries', in: H. Birnbaum and S. Vryonis (Eds.), *Aspects of the Balkans: Continuity and Change*, Paris/The Hague, Mouton, 1972.

29   Benjamin Braude and Bernard Lewis, *Christians and Jews in the Ottoman Empire*, New York/London, Holmes & Meier Publishers, 1982, pp. 4–8; Inalcik with Quataert, *An Economic and Social History of the Ottoman Empire*, p. 32.

30   The Turkish name of Constantinople ('Konstaniniyye') was used by Ottomans along-side with Istanbul – originally Greek for 'in the city' ('stin-poli'), later turned into 'Is-lambol' (Ottoman for 'abounding with Islam') – which became the official name of the city only in 1930 (Finkel, *Osman's Dream*, p. 57).

31   Finkel, *Osman's Dream*, p. 56; See Eric Dursteler, *Venetians in Constantinople: Nation, Identity, and Coexistence in the Early Modern Mediterranean*, Boston, John Hopkins University Press, 2006, pp. 153 ff. on the coexistence of these communities within the city.

32   Quataert, *The Ottoman Empire*, p. 21; Finkel, *Osman's Dream*, p. 56; The same percentages of Muslims, Christians and Jews were recorded in the surveys of 1535 and 1550: Robert Mantran, *Istanbul dans la seconde moité du XVIIe siecle*, Paris, Libaraire Adrien Maison-neuve, 1986, pp. 44–45; Barkan, 'Essay sur les donnees statistiques des registres de re-censement dans l'empire Ottoman', pp. 9–36.

33   Mark Mazower, *The Balkans. A short History*, New York, The Modern Library, 2002, p. 25.

34   Donia and Fine, *Bosnia and Hercegovina*, pp. 37, 41.

35   Anton Minkov, *Conversion to Islam in the Balkans, Kisve bahasi petitions and Ottoman social life, 1670–1730*, Leiden/Boston, Brill, 2004, p. 193.

36   Donia and Fine, *Bosnia and Hercegovina*, pp. 41–45; Minkov, *Conversion to Islam in the Balkans*, p. 193.

37   Donia and Fine, *Bosnia and Hercegovina*, pp. 41–45.

38   Donia and Fine, *Bosnia and Hercegovina*; Tijna Krstic, *Contested Conversions to Islam: Narratives of Religious Change in the Early Modern Ottoman Empire*, Stanford, Stanford University Press, 2011; Anton Minkov, *Conversion to Islam in the Balkans*; Speros Vryonis, *The Decline of Medieval Hellenism in Asia Minor and the Process of Islamization from the Eleventh through the Fifteenth Century*, Berkeley/Los Angeles, University of California Press, 1971.

39   Inalcik with Quataert, *An Economic and Social History of the Ottoman Empire*, p. 66, refer-ring to Barkan, 'Essai sur les données statistiques des registers de recensement dans l'empire ottoman au XVe siecle'; Peter Sugar (*South-eastern Europe under ottoman Rule, 1354–1804*) mentions the much higher figure of 42,3 percent, which is probably a mis-reading of Barkan's figures who mentions that the tax collected in the European prov-inces amounted to the sum (not the percentage) of 42,29 million akça.

40   Donia and Fine, *Bosnia and Hercegovina*, 41–43.

41   Emphasized by Sugar as the most important reason for the conversions in the Balkans: Sugar, *South-Eastern Europe under Ottoman Rule*, p. 52–54; Vryonis holds a slightly dif-ferent opinion, arguing that converted Christians passed on Christian cult practices into Islam, like the celebration of Christian holidays, the veneration of Christian saints and even baptism, which was extensively practised among Muslims; in this way many forms of syncretism between Islam and Christianity emerged in the Balkans (Speros

Vryonis, 'Religious change and continuity in the Balkans and Anatolia from the four-teenth through the sixteenth century,' in: Speros Vyronis Jr. (ed.), *Islam and Cultural Change in the Middle Ages*, Wiesbaden, Otto Harrassowitz, 1973, p. 139).

42 Sugar, *South-Eastern Europe under Ottoman Rule*, pp. 11–12.

43 Donia and Fine, *Bosnia and Hercegovina*, pp. 38–39.

44 The boy levy was not indiscriminate: there was a preference for Albanian, Bosnian, Greek, Bulgar, Serbian and Croatian boys; Jews, Turks, Kurds, Persians, Ruthenian (Ukranian), Muscovite and Georgians were exempted; Armenians only for palace ser-vice, not military service (Finkel, *Osman's Dream*, p. 74).

45 Estimates of Sugar, *South-eastern Europe under Ottoman Rule*, p. 56.

46 Daniel Goffman, *The Ottoman Empire and Early Modern Europe*, Cambridge, Cambridge University Press, 2002, p. 65; Minkov, *Conversion to Islam in the Balkans*, pp. 66–77; Sugar, *South-Eastern Europe under Ottoman Rule*, pp. 56–58; Finkel, *Osman's Dream*, pp. 74–75, 233; Godfrey Goodwin, *The Janissaries*, London, Saqi, 1994.

47 Minkov, *Conversion to Islam in the Balkans*, pp. 71–72.

48 Goffman, *The Ottoman Empire and Early Modern Europe*, p. 68; Minkov, *Conversion to Islam in the Balkans*, p. 75; Sugar, *South-eastern Europe under Ottoman Rule*, p. 58.

49 Sugar, *South-Eastern Europe under Ottoman Rule*, p. 58.

50 George G. Arnakis, 'The role of religion in the development of Balkan nationalism', in: Barbara and Charles Jelavich (eds.), *The Balkans in Transition. Essays on the development of Balkan life and politics since the eighteenth century*, Berkeley, University of California Press, 1963, p. 23.

51 Benjamin Baude makes it clear that the term millet came into use only in the nine-teenth century, and was until then not a developed institution but rather a set of arrangements and policies that differed with time and place: Benjamin Braude, 'Foun-dation Myths of the Millet System', in: Benjamin Braude and Bernard Lewis, *Christians and Jews in the Ottoman Empire*, New York/London, Holmes & Meier Publishers, 1982, pp. 69–87.

52 Most literature on the millet system deals with its situation and transformations dur-ing the nineteenth century, of which we will speak in the next chapter. For the period between 1500 and 1700, the main volume of literature is that of Benjamin Braude and Bernard Lewis, *Christians and Jews in the ottoman Empire*, New York/London, Holmes & Meier Publishers, 1982.

53 See, e.g., Sugar, *South-Eastern Europe under Ottoman Rule*, p. 45.

54 Braude, 'Foundation Myths of the Millet System.'

55 Kemal H. Karpat, 'Millets and Nationality: The Roots of the Incongruity of Nation and State in the Post-Ottoman Era', in: Benjamin Braude and Bernard Lewis, *Christians*

and Jews in the Ottoman Empire, New York/London, Holmes & Meier Publishers, 1982, pp. 141–169.

56 Sugar, South-Eastern Europe under Ottoman Rule, p. 108.

57 Finkel, Osman's Dream, p. 193; Mazower, The Balkans, p. 67.

58 Gülru Necipoglu, 'The Life of an Imperial Monument: Hagia Sophia after Byzantium', in: R. Mark and A. Çakmak (eds.), Hagia Sophia from the Age of Justinian to the Present Day, Cambridge MA, Cambridge University Press, 1992.

59 Aleksandar Fotic, 'The Official Explanations for the Confiscation and Sale of Monasteries (Churches) and their Estates at the Time of Selim II', Turcica, 1994 (Vol. 26), pp. 33–54.

60 Sugar, South-Eastern Europe under Ottoman Rule, p. 108; Mischa Glenny, The Balkans: Nationalism, War and the Great Powers, 1804–1999, London, Viking Penguin, 2000, pp. 9, 72.

61 Mazower, The Balkans, p. 67.

62 Sugar, South-eastern Europe under Ottoman Rule, pp. 31 ff.

63 Mazower, The Balkans, pp. 39, 42.

64 Especially Jews were close to the Ottoman ruling class as physicians, advisors, diplomats: Finkel, Osman's Dream, pp. 190–191.

65 Sugar, South-Eastern Europe under Ottoman Rule, p. 109; Donald Quataert, The Ottoman Empire 1700–1922, pp. 143–144.

66 Goffman, The Ottoman Empire and Early Modern Europe, p. 110.

67 Mark Mazower, Salonica, City of Ghosts. Christians, Muslims and Jews, 1430–1950, New York: Vintage, 2006.

68 Goffman, The Ottoman Empire and Early Modern Europe, p. 90; Also Edham Eldem, Daniel Goffman and Bruce Masters, The Ottoman city between East and West: Aleppo, Izmir and Istanbul, Cambridge, Cambridge University Press, 1999; Quataert, The Ottoman Empire, pp. 179–183.

69 For instance, in the case of Jews, see Aryeh Shmuelevitz, The Jews of the Ottoman Empire in the Late Fifteenth and the Sixteenth Century, Leiden: Brill, 1984, pp. 67, 72; Mazower, Salonica, City of Ghosts, pp. 60–61.

70 The following is taken from Finkel, Osman's Dream, pp. 181, 191–193.

71 Sugar, South-eastern Europe under Ottoman Rule, pp. 94, 110.

72 Leonard P. Harvey, Muslims in Spain, 1500 to 1614, Chicago, The University of Chicago Press, 2005.

73 Mary Elizabeth Perry, The handless maiden: Moriscos and the politics of religion in early modern Spain, Princeton, Princeton University Press, 2005, pp. 65 ff.

74 Louis Cardaillac (ed.), Les Morisques et l'Inquisition, Paris, Editions Publisud, 1990, pp. 24–25; Harvey, Muslims in Spain, pp. 10–13.

75   Harvey, *Muslims in Spain*, p. 7; Toby Green, *Inquisition. The Reign of Fear*, London, Macmillan, 2007, p. 180.

76   Harvey, *Muslims in Spain*, pp. 7–10.

77   The following is based on English literature, which makes reference to the vast Spanish literature on Moriscos.

78   Green, *Inquisition*, pp. 24–25, 32.

79   Cardaillac, *Les Morisques et l'Inquisition*, p. 17.

80   Green, *Inquisition*, p. 170.

81   For examples and cases see e.g., Green, *Inquisition*; Cardaillac, *Les Morisques et l'Inquisition*, Anwar Chejne, *Islam and the West: The Moriscos, a Cultural and Social History*, Albany, State University of New York Press, 1983; Henry C. Lea, *A History of the Inquisition in Spain (Volumes 1–3)*, New York, MacMillan, 1906–1907; Mary E. Perry, *The handless maiden: Moriscos and the politics of religion in early modern Spain*, Princeton, Princeton University Press, 2005.

82   Green, *Inquisition*, pp. 126, 169.

83   Andrew C. Hess, 'The Moriscos: An Ottoman Fifth Column in Sixteenth-Century Spain?' *The American Historical Review*, 1968 (Vol. 74, No. 1), p. 13.

84   Harvey, *Muslims in Spain*, pp. 12–13.

85   Henry C. Lea, *The Moriscos of Spain. Their Conversion and Expulsion*, Philadelphia, Lea Brothers and Co., 1901, pp. 278–279.

86   Harvey, *Muslims in Spain*, p. 13.

87   Chejne, *Islam and the West*, p. 10.

88   Hess, 'The Moriscos: An Ottoman Fifth Column in Sixteenth-Century Spain?' pp. 17–20; See also Andrew C. Hess, *The Forgotten Frontier. A History of the Sixteenth-Century Ibero-African Frontier*, Chicago/London, The University of Chicago Press, 1978.

89   See for references: Perry, *The Handless Maiden*, p. 138.

90   Hess, 'The Moriscos: An Ottoman Fifth Column in Sixteenth-Century Spain?' pp. 15, 19; Alexander H. de Groot, *The Ottoman Empire and the Dutch Republic: A History of the Earliest Diplomatic Relations, 1610–1630*, Leiden/Istanbul, Nederlands Historisch-Archaelogisch Instituut, 1978, pp. 84–85.

91   Harvey, *Muslims in Spain*, p. 343.

92   See for an overview of these reports Henry Charles Lea, *The Moriscos of Spain. Their Conversion and Expulsion*, pp. 278–290.

93   Green, *Inquisition*, pp. 137–138.

94   Chejne, *Islam and the West*, pp. 10.

95   Green, *Inquisition*, pp. 171.

96   Chejne, *Islam and the West*, pp. 9–11.

97 Cardaillac, *Les Morisques et l'Inquisition*, p. 24; Harvey, *Muslims in Spain*, pp. 12–13.

98 Chejne, *Islam and the West*, p. 15.

99 Catherine W. Bracewell, *The Uskoks of Senj: Piracy, Banditry, and holy war in the sixteenth century Adriatic*, Ithaca/London, Cornell University Press, 1992, p. 13.

100 See Bracewell, *The Uskoks of Senj*; Peter Earle, *Corsairs of Malta And Barbary*, London, Sidgwick & Jackson, 1970; Andrew Hess, *The Forgotten Frontier. A History of the Sixteenth-Century Ibero-African Frontier*, Chicago/London, The University of Chicago Press, 1978; William H. McNeill, *Europe's Steppe Frontier 1500–1800*, Chicago/London, The University of Chicago Press, 1964.

101 See the chapter 'What could the terms Gaza and Gazi have meant?' in Heath W. Lowry, *The nature of the early Ottoman state*, Albany, State University of New York Press, 2003.

102 Finkel, *Osman's Dream*, p. 15. For a similar view see also: Çelik, Nihat, 'Muslims, Non-Muslims and Foreign Relations: Ottoman Diplomacy', *International Review of Turkish Studies*, 2011 (Vol. 1, No. 3), pp. 8–31.

103 Lowry, *The nature of the early Ottoman state* pp. 51–54; Sugar, *South-eastern Europe under Ottoman Rule*, p. 20.

104 Lowry, *The nature of the early Ottoman state*, pp. 50, 57, 95–96; Finkel, *Osman's Dream*, p. 10.

105 Andrew Wheatcroft, *The Enemy at the Gate: Habsburgs, Ottomans and the Battle for Europe*, London, Pimlico, 2009, p. 44.

106 Cemal Kafadar, *Between Two Worlds: The Construction of the Ottoman State*, Berkeley, University of California Press, 1995, pp. 79–80.

107 Finkel, *Osman's Dream*, p. 119.

108 Kafadar, *Between Two Worlds*, p. 80, referring to James T. Johnson and John Kelsay, *Just War and Jihad: Historical and Theoretical Perspectives on War and Peace in Western and Islamic Thought*, New York, Greenwood Pub Group, 1991; Rudolph Peters, *Jihad in Medieval and Modern Islam*, Leiden, Brill, 1977.

109 Sugar, *South-eastern Europe under Ottoman Rule*, p. 21.

110 Suraiya Faroqhi, *The Ottoman Empire and The World Around It*, London/ New York, Tauris, 2007.

111 See Christine Isom-Verhaaren, 'Barbarossa and his army who came to succor all of us: Ottoman and French Views of Their Joint Campaign of 1543–1544', *French Historical Studies*, 2007 (Vol. 30, No. 3), pp. 395–425, and references there.

112 Finkel, *Osman's Dream*, pp. 11, 15; Lowry, *The nature of the early Ottoman state*, p. 132.

113 *Weekly Standard*, 4 Oct 2004.

114 Discussed in Kenneth M. Setton, *Western Hostility to Islam and Prophecies of Turkish Doom*, Philadelphia, American Philosophical Society, 1992, pp. 29 ff.

115 Sugar, *South-Eastern Europe under Ottoman Rule*, p. 21.

116 The siege of 1529 "was not part of a Turkish plan to conquer Germany. It was intended to warn the Habsburgs that interference in Hungary, the western bastion of the Ottoman Empire, would not pass unchallenged." (Stephen A. Fisher-Galati, *Ottoman Imperialism and German Protestantism, 1521–1555*, Cambridge: Harvard University Press, 1959, p. 38).

117 John Stoye, *The Siege of Vienna: The Last Great Trial Between Cross & Crescent*, New York, Pegasus Books, 2007, pp. 10–12.

118 Andrew Wheatcroft, *The Enemy at the Gate: Habsburgs, Ottomans and the Battle for Europe*, London, Pimlico, 2009, p. 18.

119 Wheatcroft, *The Enemy at the Gate*, pp. 165–167.

120 See, e.g., Godfrey Fisher, *Barbary Legend. War, Trade and Piracy in North Africa 1415–1830*, Oxford, Clarendon Press, 1957; Leïla Maziane, *Salé et ses corsaires, 1666–1727: un port de course marocain au XVIIe siècle*, Havre, Université de Rouen, 2007; Daniel Panzac, *Barbary Corsairs: The End of a Legend, 1800–1820*, Leiden, Koninklijke Brill, 2005; Adrian Tenniswood, *Pirates of Barbary: Corsairs, Conquests and Captivity in the Seventeenth-Century Mediterranean*, London, Riverhead Trade, 2011.

121 Ernle Bradford, *The Sultan's Admiral. Barabarossa, Pirate and Empire-Builder*, London, Tauris, 2009.

122 Earle, *Corsairs of Malta And Barbary*, p. 10; Fisher, *Barbary Legend*, p. 7.

123 McNeill, *Europe's Steppe Frontier*, p. 49.

124 Matsuki Eizo, 'The Crimean Tatars and their Russian-Captive Slaves. An Aspect of Muscovite-Crimean Relations in the 16th and 17th centuries', *Mediterranean World*, 2006 (Vol. 18), pp. 171–182.

125 Bracewell, *The Uskoks of Senj*, pp. 189–190.

126 Bracewell, *The Uskoks of Senj*, pp. 199–200.

127 Earle, *Corsairs of Malta And Barbary*, p. 109

128 Garrett Mattingly, *Renaissance Diplomacy*, Dover Publications, 1988 (first published by Houghton Mifflin Company, Boston, 1955), pp. 105 ff.

129 Also: Maxime Rodinson, *Europe and the Mistique of Islam*, pp. 32–33.

130 See, e.g., D.L. Jensen, 'The Ottoman Turks in Sixteenth Century French Diplomacy', *The Sixteenth Century Journal*, 1985 (Vol. 16, No. 4), pp. 451–470.

131 William E. Watson, *Tricolor and Crescent: France and the Islamic World*, Westport, Praeger Publishers, 2003, p. 11.

132 Isom-Verhaaren, 'Barbarossa and His Army Who Came to Succor All of Us'; Jean Dény and Jane Laroche, 'L' expédition en Provence de l' armée de mer de Sultan Suleyman sous le commandement de l' amiral Hayreddin Pacha dit Barbarousse', *Turcica*, 1969 (Vol. 1), pp. 161–211.

133 The following paragraph is mostly based on Abdelkader Benali and Herman Obdeijn, *Marokko door Nederlandse ogen, 1605–2005*, Amsterdam, Arbeiderspers, 2005.

134 Mercedes Garcia-Arenal & Gerard Wiegers, *A Man of Three Worlds. Samuel Pallache, a Moroccan Jew in Catholic and Protestant Europe*, Baltimore, John Hopkins University Press, 2003.

135 Geraud Poumarède, *Pour en Finir avec la Croisade: mythes et réalités de la lutte contre les Turcs aux XVIe et XVIIe sciècles*, Paris, Presses Universitaires de France, 2004, p. 314.

136 Eric Dursteler, *Venetians in Constantinople: Nation, Identity, and Coexistence in the Early Modern Mediterranean*, Boston, John Hopkins University Press, 2006, pp. 3–4.

137 Faroqhi, *The Ottoman Empire and The World Around It*, pp. 137–160; Inalcik with Quataert, *An Economic and Social History of the Ottoman Empire*, pp. 209–216.

138 Nabil Matar, *Europe through Arab Eyes, 1578–1727*, New York, Columbia University Press, 2009.

139 See on the Turkish presence in Venice: Bernard Lewis, *The Muslim Discovery of Europe*, New York/London, W.W. Norton, 1982, pp. 121–124.

140 See for the special case of Ragusa/Dubrovnik: Inalcik with Quataert, *An Economic and Social History of the Ottoman Empire*, p. 256–270; Sugar, *South-eastern Europe under Ottoman Rule*, pp. 168–183; Traian Stoianovich, 'The conquering Balkan Orthodox Merchant', *Journal of Economic History*, 1960 (Vol. 20, No. 2), pp. 234–313.

141 The earlier treaty of 1536 was drafted but never ratified by the Ottoman Sultan: Inalcik with Quataert, *An Economic and Social History of the Ottoman Empire*, p. 194.

142 Inalcik with Quataert, *An Economic and Social History of the Ottoman Empire*, p. 194.

143 Goffman, *The Ottoman Empire and Early Modern Europe*, p. 195.

144 D.L. Jensen, 'The Ottoman Turks in Sixteenth Century French Diplomacy', *The Sixteenth Century Journal*, 1985 (Vol. 16, No. 4), p. 464.

145 Robert C. Davis, 'The Geography of Slaving in the Early Modern Mediterranean, 1500–1800', *Journal of Medieval and Early Modern Studies*, 2007 (Vol. 37, No. 1), pp. 58–74.

146 Davis, *Christian Slaves, Muslim Masters*, p. 23: He bases this figure on extensive calculations (p. 3–26) whereby he estimates that during the period between 1580 and 1680 CE an average of 35,000 European slaves were held at any given time in all Barbary (p. 15); this estimate corroborates the similar estimate given by Stephen Clissold, *The Barbary Slaves*, London, Elek, 1977, pp. 17–25.

147 Ellen Friedman, 'Christian Captives at 'Hard labor' in Algiers, 16th–18th centuries', *The International Journal of African Historical Studies*, 1980 (Vol. 13, No. 4), pp. 616–632.

148 Inalcik with Quataert, *An Economic and Social History of the Ottoman Empire*, p. 284.

149 Sugar, *South-Eastern Europe under Ottoman Rule*, pp. 56–57.

150 Inalcik with Quataert, *An Economic and Social History of the Ottoman Empire*, p. 284; See

for a description of slave market practices in the Ottoman Empire: Alan W. Fisher, 'The sale of slaves in the Ottoman Empire: Markets and State taxes on slave sales, some preliminary considerations', *Beseri Bilimler – Humanities*, 1978 (Vol. 6), pp. 149–174.

151 Robert C. Davis, *Christian Slaves, Muslim Masters: White Slavery in the Mediterranean, the Barbary Coast and Italy, 1500–1800*, Basingstoke, Palgrave Macmillan, 2004.

152 Géza Dávid and Pál Fodor, *Ransom Slavery along the Ottoman Borders*, Leiden/Boston, Brill, 2007.

153 Daniel J. Vitkus (ed.), *Piracy, Slavery, and Redemption: Barbary Captivity Narratives from Early Modern England*, New York, Columbia University Press, 2001.

154 E.g., Earle, *Corsairs of Malta And Barbary*, p. 92.

155 These reactions are extensively discussed for England, France, Italy and Spain in, respectively Nabil Matar, *Islam in Britain, 1558–1685*, Cambridge, Cambridge University Press, 1998; Bartolome and Lucile Bennassar, *Les chretiens d'Allah, L'histoire extraordinaire des renigats, XVI–XVIIe siècles*, Paris, Perrin, 1989; Gino Benzoni, 'Il 'farsi turco', ossia lombra del rinnegato', *Venezia e i Turchi*, Milan, Electa Editricce, 1985, p. 91–134; Ellen G. Friedman, *Spanish Captives in North Africa in the Early Modern Period*, Madison, University of Wisconsin Press, 1983.

156 Davis, *Christian Slaves, Muslim Masters*, p. 21.

157 Setton, *Western Hostility to Islam and Prophecies of Turkish Doom*, p. 17.

158 The earliest is probably the *Tractate on the customs and conducts of the Turcs* (origin in Latin) by the escaped slave Georgius de Hungaria, published in 1481 (Albrecht Classen, 'The World of the Turks Described by an Eye-Witness: Georgius de Hungaria's Dialectical Discourse on the Foreign World of the Ottoman Empire', *Journal of Early Modern History*, 2003 (Vol. 7, No. 3)).

159 Kenneth M. Setton, *Western Hostility to Islam and Prophecies of Turkish Doom*, Philadelphia, American Philosophical Society, 1992, p. 51.

160 The most famous were the *Turkish Letters* (1555–1562) by Ogier Ghiselin de Busbecq, ambassador of the Holy Roman Emperor to the Ottoman Empire, and the writings of Barthomolaeus Georgievicz who had spent a decade as a slave in various parts of the Ottoman Empire.

161 See, e.g., Jonathan Burton, *Traffic And Turning: Islam And English Drama, 1579–1624*, Newark, University of Delaware Press, 2005; Clarence D. Bouillard, *The Turk in French History, Thought, and Literature (1550–1660)*, Paris, 1938; Albert Mas, *Les Turcs dans la littérature espagnole du Siecle d'Or* (2 vols.), Paris, 1967; Mahmoud Rais, *The Representation of the Turk in English Renaissance Drama*, Cornell University, 1973; Setton, *Western Hostility to Islam and Prophecies of Turkish Doom*.

162   Bernard Lewis, *Islam and the West*, pp. 78–81.

163   E.g., Christine Isom – Verhaaren, "An Ottoman report about Martin Luther and the Emperor: New evidence of the Ottoman interest in the Protestant challenge to the power of Charles V" in *Turcica*, 1996 (Vol. 28), pp. 299–318.

164   Franklin L. Baumer, 'England, the Turk, and the Common Corps of Christendom' in *The American Historical Review*, 1944 (Vol. 50, No. 1), pp. 26–48; Denys Hays, *Europe. The Emergence of an Idea*, Edinburgh: Edinburgh University Press, 1957, pp. 113–114.

165   Fisher-Galati, *Ottoman Imperialism and German Protestantism*, pp. 5–11; Robert Schoebel, *The Shadow of the Crescent: The Renaissance Image of the Turk*, Nieuwkoop, 1967, pp. 218–219.

166   A.S. Francisco, *Martin Luther and Islam. A Study in Sixteenth-Century Polemics and Apologetics*, Leiden: Brill, 2007, pp. 43–44, 64–65.

167   A.S. Francisco, *Martin Luther and Islam*, pp. 45–46, 64–65.

168   Baumer, 'England, the Turk, and the Common Corps of Christendom,' pp. 31–33.

169   Voetius, 'Over het mohammedanisme', in: J. van Amersfoort and W.J. van Asselt (Eds.), *Liever Turks dan Paaps? De visies van Johannes Coccejus, Gisbertus Voetius en Adrianus Relandus op de islam*, Zoetermeer, Uitgeverij Boekencentrum, 1997, pp. 59–100.

170   Helmut-Wolfhardt Vielau, *Luther und der Türke*, Gottingen, 1936, p. 15; Ahmad Gunny, 'Protestant Reactions to Islam in late Seventeenth-Century French Thought', *French Studies*, 1986 (Vol. 40, No. 2), pp. 129–140. See also Johannes Ehmann, *Luther, Türken und Islam*, Heidelberg: Gütersloher Verlagshaus, 2008; Ludwig Hagemann, *Martin Luther und der Islam*, Altenberge: Verlag für Christlich-Islamisches Schrifttum, 1983.

171   Halil Inancik, 'The Turkish Impact on the Development of Modern Europe,' in: Kemal H. Karpat (ed.), *The Ottoman state and its place in world history*, Leiden, Brill, 1974, p. 53. See for similar scheming letters by Sulayman's successor, Selim II: Andrew C. Hess, 'The Moriscos: An Ottoman fifth Column in Sixteenth-Century Spain?', pp. 19–21.

172   Quote from Jonathan Burton, *Traffic And Turning: Islam And English Drama*, p. 62.

173   Jonas Otterbeck, 'The Depiction of Islam in Sweden', *The Muslim World*, 2002 (Vol. 92), pp. 143–156.

174   Martin Luther, *Vom Kriege wider die Türken*, 1528, WA 30 II, pp. 107–148.

175   Vielau, *Luther und der Türke*, p. 23. See also Francisco, *Martin Luther and Islam*, pp. 69–82.

176   *Vom Kriege wider die Türken*, WA 30 II, pp. 107–148.

177   *Vom Kriege wider die Türken*, WA 30 II, pp. 107–148; *Verlegen des Alcoran*, Wittemberg, 1542: 'Und ich halt der Mahmet nicht fur den Endechrist. Er machts zu grob ... Aber der Bapst bey uns ist der rechte Endechrist, der hat den hohen, subtilem, schönen gelissenden Teuffel. Der sitzt inwendig in der Christenheit' (fol. X).

178   Described by Kenneth D. McRae (ed.) *The six books of a commonweale*, New York, 1979.

179   Setton, *Western Hostility to Islam and Prophecies of Turkish Doom*, p. 51.

4. Powerfull Europe (1700–1950 CE)

1 Kemal Karpat, *Ottoman population, 1830–1914: demographic and social characteristics*, Madison, University of Wisconsin Press, 1985, pp. 109–114. See for discussions on the censuses during this period: Justin McCarthy, 'Muslims in Ottoman Europe: Population from 1800 to 1912', *Nationalities Papers: The Journal of Nationalism and Ethnicity*, 2000 (Vol. 28, No. 1), pp. 29–43; M. Kabadayi, *Inventory for the Ottoman Empire/Turkish Republic 1500–2000*, online publication of the International Institute of Social History: http://www.iisg.nl/research/labourcollab/turkey.pdf; Kemal Karpat, 'Ottoman Population Records and the Census of 1881/82–1893', *International Journal of Middle Eastern Studies*, 1978 (Vol. 9, No. 2), pp. 237–274; Stanford Shaw, 'The Ottoman Census System and Population, 1831–1914', *International Journal of Middle Eastern Studies*, 1978 (Vol. 9, No. 3), p. 323–338.

2 Karpat, *Ottoman population*, p. 148–149; Charles P. Issawi, *The economic history of Turkey, 1800–1914*, Chicago/London, University of Chicago Press, 1980, p. 18.

3 McCarthy, 'Muslims in Ottoman Europe: Population from 1800 to 1912', pp. 36–37 which summarizes his work *Death and Exile. The Ethnic Cleansing of Ottoman Muslims, 1821–1922*, Princeton, The Darwin Press, 1995. Also Edham Eldem, Daniel Goffman and Bruce Masters, *The Ottoman city between East and West: Aleppo, Izmir and Istanbul*, Cambridge, Cambridge University Press, 1999.

4 Karpat, *Ottoman population*, p. 254.

5 Donald Quataert, *The Ottoman Empire 1700–1922*, Cambridge, Cambridge University Press, 2005, p. 175. Also Daniel Goffman, *The Ottoman Empire and Early Modern Europe*, Cambridge, Cambridge University Press, 2002, p. 90. The opposing view is voiced, e.g., by Charles and Barbara Jelavich who have written several seminal works on the Balkans.

6 Quataert, *The Ottoman Empire 1700–1922*, pp. 46–47.

7 Halil Inalcik with Donald Quataert, *An Economic and Social History of the Ottoman Empire, Vol. 1, 1300–1600*, Cambridge, Cambridge University Press, 1994, p. 769.

8 Quataert, *The Ottoman Empire 1700–1922*, p. 45.

9 Inalcik with Quataert, *An Economic and Social History of the Ottoman Empire*, p. 702 & 764.

10 Charles and Barbara Jelavich, *The Establishment of the Balkan National States, 1804–1920*, Seattle/ London, University of Washington Press, 1977, pp. 13–14.

11 Quataert, *The Ottoman Empire 1700–1922*, p. 148.

12 Quataert, *The Ottoman Empire 1700–1922*, p. 148.

13 Jelavich, *The Establishment of the Balkan National States*, pp. 5–6.

14   Mark Mazower, *Salonica, City of Ghosts. Christians, Muslims and Jews, 1430–1950*, New York: Vintage, 2006, p. 72.

15   This paragraph is based on Misha Glenny, *The Balkans. Nationalism, War and the Great Powers, 1804–1999*, London: Viking Penguin, 2000, pp. 9–10, 22–26, 32–33. See also Charles Issawi's chapter 'The Greeks in the Middle East' in his *Cross-Cultural Encounters and Conflicts*. Oxford: Oxford University Press, 1998.

16   See, e.g., Mazower, *Salonica, City of Ghosts*, pp. 46 ff., 114 ff.

17   Ahmad Feroz, 'Ottoman Perceptions of the Capitulations, 1800–1912', *Journal of Islamic Studies*, 2000 (Vol. 11, No. 1), pp. 1–20.

18   E. Nathalie Rothman, 'Interpreting Dragomans: Boundaries and Crossings in the Early Modern Mediterranean', *Comparative Studies in Society and History*, 2009 (Vol. 51, No. 4), pp. 771–800.

19   Maurits H. van den Boogert, *The Capitulations and the Ottoman Legal System. Qadis, Consuls and Berats in the 18th Century*, Leiden, Brill, 2005.

20   Goffman, *The Ottoman Empire and Early Modern Europe*, pp. 196–197.

21   Geoffrey L. Lewis, *Modern Turkey*, New York, Praeger, 1955, p. 24.

22   See Robert J. Donia, *Islam Under the Double Eagle: The Muslims of Bosnia and Hercegovina, 1878–1914*, New York, Columbia University Press, 1981; Mark Pinson (ed.), *The Muslims of Bosnia-Herzegovina. Their Historic Development from the Middle Ages to the Dissolution of Yugoslavia*, Harvard, Harvard University Press, 1993.

23   Mark Pinson, 'The Muslims of Bosnia-Hercegovina under Austro-Hungarian Rule, 1878–1918', in: Mark Pinson (ed.), *The Muslims of Bosnia-Herzegovina*, pp. 100–102.

24   Inalcik with Quataert, *An Economic and Social History of the Ottoman Empire*, p. 766.

25   Carter V. Findley, 'The Acid Test of Ottomanism: the Acceptance of Non-Muslims in the late Ottoman Bureaucracy', in: Benjamin Braude and Bernard Lewis (eds.), *Christians and Jews in the Ottoman Empire*, New York/London, Holmes & Meier Publishers, 1982, p. 339–368.

26   Edin Hajdarpasic, 'Out of the Ruins of the Ottoman Empire: Reflections on the Ottoman Legacy in South-eastern Europe', *Middle Eastern Studies*, Vol. 44, No. 5, 2008, p. 722.

27   Quataert, *The Ottoman Empire 1700–1922*, p. 68.

28   Kamel S. Abu Jaber, 'The Millet system in the nineteenth-century Ottoman Empire', *The Muslim World*, 1976 (Vol. 57, No. 3), p. 221.

29   Kemal Karpat, 'Millets and Nationality: The Roots of the Incongruity of Nation and State in the Post-Ottoman Era', in: Benjamin Braude and Bernard Lewis (eds.), *Christians and Jews in the Ottoman Empire*, New York/London, Holmes & Meier Publischers, 1982, pp. 141–169.

30 See above; also Charles Issawi, 'The Transformation of the Economic Position of the Mil-
    lets in the Nineteenth Century', in: Benjamin Braude and Bernard Lewis (eds.), *Christians
    and Jews in the Ottoman Empire*, New York/London, Holmes & Meier Publishers, 1982,
    pp. 261–285.

31 George Arnakis, 'The role of religion in the development of Balkan nationalism', in:
    Barbara and Charles Jelavich (eds.), *The Balkans in Transition. Essays on the development of
    Balkan life and politics since the eighteenth century*, Berkeley, University of California Press,
    1963, pp. 118–119. ·

32 Michael B. Petrovich, *A History of Modern Serbia: 1804–1918*, New York, Harcourt Brace
    Javanovich, 1976, pp. 28–29.

33 Mischa Glenny, *The Balkans: Nationalism, War and the Great Powers, 1804–1999*, London,
    Viking Penguin, 2000, pp. 80–83.

34 Giannes Koliopoulos, *Brigands with a Cause: Brigandage and Irredentism in Modern Greece,
    1821–1912*, Oxford, Clarendon Press, 1987; Barbara Jelavich, *History of the Balkans, 18th and
    19th centuries*, New York, Cambridge University Press, 1983.

35 Virginia H. Aksan, *Ottoman Wars, 1700–1870: An Empire Besieged*, New York, Pearson
    Longman, 2007, p. 4.

36 Snouck Hurgronje, *The Holy War, Made in Germany*, New York/London, The Knicker-
    bocker Press, 1915; See also Tilman Lüdke, *Jihad Made in Germany: Ottoman and Ger-
    man Propaganda and Intelligence in the First World War*, Münster, Lit, 2005; Wolfgang
    G. Schwanitz, *Djihad made in Germany: Deutsche Islampolitik im 19. Und 20. Jahrhundert.
    Politik, Wirtschaft, Militär und Kultur*, Berlin: Trafo, 2005.

37 For a critical evaluation see Gottfried Hagen, 'German Heralds of Holy War: Oriental-
    ists and Applied Oriental studies', *Comparative Studies of South Asia, Africa and the Middle
    East*, 2004 (Vol. 24, No. 2), pp. 145–162; Aksakal, ' 'Holy War Made in Germany'? Ottoman
    Origins of the 1914 Jihad', pp. 184–199.

38 Mustafa Aksakal, ' 'Holy War Made in Germany'? Ottoman Origins of the 1914 Jihad',
    War in History, 2011 (Vol. 18, No. 2), pp. 189–190 identified official calls for jihad against
    Russia (twice, 1773, 1829), Serbs (1809), Greeks (1897), European Allies (1914) and Greece
    (1919).

39 The *fatwa* was made up of questions and answers, and the question relating to the
    colonies read: "The Moslem subjects of Russia, of France, of England and of all the
    countries that side with them in their land and sea attacks dealt against the Caliphate
    for the purpose of annihilating Islam, must these subjects, too, take part in the holy
    War against the respective governments from which they depend?" The answer in the
    fatwa was a brief "Yes". (Source: Charles F. Horne (ed.), *Records of the Great War, Vol. III*,
    National Alumni, 1923.)

40 Report of the International Commission to Inquire into the Causes and Conduct of the Balkan Wars, Washington, D.C., Carnegie Endowment for International Peace, 1914, pp. 154–155.

41 Report of the International Commission to Inquire into the Causes and Conduct of the Balkan Wars, p. 148.

42 M. Edith Durham, The burden of the Balkans, London, E. Arnold, 1905, p. 104.

43 Machiel Kiel, Studies on the Ottoman Monuments of the Balkans, Aldershot, Variorum, 1990; H. Kalesi, 'Oriental Culture in Yugoslav Countries from the 15th century till the End of the 17th Century', in: Jaroslav Cesar, Ottoman Rule in Middle Europe and Balkan in the 16th and 17th Centuries, Prague, Oriental Institute Publishing House, 1978, p. 363.

44 Mazower, The Balkans, 2002.

45 E.g., Barbara Jelavich, The establishment of the Balkan national states, 1804–1920, Seatle, University of Washington Press, 1977; McCarthy Justin, Death and Exile. The Ethnic Cleansing of Ottoman Muslims, 1821–1922, Princeton, The Darwin Press, 1995; Stephen-Pericles Ladas, The Exchange of Minorities: Bulgaria, Greece and Turkey, New York, Macmillan, 1932; Safiye B. Temel, Greek-Turkish Population Exchange: An Analysis of the Conflict Leading to the Exchange, Thesis Standfort University, 1949; Vesselin Mintchev, 'External Migration and External Migration Policies in Bulgaria', South-East Europe Review for Labour and Social Affairs, 1999 (Vol. 3), pp. 123–150; Alexandre Toumarkine, Les Migrations des Populations Musulmanes Balkaniques en Anatolie (1876–1913), Istanbul, Editions Isis, 1995; Joseph B. Schechtman, 'Compulsory Transfer of the Turkish Minority from Bulgaria,' Journal of Central European Affairs, 1952 (Vol. 12), pp. 154–169; Karpat, Ottoman population.

46 Toumarkine, Les Migrations des Populations Musulmanes Balkaniques en Anatolie, p. 4.

47 Onur Yıldırım, Diplomacy and Displacement: Reconsidering the Turco-Greek Exchange of Populations, 1922–1934, New York, Routledge, 2006, pp. 90, 106.

48 McCarthy, Death and Exile, pp. 338–339.

49 Mehmet A. Yalcinkaya, The First Permanent Ottoman Embassy in Europe, Istanbul, The Isis Press, 2010.

50 Fatma M. Göçek, East encounters West: France and the Ottoman Empire in the Eighteenth Century, New York, Oxford University Press, 1987, pp. 4–5.

51 Paula S. Fichtner, Terror and Toleration: the Habsburg Empire confronts Islam, 1526–1850, London, Reaktion Books, 2008, pp. 88–101; Ivan Parvev, Habsburgs and Ottomans between Vienna and Belgrade, 1683–1789, New York, Columbia University Press, 1995, pp. 139 ff.

52 Göçek, East encounters West, pp. 4–7; Inalcik with Quataert, An Economic and Social History of the Ottoman Empire, p. 766.

53 Arnold J. Toynbee, The Western Question in Greece and Turkey. A Study in the Contact of Civilizations, London, 1922, pp. 17–19.

54   H. Pfusterschmid-Hardtenstein, *A Short History of the Diplomatic Academy of Vienna*, Vienna, Diplomatic Academy of Vienna, 2008. See also Fichtner, *Terror and Toleration*, pp. 126–127. In 1897, the Academy became the general training institute for all diplomats, henceforth called the Consular Academy, and in 1964 was restructured and renamed as the Diplomatic Academy of Vienna.

55   Robert Mantran, 'The transformation of trade in the Ottoman empire in the eighteenth century', in: Thomas Naff and Roger Owen (eds.), *Studies in eighteenth century Islamic history*, Carbondale, Southern Illinois University Press, 1977, pp. 217–235.

56   Inalcik with Quataert, *An Economic and Social History of the Ottoman Empire*, p. 724.

57   Traian Stoianovich, 'The conquering Balkan Orthodox Merchant', *Journal of Economic History*, 1960 (Vol. 20, No. 2), pp. 234–313.

58   Inalcik with Quataert, *An Economic and Social History of the Ottoman Empire*, p. 699; Bruce McGowan, *Economic Life in Ottoman Europe: taxation, trade, and the struggle for land, 1600–1800*, Cambridge/New York, Cambridge University Press, 1981, pp. 28–44.

59   McGowan, *Economic Life in Ottoman Europe*, p. 21; Goffman, *The Ottoman Empire and Early Modern Europe*, pp. 201–203.

60   McGowan, *Economic Life in Ottoman Europe*, p. 18; Inalcik with Quataert, *An Economic and Social History of the Ottoman Empire*, pp. 727–729.

61   Alison Frank, 'The Children of the Desert and the Laws of the Sea: Austria, Great Britain, the Ottoman Empire, and the Mediterranean Slave Trade in the Nineteenth Century', *The American Historical Review*, 2012 (Vol. 117, No. 2), pp. 410–444.

62   Inalcik with Quataert, *An Economic and Social History of the Ottoman Empire*, p. 771.

63   Albert Hourani: *Arabic Thought in the Liberal Age, 1798–1939*, Cambridge: Cambridge University Press, 1983.

64   *Takhlish al-Ibriz fi Takhlish Bariz* (English translation by David L. Newman, *An Imam in Paris: Al-Tahtawi's visit to France (1826–31)*, London: Saqi Books, 2004).

65   Mark Sedgwick, *Muhammad Abduh*, London: Oneworld Publications, 2009.

66   W.L. Cleveland, *Islam against the West: Shakîb Arslân and the campaign for Islamic nationalism the West*, Austin: University of Texas Press, 1985; Martin Kramer, *Islam Assembled, the Advent of the Muslim Congresses*, New York: Colombia University Press, 1986.

67   Sabine Kraft, *Neue Sakralarchitectur des Islam in Deutschland* (PhD thesis), Theology Faculty, Marburg, 2000.

68   A small Ahmadiyya community built the first modest brickstone mosque with private funds in The Hague in 1955.

69   L. Hirszowicz, *The Third Reich and the Arab East*, Toronto, 1966.

70   Götz Nordbruch, *Nazism in Syria and Lebanon: The Ambivalence of the German Option, 1933–1945*, Routledge, 2009.

71 Philip Mattar, *The Mufti of Jerusalem: Al-Hajj Amin al-Husayni and the Palestinian national movement*, New York: Columbia University Press, 1988; Francis R. Nicosia, *The Third Reich and the Palestine Question*, London: Tauris, 1985; Yehuda Taggar, *The Mufti of Jerusalem and Palestine Arab Politics, 1930–1937*, Garland Pub, 1987.

72 Clifford D. Rosenberg, *Policing Paris: The Origins of Modern Immigration Control Between the Wars*, Cornell: Cornell University Press, 2006. Also: Brigitte Maréchal, 'Introduction: From past to present.' In Brigitte Maréchal, Stefano Allievi, Felice Dassetto, Jørgen Nielsen (eds.), *Muslims in the Enlarged Europe (Muslim Minorities, Volume 2)*, Leiden/Boston: Brill, 2003, p. xxi.

73 Sebastian Balfour, *Deadly Embrace: Morocco and the road to the Spanish Civil War*, Oxford, 2002.

74 Humayun Ansari, "Between Collaboration and Resistance: Muslim Soldiers' Identities and Loyalties in the two World Wars," *Arches Quarterly*, 2011 (Vol. 4), pp. 18–29.

75 Issawi, Charles, *Cross-Cultural Encounters and Conflicts*, p. 143.

76 Nebahat Avcioğlu, *Turquerie and the Politics of Representation, 1728–1876*, Farnham/Burlington, Ashgate Publishing, 2011.

77 Jurgen Habermas, *The Structural Transformation of the Public Sphere: An Inquiry into a Category of Bourgeois Society*, Cambridge, Polity Press, 1962, English translation: 1989.

78 William J. Bernstein, *A Splendid Exchange: How Trade Shaped the World*, New York, Atlantic Monthly Press, 2008, p. 247; Göçek, *East encounters West*, p. 9.

79 Peter M. Garber, 'Tulipmania', *Journal of Political Economy*, 1989 (Vol. 97, No. 3), pp. 535–560; Anne Goldgar, *Tulipmania: Money, Honor, and Knowledge in the Dutch Golden Age*, Chicago, University of Chicago Press, 2007.

80 Eve R. Meyer, 'Turquerie and Eighteenth-Century Music', *Eighteenth-Century Studies*, 1974 (Vol. 7, No. 4), pp. 474–488.

81 Albert Hourani, *Islam in European thought*, pp. 136 ff.; Bernard Lewis, *Islam and the West*, pp. 89–95; Maxime Rodinson, *Europe and the Mystique of Islam*, pp. 83 ff.

82 Francisco, *Martin Luther and Islam*, p. 54.

83 Rodinson, *Europe and the Mystique of Islam*, p. 48.

84 E.g., Carol Appadurai Breckenridge & Peter van der Veer (eds), *Orientalism and the Postcolonial Predicament: Perspectives on South Asia*, University of Pennsylvania Press, 1993.

85 Simon During, *Cultural studies: a critical introduction*, London: Routledge, 2005.

86 E.g., R.G. Latham, 'Contributions to the Minute Ethnology of Europe, with Special Reference to a Treatise by Biondelli, Entitled Prospecto Topographico-Statisco delle Colonie Straniere d' Italia', *Transactions of the Ethnological Society of London*, 1861 (Vol. 1), pp. 105–111.

87 Mark Mazower, *The Balkans*.

88 John A.R. Marriott, *The Eastern Question. A Historical Study in European Diplomacy*, Oxford, Clarendon Press, 1940, pp. 1–3.

89 Nuri Yurdesev, 'Perceptions and Images in Turkish (Ottoman)-European Relations' in Tareq Yousif Ismael & Mustafa Aydin (eds.), *Turkey's Foreign Policy in the Twenty-First Century: A Changing Role in the World*, Aldershot: Ashgate Publishing Ltd, 2003, pp. 77–100.

90 Erik Jan Züricher, *Turkey: a modern history*, London, I.B. Tauris & Co, 1993, repr. 2005.

91 George G. Arnakis, 'The Role of Religion in the Development of Balkan Nationalism', p. 124.

92 Goffman, *The Ottoman Empire and Early Modern Europe*, pp. 64, 222–224.

93 Mary Anne Perkins, *Christendom And European Identity: The Legacy Of A Grand Narrative Since 1789*, Berlin; New York: Walter de Gruyter, 2004, p. 187.

94 Burak Akçapa, *Turkey's New European Era: Foreign Policy on the Road to EU Membership*, Plymoouth, Rowman & Littlefield, 2007, p. 36.

95 E.g., Edward Said, *Orientalism*, New York, Pantheon Books, 1978; and a critical reaction by Ibn Warraq, *Defending the West: A Critique of Edward Said*, Prometheus Books, 2007; See also Alexander L. Macfie, *Orientalism: A Reader*, New York, New York University Press, 2001.

96 Ernest Renan is one of the main proponents of this argument, in particular in his *L'Islamisme et la Science* (Paris: Calmann Levy, 1883).

97 See for descriptions of this discipline: Albert Hourani, *Islam in European thought*; Bernard Lewis, *Islam and the West*; Maxime Rodinson, *Europe and the Mystique of Islam*.

98 See for a discussion of these studies: David Motadel, 'Islam and the European Empires,' *The Historical Journal*, 2012 (Vol. 0, No. 03), pp. 831–856.

99 See, e.g., Allan Christelow, *Muslim law courts and the French colonial state in Algeria*, Princeton, NJ: Princeton University Press, 1985; J.R. Henry & F. Balique, *La doctrine coloniale du droit musulman algérien. Bibliographie systématique et introduction critique*, Paris: Editions de CNRS, 2003; Hooker, M.B., 'Muhammadan Law and Islamic Law' in M.B. Hooker (ed.), *Islam in South-East Asia*, Leiden: Brill, 1983.

100 See for these theories and notions: Albert Hourani, *Islam in European thought*; Bernard Lewis, *Islam and the West*; Maxime Rodinson, *Europe and the Mystique of Islam*.

101 E.g. Norman Daniel, *Islam, Europe and Empire*, Edinburgh, Edinburgh University Press, 1966; Jacques J. Waardenburg, *L'Islam dans le miroir de l'Occident: Comment quelques orientalistes occidentaux se sont penchés sur l'Islam et se sont formé une image de cette religion: I. Goldziher, C. Snouck Hurgronje, C.H. Becker, D.B. MacDonald, Louis Massignon*, Paris, Mouton, 1963.

5. Struggling Europe (1950–)

1   See, e.g., Bruce Bawer, *While Europe Slept: How Radical Islam is Destroying Europe from Within* (New York: Doubleday, 2006); Claire Berlinski *Menace in Europe: Why the Continent's Crisis Is America's, Too* (New York: Crown Forum, 2006); Christopher Caldwell, *Reflections on the Revolution in Europe* (New York: Anchor, 2010); Walter Laqueur, *The Last Days of Europe: Epitaph for an Old Continent* (New York: St Martin's Griffin, 2009); Mark Steyn, *Lights Out: Islam, Free Speech And The Twilight Of Europe* (Montreal: Stockade Books, 2009); Bruce Thornton, *Decline & Fall: Europe's Slow Motion Suicide* (New York: Encounter Books, 2007); Bat Ye'or, *Eurabia: The Euro-Arab Axis* (Madison (NJ): Fairleigh Dickinson University Press, 2005).

2   See, e.g., Jørgen S. Nielsen, *Muslims In Western Europe*, Edinburgh: Edinburgh University Press, 2004 (3d ed.), and Jørgen S. Nielsen et al. (eds.), *Yearbook of Muslims in Europe* (Volumes 1–5), Leiden: Brill, 2009–2013.

3   Austria is a special case: while the number of Muslims and the Islamic heritage is limited, it still has a political-legal infrastructure regarding Muslims and Islam that is a legacy from the imperial times when Austria ruled Bosnia and other regions with Muslim populations (see Robert Hunt, 'Islam in Austria' in *The Muslim World*, 2002 (Vol. 92, Nos. 1–2), pp. 115–128; Richard Potz, 'Covenental and Non-Covenental Cooperation of State and Religions in Austria' in Richard Puza & Norman Doe (eds.), *Religion and Law in Dialogue*, Leuven: Uitgeverij Peeters, 2006, pp. 11–19).

4   Mandaville, Peter, 'Muslim Transnational Identity and State Responses in Europe and the UK after 9/11: Political Community, Ideology and Authority' *Journal of Ethnic and Migration Studies*, 2009 (Vol. 35, No. 3), pp. 491–506.

5   See Steven Vertovic, *Transnationalism*, London: Routledge, 2009; Stefano Allievi & Jørgen Nielsen (eds.), *Muslim Networks and Transnational Communities in and across Europe*, Leiden/Boston: Brill, 2003.

6   Allievi, Stefano, 'Islam in the Public Space: Social Networks, Media and Neo-Communities' in Stefano Allievi & Jorgen Nielsen (eds.), *Muslim Networks and Transnational Communities in and across Europe*, Leiden: Brill, 2003, pp. 1–27; John Bowen, 'Beyond Migration: Islam as a Transnational Public Space,' *Journal of Ethnic and Migration Studies*, 2004 (Vol. 30, No. 5), pp. 879–894.

7   Akbar S. Ahmed & Donnan, Hastings (eds) *Islam, Globalization and Postmodernity*, London: Routledge, 1994; Jocelyne Cesari, 'Islam in the West: From Immigration to Global Islam' in *Harvard Middle Eastern and Islamic Review*, 2009 (Vol. 8), pp. 148–175; Peter Mandaville, *Transnational Politics. Reimagining the umma*, London/New York: Routledge, 2001 and *Global Political Islam*, London: Routledge, 2007; Ina Merdjanova, *Rediscovering the*

Umma. Muslims in the Balkans between Nationalism and Transnationalism, Oxford: Oxford University Press, 2013; Olivier Roy, *Globalized Islam: The Search for a New Ummah*, Columbia: Columbia University Press, 2006.

8   Olivier Roy describes the *umma* as an "imaginary" community that is abstract and deterriorialized (*Globalized Islam*), Mandaville speaks of a "virtual" *umma* that is the process of being continuously reimagined (*Reimagining the umma*), while Allievi conceives of it as both a real local community and a symbolic meta-community ('Islam in the Public Space').

9   Kasturi Sen and A. Yunas Samad, *Islam in the European Union. Transnationalism, Youth and the War on Terror*, Oxford: Oxford University Press, 2007.

10   S. Sayyid, 'Beyond Westphalia: Nations and Diasporas – the Case of the Muslim Umma' in B. Hesse, *Unsettled Multiculturalisms: Diasporas, Entanglements, Transruptions* (New York: Zed Books, 2000).

11   Steven Vertovic, 'Diaspora, Transnationalism and Islam', in Stefano Allievi & Jørgen Nielsen (eds.), *Muslim Networks and Transnational Communities in and across Europe*, Leiden/Boston: Brill, 2003 (pp. 312–326), p. 315.

12   B. Parekh, *Rethinking Multiculturalism: Cultural Diversity and Political Theory*, Houndmills and London: Macmillan Press, 2000.

13   Tariq Modood, 'The Place of Muslims in British Secular Multiculturalism' in Alsayyad, N, Castells, M and Michalak, L (eds.) *Islam and the Changing Identity of Europe* (University Press of America, Lexington Books, 2000); P. Werbner, *Imagined Diasporas Among Manchester Muslims: The Public Performance of Pakistani Transnational Identity Politics*, James Currey, 2002.

14   Vertovic, *Transnationalism*, pp. 99–100.

15   See, e.g., Jocelyne Cesari, *The Securitisation of Islam in Europe*, Centre for European Policy Studies: CHALLENGE Research Paper No. 14, April 2009.

16   Interview with German daily *Die Welt*, 28 July 2004.

17   Bernard Lewis, *Europe and Islam*, Washington: The AEI Press, 2007, p. 19.

18   Closer inspection shows that the references all lead to the authoritative report by the economist Karoly Lorant (*The demographic challenge in Europe* (Brussels: European Parliament, 2005)). However, the report shows that these figures are not Lorant's, but he has used them under the heading 'Those who are worrying about the growing Muslim population usually emphasize the following arguments' and for this particular statement refers on page 12 of the report to the article by Timothy M. Savage, 'Europe and Islam: Crescent Waxing, Cultures Clashing' (*The Washington Quarterly* 2004 (Vol. 27, No. 3), pp. 25–50).

19   See for elaborate studies on this topic Göran Larsson, 'The Fear of Small Numbers:

Eurabian Literature and Censuses on Religious Belonging' *Journal of Muslims in Europe*, 2012 (Vol. 1, No. 2), pp. 142–165; Birgitte Schepelern Johansen and Riem Spielhaus, 'Counting Deviance: Revisiting a Decade's Production of Surveys among Muslims in Western Europe' *Journal of Muslims in Europe*, 2012 (Vol. 1, No. 1), pp. 81–112.

20   The rise in the number of Muslims was caused by the fact that the statistical office had previously focused only on the first generation of immigrants, but now also included their descendants. See Sonja Haug, Stephanie Müssig, Anja Stichs, *Muslimisches Leben in Deutschland*, Berlin: Bundesamt für Migration und Flüchtlinge, 2009, p. 80.

21   CBS [Central Agency for Statistics], press release "Ruim 850 duizend islamieten in Nederland" Wednesday 24 October 2007.

22   UK: 1.7 million, 3% (2001 Census); France: 3.5–5 million, 6–8.5% (Sonia Tebbakh, *Muslims in the EU – Cities Report: France*, Open Society Institute, 2007, 11–13); Belgium: 0.4–0.45 million, 4% (Rijksregister, 2006); Sweden: 0.25–.35 million, 1.8–3.5% (Göran Larsson, *Muslims in the EU – Cities Report: Sweden*, Open Society Institute, 2007, pp. 9–11).

23   Author's calculations based on numbers and percentages that average what government and independent agencies have produced so far.

24   Numbers listed by the Centraal Bureau voor Statistiek [Central Statistics Agency], 25 May 2011.

25   See the European city profiles in the online studies of Open Society Foundations (www.soros.org).

26   M. Brown, 'Quantifying the Muslim Population in Europe: Conceptual and Data Issues,' *Journal of Social Research Methodology*, 2000 (Vol. 3), pp. 87–101.

27   Marieke van Herten, 'Het aantal islamieten in Nederland,' in *Religie aan het begin van de 21ste eeuw*, Den Haag: CBS, 2009, pp. 35–40.

28   Kaya, Ayhan and Ferhat Kentel, *Euro-Turks. A Bridge or a Breach between Turkey and the European Union? A Comparative Study of German Turks and French Turks*, Brussels: Centre for European Policy Studies, 2005, p. 61.

29   Haug et al. *Muslimisches Leben in Deutschland*, 2009, pp. 12, 87, 302–320.

30   Sylvain Brouard and Vincent Tiberj, *Français comme les autres: enquête sur les citoyens d'origine maghrébine, africaine et turque*, Paris: Les Presses de Sciences Po, 2005, p. 23.

31   Mentioned in Göran Larsson, *Muslims in the EU – City Report: Sweden*, Open Society Institute, 2007, p. 11.

32   Xavier Bougarel, 'The role of Balkan Muslims in building a European Islam,' EPC Issue Paper No. 43, Brussels: European Policy Centre, 23 November 2005, p. 16; Gyorgy Lederer, 'Contemporary Islam in East Europe,' online publication by NATO Academic Forum, May 1999 (http://www.nato.int/acad/fellow/97--99/lederer.pdf).

33   S. Akgönül, *Une communauté, deux Etats: La minorité turco-musulmane de Thrace occidentale*,

Istanbul: Isis, 1999; J. Dalègre, *La Thrace grecque. Populations et territoire*, Paris: L'Harmattan, 2001.

34   Brigitte Maréchal, 'The Question of belonging' in: Brigitte Maréchal, Stefano Allievi, Felice Dassetto, Jørgen Nielsen (eds.), *Muslims in the Enlarged Europe (Muslim Minorities, Volume 2)*, Leiden/Boston: Brill, 2003 (pp. 5–18), p. 9. See also: Hargreaves, A.G., *Immigration, 'Race' and Ethnicity in Contemporary France*, London: Routledge, 1995; Dassetto, F., *La construction de l'islam europeen. Approche socio-anthropologique*, Paris: L'Harmattan, 1996; Shadid, W. & P.S. van Koningsveld: (red.), *Muslims in the margin. Political responses to the presence of Islam in Western Europe*, Kampen: Kok Pharos, 1996.

35   J. Jacobson, *Islam in Transition – Religion and Identity among British Pakistani Youth*, London/New York: Routledge, 1998; Peter Mandaville, 'Towards a critical Islam' in Stefano Allievi & Jørgen Nielsen (eds.), *Muslim Networks and Transnational Communities in and across Europe*, Leiden/Boston: Brill, 2003, pp. 127–145; Bhikhu Parekh, *Europe, Liberalism and the "Muslim Question"*, Leiden: ISIM & Amsterdam University Press, 2008, p. 17; Olivier Roy, 'A Clash of Cultures or a Debate on Europe's Values' *ISIM Newsletter*, 2005 (Vol. 15).

36   Nielsen, Jørgen, *Muslims in Western Europe*, Edingburgh: Edingburgh University Press, 1992; Jocelyne Cesari, *Musulmans et republicains. Les jeunes, l'islam et la France*, Bruxelles/Paris: Editions Complexe, 1998.

37   Peter Mandaville, 'Towards a critical Islam', pp. 127–145.

38   Dasseto 1996; Babes, B., *L'Islam positif – La religion des jeunes musulmans de France*, Paris: Editions de l'Atelier, 1997; Olivier Roy, *Vers un islam europeen*, Paris: Editions Esprit, 1999; Jacobson, *Islam in Transition*, p. 153.

39   Babes, *L'Islam positif*; 1997, Dassetto 1996, Peev, Y, 'Courants islamiques en Bulgarie' in *Les Annales de l'Autre Islam*, 1997 (no. 4), pp. 183–197.

40   R. Khosrokhavar, *L'islam des jeunes*, Paris: Flammarion, 1997; Brigitte Maréchal, 'The Question of belonging', p. 15.

41   A. Kaya, *Constructing Diasporas: Turkish Hip-Hop Youth in Berlin* (PhD thesis), University of Warwick, 1997; Miriam Cooke & Bruce B. Lawrence, *Muslim Networks: From Hajj to Hip Hop*, University of North Carolina Press, 2005; Miriam Gazzah, 'European Muslim youth: Towards a cool Islam?' in Nielsen, Jørgen S., Samim Akgonül, Ahmet Alibašić, Brigitte Maréchal & Christian Moe (eds.), *Yearbook of Muslims in Europe (Volume 1)*, London/Boston: Brill, 2009, pp. 403–427.

42   X. Bougarel & N. Clayer, *Le nouvel Islam balkanique – Les musulmans, acteurs du post-communisme 1990–2000*, Paris: Maisonneuve & Larose, 2001; Harun Karcic, 'Islamic Revival in Post-Socialist Bosnia and Herzegovina: International Actors and Activities', *Journal of Muslim Minority Affairs*, 2010 (Vol. 30, No. 4), pp. 519–534.

43 H.R. Ebaugh and J.S. Chafez, *Religion and the New Immigrants – Continuities and Adaptations in Immigrant Congregations*, Oxford: Alta Mira Press, 2000; R.S. Warner and J.G. Wittner, ed., *Gatherings in Diaspora – Religious communities and, the New Immigration*, Philadelphia, PA: Temple University Press, 1998; G.M. Mirdal, 'The Construction of Muslim Identities in Contemporary Europe,' in F. Dassetto (ed.), *Paroles d' Islam-Individus, Societes et Discours dans l' Islam Europeen Contemporain*, Paris: Maisonneuve et Larose, 2000, pp. 35–49.

44 L. Lucassen & C. Laarman, 'Immigration, intermarriage and the changing face of Europe in the post war period,' in *The History of the Family*, 2009 (Vol. 14, No. 1), pp. 52–68.

45 A. Duderija, 'Factors Determining Religious Identity Construction among Western-born Muslims: Towards a Theoretical Framework' *Journal of Muslim Minority Affairs*, Vol. 28, No. 3, December 2008, p. 371–399.

46 T. Savage, 'Europe and Islam: Crescent Waxing, Cultures Clashing', p. 28.

47 Survey by *Faith Matters*, published online on 6 January 2011 (http://faith-matters.org/press/223-surge-in-britons-converting-to-islam).

48 'More in France are turning to Islam,' *New York Times*, 3 February 2013.

49 Anne Sofie Roald, *New Muslims in the European Context: The Experience of Scandinavian Converts*, Leiden: Brill, 2004, and 'The conversion process in stages: new Muslims in the twenty-first century,' *Islam and Christian–Muslim Relations*, 2012 (Vol. 23, No. 3), pp. 347–362; John Lofland & Norman Skonovd, 'Conversion Motifs,' *Journal for the Scientific Study of Religion*, 1981 (Vol. 20, No. 4), pp. 373–385; Ali Köse & Kate Miriam Loewenthal, 'Conversion Motifs Among British Converts to Islam,' *International Journal for the Psychology of Religion*, 2000 (Vol. 10, No. 2), pp. 101–110; Mounia Lakhdar, Genevive Vinsonneau, Michael J. Apter & Etienne Mullet, 'Conversion to Islam Among French Adolescents and Adults: A Systematic Inventory of Motives,' *International Journal for the Psychology of Religion*, 2007 (Vol. 17, No. 1), pp. 1–15; Karin van Nieuwkerk, *Women embracing Islam: gender and conversion in the West*, Austin: University of Texas Press, 2006.

50 Roald, *New Muslims in the European Context*, p. 53 ff.

51 Köse & Loewenthal, 'Conversion Motifs Among British Converts,' pp. 109–110; Van Nieuwkerk, *Women embracing Islam*, p p. 432.

52 E. Özyürek, 'Convert alert: German Muslims and Turkish Christians as threats to security in the new Europe', *Comparative Studies in Society and History*, 2009 (Vol. 51, No. 1) 9, pp. 91–116.

53 Olivier Roy, 'Islam in Europe: Clash of religions or convergence of religiosities?' in Krzysztof Michalski (ed.), *Religion in the New Europe, Volume 2*, New York: Central European University Press, 2006, pp. 131–142. See also Malise Ruthven, '"Born-again" Mus-

lims: cultural schizophrenia' *Open Democracy* (online publication), 10 September 2009 (http://www.opendemocracy.net/faith-islamicworld/article_103.jsp).

54   Ruthven, idem.

55   Martin Baumann, 'Anxieties, Banning Minarets and Populist Politics in Switzerland – a Preliminary Analysis,' *Pluralism Project at Harvard University*, 2009; Thijl Sunier, 'Constructing Islam: Places of Worship and the Politics of Space in the Netherlands' *Journal of Contemporary European Studies*, 2005 (Vol. 13, No. 3), pp. 317–334.

56   Avcioglu, Nebahat, 'Identity-as-Form: The Mosque in the West' *Cultural Analysis*, 2007 (Vol. 6), (pp. 91–112), p. 103; Allievi, Stefano, *Conflicts over Mosques in Europe: Policy Issues and Trends*, Alliance Publishing Trust, 2009, p. 45; Gölle, Nilüfer, 'The Public Visibility of Islam and European Politics of Resentment: The Minarets mosques debate,' *Philosophy & Social Criticism*, 2011 (Vol. 37, No. 4), pp. 383–392.

57   Stefano Allievi, *Conflicts over Mosques in Europe*, pp. 45–46; Jocelyne Cesari, 'Mosque Conflicts in European Cities: Introduction,' *Journal of Ethnic and Migration studies* 2005 (Vol. 31), pp. 1015–1024.

58   Bauman, 'Anxieties, Banning Minarets,' 2009; Stéphane Lathion, 'The impact of the minaret vote in Switzerland,' in Stefano Allievi (ed), *Mosques in Europe. Why a solution has become a problem*, London: Alliance Publishing Trust, 2010, pp. 217–233.

59   Maussen, Marcel, *Constructing Mosques: The governance of Islam in France and the Netherlands*, Amsterdam: University of Amsterdam, 2009, p. 235.

60   Azra Aksamija, 'Contested identities: identity politics and contemporary mosques in Bosnia and Herzegovina', in Stefano Allievi (ed), *Mosques in Europe. Why a solution has become a problem*, pp. 318–354.

61   Eric Roose, 'Fifty Years of Mosque Architecture in the Netherlands,' *Electronic Journal of Oriental Studies*, 2005 (Vol.), pp. 1–46.

62   The literature on the headscarf in Europe is extensive. Jennifer Selby, 'Hijab' in Jocelyne Cesari (ed.), *The Oxford Handbook of European Islam*, Oxford: Oxford University Press, 2013 provides an overview and an extensive bibliography.

63   The two cases were Dahlab vs. Switzerland (ECHR, 15 February 2001, No. 42393/98) and Sahin vs. Turkey (ECHR, 10 November 2005, No. 44774/98). For a critical review of these, cases see Carolyn Evans, 'The "Islamic Scarf" in the European Court of Human Rights' *Melbourne Journal of International Law*, 2006 (Vol. 7), pp. 52–73.

64   Velko Attanassof, *Islamic Revival in the Balkans* (thesis), Monterey: Naval Postgraduate School, March 2006; Kenneth Morrison, *Wahhabism in the Balkans*, Shrivenham: Cranfield University, Defence Academy of the United Kingdom, Advanced Research and Assessment Group, 2008.

65   Rafic Banawi & Rex Stockton, 'Islamic values relevant to group work, with practical

implications for the group leader,' *The Journal for Specialists in Group Work*, 1993 (Vol. 18), record first published in 2008, pp. 151–160.

66   Tabassum Fatima Rehman & Sophia F. Dziegielewski, 'Women Who Choose Islam. Issues, Changes, and Challenges in Providing Ethnic-Diverse Practice,' *International Journal of Mental Health*, 2003 (Vol. 23), pp. 31–49.

67   Literature on this subject is extensive. See, e.g., Jørgen S. Nielsen et al. (eds.) *Yearbook of Muslims in Europe* (Volumes 1–5), Leiden: Brill, 2009–2013.

68   Jonas R. Kunst & David L. Sam, 'Relationship between perceived acculturation expectations and Muslim minority youth's acculturation and adaptation,' in *International Journal of Intercultural Relations*, 2013 (Vol. 37), pp. 477–490.

69   Literature on secularism in Europe is extensive, also when discussed in relation to Muslims and Islam. See, e.g., Jocelyne Cesari & Sean McLoughlin (eds.), *European Muslims and the Secular State*, Aldershot: Ashgate, 2005; Jytte Klausen, *The Islamic Challenge: Politics and Religion in Western Europe*, Oxford: Oxford University Press, 2005; Olivier Roy, *Secularism confronts Islam*, New York: Columbia University Press, 2007; Joel S. Fetzer & J. Christopher Soper, *Muslims and the State in Britain, France, and Germany*, Cambridge: Cambridge University Press, 2005.

70   See for an overview of the European state systems the country summaries in *Yearbook of Muslims in Europe* (Volumes 1–5, edited by Jørgen S. Nielsen et al., Leiden: Brill, 2009–2013).

71   Sean McLoughlin, 'The State, New Muslim Leadership and Islam as a Resource for Public Engagement in Britain' in Jocelyne Cesari & Sean McLoughlin (eds.), *European Muslims and the Secular State*, p. 53–69; Alexandre Caiero, 'Religious Authorities or Public Actors? The Muslim Leaders of the French Representative Body of Islam' Jocelyne Cesari & Sean McLoughlin (eds.), *European Muslims and the Secular State*, p. 71–84; Yvonne Haddad & Tyler Golson, 'Overhauling Islam: Representation, Construction, and Cooption of 'Moderate' Islam in Europe' *Journal of Church & State*, Vol. 49, No. 3, 2007, p. 487–515.

72   This is the concept of the state as the 'neutral organizer' (e.g., ECHR, Kokkinakis v. Greece, Nr. 14307/88, 25 May 1993).

73   See Jørgen S. Nielsen et al (eds.), *Yearbook of Muslims in Europe*, Volumes 1–5.

74   Maurits Berger, 'Shari'a in Europe' in J. Brown (ed.), *Oxford Encyclopedia of Islam and Law*, Oxford: Oxford University Press, *forthcoming in 2014*.

75   See, e.g., Samia Bano, *Islamic Dispute Resolution and Family Law*, London: PalgraveMacMillan, 2011; Sonia Nurin Shah-Kazemi, *Untying the Knot, Muslim Women, Divorce and the Shariah*, Nuffield Foundation, 2001.

76   See for discussions on the issue of 'sharia in the West': Rex Ahdar and Nicholas Aroney (eds.), *Shari'a in the West*, Oxford: Oxford University Press, 2011; Maurits Berger (ed.),

Applying Shari'a in the West: Facts, Fears and Figures, Leiden: Leiden University Press, 2013; Andrea Büchler, *Islamic Law in Europe? Legal Pluralism and its Limits in European Family Laws*, Burlington: Ashgate, 2011; Robin Griffith-Jones (ed.), *Islam and English Law: Rights, Responsibilities and the Place of Shari'a*, Cambridge: Cambridge University Press, 2013; Jørgen Nielsen and Lisbet Christiffersen (eds.), *Shari'a as a Discourse: Legal Traditions and the Encounter with Europe*, Burlington: Ashgate, 2010; Matthias Rohe, *Muslim Minorities and the Law in Europe: Chances and Challenges*, Global Media Publications, 2007.

77 Stefano Allievi, 'Muslims and Politics' in Brigitte Maréchal, Stefano Allievi, Felice Dassetto, Jørgen Nielsen (eds.), *Muslims in the Enlarged Europe (Muslim Minorities, Volume 2)*, Leiden/Boston: Brill, 2003 (pp. 183–216), pp. 188–194.

78 Article 62 sub 2 of the 2003 Constitution stipulates: "Organizations of citizens belonging to national minorities, which fail to obtain the number of votes for representation in Parliament, have the right to one Deputy seat each, under the terms of the electoral law. Citizens of a national minority are entitled to be represented by one organization only."

79 See, e.g., the omission of religious minorities in the 1995 European Framework Convention for the Protection of National Minorities.

80 Yusuf Al-Qaradawi, *Fiqh of Muslim Minorities: Contentious Issues & Recommended Solutions*, Al-Falah for Translation Publications Distribution, 2003.

81 Tariq Ramadan, *Western Muslims and the Future of Islam*, Oxford: Oxford University Press, 2005.

82 Religious minority rights are mostly discussed in non-European contexts (see, e.g., publications in *Journal of Muslim Minority Affairs*). Within the Western European context Muslim minority rights are mostly discussed in ethnic terms, i.e. as the rights of Turks, Pakistanis, Moroccans more than the rights of Muslims (see, e.g., Tariq Modood, *Ethnicity, nationalism, and minority rights*, Cambridge: Cambridge University Press, 2004; Jonathan Laurence, *The emancipation of Europe's Muslims: the state's role in minority integration*, Princeton: Princeton University Press, 2012). For an Islamic legal perspective see Andrew March, *Islam and Liberal Citizenship: The search for an overlapping consensus*, Oxford: Oxford University Press, 2009.

83 *Perceptions of Discrimination and Islamophobia. Voices from Members of Muslim Communities in the European Union* by the European Monitoring Centre on Racism and Xenophobia (EUMC), 2006.

84 For authors who advocate such tolerance within a legal setting, see Silvio Ferrari, 'The New Wine and the Old Cask. Tolerance, Religion, Religion and the Law in Contemporary Europe', *Ratio Juris*, 1997 (Vol. 10, No. 1), pp. 75–89; Marie-Claire Foblets, 'Accomodating Islamic Family Law(s): A Critical Analysis of Some Recent Developments and

Experiments in Europe' in: Maurits S. Berger (ed.), 'Applying Shari'a in the West' in *Applying Shari'a in the West. Facts, fears and figures*, Maurits S. Berger (ed.) (Leiden: Leiden University Press, 2013, pp. 207-226).

85   Under 'Scope' in the Appendix to the Recommendation No. R (97) 20 of the Committee of EU Ministers to member states on "hate speech" (Adopted by the Committee of Ministers on 30 October 1997) it is explicitly mentioned that hate speech can be punishable only when directed against people, not abstractions like religion.

86   Article 10, Paragraph 2 of the European Convention for Human Rights. See also Bahia Tahzib-Lie, 'The European definition of freedom of religion or belief', in: *Helsinki Monitor*, 1998 (Vol. 9), pp. 17-27.

87   ECHR, 7 December 1976 (*Handyside*).

88   Peev, Y, 'Courants islamiques en Bulgarie' in *Les Annales de l'Autre Islam*, 1997 (no. 4), pp. 183-197.

89   Ilchev, I. & D. Perry, 'The Muslims of Bulgaria' in G. Nonneman, T. Niblock & B. Szajkowski, *Muslim Communities in Europe*, London: Ithaca Press, 1996, pp. 115-138.

90   Samuel Huntington, *The Clash of Civilizations and the Remaking of World Order*, New York: Simon and Schuster, 2007, p. 35.

91   Srdjan Vrcan, 'The War in ex-Yugoslavia and Religion', *Social Compass*, 1994 (Vol. 41, No. 3), (pp. 413-422), p. 414.

92   Louis Sell, *Slobadan Milosevic and the destruction of Yugoslavia*. Durham/London: Duke University Press, 2002; Dusan Kecmanovic, *Ethnic Times. Exploring Ethnonationalism in the former Yugoslavia*. Westpot/Connecticut/London: Praeger, 2002; Ann Lane, *Yugoslavia. When ideals collide*. New York: Palgrave Macmillan: 2004; Gerard F. Powers, 'Religion, Conflict and Prospects for Peace in Bosnia, Croatia and Yugoslavia', *Journal of International Affairs*, 1996 (Vol. 50, No. 1).

93   Ivekovic, Ivan, 'Nationalism and the Political Use and Abuse of Religion: The Politicization of Orthodoxy, Catholicism and Islam in Yugoslave Successor States', in *Social Compass*, 2002 (Vol. 49, No. 4).

94   Vjekoslav Perica, *Balkan Idols. Religion and Nationalism in Yugoslav States*. Oxford: Oxford University Press, 2002.

95   Douglas Johnston and Jonathan Eastvold, 'History Unrequited. Religion as Provocateur and Peacemaker in the Bosnian Conflict', in Harold Coward & Gordon S. Smith, *Religion and Peacebuilding*, New York: SUNY Press, 2004, pp. 213-242.

96   Srdjan Vrcan, 'The War in ex-Yugoslavia and Religion', p. 414, quoting F. Vreg, 'Iluzije o evropskem multikulturalizmu', *Teorija in praksa*, 1993 (Vol. 30 Nos. 7-8), p. 664.

97   Michael Sells, 'Crosses of Blood: Sacred Space, Religion, and Violence in Bosnia-Hercegovina', *Sociology of Religion*, 2003 (Vol. 64, No. 3), pp. 309-331.

98   Aydin Babuna, 'The Albanians of Kosovo and Macedonia: ethnic identity superseding Religion', *Nationality Papers*, 2000 (Vol. 28, No. 1); and 'The Bosnian Muslims and Albanians: Islam and nationalism', *The Journal of Nationalism and Ethnicity*, 2004 (Vol. 32, No. 2), pp. 287–332.

99   Bougarel, X. & N. Clayer, *Le nouvel Islam balkanique – Les musulmans, acteurs du postcommunisme 1990–2000*, Paris: Maisonneuve & Larose, 2001; Harun Karcic, 'Islamic Revival in Post-Socialist Bosnia and Herzegovina: International Actors and Activities', *Journal of Muslim Minority Affairs*, 2010 (Vol. 30, No. 4), pp. 519–534; Attanassof, Velko, *Islamic Revival in the Balkans* (thesis), Monterey: Naval Postgraduate School, March 2006.

100   A. Izetbegovic, *Islam Between East and West*, American Trust Publications, 1985; and *The Islamic Declaration*, 1991 (not published, but available in English translation on manifique.free.fr/allhere/ezati.pdf).

101   See also Dzemal Sokolovic, 'How to Conceptualize the Tragedy of Bosnia: Civil, Ethnic, Religious War or ...?', *War Crimes, Genocide, & Crimes against Humanity*, 2005 (Vol. 1, No. 1), pp. 115–130; Ramet, Sabrina Petra, *Balkan Babel. Politics, Culture, and Religion in Yugoslavia*, Boulder/San Francisco/Oxford: Westview Press, 1992.

102   Anastas Vangeli, 'Religion, Nationalism and Counter-secularization: The Case of the Macedonian Orthodox Church' in *Identity Studies*, 2010 (Vol. 2), pp. 1–15.

103   E.g., Thomas. M. Pick, Anne Speckhard, Beatrice Jacuch, *Home-Grown Terrorism: Understanding and Addressing the Root Causes of Radicalisation Among Groups With an Immigrant Heritage in Europe*, IOS Press, 2009; Daveed Gartenstein-Ross, & Laura Grossman, *Homegrown Terrorists in the U.S. and U.K. An Empirical Examination of the Radicalization Process*, Washington DC: FDD's Center for Terrorism Research, 2009.

104   J. Githens-Mazer, J., 'The rhetoric and the reality: radicalisation and political discourse', *International Political Sciences Review*, 2012 (Vol. 33, No. 5), pp. 556–567; M. Sedgwick, 'The Concept of Radicalization as a Source of Confusion,' *Terrorism and Political Violence*, 2010 (Vol. 22, No. 4), pp. 479–494; L. Richardson, *What Terrorists Want. Understanding the Enemy, Containing the Threat*, London: Random House, 2007; Edwin Bakker, *Jihadi terrorists in Europe. Their characteristics and the circumstances in which they joined the jihad: an exploratory study*, The Hague: Clingendael Institute, December 2006. See also CRS Report RL33166 for Congress, 'Muslims in Europe: Integration Policies in Selected Countries', 2005: "While there is no sharply developed tendency towards radicalism, it is likely that young Muslims above all have in recent years grown alienated from the European societies in which they live." (p. 2).

105   There are many reports on this issue. For the sake of brevity I refer here to the recent report series by the Open Society Institute's EUMAP-initiative called *Muslims in EU Cities: Background Research Reports*, which in early 2009 listed downloadable reports on

Belgium, Denmark, France, Germany, The Netherlands, Sweden and United Kingdom (www.eumap.org/topics/minority/reports/eumuslims/background_reports).

106 *Muslims in Europe: Integration Policies in Selected Countries* CRS Report RL33166 for Congress, by Paul Gallis, coordinator, November 18, 2005.

107 European Monitoring Centre on Rascism and Xenophobia (EUMC), *Perceptions of Discrimination and Islamophobia*, 2006.

108 Open Society Institute, *Muslims in the UK: Policies for Engaged Citizens*, November 2004; UK Home Office, *Improving Opportunity; Strengthening Society: The Government's strategy to increase race equality and community cohesion*, January 2005. Bundesamt für Verfassungsschutz (Federal Office for the Protection of the Constitution), *Integration als Extremismus- und Terrorismusprävention. Zur Typologie islamistischer Radikalisierung und Rekrutierung*, January 2007.

109 M.S. Berger, 'Jihad and counter-jihad: Western Legal Responses to Islamic Militancy,' in: Bassiouni, M.C. & Guellali, A. (eds.), *Jihad and its Challenges to International and Domestic Law*, The Hague: Hague Academic Press, 2010; James Brandon & Lorenzo Vidino, *Countering Radicalization in Europe*, London: International Centre for the Study of Radicalisation and Political Violence (ICSR), 2012; Daniela Pisoiu, *Islamist Radicalisation in Europe: An Occupational Change Process*, London: Routledge, 2013.

110 'Gelingende Integration = Extremismus- und Terrorismusprävention' in: *Integration als Extremismus-und Terrorismusprävention. Zur Typologie islamistischer Radikalisierung und Rekrutierung*, Bundesamt für Verfassungsschutz (Federal Office for the Protection of the Constitution), January 2007, p. 7.

111 In the Netherlands, with a strong tradition of municipal autonomy, cities like Amsterdam and Rotterdam have developed their own strategic plans, with a lot of financial and staff support (see Amsterdam's *Wij Amsterdammers*, 2004 and *Amsterdam tegen Radicalisering*, 2007, and Rotterdam's *Meedoen of Achterblijven*, 2005). In England, municipalities lack such powers and resources, but similar activities are nevertheless taking place in West London, West Yorkshire, Leicester and Birmingham (see *The Prevent Strategy: A Guide for Local Partners in England. Stopping people becoming or supporting terrorists and violent extremists*, H.M. Government, May 2008). For the little information in English available about Spain see *Muslims in Europe: Integration Policies in Selected Countries*, CRS Report to Congress, November 18, 2005, p. 38 *ff*.

112 Idem.

113 Observed by the author.

114 Jocelyne Cesari, *The Securitization of Islam in Europe*, Research Paper No. 15 in CEPS CHALLENGE Programme, April 2009 (available online at www.ceps.eu); E. Schlueter, B. Meuleman & E. Davidov, 'Immigrant integration policies and perceived Group Threat: A

multilevel study of 27 Western and Eastern European Countries' in *Social Science Research*, 2013 (Vol. 42).

115 See, e.g., the 1997 special of *Mediterranean Politics* (Vol. 2, No. 1).

116 Stefano Allievi, 'The International Dimension' (Chapter twelve in Part Three: 'Islam and Society: Public Space and Integration'), in Brigitte Maréchal, Stefano Allievi, Felice Dassetto, Jørgen Nielsen (eds.), *Muslims in the Enlarged Europe* (*Muslim Minorities, Volume 2*), Leiden/Boston: Brill, 2003 (pp. 449–488), pp. 479–488; C. Spencer, 'Europe and political Islam: defining threats and evolving policies,' in: M. Kramer (ed.), *The Islamism Debate*, Tel Aviv: Moshe Dayan Center for Middle Eastern and African Studies, Tel Aviv University, 1997.

117 Declaration No. 11 of the Amsterdam Treaty (1997) which has been reaffirmed in Article 17 of the Treaty on the Functioning of the European Union (see Sergio Carrera and Joanna Parkin, 'The Place of Religion in the European Union Law and Policy (2008). Competing Approaches and Actors inside the European Commission', in *Justice and Home Affairs*, RELIGARE Working Document No. 1, September 2010 (online publication, available at http://www.ceps.be/book/place-religion-european-union-law-and-policy-competing-approaches-and-actors-inside-european-co)).

118 Sara Silvestri, 'EU Relations with Islam in the Context of the EMP's Cultural Dialogue' in *Mediterranean Politics*, 2005 (Vol. 10, No. 3), pp. 385–405.

119 The 'intercultural dialogue' was the so-called third basket of the Barcelona Declaration, 1995. See Michelle Pace, Imagining Co-presence in Euro-Mediterranean Relations: The Role of 'Dialogue', in *Mediterranean Politics*, 2005 (Vol. 10, No. 3), pp. 291–312.

120 Stefano Allievi, 'The International Dimension', pp. 481–482.

121 Sara Silvestri, 'EU Relations with Islam', 2005.

122 Gillespie, R., 'Reshaping the agenda? The internal politics of the Barcelona Process in the aftermath of September 11,' *Mediterranean Politics*, 2003 (Vol. 8, Nos. 2–3), pp. 21–36; Volpi, F., 'Regional community building and the transformation of international relations: the case of the Euro-Mediterranean Partnership,' *Mediterranean Politics*, 2004 (Vol. 9, No. 2), pp. 145–164.

123 Speech of 6 November 2003 for the National Endowment for Peace.

124 See, e.g., *Changing Minds, Winning Peace, A New Strategic Direction for U.S. Public Diplomacy in the Arab & Muslim World*, Report of the Advisory Group on Public Diplomacy for the Arab and Muslim World, October 1, 2003. Also M.S. Berger, 'Islam and Islamic law in Contemporary International Relations' in M.-L. Frick. & A.Th. Mueller (eds.), *Islam and International Law. Engaging Self-Centrism from a Plurality of Perspectives* (Arab and Islamic Law Series), Leiden/Boston: Brill/Martinus Nijhoff Publishers, pp. 393–413.

125 Muslims in Europe: Integration Policies in Selected Countries CRS Report RL33166 for Congress, by Paul Gallis, coordinator, November 18, 2005, pp. 11–12.

126 Gary R. Bunt, Islam in the Digital Age: E-Jihad, Online Fatwas and Cyber Islamic Environments, London and Sterling, Virginia: Pluto Press, 2003; B. Gräf & J. Skovgaard-Petersen, Global mufti: the phenomenon of Yūsuf al-Qaraḍāwi, Columbia University Press, 2009.

127 This has been observed in the cases of Morocco and Turkey vis-à-vis their nationals in the Netherlands (Sunier, T. & N. Landman, Diyanet, the Turkish Directorate for Religious Affairs in a changing environment, Amsterdam/Utrecht: VU University and Utrecht University, 2011; M. Kahmann, Ontmoetingen tussen Marokkaanse Nederlanders en de Marokkaanse Overheid, Leiden (PhD thesis), 2014).

128 Brigitte Maréchal, 'Mosques, organisations and leadership' in Brigitte Maréchal, Stefano Allievi, Felice Dassetto, Jørgen Nielsen (eds.), Muslims in the Enlarged Europe (Muslim Minorities, Volume 2), Leiden/Boston: Brill, 2003 (pp. 79–150), pp. 85 ff.; Dassetto, La construction de l'islam europeen; M. Reeber., 'Les khutbas de la diaspora: enquete sur les tendencies de la predication dans les mosques en France et dans plusieurs pays d'Europe occidentale' in F. Dassetto, Paroles d'Islam – Individus, Societes et Discours dans l'Islam europeen contemporain / Islamic Words – Individuals, Societies and Discourse in Contemporary European Islam, Paris: Maisonneuve & Larose, 2000: 236 ff.; Fregosi, F, La formation des cadres religieuz musulmans en France – Approahces socio-juridiques, Paris: L'Harmattan, 1998, p. 203.

129 Meijer, Roel & Edwin Bakker (eds.), The Muslim Brotherhood in Europe, New York: Columbia University Press, 2013.

130 Pargeter, Alison, The New Frontiers of Jihad: Radical Islam in Europe, London/New York: I.B. Tauris, 2008. Also: Maréchal, Brigitte, The Muslim Brothers in Europe: Roots and Discourse (Muslim Minorities, 8), Leiden: Brill, 2008.

131 Brigitte Maréchal, 'Mosques, organisations and leadership' in Brigitte Maréchal, Stefano Allievi, Felice Dassetto, Jørgen Nielsen (eds.), Muslims in the Enlarged Europe (Muslim Minorities, Volume 2), Leiden/Boston: Brill, 2003, pp. 109–111.

132 Harun Karcic, 'Islamic Revival in Post-Socialist Bosnia and Herzegovina: International Actors and Activities', Journal of Muslim Minority Affairs, 2010 (Vol. 30, No. 4), pp. 519–534; Kullolli, Arben, Proselytization in Albania by Middle Eastern Islamic Organizations (thesis), Monterey: Naval Postgraduate School, March 2009

133 X. Bougarel, X. & N. Clayer, Le nouvel Islam balkanique.

134 Pancevski, Bojan, 'Saudis fund Balkan Muslims spreading hate of the West' in TimesOnline, March 28, 2010; Defense & Foreign Affairs Special Analysis (no author), 'Wahhabism and Islamic Extremism in Former Yugoslav Republic of Macedonia: a General

Overview', June 1, 2006; Somun, Hajrudin, 'Wahhabism in the Balkans: a threat to regional stability?' in *Today's Zaman*, 4 March 2010.

135 For an overview, see Ozay Mehmet, 'Turkey and the European Union: A Troubled Relationship or a Historic Partnership?' in Tareq Yousif Ismael & Mustafa Aydin (eds.), *Turkey's Foreign Policy in the Twenty-First Century: A Changing Role in the World*, Aldershot: Ashgate Publishing Ltd, 2003, pp. 41–58.

136 Interview in *Time Magazine*, European edition, 20 November 1995.

137 Z. Öniz, 'Globalization and Party Transformation: Turkey's JDP in Perspective', in: Peter Burnell (ed.), *Globalizing Democracy: Party Politics in Emerging Democracies*, London: Routledge, 2006 (pp. 1–27), p. 18. Ahyan Kaya, 'Turkey-EU relations: The impact of Islam on Europe' in Nielsen, Jørgen S., Samim Akgonül, Ahmet Alibašić, Brigitte Maréchal & Christian Moe (eds.), *Yearbook of Muslims in Europe (Volume 1)*, London/Boston: Brill, 2009 (pp. 377–402), p. 380.

138 See examples mentioned in Thomas Diez, 'Europe's Others and the Return to Geopolitics' in *Cambridge Review of International Affairs*, 2004 (Vol. 17, No. 2), pp. 319–335.

139 Interview with BBC Radio 4 on 16 October 2002.

140 Interview in *The Guardian*, 27 November 2002.

141 Ahyan Kaya & Kentel, Ferhat, *Euro-Turks: A Bridge, or a Breach between Turkey and the EU* (Brussels: Centre for European Policy Studies, 2005).

142 In 2006 restructured and named the Human Rights Council.

143 European Monitoring Centre on Racism and Xenophobia (EUMC), *Summary Report into Islamophobia in the EU following 11 September 2001* (Vienna: EUMC, 2002).

144 Human Rights Council resolution 16/18 on Combating Intolerance, Discrimination, and Violence Based on Religion or Belief.

145 Mary Anne Perkins, *Christendom And European Identity: The Legacy Of A Grand Narrative Since 1789*, Berlin/New York: Walter de Gruyter, 2004; Talal Assad, *Formations of the Secular. Christianity, Islam, Modernity*, Stanford: Stanford University Press, 2003 p. 165.

146 Talal Asad, *Formations of the Secular*, p. 159.

147 Nezar AlSayyad & Manuel Castells (eds.), *Muslim Europe or Euro-Islam. Politics, Culture, and Citizenship in the Age of Globalization*, Lanham: Lexington Books, 2002, p. 182.

148 For a discussion of Jurgen Habermas' *Die Einbeziehung des Anderen* (Frankfurt: Suhrkamp, 1996) and Alain Touraine's *Pourrons-nous vivre ensemble? Egaux et Differents* (Paris: Fayard, 1997) see AlSayyad, Nezar & Manuel Castells (eds.), *Muslim Europe or Euro-Islam. Politics, Culture, and Citizenship in the Age of Globalization*, Lanham: Lexington Books, 2002, pp. 182–187. For Charles Taylor, see his "Multiculturalism and 'The Politics of Recognition': an essay" in A. Guttmann (ed.), *Multiculturalism and the Politics of Recognition*, (Princeton: Princeton University Press, 1992). For Will Kymlicka, see his

Multicultural Citizenship: A Liberal Theory of Minority Rights (Oxford: Oxford University Press, 1995).

149 Perkins, *Christendom And European Identity*, p. 187.

150 Jocelyne Cesari and Sean McLoughlin, *European Muslims and the Secular State*, London: Ashgate Publishing, 2005; Sarah Bracke & Nadia Fadil, *Islam and Secular Modernity under Western Eyes: A Geneaology of a Constitutive Relationship*, Florence: European University Institute, Working Paper RSCAS No. 5, 2008.

151 Ciftci, 'Islamophobia and Threat Perceptions,' 2012, p. 303–306.

152 The most renown parties are the British National Party in the United Kingdom, *Vlaams Blok* in Belgium, the *Party for Freedom* in the Netherlands, the *People's Party* in Denmark, the Northern League in Italy, the Freedom Party in Austria (for an analysis of the last three see Susi Meret, *The Danish People's Party, the Italian Northern League and the Austrian Freedom Party in a Comparative Perspective: Party Ideology and Electoral Support* (PhD thesis), Aalborg University, 2009).

153 The first study on Islamophobia was report by The Runnymede Trust: *Islamophobia: A Challenge for Us All* (London: Runnymede Trust, 1997), followed by F. Halliday, 'Islamophobia reconsidered' (*Ethnic and Racial Studies*, 1999 (Vol. 22, No. 5), pp. 892–902). See also, in chronological order: Salman Sayyid, *Thinking Through Islamophobia* London: Hurst & Co., 2010; Andrew Shryock, *Islamophobia/Islamophilia: Beyond the Politics of Enemy and Friend*, Bloomington: Indiana University Press, 2010, John L. Esposito, Ibrahim Kalin, *Islamophobia. The Challenge of Pluralism in the 21st Century*, Oxford: Oxford University Press, 2011. Two comprehensive analyses are: F. Bravo López T., 'Towards a definition of Islamophobia: approximations of the early twentieth century', Ethnic and Racial Studies, 2011 (Vol. 34, No. 4), pp. 556–573; Sabri Ciftci, 'Islamophobia and Threat Perceptions: Explaining Anti-Muslim Sentiment in the West', *Journal of Muslim Minority Affairs*, 2012 (Vol. 32, No. 3), pp. 293–309; H. Ansari, & F. Hafez, *From the Far Right to the Mainstream: Islamophobia in Party Politics and the Media*, Frankfurt-am-Main: Campus Verlag GmbH, 2012. Reports commissioned by governments are the Commission on British Muslim and Islamophobia, *Islamophobia: Issues, Challenges and Action*, Stoke-on-Trent and Sterling, VA: Trentham Books, 2004; *Perceptions of Discrimination and Islamophobia. Voices from Members of Muslim Communities in the European Union* by the European Monitoring Centre on Racism and Xenophobia (EUMC), 2006.

154 Some of these Muslims become staunch critics themselves. A scholar specializing in Islamophobia makes the comparison with Jewish converts: "It is common knowledge that the best way of proving that one is no longer a Muslim is to become an Islamophobe. The history of anti-Semitism is full of examples of converts who became anti-Semites and who were accepted by anti-Semites as one of them." (F. Bravo López, 'To-

wards a definition of Islamophobia', 2004, in which she refers to her PhD dissertation 'Islamofobia y antisemitismo: la construccion discursiva de las amenazas islamica y judia', Department of Arab, Islamic and Oriental Studies, Universidad Auto'noma de Madrid, Madrid, 2009, pp. 281–284).

155 Bernard Lewis, 'The Third Wave: Muslim Migration to Europe,' *New Perspectives Quarterly*, 2007 (Vol. 24), pp. 30–35; Bassam Tibi, *Political Islam, World Politics and Europe* (New York: Routledge, 2008), p. 1.

156 See Chapter 1, *The Battle of Poitiers*.

157 See Chapter 3, *Vienna 1683*.

158 Excerpt from television interview in the Al-Jazeera programme Bi-la Hudud on 13 August 2007 (available at http://www.youtube.com/watch?v=RDLinMUhn3Q).

159 Secretary-general Willy Claes, interview in the *Süddeutche Zeitung* of 2 February 2009.

160 See literature in footnote XX (Eurabia etc.).

161 See contributions in Section III of *European Muslims and the Secular State*, Jocelyne Cesari and sean McLoughlin (eds) (London: Ashgate, 2005), 129–196. Also: Felice Dassetto (ed.), *Paroles d'islam: individus, sociétés, discours dans l'islam européen contemporain* (Paris: Maisonneuve et Larose, 2000). For categorizations of forms of Islamic religiosity among European Muslims see Brigitte Maréchal, 'The Question of Belonging' pp. 6–18; Jocelyne Cesari, *When Islam and Democracy Meet: Muslims in Europe and the United States*, New York: Palgrave Macmillan, 2004, pp. 43–64.

162 This observation is not without discussion and controversy. See, e.g., J. Raz, *The Morality of Freedom*, Oxford: Oxford University Press, 1986; J. Rawls, 'The priority of rights and the idea of good', *Philosophy and Public Affairs*, 1988 (Vol. 17), pp. 251–276; W. Kymlicka, *Multicultural Citizenship: A Liberal Theory of Minority Rights*, Oxford: Clarendon Press, 1995, pp. 129–131; Erhard Denninger, ''Security, Diversity, Solidarity' Instead of 'Freedom, Equality, Fraternity',' *Constellations* 2000 (Vol. 7, No. 4), pp. 507–521; P. Shah, *Legal Pluralism in Conflict: Coping with Cultural Diversity in Law*. London: Cavendish, Glasshouse, 2005.

163 See country reports in Jocelyne Cesari (ed.), *The Oxford Handbook of European Islam*, and the online country studies of Open Society Foundations (www.soros.org). Also: Gallup World Poll, *Muslims in Europe: Basis for Greater Understanding Already Exists* (Princeton: The Gallup Organization, 2007).

164 Maurits S. Berger, 'Introduction to Applying Sharia in the West,' and Matthias Rohe, 'Reasons for the Application of Sharia in the West' in: Maurits S. Berger (ed.), 'Applying Shari'a in the West' in *Applying Shari'a in the West. Facts, fears and figures*, Maurits S. Berger (ed.) (Leiden: Leiden University Press, 2013).

165 Ayelet Shachar, "Privatizing Diversity: A Cautionary Tale from Religious Arbitration in Family Law" *Theoretical Inquiries in Law*, 2008 (Vol. 9), pp. 573–607. Similar observations

were made by Samia Bano, *Islamic Dispute Resolution and Family Law*, London: Palgrave-MacMillan, 2011.

166 In the Greek province of Thrace, the existing practice of legal autonomy for Muslim family matters is being criticized as 'neo-milletanism' (see K. Tsitselikis, *Old and New Islam in Greece: From Historical Minorities to Immigrant Newcomers*, Leiden: Martinus Nijhoff Publishers, 2012; Angeliki Ziaki, 'Greece: Debate and Challenges' in Maurits S. Berger (ed.), 'Applying Shari'a in the West' in *Applying Shari'a in the West. Facts, fears and figures*, Leiden: Leiden University Press, 2013, pp. 125–139).

167 James O'Connell, *The Making of Modern Europe: Strengths, Constraints and Resolutions*, University of Bradford Peace Research Report no. 26 (Bradford: University of Bradford, 1991); Hugh Trevor-Roper, *The Rise of Christian Europe*, London: Thames and Hudson, 1965; Michael Wintle (ed.), *Culture and Identity in Europe*, Aldershot: Avebury, 1996.

168 See, e.g., Talal Asad, *Formations of the Secular: Christianity, Islam, Modernity* (Stanford: Stanford University Press, 2003); Cesari and McLoughlin, *European Muslims and the Secular State*, 2005; Jose Casanova, "Religion, European secular identities, and European integration", *Transit* 27 (2004), 1–17; Jytte Klausen, *The Islamic Challenge: Politics and Religion in Western Europe* (Oxford: Oxford University Press, 2005); Olivier Roy, *Secularism confronts Islam* (New York: Columbia University Press, 2007); Armando Salvatore, "Power and Authority within European Secularity: From the Enlightenment Critique of Religion to the Contemporary Presence of Islam" in, 543–561.

169 For comparative analyses, see e.g., Peter L. Berger, Grace Davie, Effie Fokkas, *Religious America, Secular Europe?: A Theme and Variation*, London: Ashgate, 2008; Jackson, Pamela Irving & Peter A. Zervakis, *The Integration of Muslims in Germany, France and the United States: Law, Politics and Public Policy*, Paper prepared for 2004 annual meeting of the American sociological Association (pdf-file online only), 2004; Jocelyne Cesari, *When Islam and Democracy Meet*; Barbara Metcalf, *Making Muslim Space in North America and Europe* (Berkeley/London: University of California Press, 1996).

170 See also Jytte Klaus, *The Islamic Challenge: Politics and Religion*, Oxford: Oxford University Press, 2005, pp. 204 ff.

171 Conseil d'Etat, *Etude relative aux possibilités juridiques d'interdiction du port du voile intégral*, 25 March 2010 (available online at: www.conseil-etat.fr/cde/media/document/avis/etude_vi_30032010.pdf).

172 See the explanations of their respective law proposals by the Cabinet (*Projet de loi interdisant la dissimulation du visage dans l'espace public* (No. 2520, 19 May 2010)) and by the Socialist Party (*Proposition de loi visant à fixer le champ des interdictions de dissimuler son visage liées aux exigences des services publics, à la prévention des atteintes à l'ordre public* (No. 2544, 20 May 2010)).

173   For an insightful and critical survey and analysis of methods used by the early and modern scholars of Muslim societies and Islam, see Maxime Rodinson, *Europe and the Mystique of Islam*, London, Tauris, 1988; J. Waardenburg, *Muslims as Actors: Islamic Meanings and Muslim Interpretations in the Perspective of the Study of Religions*, Berlin: Walter de Gruyter, 2007.

174   Edward Said, *Orientalism*, New York: Vintage Books, 1979.

175   See for critical responses: Bernard Lewis, *Islam and the West*, 1993, pp. 99–118; Ibn Warraq, Defending the West: a critique of Edward Said's Orientalism, Amerherst (N.Y.): Prometheus Books, 2007; Daniel Martin Varisco, *Reading Orientalism: Said and the Unsaid*, Seattle: Washington University Press, 2007.

176   M.S. Berger, *Islam and the Uncertainty Principle*, Den Haag: Boom Juridische Uitgeverij, 2009.

177   For instance, Jocelyne Cesari, 'Islam in France: The Shaping of a Religious Minority', in Yvonne Haddad-Yazbek (ed.), *Muslims in the West: From Sojourners to Citizens*, Oxford: Oxford University Press, 2002.

178   Jørgen S. Nielsen remarked in 2012: "My own simple thematic search on the website of the UK Economic and Social Research Council using the search term 'Islam' in the category 'Security and conflict' indicates that no research grants meeting these criteria were awarded in the period 1982 (when the record starts) till 2000, although if all subject categories are included there were 18 grants. If, however, the same search is made for the years 2001 till the present, it appears that a total of 40 research grants were awarded in all categories, of which 32 were in the category 'Security and conflict'." (in: Book Reviews, *Journal of Muslims in Europe*, 2012 (Vol. 1), p. 217).

179   See the bibliographical references in the country studies in Jocelyne Cesari, *Handbook of Islam in Europe*.

180   W.B. Drees & S. van Koningsveld, *The Study of Religion and the Training of Muslim Clergy in Europe: Academic and Religious Freedom in the 21st Century*, Leiden: Leiden University Press, 2008.

181   See, e.g., Martin van Bruinessen, 'Making and unmaking Muslim religious authority in Western Europe', Paper presented at the Fourth Mediterranean Social and Political Research Meeting, Florence & Montecatini Terme 19–23 March 2003, organized by the Mediterranean Programme of the Robert Schuman Centre for Advanced Studies at the European University Institute.

182   N. Ragaru, 'Islam et coexistence communautaire en Bulgarie' in X. Bougarel, & N. Clayer, *Le nouvel Islam balkanique*, pp. 241–288.

183   E.g. Alexandre Caeiro, *Fatwas for European Muslims: The Minority Fiqh Project and the Integration of Islam in Europe* (PhD thesis), Utrecht: Utrecht University Press, 2011; Dilwar

Hussain, 'Muslim Political Participation in Britain and the "Europeanisation" of Fiqh,' *Die Welt des Islams* 2004 (Vol. 44, No. 3), pp. 376–401; Fiqh Council of the Muslim World League, 'A message from Muslim scholars to Muslim Minorities in the West', *Daawah*, 2002, (No. 4); Shammai Fishman, 'Fiqh al-Aqalliyyat: A Legal Theory for Muslim Minorities', Center on Islam, Democracy, and the Future of the Muslim World, Research Monograph, 2006 (No. 2).

184 See for these and other examples: M. Berger, 'Buying houses, donating organs and fighting wars – the changing role of muftis', Pauline Kruiniger (ed.) *Recht van de Islam*, Den Haag: Boom Uitgeverij, 2011.

185 Organizations that issue *fatwas* on questions regarding Muslims living in Western societies are the European Council of Fatwa and Research focuses (www.e-cfr.org) and the Fiqh Council of North America (www.fiqhcouncil.org). For other organizations see Berger, 'Buying houses, donating organs', 2011.

186 Martin van Bruinessen and Stefano Allievi (eds.), *Producing Islamic Knowledge: Transmission and Dissemination in Western Europe*, London: Routledge, 2010.

187 See, e.g., Tariq Ramadan, *Western Muslims and the future of Islam* (Oxford: Oxford University Press, 2004) and *Radical Reform: Islamic Ethics and Liberation* (Oxford: Oxford University Press, 2009). Also, Abdullah Saeed, 'Reflections on the Development of the Discourse of Fiqh for Minorities and Some of the Challenges It Faces' in Maurits S. Berger (ed.), *Applying Shari'a in the West. Facts, fears and figures*, Leiden: Leiden University Press, 2013, pp. 241–254.

188 Bernard Lewis, *Islam and the West*, New York/Oxford: Oxford University Press, 1993: p. 10.

189 Idem.

190 Idem.

191 Neumann uses the opposites 'dialogical' and 'dialectical' Other (Iver B. Neumann, *Uses of the Other. 'The East' in European Identity Formation*, Minneapolis: University of Minnesota Press, 1999, p. 3).

192 See, for instance, the Pew Research Centre in its survey of 12 June 2013: an average of 50% of Americans find religion very important, pray at least once a day and find it necessary to believe in God to be moral, as opposed to an average of 30% Italians, 20% Germans and 13% Frenchmen (http://www.pewresearch.org/fact-tank/2013/06/12/americans-are-less-accepting-of-homosexuality-than-canadians-western-europeans-and-religion-may-be-one-explanation).

193 Fabian, J., *Time and the Other. How Anthropology makes its Object*, NY: Colombia university press, 2002.

194 Houtum, H. van, & T. van Naerssen, 'Bordering, Ordering and Othering,' *Tijdschrift voor Economische en Sociale Geografie*, 2002 (Vol. 93, No. 2).

195   Walzer, *On Toleration*, p. 15.

196   Inayatullah & Blaney, *International Relations and the Problem of Difference*, pp. 22–23.

197   Asad, *Formations of the Secular*. p. 161.

198   See, e.g., Tariq Ramadan, 'Europeanization of Islam or the Islamization of Europe', in: *Islam, Europe's Second Religion*, Shireen T. Hunter (ed.) (Westport, Praeger Publishers, 2002), pp. 202–218; Bassam Tibi, 'Europeanizing Islam or the Islamization of Europe: political democracy vs. cultural difference', in *Religion in an Expanding Europe*, Timothy A. Byrnes & Peter J. Katzenstein (eds.) (Oxford: Oxford University Press, 2006), pp. 204–224.

199   Nathalie Clayer & Eric Germain, 'Towards the building of a "European Islam"', in Nathalie Clayer & Eric Germain (eds.), *Islam in Inter-War Europe*, London: Hurst, 2008, p. 119–127.

200   Ina Merdjanova, *Rediscovering the Umma. Muslims in the Balkans between Nationalism and Transnationalism*, Oxford: Oxford University Press, 2013, p. 109

201   See, e.g., Ahmet Alibašić, 'The Profile of Bosnian Islam and How West European Muslims Could Benefit from It,' *Islam in Southeast Forum*, June 29, 2010 (online publication: iseef.net); Xavier Bougarel, 'The Role of Balkan Muslims in Building a European Islam', EPC Issue Paper 43, European Policy Centre and King Badouin Foundation, 2005; Enes Karić, 'Is Euro-Islam a Myth, Challenge or a Real Opportunity for Muslims in Europe?' *Journal for Muslim Minority Affairs*, Vol. 22, No. 2, 2002 (p. 435–442), p. 436; Merdjanova, *Rediscovering the Umma*, pp. 121–127.

Bibliography

Abu-Jaber, Kamel, 'The Millet system in the nineteenth-century Ottoman Empire', *The Muslim World*, 1976 (Vol. 57, No. 3), pp. 212–223.

Abulafia, David, 'Monarchs and Minorities in the Christian Western Mediterranean around 1300: Lucera and its Analogues' in: Scott Waugh & Peter Diehl (eds.), *Christendom and its Discontents: Exclusion, Persecution and Rebellion, 1000–1500*, Cambridge: Cambridge University Press, 1996.

————, *The Great Sea: a human history of the Mediterranean*, London: Allen Lane, 2011.

Abu-Shahlieh, Sami, *L'Impact de la religion sur l'ordre juridique: cas de l'Égypte: non-musulmans en pays d'Islam*, Fribourg: Éditions universitaires, 1979.

Advisory Group on Public Diplomacy for the Arab and Muslim World, *Changing Minds, Winning Peace, A New Strategic Direction for U.S. Public Diplomacy in the Arab & Muslim World*, October 1, 2003.

Ahdar, Rex & Nicholas Aroney (eds.), *Shari'a in the West*, Oxford: Oxford University Press, 2011.

Ahmed, Akbar S. & Donnan Hastings (eds.), *Islam, Globalization and Postmodernity*, London: Routledge, 1994.

Akgönül, S., *Une communauté, deux Etats: La minorité turco-musulmane de Thrace occidentale*, Istanbul: Isis, 1999.

Akiner, Shirin, 'Oriental Borrowings in the Language of the Byelorussian Tatars', *SEER*, 1978 (Vol. 56, No. 2), pp. 224–241.

Aksakal, Mustafa, ''Holy War Made in Germany'? Ottoman Origins of the 1914 Jihad', *War in History*, 2011 (Vol. 18, No. 2), pp. 184–199.

Aksamija, Azra, 'Contested identities: identity politics and contemporary mosques in Bosnia and Herzegovina' in: Stefano Allievi (ed.), *Mosques in Europe. Why a solution has become a problem*, London: Alliance Publishing Trust, 2010, pp. 318–354.

Aksan, Virginia, *Ottoman Wars, 1700–1870: An Empire Besieged*, New York: Pearson Longman, 2007.

Alibašić, Ahmet, 'The Profile of Bosnian Islam and How West European Muslims Could Benefit from It', *Islam in Southeast Forum*, June 29 2010 (online publication: iseef.net).

Allievi, Stefano, *Conflicts over Mosques in Europe. Policy issues and trends*, London: Alliance Publishing Trust, 2009.

———, 'Islam in the Public Space: Social Networks, Media and Neo-Communities' in: Stefano Allievi & Jorgen Nielsen (eds.), Muslim Networks and Transnational Communities in and across Europe, Leiden: Brill, 2003, pp. 1–27.

———, 'Muslims and Politics' in: Brigitte Maréchal, Stefano Allievi, Felice Dassetto, Jørgen Nielsen (eds.), Muslims in the Enlarged Europe (Muslim Minorities, Volume 2), Leiden/Boston: Brill, 2003, pp. 183–216.

———, 'The International Dimension' in: Brigitte Maréchal, Stefano Allievi, Felice Dassetto, Jørgen Nielsen (eds.), Muslims in the Enlarged Europe (Muslim Minorities, Volume 2), Leiden/Boston: Brill, 2003, pp. 449–488.

——— & Jorgen Nielsen (eds.), Muslim Networks and Transnational Communities in and across Europe, Leiden: Brill, 2003.

Aluffi, Roberta & Giovanna Zincone, The Legal Treatment of Islamic Minorities in Europe, Leuven: Peeters, 2004.

Ansari, Humayun, 'Between Collaboration and Resistance: Muslim Soldiers' Identities and Loyalties in the two World Wars', Arches Quarterly, 2011 (Vol. 4), pp. 18–29.

——— & F. Hafez, From the Far Right to the Mainstream: Islamophobia in Party Politics and the Media, Frankfurt-am-Main: Campus Verlag GmbH, 2012.

Arnakis, George, 'The role of religion in the development of Balkan nationalism' in: Barbara & Charles Jelavich (eds.), The Balkans in Transition. Essays on the development of Balkan life and politics since the eighteenth century, Berkeley: University of California Press, 1963, pp. 115–144.

Asad, Talal, Formations of the Secular. Christianity, Islam, Modernity, Stanford: Stanford University Press, 2003.

———, 'The Construction of Religion as an Anthropological Category' in: Talal Asad, Genealogies of Religion; Discipline and Reasons of Power in Christianity and Islam, Baltimore MD: Johns Hopkins University Press, 1993 (1st ed. 1982), pp. 27–54.

Asbridge, Thomas, The Crusades. The War for the Holy Land, London: Simon and Schuster, 2010.

———, The First Crusade: A new History, Oxford: Oxford University Press, 2004.

Ashtor, Eliyahu, Studies on the Levantine Trade in the Middle Ages, London: Collins, 1978.

Assman, Jan, 'Collective Memory and Cultural Identity' in: Jan Assman & Tonio Hölscher (eds.), Kultur und Gedachtnis, Frankfurt/Main: Suhrkamp, 1988, pp. 9–19.

Atiyah, A.S., Crusade, Commerce and Culture, Indiana/Oxford: Indiana University Press, 1996.

Attanassof, Velko, Islamic Revival in the Balkans (thesis), Monterey: Naval Postgraduate School, 2006.

Avcioğlu, Nebahat, 'Identity-as-Form: The Mosque in the West', Cultural Analysis, 2007 (Vol. 6), pp. 91–112.

———, Turquerie and the Politics of Representation, 1728–1876, Farnham/Burlington: Ashgate Publishing, 2011.

Aziz, Ahmad, *A history of Islamic Sicily*, Edinburgh: Edinburgh University Press, 1975.

Azmeh, Aziz Al- & Effie Fokas (eds.), *Islam in Europe: Diversity, Identity and Influence*, Cambridge: Cambridge University Press, 2007.

Babes, B., *L' Islam positif – La religion des jeunes musulmans de France*, Paris: Editions de l'Atelier, 1997.

Babuna, Aydin, 'The Albanians of Kosovo and Macedonia: Ethnic Identity superseding Religion', *Nationality Papers*, 2000 (Vol. 28, No. 1), pp. 67–92.

————, 'The Bosnian Muslims and Albanians: Islam and Nationalism', *The Journal of Nationalism and Ethnicity*, 2004 (Vol. 32, No. 2), pp. 287–32.

Backman, Clifford, *The decline and fall of medieval Sicily: politics, religion, and economy in the reign of Frederick III, 1296–1337*, Cambridge: Cambridge University Press, 1995.

Badr, Gamal, 'Islamic Law: Its Relation to Other Legal Systems', *The American Journal of Comparative Law*, 1978 (Vol. 26, No. 2), pp. 187–198.

Baer, Marc David, *Honored by the Glory of Islam. Conversion and Conquest in Ottoman Europe*, Oxford: Oxford University Press, 2008.

Bakker, Edwin, *Jihadi terrorists in Europe. Their characteristics and the circumstances in which they joined the jihad: an exploratory study*, The Hague: Clingendael Institute, December 2006.

Balfour, Sebastian, *Deadly Embrace: Morocco and the road to the Spanish Civil War*, Oxford: Oxford University Press, 2002.

Banaji, Jairus, 'Islam, the Mediterranean and the rise of capitalism', *Journal of Historical Materialism*, 2007 (Vol. 15, No. 1), pp. 47–74.

Banawi, Rafic & Rex Stockton, 'Islamic values relevant to group work, with practical implications for the group leader', *The Journal for Specialists in Group Work*, 1993 (Vol. 18), pp. 151–160.

Bano, Samia, 'In Pursuit of Religious and Legal Diversity: A Response to the Archbishop of Canterbury and the 'Sharia Debate' in Britain', *Ecclesiastical Law Journal*, 2008 (Vol. 10, No. 3), pp. 283–309.

————, *Islamic Dispute Resolution and Family Law*, London: PalgraveMacMillan, 2011.

————, 'Islamic Family Arbitration, Justice and Human Rights in Britain', *Law, Social Justice & Global Development Journal* (LGD), 2007 (Vol. 1), pp. 1–26.

Bărbulescu, Iordan & Gabriel Andreescu, 'References to God and the Christian Tradition in the Treaty Establishing a Constitution for Europe: An Examination of the Background', *Journal for the Study of Religions and Ideologies*, 2009 (Vol. 8, Nr. 24), pp. 207–223.

Barkan, Omer, 'Essai sur les données statistiques des registres de recensement dans l' empire Ottoman au XVe et XVIe siècles', *Journal of the Economic and Social History of the Orient*, 1958 (Vol. 1, No. 1), pp. 9–36.

Barker, Francis et al, *Europe and Its Others*, Colchester: University of Essex, 1985.

Barnes, John, *An introduction to the religious foundations of the Ottoman empire*, Leiden: Brill, 1986.

Bartlett, Robert, *The Making of Europe. Conquest, Colonization and Cultural Change, 950–1350*, London: Penguin Books, 1995.

Baumann, Martin, 'Anxieties, Banning Minarets and Populist Politics in Switzerland – a Preliminary Analysis', *Pluralism Project at Harvard University*, 2009. (available online at: http://www.pluralism.org/files/spotlight/Baumann_Swiss-ban-on-minarets_Nov09.pdf)

Baumer, Franklin L., 'England, the Turk, and the Common Corps of Christendom', *The American Historical Review*, 1944 (Vol. 50, No. 1), pp. 26–48.

Bawer, Bruce, *While Europe Slept: How Radical Islam is Destroying Europe from Within*, New York: Doubleday, 2006.

Benali, Abdelkader & Herman Obdeijn, *Marokko door Nederlandse ogen, 1605–2005*, Amsterdam: Arbeiderspers, 2005.

Bennassar, Bartolome & Lucile Bennassar, *Les chrétiens d' Allah, L' histoire extraordinaire des renigats, XVI–XVIIe siècles*, Paris: Perrin, 1989.

Bennett, Christopher, *Yugoslavia's Bloody Collapse, Causes, Course and Consequences*, New York: New York University Press, 1995.

Berger, Maurits S., (ed.), *Applying Shari'a in the West: Facts, Fears and Figures*, Leiden: Leiden University Press, 2013.

———, 'Buying houses, donating organs and fighting wars – the changing role of muftis' in: Pauline Kruiniger (ed.), *Recht van de Islam*, Den Haag: Boom Uitgeverij, 2011.

———, 'Introduction to Applying Sharia in the West' in: Maurits S. Berger (ed.), *Applying Shari'a in the West. Facts, fears and figures*, Leiden: Leiden University Press, 2013, pp. 7–22.

———, 'Islam and Islamic law in Contemporary International Relations' in Marie-Luisa Frick & Andreas Th. Muller, *Islam and International Law. Engaging Self-Centrism from a Plurality of Perspectives*, Leiden/Boston: Brill / Martinus Nijhoff Publishers, 2013, pp. 393–413.

———, *Islam and the Uncertainty Principle*, Den Haag: Boom Juridische Uitgeverij, 2009.

———, 'Jihad and counter-jihad: Western Legal Responses to Islamic Militancy' in: M.C. Bassiouni & A. Guellali (eds.), *Jihad and its Challenges to International and Domestic Law*, The Hague: Hague Academic Press, 2010, pp. 229–247.

———, 'Shari'a in Europe' in: J. Brown (ed.), *Oxford Encyclopedia of Islam and Law*, Oxford: Oxford University Press, *forthcoming in 2013*.

Berger, Peter L., Grace Davie, Effie Fokkas, *Religious America, Secular Europe? A Theme and Variation*, London: Ashgate, 2008.

Berlinski, Claire, *Menace in Europe: Why the Continent's Crisis Is America's, Too*, New York: Crown Forum, 2006.

Berman, Harold, *Faith and Order: The Reconciliation of Law and Religion*, Cambridge: Scholars Press for Emory University, 1993.

————, Law and Revolution: The Formation of the Western Legal Tradition, Cambridge (Mass)/ London: Harvard University Press, 1983.

Bernstein, William, A Splendid Exchange: How Trade Shaped the World, New York: Atlantic Monthly Press, 2008.

Bisaha, Nancy, Creating East and West: Renaissance humanists and the Ottoman Turks, Philadelphia: University of Pennsylvania Press, 2004.

Blanks, David & Michael Frassetto, Western views of Islam in medieval and early modern Europe: perceptions of the other, Basingstroke: Macmillan, 1999.

Blommaert, Jan & Chris Bulcaen, 'Critical Discourse Analysis', Annual Review of Anthropology, 2000 (Vol. 29), pp. 447–466.

Boisard, Marcel, 'On the probable Influence of Islam on Western Public and International Law', International Journal of Middle East Studies, 1980 (Vol. 11, No. 4), pp. 429–450.

Bonner, Michael, Jihad in Islamic History: Doctrines and Practice, Princeton: Princeton University Press, 2006.

Boogert, Maurits van den, The Capitulations and the Ottoman Legal System. Qadis, Consuls and Beraths in the 18th Century, Leiden: Brill, 2005.

Bougarel, Xavier, The role of Balkan Muslims in building a European Islam, European policy Centre Issue, Paper No. 43, 23 November 2005.

———— & N. Clayer, Le nouvel Islam balkanique – Les musulmans, acteurs du post-communisme 1990–2000, Paris: Maisonneuve & Larose, 2001.

Bowen, John R., 'Beyond Migration: Islam as a Transnational Public Space', Journal of Ethnic and Migration Studies, 2004 (Vol. 30, No. 5), pp. 879–894.

Boyd, Marion, Dispute Resolution in Family Law: Protecting Choice, Promoting Inclusion, Ontario, December 2004, available online: http://www.attorneygeneral.jus.gov.on.ca/english/about/pubs/boyd/.

Bracewell, Catherine, The Uskoks of Senj: Piracy, Banditry, and holy war in the sixteenth century Adriatic, Ithaca/London: Cornell University Press, 1992.

Bradford, Ernle, The Sultan's Admiral. Barbarossa, Pirate and Empire-Builder, London: Tauris, 2009.

Brandon, James & Lorenzo Vidino, Countering Radicalization in Europe, London: International Centre for the Study of Radicalisation and Political Violence (ICSR), 2012.

Braude, Benjamin & Bernard Lewis, Christians and Jews in the ottoman Empire, New York/London: Holmes & Meier Publishers, 1982.

Breckenridge, Carol Appadurai & Peter van der Veer (eds.), Orientalism and the Postcolonial Predicament: Perspectives on South Asia, University of Pennsylvania Press, 1993.

Bresc, Henri, La Méditerranée entre pays d' Islam et monde latin, Paris: Sedes, 2001.

Brodman, James, Ransoming Captives in Crusader Spain: The Order of Merced on the Christian-Islamic Frontier, Philadelphia: University of Pennsylvania Press, 1986.

Brouard, Sylvain & Vincent Tiberj, *Français comme les autres: enquête sur les citoyens d'origine maghrébine, africaine et turque*, Paris: Les Presses de Sciences Po, 2005.

Brown, M., 'Quantifying the Muslim Population in Europe: Conceptual and Data Issues', *Journal of Social Research Methodology*, 2000 (Vol. 3), pp. 87–101.

Brown, Wendy, *Regulating Aversion. Tolerance in the Age of Identity and Empire*, Princeton: Princeton University Press, 2006.

Bruinessen, Martin van, 'Making and unmaking Muslim religious authority in Western Europe', Paper presented at the Fourth Mediterranean Social and Political Research Meeting, Florence & Montecatini Terme 19–23 March 2003, organised by the Mediterranean Programme of the Robert Schuman Centre for Advanced Studies at the European University Institute.

————— & Stefano Allievi (eds.), *Producing Islamic Knowledge: Transmission and Dissemination in Western Europe*, London: Routledge, 2010.

————— & Stefano Allievi (eds.), *Production and Dissemination of Islamic Knowledge in Western Europe*, London: Routledge, 2006.

Brummett, Palmira, *Ottoman Seapower and Levantine diplomacy in the age of discovery*, Albany: State University of New York Press, 1994.

Brundage, James A., 'Intermarriage Between Christians and Jews in Medieval Canon Law', *Jewish History*, 1988 (Vol. 3, No. 1), pp. 25–40.

—————, 'Prostitution, Miscegenation, and Sexual Purity in the First Crusade' in: Peter W. Edbury, *Crusade and Settlement*, Cardiff: University College Cardiff Press, 1985, pp. 57–65.

Buaben, Jabal, *Image of the Prophet Muhammad in the West: A study of Muir, Margoliouth and Watt*, Leicester: The Islamic Foundation, 1996.

Büchler, Andrea, *Islamic Law in Europe? Legal Pluralism and its Limits in European Family Laws*, Burlington: Ashgate, 2011.

Buijs, Frank & Jan Rath, *Muslims in Europe: The State of Research*, New York: Russell Sage Foundation, 2003.

Bulliet, Richard, *Conversion to Islam in the Medieval Period: An Essay in Quantitative History*, Cambridge MA: Harvard University Press, 1979.

—————, *The Case for a Islamo-Christian Civilization*, Columbia: Columbia University Press, 2006.

Bundesamt für Verfassungsschutz (Federal Office for the Protection of the Constitution), *Integration als Extremismus-und Terrorismusprävention. Zur Typologie islamistischer Radikalisierung und Rekrutierung*, January 2007.

Bunt, Gary R., *Islam in the Digital Age: E-Jihad, Online Fatwas and Cyber Islamic Environments*, London/Sterling/Virginia: Pluto Press, 2003.

Burnett, Charles, *Islam and the Italian Renaissance*, London: The Warburg Institute, University of London, 1999.

Burton, Jonathan, *Traffic And Turning: Islam And English Drama, 1579–1624*, Newark: University of Delaware Press, 2005.

Bury, J., H. Gwatkin & J. Hussey, *The Cambridge Medieval History. Volume IV: The Byzantine Empire (717–1453)*, 2nd edition, Cambridge: Cambridge University Press, 1966–1967.

Butterworth, Charles E. & Blake Andree Kessel (eds.), *The Introduction of Arabic Philosophy into Europe*, Leiden/New Jork, Köln: E.J. Brill, 1993

Caeiro, Alexandre, *Fatwas for European Muslims: The Minority Fiqh Project and the Integration of Islam in Europe* (PhD thesis), Utrecht: Utrecht University Press, 2011.

————, 'Religious Authorities or Public Actors? The Muslim Leaders of the French Representative Body of Islam' in: Jocelyne Cesari & Sean McLoughlin (eds.), *European Muslims and the Secular State*, London: Ashgate, 2005, pp. 71–84.

Caldwell, Christopher, *Reflections on the Revolution in Europe*, New York: Anchor, 2010.

Canard, Marius, *Byzance et les musulmans du Proche Orient*, London: Variorum Reprints, 1973.

————, 'Les relations politiques et sociales entre Byzance et les Arabes', *Dumbartons Oaks Papers*, 1964 (Vol. 18), pp. 33–56.

Cantarino, Vicente, 'The Spanish Reconquest: A Cluniac Holy War against Islam?' in: Khalil Semaan (ed), *Islam and the Medieval West. Aspects of Intercultural Relations*, Albany: State University of New York Press, 1980.

Carboni, Stefano, *Venice and the Islamic World 828–1797*, New Haven: Yale University Press, 2007.

Cardaillac Louis, (ed.), *Les Morisques et leur Temps*, Paris: Editions du CNRS, 1983.

———— (ed.), *Les Morisques et l' Inquisition*, Paris: Editions Publisud, 1990.

Cardini, Franco, *Europe and Islam*, London: Wiley-Blackwell, 2001.

Carey, George, 'Tolerating religion' in: Susan Mendus (ed.), *The Politics of Tolerance in Modern Life*, Durham: Duke University Press, 2000, pp. 45–46.

Carr, Matthew, *Blood and Faith. The Purging of Muslim Spain*, New York/London: The New Press, 2009.

Carrera, Sergio & Joanna Parkin, 'The Place of Religion in the European Union Law and Policy: Competing Approaches and Actors inside the European Commission', in *Justice and Home Affairs*, RELIGARE Working Document No. 1, September 2010 (online publication, available at http://www.ceps.be/book/place-religion-european-union-law-and-policy-competing-approaches-and-actors-inside-european-co).

Casanova, Jose, 'Religion, European secular identities, and European integration', *Transit*, 2004 (Vol. 27), pp. 1–17.

Castells, Manuel, *The Power of Identity: The Information Age: Economy, Society and Culture*, Malden: Wiley-Blackwell, A John Wiley & Sons, Ltd. Publication, 1997 (2nd edition 2004).

CBS [Central Agency for Statistics], press release "Ruim 850 duizend islamieten in Nederland" Wednesday 24 October 2007.

Çelik, Nihat, 'Muslims, Non-Muslims and Foreign Relations: Ottoman Diplomacy', *International Review of Turkish Studies*, 2011 (Vol. 1, No. 3), pp. 8–31.

Cesari, Jocelyne, 'Islam in France: The Shaping of a Religious Minority' in: Yvonne Haddad-Yazbek (ed.), *Muslims in the West: From Sojourners to Citizens*, Oxford: Oxford University Press, 2002.

——, 'Islam in the West: From Immigration to Global Islam', *Harvard Middle Eastern and Islamic Review*, 2009 (Vol. 8), pp. 148–175.

——, 'Mosque Conflicts in European Cities: Introduction', *Journal of Ethnic and Migration studies*, 2005 (Vol. 31), pp. 1015–1024.

——, *Musulmans et republicains. Les jeunes, l'islam et la France*, Bruxelles/Paris: Editions Complexe, 1998.

——, *The Securitisation of Islam in Europe*, Centre for European Policy Studies: Research Paper No. 14–15 CEPS CHALLENGE Research Program, April 2009. (available online at www.ceps.eu).

—— (ed.), *The Oxford Handbook of European Islam*, Oxford: Oxford University Press (*forthcoming in 2014*).

——, *When Islam and Democracy Meet: Muslims in Europe and the United States*, New York: Palgrave Macmillan, 2004.

—— & Sean McLoughlin (eds.), *European Muslims and the Secular State*, London: Ashgate, 2005.

Chabry, Laurent & Annie Chabry, *Politique et minorités au Proche-Orient*, Paris: Maisonneuve & Larose, 1984.

Cheich, Nadia El-, *Byzantium viewed by the Arabs*, Cambridge: Cambridge University Press, 2004.

Chejne, Anwar, *Islam and the West: The Moriscos, a Cultural and Social History*, Albany: State University of New York Press, 1983.

——, 'Islamization and Arabization in al-Andalus' in: Vyronis Speros Jr. (ed.), *Islam and Cultural Change in the Middle Ages*, Wiesbaden: Harrassowitz, 1973.

Christelow, Allan, *Muslim law courts and the French colonial state in Algeria*, Princeton/New Yok: Princeton University Press, 1985.

Ciftci, Sabri, 'Islamophobia and Threat Perceptions: Explaining Anti-Muslim Sentiment in the West', *Journal of Muslim Minority Affairs*, 2012 (Vol. 32, No. 3), pp. 293–309.

Çirakman, Asli, 'From tyranny to despotism: the enlightenment unenlightened image of the Turks', *International Journal of Middle East Studies*, 2001 (Vol. 33, No. 1), pp. 49–68.

Clayer, Nathalie & Eric Germain (eds.), *Islam in Inter-War Europe*, London: Hurst, 2008.

Cleveland, W.L., *Islam against the West: Shakíb Arslân and the campaign for Islamic nationalism the West*, Austin: University of Texas Press, 1985.

Clissold, Stephen, *The Barbary Slaves*, London: Elek, 1977.

Cohn, Norman, *The Pursuit of the Millennium* (rev. and exp. ed.), Oxford: Oxford University Press, 1970.

Coles, Paul, *The Ottoman impact on Europe*, London: Thames and Hudson, 1968.

Commission on British Muslim and Islamophobia, *Islamophobia: Issues, Challenges and Action*, Stoke-on-Trent and Sterling, VA: Trentham Books, 2004.

Confino, Alon, 'Collective Memory and Cultural History: Problems of Method', *The American Historical Review*, 1997 (Vol. 102, No. 5), pp. 1386–1403.

Conseil d' Etat, *Etude relative aux possibilités juridiques d' interdiction du port du voile intégral*, 25 March 2010 (available online at: www.conseil-etat.fr/cde/media/document/avis/etude_vi _30032010.pdf.).

Constable, Olivia, 'Funduq, Fondaco, and Khan' in: Angeliki Laiou & Roy Mottahedh (eds.), *The Crusades from the Perspective of Byzantium and the Muslim World*, Washington: Dumbarton Oaks, 2001.

Conyers, A.J., *The Long Truce: How Tolerance made the World Safer for Power and Profit*, Dallas: Spencer Publishing Company, 2001.

Cook, David, *Understanding Jihad*, Berkeley: University of California Press, 2005.

Cook, Robert, *The Sense of the Song of Roland*, New York: Ithaca Press, 1987.

Cooke, Miriam & Bruce B. Lawrence, *Muslim Networks: From Hajj to Hip Hop*, University of North Carolina Press, 2005.

Coope, Jessica, *The Martyrs of Cordoba: Community and Family Conflict in an Age of Mass Conversion*, Lincoln: University of Nebraska, 1995.

Courbage, Youssef & Philippe Fargues, *Christians and Jews Under Islam*, London: Tauris, 1997.

Cowley, Robert & Geoffrey Parker, *The Reader's Companion to Military History*, Boston: Houghton Mifflin, 2001.

Creasy, Edward, *Fifteen decisive battles of the world: from Marathon to Waterloo* (orig. 1851), repr. Da Capo Press, 1994.

Crensaw, Martha, ' "New" versus "old" Terrorism', *Palestine-Israel Journal*, 2003 (Vol. 10, No. 1) online publication at www.pij.org.

Cutler, Alan, 'Innocent III and the Distinctive Clothing of Jews and Muslims', *Studies in Medieval Culture*, 1970 (Vol. 3), pp. 92–116.

Dalègre, J., *La Thrace grecque. Populations et territoire*, Paris: L' Harmattan, 2001.

Dalli, Charles, 'From Islam to Christianity: the Case of Sicily' in: Joaquim Carvallo (ed.), *Religion, Ritual and Mythology: Aspects of Identity Formation in Europe*, Pisa: Pisa University Press, 2006.

Daniel, Norman, *Islam and the West. The Making of an Image*, Edinburgh: Edinburgh University Press, 1960.

————, *Islam, Europe and Empire*, Edinburgh: Edinburgh University Press, 1966.

Dassetto, Felice, *La construction de l' islam europeen. Approche socio-anthropologique*, Paris: L'Harmattan, 1996.

———— (ed.), *Paroles d' Islam-Individus, Societes et Discours dans l' Islam Europeen Contemporain*, Paris: Maisonneuve et Larose, 2000.

Dávid, Géza & Pál Fodor, *Ransom Slavery along the Ottoman Borders*, Leiden/Boston: Brill, 2007.

Davis, Paul, *100 Decisive Battles from Ancient Times to the Present: The World's Major Battles and How They shaped History*, Oxford: Oxford University Press, 1999.

Davis, Robert, *Christian Slaves, Muslim Masters: White Slavery in the Mediterranean, the Barbary Coast and Italy, 1500–1800*, Basingstoke: Palgrave Macmillan, 2004.

————, 'The Geography of Slaving in the Early Modern Mediterranean, 1500–1800', *Journal of Medieval and Early Modern Studies*, 2007 (Vol. 37, No. 1), pp. 58–74.

Day, Gerald, *Genoa's Response to Byzantium, 1155–1204: commercial expansion and factionalism in a medieval city*, Chicago: University of Illinois Press, 1988.

Deanesly, Margaret, *A History of Early Medieval Europe, from 476 to 911*, London: Taylor & Francis, 1963.

Dennett, Daniel, *Conversion and the Poll Tax in Early Islam*, Cambridge MA: Harvard University Press, 1950.

Denninger, Erhard, ''Security, Diversity, Solidarity' Instead of 'Freedom, Equality, Fraternity'', *Constellations*, 2000 (Vol. 7, No. 4), pp. 507–521.

Dény, Jean & Jane Laroche, 'L' expédition en Provence de l' armée de mer de Sultan Suleyman sous le commandement de l' amiral Hayreddin Pacha dit Barbarousse', *Turcica*, 1969 (Vol. 1), pp. 161–211.

Diez, Thomas, 'Europe's Others and the Return to Geopolitics', *Cambridge Review of International Affairs*, 2004 (Vol. 17, No. 2), pp. 319–335.

Donia, Robert, *Islam Under the Double Eagle: The Muslims of Bosnia and Hercegovina, 1878–1914*, New York: Columbia University Press, 1981.

———— & John Fine, *Bosnia and Hercegovina. A Tradition Betrayed*, London: Hurst and Company, 1994.

Drees, W.B. and P.S. van Koningsveld, *The Study of Religion and the Training of Muslim Clergy in Europe: Academic and Religious Freedom in the 21st Century*, Leiden: Leiden University Press, 2008.

Duderija, Adis, 'Factors Determining Religious Identity Construction among Western-born Muslims: Towards a Theoretical Framework', *Journal of Muslim Minority Affairs*, 2008 (Vol. 28, No. 3), pp. 371–400.

Durham, Edith, *The burden of the Balkans*, London: E. Arnold, 1905.

During, Simon, *Cultural studies: a critical introduction*, London: Routledge, 2005.

Dursteler, Eric, *Venetians in Constantinople: Nation, Identity, and Coexistence in the Early Modern Mediterranean*, Boston: John Hopkins University Press, 2006.

Dziekan, Marek, 'History and Culture of Polish Tatars' in: Katarzyna Gorak-Sosnowska (ed.), *Muslims in Poland and Eastern Europe. Widening the European Discourse on Islam*, Warsaw: University of Warsaw Press, 2011.

Earle, Peter, *Corsairs of Malta And Barbary*, London: Sidgwick & Jackson, 1970.

Earle, T. & K. Lowe (ed.), *Black Africans in Renaissance Europe*, Cambridge: Cambridge University Press, 2010.

Ehmann, Johannes, *Luther, Türken und Islam*, Heidelberg: Gütersloher Verlagshaus, 2008.

Eldem, Edham, Daniel Goffman & Bruce Masters, *The Ottoman city between East and West: Aleppo, Izmir and Istanbul*, Cambridge: Cambridge University Press, 1999.

Elgeddawy, Kessmat, *Relations entre systèmes confessionnels et laïque en Droit International Privé*, Paris: Dalloz, 1971.

Emon, Anver M., *Religious Pluralism and Islamic Law. Dhimmis and Others in the Empire of Law*, Oxford: Oxford University Press, 2012.

Epalza, Mikel de, 'Mozarabs: An Emblematic Christian Minority in Islamic Al-Andalus' in: Salma Khadra Jayyusi (ed), *The Legacy of Muslim Spain*, Leiden: Brill, 1992, pp. 149–170.

European Monitoring Centre on Racism and Xenophobia (EUMC), *Perceptions of Discrimination and Islamophobia. Voices from Members of Muslim Communities in the European Union*, Vienna: EUMC, 2006.

———, *Summary Report into Islamophobia in the EU following 11 September 2001*, Vienna: EUMC, 2002.

Evans, Carolyn, 'The "Islamic Scarf" in the European Court of Human Rights' *Melbourne Journal of International Law*, 2006 (Vol. 7), pp. 52–73.

Evstatiev, Simeon, *Public Islam on the Balkans in a Wider Europe Context*, Central European University Center For Policy Studies, July 2006.

Fabian, J., *Time and the Other. How Anthropology makes its Object*, New York: Colombia University Press, 2002.

Fadil, Sarah & Nadia Fadil, *Islam and Secular Modernity under Western Eyes: A Geneaology of a Constitutive Relationship*, Florence: European University Institute, Working Paper RSCAS No. 5, 2008.

Fairclough, Norman, 'Critical Discourse Analysis in Transdisciplinary Research' in: P. Chilton & R. Wodak (eds.), *A New Agenda in (Critical) Discourse Analysis*, Amsterdam: John Benjamins, 2005, pp. 53–69.

Farmer, Henry, *Historical facts for the Arabian Musical Influence*, London: William Reeves, 1930.

Faroqhi, Suraiya, *The Ottoman Empire and The World Around It*, London/ New York: Tauris, 2007.

Fattal, Antoine, *Le statut légal des non-musulmans en pays d'Islam*, Beirut: Imprimerie Catholique, 1958.

Feroz, Ahmad, 'Ottoman Perceptions of the Capitulations, 1800–1912', *Journal of Islamic Studies*, 2000 (Vol. 11, No. 1), pp. 1–20.

Ferrari, Silvio, 'The New Wine and the Old Cask. Tolerance, Religion, Religion and the Law in Contemporary Europe', *Ratio Juris*, 1997 (Vol. 10, No. 1), pp. 75–89.

Fetzer, Joel S. & J. Christopher Soper, *Muslims and the State in Britain, France, and Germany*, Cambridge: Cambridge University Press, 2005.

Fichtner, Paula Sutter, *Terror and Toleration: The Habsburg Empire confronts Islam, 1526–1850*, London: Reaktion Books, 2008.

Findley, Carter, 'The Acid Test of Ottomanism: the Acceptance of Non-Muslims in the late Ottoman Bureaucracy' in: Benjamin Braude & Bernard Lewis (eds.), *Christians and Jews in the Ottoman Empire*, New York/London: Holmes & Meier Publishers, 1982.

Finkel, Caroline, *Osman's Dream. The History of the Ottoman Empire*, New York: Basic Books, 2005.

Fiqh Council of the Muslim World League, 'A message from Muslim scholars to Muslim Minorities in the West', *Daawah*, 2002, (No. 4).

Fisher, Alan, *A Precarious Balance: Conflict, Trade and Diplomacy on the Russian-Ottoman Frontier*, Istanbul: Isis Press, 1999.

———, 'The sale of slaves in the Ottoman Empire: Markets and State taxes on slave sales, some preliminary considerations', *Beseri Bilimler – Humanities*, 1978 (Vol. 6), pp. 149–174.

Fisher, Godfrey, *Barbary Legend. War, Trade and Piracy in North Africa 1415–1830*, Oxford: Clarendon Press, 1957.

Fisher-Galati, Stephen A., *Ottoman Imperialism and German Protestantism, 1521–1555*, Cambridge: Harvard University Press, 1959.

Fishman, Shammai, 'Fiqh al-Aqalliyyat: A Legal Theory for Muslim Minorities', Center on Islam, Democracy, and the Future of the Muslim World, Research Monograph, 2006 (No. 2).

Fletcher, Richard, *Moorish Spain*, London: Phoenix, 1992.

Foblets, Marie-Claire, 'Accomodating Islamic Family Law(s): A Critical Analysis of Some Recent Developments and Experiments in Europe' in: Maurits S. Berger (ed.), *Applying Shari'a in the West. Facts, fears and figures*, Leiden: Leiden University Press, 2013, pp. 207–226.

Fotic, Aleksandar, 'The Official Explanations for the Confiscation and Sale of Monasteries (Churches) and their Estates at the Time of Selim II', *Turcica*, 1994 (Vol. 26), pp. 33–54.

Francisco, Adam S., *Martin Luther and Islam: A Study in Sixteenth-Century Polemics and Apologetics*, Leiden: Brill, 2007.

Frank, Alison, 'The Children of the Desert and the Laws of the Sea: Austria, Great Britain, the Ottoman Empire, and the Mediterranean Slave Trade in the Nineteenth Century', *The American Historical Review*, 2012 (Vol. 117, No. 2), pp. 410–444.

Frank, Allen, *Islamic historiography and 'Bulghar' identity among the Tatars and Bashkirs of Russia*, Leiden: Brill, 1998.

Frazee, Charles, *Catholics and Sultans. The church and the Ottoman Empire 1453–1923*, London: Cambridge University Press, 1983.

Fregosi, Frank, (ed.), *La formation des cadres religieux musulmans en France: approaches socio-juridiques*, Paris: L'Harmattan, 1998.

——, *Penser l'islam dans la laïcité. Les musulmans de France et la République*, Paris: Fayard, 2008.

Fregosi, Paul, *Jihad in the West. Muslim Conquests from the 7th to the 21st Centuries*, New York: Prometheus Books, 1998.

Friedman, Ellen, 'Christian Captives at 'Hard labor' in Algiers, 16th–18th centuries', *The International Journal of African Historical Studies*, 1980 (Vol. 13, No. 4), pp. 616–632.

——, *Spanish Captives in North Africa in the Early Modern Period*, Madison: University of Wisconsin Press, 1983.

Fuller, John, *The Decisive Battles of the Western World*, London: Eyre & Spottiswoode, 1954.

Gabrielli, Fransesco, *Arab Historians of the Crusades*, Los Angeles: University of California Press, 1984.

Gallis, Paul, 'Muslims in Europe: Integration Policies in Selected Countries', Congressional Research Service Report RL33166 for Congress, November 18, 2005.

Gallup World Poll, *Muslims in Europe: Basis for Greater Understanding Already Exists*, Princeton: The Gallup Organization, 2007.

Garber, Peter, 'Tulipmania', *Journal of Political Economy*, 1989 (Vol. 97, No. 3), pp. 535–560.

Garcia-Arenal, Mercedes, *Los Moriscos*, Granada: Universidad de Granada, 1975 (repr. 1996).

—— & Gerard Wiegers, *A Man of Three Worlds. Samuel Pallache, a Moroccan Jew in Catholic and Protestant Europe*, Baltimore: John Hopkins University Press, 2003.

Gartenstein-Ross, Daveed & Laura Grossman, *Homegrown Terrorists in the U.S. and U.K. An Empirical Examination of the Radicalization Process*, Washington DC: FDD's Center for Terrorism Research, 2009.

Gazzah, Miriam, 'European Muslim youth: Towards a cool Islam?' in: Jørgen S. Nielsen, Samim Akgonül, Ahmet Alibašić, Brigitte Maréchal & Christian Moe (eds.), *Yearbook of Muslims in Europe (Volume 1)*, London/Boston: Brill, 2009, pp. 403–427.

Geaves, R., T. Gabriel, Y. Haddad & J. Idleman Smith (eds.), *Islam and the West Post 9/11*, Ashgate: Routledge, 2004.

Geertz, Clifford, 'Religion as a Cultural System' in: Michael Banton (ed.), *Anthropological Approaches to the Study of Religion*, ASA Monographs, 3, London: Tavistock Publications, 1966, pp. 1–46.

Geisser, Vincent & Françoise Lorcerie, *La nouvelle islamophobie*, Paris: La Decouverte, 2005.

Gerholm, T. & Y.G. Lithman (eds.), *The New Islamic Presence in Western Europe*, London: Mansell, 1988.

Gervers, Michael & Ramzi Bikhazi, *Conversion and continuity: indigenous Christian communities in Islamic lands: eight to eighteenth century*, Toronto: Pontifical Institute of Mediaeval Studies, 1990.

Ghazanfar, S.M. (ed.), *Medieval Islamic Economic Thought. Filling the "Great Gap" in European Economics*, London: Routledge, 2003.

Gibb, H., 'Constantinople', *The Encyclopedia of Islam*, 1982 (Vol. 2, Part 2).

Gibbon, Edward (ed.), *The History of the Decline and Fall of the Roman Empire*, New York: J&J Harper, 1829, repr. 1993 by Everyman's Library.

Gilchrist, John, *The church and economic activity in the Middle Ages*, London: Macmillan, 1969.

Gillespie, R., 'Reshaping the agenda? The internal politics of the Barcelona Process in the aftermath of September 11', *Mediterranean Politics*, 2003 (Vol. 8, No. 2–3), pp. 21–36.

Githens-Mazer, Jonathan, 'The rhetoric and reality: radicalization and political discourse', *International Political Science Review*, 2012 (Vol. 33, No. 5), pp. 556–567.

Glenny, Mischa, *The Balkans: Nationalism, War and the Great Powers, 1804–1999*, London: Viking Penguin, 2000.

Glick, Thomas, *Islamic and Christian Spain in the Early Middle Ages*, Princeton: Princeton University Press, 1979.

Göçek, Fatma Muge, *East Encounters West: France and the Ottoman Empire in the Eighteenth Century*, New York: Oxford University Press, 1987.

Goddard, Hugh, *A history of Christian-Muslim relations*, Edinburgh: Edinburgh University Press, 2000.

Goff, Jacques Le, *La civilization de l' Occident Médiéval*, Paris: Editions Arthaud, 1984.

Goffman, Daniel, 'Ottoman millets in the early seventeenth century', *New Perspectives on Turkey*, 1994 (Vol. 11, No. 3), pp. 135–158.

———, *The Ottoman Empire and Early Modern Europe*, Cambridge: Cambridge University Press, 2002.

Goitein, S., 'Mediterranean Trade in the Eleventh Century: Some Facts and Problems' in: Michael Cook, *Studies in the Economic History of the Middle East: from the rise of Islam to the present day*, London: Oxford University Press, 1970, pp. 51–62.

Golb, Norman & Omeljan Pritsak, *Khazarian Hebrew documents of the tenth century*, Ithaca/London: Cornell University Press, 1982.

Goldgar, Anne, *Tulipmania: Money, Honor, and Knowledge in the Dutch Golden Age*, Chicago: University of Chicago Press, 2007.

Gölle, Nilüfer, 'The Public Visibility of Islam and European Politics of Resentment: The Minarets mosques debate', *Philosophy & Social Criticism*, 2011 (Vol. 37, No. 4), pp. 383–392.

Goodwin, Godfrey, *The Janissaries*, London: Saqi, 1994.

Gorak-Sosnowska, Katarzyna (ed.), *Muslims in Poland and Eastern Europe. Widening the European Discourse on Islam*, Warsaw: University of Warsaw Press, 2011.

Gräf, B. & J. Skovgaard-Petersen, *Global mufti: the phenomenon of Yūsuf al-Qaraḍāwi*, New York: Columbia University Press, 2009.

Graham, Mark, *How Islam created the Modern World*, Beltsville (Ml): Amana Publications, 2006.

Green, Toby, *Inquisition. The Reign of Fear*, London: Macmillan, 2007.

Greenblatt, Mariam, *Charlemagne and the Early Middle Ages*, New York: Benchmark Books, 2002.

Griffith-Jones, Robin (ed.), *Islam and English Law: Rights, Responsibilities and the Place of Shari'a*, Cambridge: Cambridge University Press, 2013.

Groot, Alexander de, *The Ottoman Empire and the Dutch Republic: A History of the Earliest Diplomatic Relations, 1610–1630*, Leiden/Istanbul: Nederlands Historisch-Archaelogisch Instituut, 1978.

Guichard, Pierre, *L'Espagne et la Sicile Musulmanes aux XIe et XIIe siècles*, Lyon: Presses Universitaires de Lyon, 1991.

Gunny, Ahmad, 'Protestant Reactions to Islam in late Seventeenth-Century French Thought', *French Studies*, 1986 (Vol. 40, No. 2), pp. 129–140.

Gutas, Dimitri, *Greek Thought, Arabic Culture: The Graeco-Arabic Translation Movement in Baghdad and Early Abbasid Society*, London: Routledge, 1998.

Haaren, John & Addison Poland, *Famous Men of the Middle Ages* (orig. 1904), repr. Yesterday's Classics, 2006.

Habermas, Jurgen, *The Structural Transformation of the Public Sphere: An Inquiry into a Category of Bourgeois Society*, Cambridge: Polity Press, 1962, English transl. 1989.

Haddad-Yazbek, Yvonne

———— (ed.), *Muslims in the West: From Sojourners to Citizens*, Oxford: Oxford University Press, 2002.

———— & Tyler Golson, 'Overhauling Islam: Representation, Construction, and Cooption of 'Moderate' Islam in Europe', *Journal of Church & State*, 2007 (Vol. 49, No. 3), pp. 487–515.

Hagemann, Ludwig, *Martin Luther und der Islam*, Altenberge: Verlag für Christlich-Islamisches Schrifttum, 1983.

Hagen, Gottfried, 'German Heralds of Holy War: Orientalists and Applied Oriental studies', *Comparative Studies of South Asia, Africa and the Middle East*, 2004 (Vol. 24, No. 2), pp. 145–162.

Hajdarpasic, Edin, 'Out of the Ruins of the Ottoman Empire: Reflections on the Ottoman Legacy in South-eastern Europe', *Middle Eastern Studies*, 2008 (Vol. 44, No. 5), pp. 715–734.

Haldon, John, *Warfare, State and Society in the Byzantine World 565–1204*, London: Routledge, 1999.

Haliczer, Stephen, 'The Moriscos: Loyal Subjects of His Catholic Majesty Phillip III' in: Salma Khadra Jayyusi (ed.), *The Legacy of Muslim Spain*, Leiden: Brill, 1992, pp. 265–273.

Hall, Stuart, 'The West and the Rest: Discourse and Power' in: Stuart Hall & Bram Gieben (eds.), *Formations of Modernity*, Cambridge: Polity Press, 1992, pp. 276–320.

Halliday, F., 'Islamophobia reconsidered', *Ethnic and Racial Studies*, 1999 (Vol. 22, No. 5), pp. 892–902.

Halpern, Joel M. & David A. Kideckel (eds.), *Neighbors at War. Anthropological Perspectives on Yugoslav Ethnicity, Culture, and History*, Pennsylvania: The Pennsylvania State University Press, 2000.

Hamarneh, Ala Al- & Jörn Thielmann (eds), *Islam and Muslims in Germany* (Muslim Minorities, 7), Leiden/Boston: Brill, 2008.

Hamilton, Bernard, *The Medieval Inquisition*, New York: Holmes & Meier Publishers, 1989.

Hargreaves, A.G., *Immigration, 'Race' and Ethnicity in Contemporary France*, London: Routledge, 1995.

Harrison, Alwyn, 'Behind the Curve: Bulliet and Conversion to Islam in al-Andalus Revisited', *Al-Masaq: Islam and the Medieval Mediterranean*, 2012 (Vol. 24, No. 1), pp. 35–51.

Harvey, Leonard, *Islamic Spain, 1250 to 1500*, Chicago: Chicago University Press, 1990.

————, *Muslims in Spain, 1500 to 1614*, Chicago: Chicago University Press, 2005.

Haug, Sonja, Stephanie Müssig & Anja Stichs, *Muslimisches Leben in Deutschland*, Berlin: Bundesamt für Migration und Flüchtlinge, 2009.

Hawting, Gerald, *The First Dynasty of Islam: The Ummayad Caliphate AD 661–750*, London: Routledge, 1986.

Hays, Denys, *Europe. The Emergence of an Idea*, Edinburgh: Edinburgh University Press, 1957.

Heather, Peter, *Empires and Barbarians: The Fall of Rome and the Birth of Europe*, Oxford: Oxford University Press, 2010.

Heck, Gene, *Charlemagne, Muhammad and the Arab roots of Capitalism*, Berlin: De Gruyter, 2006.

Heiss, G. & G. Klingenstein, *Das Osmanische Reich und Europa 1683 bis 1789: Konflikt, Entspannung und Austausch*, Munich: R. Oldenbourg Verlag, 1983.

Henry, J.R. & F. Balique, *La doctrine coloniale du droit musulman algérien. Bibliographie systématique et introduction critique*, Paris: Editions de CNRS, 2003.

Herren, Madeleine, Martin Rüesch & Christiane Sibille, *Transcultural History. Theories, Methods, Sources*, Heidelberg/New York: Springer, 2012.

Herrin, Judith, *Byzantium. The surprising life of a medieval empire*, London: Penguin Books, 2007.

Herten, Marieke van, 'Het aantal islamieten in Nederland' in: CBS, *Religie aan het begin van de 21ste eeuw*, Den Haag: CBS, 2009, pp. 35–40.

Hess, Andrew, *The Forgotten Frontier. A History of the Sixteenth-Century Ibero-African Frontier*, Chicago/London: The University of Chicago Press, 1978.

————, 'The Moriscos: An Ottoman Fifth Column in Sixteenth-Century Spain?', *The American Historical Review*, 1968 (Vol. 74, No. 1), pp. 1–25.

Heyward, Madeleine, 'What Constitutes Europe? Religion, Law and Ideology in the Draft Constitution for the European Union', *Hanse Law Review*, 2005 (Vol. 1), pp. 227–235.

Hillenbrand, Robert, *Islamic Art and Architecture*, London: Thames and Hudson Ltd., 1999.

Hillgarth, J., *The Spanish Kingdoms, 1250–1516*, Oxford: Clarendon Press, 1976–1978.

Hirszowicz, L., *The Third Reich and the Arab East*, London: Routledge, 1966.

Hitchcock, Richard, *Mozarabs in Medieval and Early Modern Spain: Identities and Influences*, Aldershot: Ashgate, 2008.

Hitti, Philip, *Islam and the West: a historical cultural survey*, Princeton: Van Nostrand, 1962.

Hodges, Richard & David Whitehouse, *Mohammed, Charlemagne and the Origins of Europe: archeology and the Pirenne thesis*, London: Duckworth, 1983.

Hodgett, Gerald, *Social and Economical History of Medieval Europe*, London: Methuen, 1972.

Hodgson, Marshall, *The Venture of Islam, Volume 1: The Classical Age of Islam*, Chicago: University of Chicago Press, 1977.

Hooker, M.B., 'Muhammadan Law and Islamic Law' in: M.B. Hooker (ed.), *Islam in South-East Asia*, Leiden: Brill, 1983.

Horton, John (ed.), *Liberalism, Multiculturalism and Tolerance*, New York: St. Martin's Press, 1993.

Houben, Hubert, *Roger II of Sicily: A ruler between East and West*, Cambridge: Cambridge University Press, 2002.

Hourani, Albert, *Islam in European thought*, Cambridge: Cambridge University Press, 1993.

Hunt, Robert, 'Islam in Austria', *The Muslim World*, 2002 (Vol. 92, No. 1–2), pp. 115–128.

Hunter, Shireen (ed.), *Islam, Europe's Second Religion*, Westport (CT): Praeger, 2002.

Huntington, Samuel, *The Clash of Civilizations and the Remaking of World Order*, New York: Simon and Schuster, 2007.

Hurgronje Snouck, *The Holy War, Made in Germany*, New York/London: The Knickerbocker Press, 1915.

Hussain, Dilwar, 'Muslim Political Participation in Britain and the "Europeanisation" of Fiqh', *Die Welt des Islams*, 2004 (Vol. 44, No. 3), pp. 376–401.

Ilchev, I. & D. Perry, 'The Muslims of Bulgaria' in: G. Nonneman, T. Niblock & B. Szajkowski, *Muslim Communities in Europe*, London: Ithaca Press, 1996, pp. 115–138.

Imber, Colin, *The Ottoman Empire, 1300–1650: the structure of power*, Basingstoke: Palgrave Macmillan, 2002.

Inanchik, Halil, *The Ottoman Empire: Conquest, Organization and Economy, Collected Studies*, London: Variorum Prints, 1978.

———, 'The Turkish Impact on the Development of Modern Europe' in: Kemal H. Karpat (ed.), *The Ottoman state and its place in world history*, Leiden: Brill, 1974.

——— & Donald Quataert, *An Economic and Social History of the Ottoman Empire, Vol. 1, 1300–1600*, Cambridge: Cambridge University Press, 1994.

Inayatullah, Naeem & Davind L. Blaney, *International Relations and the Problem of Difference*, London/New York: Routledge, 2004.

Iriye, Akira, *Global and Transnational History*, New York: Palgrave MacMillan, 2013.

Iskhakov, Damir, 'The Tatar Ethnic Community', *Anthropology & Archeology of Eurasia*, 2004 (Vol. 43, No. 2), pp. 8–28.

Islamoglu-inan, H. (ed.), *The Ottoman Empire and the World-Economy*, Cambridge: Cambridge University Press, 1987.

Isom-Verhaaren, Christine, 'An Ottoman report about Martin Luther and the Emperor: New evidence of the Ottoman interest in the Protestant challenge to the power of Charles V', *Turcica*, 1996 (Vol. 28), pp. 299–318.

———, 'Barbarossa and his army who came to succor all of us: Ottoman and French Views of Their Joint Campaign of 1543–1544', *French Historical Studies*, 2007 (Vol. 30, No. 3), pp. 395–425.

Issawi, Charles, *Cross-Cultural Encounters and Conflicts*, Oxford: Oxford University Press, 1998.

———, *The economic history of Turkey, 1800–1914*, Chicago/London: University of Chicago Press, 1980.

———, 'The Transformation of the Economic Position of the Millets in the Nineteenth Century' in: Benjamin Braude & Bernard Lewis (eds.), *Christians and Jews in the Ottoman Empire*, New York/London: Holmes & Meier Publishers, 1982, pp. 261–285.

Ivekovic, Ivan, 'Nationalism and the Political Use and Abuse of Religion: The Politicization of Orthodoxy, Catholicism and Islam in Yugoslave Successor States', *Social Compass*, 2002 (Vol. 49, No. 4), pp. 523–536.

Iyigun, Murat, 'Luther and Süleyman', *The Quarterly Journal of Economics*, 2008 (Vol. 123, No. 4), pp. 1465–1494.

Izetbegovic, A., *Islam Between East and West*, American Trust Publications, 1985.

———, *The Islamic Declaration*, 1991 (not published, but available in English translation on manifique.free.fr/allhere/ezat1.pdf).

Jabri, Mohammed 'Abed Al-, *Islam, Modernism and the West. Cultural and Political Relations at the End of the Millenium* (ed. G.M. Munoz), New York: I.B. Tauris, 1999.

Jackson, Pamela Irving & Peter A. Zervakis, *The Integration of Muslims in Germany, France and the United States: Law, Politics and Public Policy*, Paper prepared for 2004 annual meeting of the American sociological Association (pdf-file online only at: http://www.allacademic.com/meta/p109230_index.html), 2004.

Jacobson, J., *Islam in Transition – Religion and Identity among British Pakistani Youth*, London/New York: Routledge, 1998.

Jayyusi, Salma Khadra (ed.), *The Legacy of Muslim Spain*, Leiden: Brill, 1992.

Jelavich, Barbara, *History of the Balkans, 18th and 19th centuries*, New York: Cambridge University Press, 1983.

———, *The establishment of the Balkan national states, 1804–1920*, Seatle: University of Washington Press, 1977.

Jenkins, Jennifer, 'German Orientalism: Introduction', *Comparative Studies of South Asia, Africa and the Middle East*, 2004 (Vol. 24, No. 2), pp. 97–100.

Jensen, D.L., 'The Ottoman Turks in Sixteenth Century French Diplomacy', *The Sixteenth Century Journal*, 1985 (Vol. 16, No. 4), pp. 451–470.

Johansen, Brigitte & Riem Spielhaus, 'Counting Deviance: Revisiting a Decade's Production of Surveys among Muslims in Western Europe', *Journal of Muslims in Europe*, 2012 (Vol. 1, No. 1), pp. 81–112.

Johns, Jeremy, *Arabic Administration in Norman Sicily: the Royal Diwan*, Cambridge: Cambridge University Press, 2002.

Johnson, James, *The Holy War Idea in Western and Islamic Traditions*, Pennsylvania: Pennsylvania State University Press, 1997.

——— & John Kelsay, *Just War and Jihad: Historical and Theoretical Perspectives on War and Peace in Western and Islamic Thought*, New York: Greenwood Pub Group, 1991.

Johnston, Douglas & Jonathan Eastvold, 'History Unrequited. Religion as Provocateur and Peacemaker in the Bosnian Conflict' in: Harold Coward & Gordon S. Smith, *Religion and Peace Building*, New York: SUNY Press, 2004, pp. 213–242.

Judt, Tony, *A Grand Illusion. An Essay on Europe*, London: Penguin Books, 1997.

———, 'The Pas is Another Country: Myth and Memory in Postwar Europe', *Daedalus*, 1992 (Vol. 121, No. 4), pp. 83–118.

Kabadayi, M., *Inventory for the Ottoman Empire/Turkish Republic 1500–2000*, online publication of the International Institute of Social History: http://www.iisg.nl/research/labourcollab/turkey.pdf.

Kaegi, Walter, *Byzantium and the Early Islamic Conquests*, Cambridge: Cambridge University Press, 1992.

———, *Muslim Expansion and Byzantine Collapse in North Africa*, Cambridge: Cambridge University Press, 2010.

Kafadar, Cemal, Between Two Worlds: The Construction of the Ottoman State, Berkeley: University of California Press, 1995.

Kahmann, M., Ontmoetingen tussen Marokkaanse Nederlanders en de Marokkaanse Overheid, Leiden (PhD thesis), 2014.

Kalesi, H., 'Oriental Culture in Yugoslav Countries from the 15th century till the End of the 17th Century' in: Cesar Jaroslav, Ottoman Rule in Middle Europe and Balkan in the 16th and 17th Centuries, Prague: Oriental Institute Publishing House, 1978.

Kaplan, Benjamin, Divided by faith: religious conflict and the practice of toleration in early modern Europe, Cambridge: The Belknap Press of Harvard University Press, 2007.

Karcic, Harun, 'Islamic Revival in Post-Socialist Bosnia and Herzegovina: International Actors and Activities', Journal of Muslim Minority Affairs, 2010 (Vol. 30, No. 4), pp. 519–534.

Karić, Enes, 'Is Euro-Islam a Myth, Challenge or a Real Opportunity for Muslims in Europe?', Journal for Muslim Minority Affairs, 2002 (Vol. 22, No. 2), pp. 435–442.

Karpat, Kemal, 'Millets and Nationality: The Roots of the Incongruity of Nation and State in the Post-Ottoman Era' in: Benjamin Braude & Bernard Lewis, Christians and Jews in the Ottoman Empire, New York/London: Holmes & Meier Publishers, 1982.

———, Ottoman population, 1830–1914: demographic and social characteristics, Madison: University of Wisconsin Press, 1985.

———, 'Ottoman Population Records and the Census of 1881/82–1893', International Journal of Middle Eastern Studies, 1978 (Vol. 9, No. 2), pp. 237–274.

Kasaba, Resat, Islamoglu-inan, H. (ed.), The Ottoman Empire and the World-Economy: The Nineteenth Century, Albany: State University of New York Press, 1988

Kaya, Ayhan, Constructing Diasporas: Turkish Hip-Hop Youth in Berlin (PhD thesis), University of Warwick, 1997.

———, 'Turkey-EU relations: The impact of Islam on Europe' in: Jørgen S. Nielsen, Samim Akgonül, Ahmet Alibašić, Brigitte Maréchal & Christian Moe (eds.), Yearbook of Muslims in Europe (Volume 1), London/Boston: Brill, 2009, pp. 377–402.

——— & Ferhat Kentel, Euro-Turks. A Bridge or a Breach between Turkey and the European Union? A Comparative Study of German Turks and French Turks, Brussels: Centre for European Policy Studies, 2005.

Kecmanovic, Dusan, Ethnic Times. Exploring Ethnonationalism in the former Yugoslavia. Westpot/Connecticut/London: Praeger, 2002.

Kedar, Benjamin, Crusade and Mission: European Approaches towards the Muslims, Princeton: Princeton University Press, 1984.

———, 'The subjected Muslims of the Frankish Levant' in: James M. Powell (ed.), Muslims under Latin Rule (1100–1300), Princeton: Princeton University Press, 1990, pp. 135–174.

Kennedy, Hugh, *The Great Arab Conquests: How the spread of Islam changed the world we live in*, London: Weidenfeld & Nicolson, 2007.

Khaduri, *Silat al-diblumatikiyya bayn Rashid wa Sharlaman*, Bagdad, 1939.

Khalili, Jim Al-, *The House of Wisdom: How Arabic Science Saved Ancient Knowledge and Gave Us the Renaissance*, London/NewYork: Penguin Press, 2011.

Khodarkovsky, Michael, *Russia's steppe frontier: the making of a colonial empire, 1500–1800*, Bloomington: Indiana University Press, 2001.

Khosrokhavar, R., *L'islam des jeunes*, Paris: Flammarion, 1997.

Kiel, Machiel, *Studies on the Ottoman Monuments of the Balkans*, Aldershot: Variorum, 1990.

King, Preston, *Tolerance*, London: George Allen & Unwin Ltd, 1976.

Klausen, Jytte, *The Islamic Challenge: Politics and Religion in Western Europe*, Oxford: Oxford University Press, 2005.

Koliopoulos, Giannes, *Brigands with a Cause: Brigandage and Irredentism in Modern Greece, 1821–1912*, Oxford: Clarendon Press, 1987.

Kolodziejczyk, Dariusz, *Ottoman-Polish diplomatic relations (15th–18th century): an annotated edition of ʿahdnames and other documents*, Leiden: Brill, 2000.

Koningsveld, P.S., 'Muslim Slaves and Captives in Western Europe During the Late Middle Ages', *Islam and Christian-Muslim Relations*, 1995 (Vol. 6. No. 1), pp. 5–23.

Kraft, Sabine, *Neue Sakralarchitectur des Islam in Deutschland* (PhD thesis), Theology Faculty Marburg, 2000.

Kramer, Martin, *Islam Assembled, the Advent of the Muslim Congresses*, New York: Colombia University Press, 1986

Kreutz, Barbara, 'Ships. Shipping, and the implications of change in the early medieval Mediterranean', *Viator*, 1976 (Vol. 7), pp. 79–110.

Kritzeck, James, *Peter the Venerable and Islam*, Princeton: Princeton University Press, 1964.

Krstic, Tijana, *Contested Conversions to Islam: Narratives of Religious Change in the Early Modern Ottoman Empire*, Stanford: Stanford University Press, 2011.

Kse, Ali & Kate Miriam Loewenthal, 'Conversion Motifs Among British Converts to Islam', *International Journal for the Psychology of Religion*, 2000 (Vol. 10, No. 2), pp. 101–110.

Kullolli, Arben, *Proselytization in Albania by Middle Eastern Islamic Organizations* (thesis), Monterey: Naval Postgraduate School, March 2009.

Kunst, Jonas R. & David L. Sam, 'Relationship between perceived acculturation expectations and Muslim minority youth's acculturation and adaptation,' *International Journal of Intercultural Relations*, 2013 (Vol. 37), pp. 477–490.

Kymlicka, Will, *Multicultural Citizenship: A Liberal Theory of Minority Rights*, Oxford: Oxford University Press, 1995.

Ladas, Stephen-Pericles, *The Exchange of Minorities: Bulgaria, Greece and Turkey*, New York: Macmillan, 1932.

Laiou, Angeliki, 'Byzantine trade with Muslims and Crusaders' in: Angeliki Laiou & Roy Mottahedh (eds.), *The Crusades from the Perspective of Byzantium and the Muslim World*, Washington: Dumbarton Oaks, 2001.

———— & Roy Mottahedh (eds.), *The Crusades from the Perspective of Byzantium and the Muslim World*, Washington: Dumbarton Oaks, 2001.

Lakhdar, Mounia, Genevive Vinsonneau, Michael J. Apter & Etienne Mullet, 'Conversion to Islam Among French Adolescents and Adults: A Systematic Inventory of Motives', *International Journal for the Psychology of Religion*, 2007 (Vol. 17, No. 1), pp. 1–15.

Lane, Ann, *Yugoslavia. When ideals collide*. New York: Palgrave Macmillan: 2004.

Laqueur, Walter, *The Last Days of Europe: Epitaph for an Old Continent*, New York: St Martin's Griffin, 2009.

————, 'The Terrorism To Come', *Policy Review*, 2004 (Aug-Sept), pp. 49–64.

Larsson, Göran, *Muslims in the EU – Cities Report: Sweden*, Open Society Institute, 2007.

————, 'The Fear of Small Numbers: Eurabian Literature and Censuses on Religious Belonging', *Journal of Muslims in Europe*, 2012 (Vol. 1, No. 2), pp. 142–165.

Latham, R.G., 'Contributions to the Minute Ethnology of Europe, with Special Reference to a Treatise by Biondelli, Entitled Prospecto Topographico-Statisco delle Colonie Straniere d' Italia', *Transactions of the Ethnological Society of London*, 1861 (Vol. 1), pp. 105–111.

Lathion, Stéphane, 'The impact of the minaret vote in Switzerland' in: Stefano Allievi (ed.), *Mosques in Europe. Why a solution has become a problem*, London: Alliance Publishing Trust, 2010, pp. 221–223.

Latouche, Robert, *The Birth of Western Economy. Economic Aspects of the Dark Ages*, London: Methuen, 1967.

Laurence, Jonathan, *The Emancipation of Europe's Muslims: The State's Role in Minority Integration*, Princeton: Princeton University Press, 2012.

Lea, Henry, *A History of the Inquisition in Spain (Volumes 1–3)*, New York: MacMillan, 1906–1907.

————, *The Moriscos of Spain. Their Conversion and Expulsion*, Philadelphia: Lea Brothers and Co., 1901.

Lederer, Gyorgy, 'Contemporary Islam in East Europe', NATO Academic Forum, May 1999 (online publication available at http://www.nato.int/acad/fellow/97--99/lederer.pdf).

Leiken, Robert S., *Europe's Angry Muslims*, Oxford/New York: Oxford University Press, 2012.

Lewis, Bernard, *Europe and Islam*, Washington: The AEI Press, 2007.

————, *Islam in the West*, New York/ Oxford: Oxford University Press, 1993.

————, *The Muslim Discovery of Europe*, New York/London: W.W. Norton, 1982.

————, 'The Third Wave: Muslim Migration to Europe', *New Perspectives Quarterly*, 2007 (Vol. 24), pp. 30–35.

———— & D. Schnapper (eds.), *Muslims in Europe*, London: Pinter, 1994.

Lewis, David, *God's Crucible: Islam and the Making of Europe*, New York: Norton & Company, 2008.

Lewis, Geoffrey, *Modern Turkey*, New York: Praeger, 1955.

Lewis, Philip, *Islamic Britain: Religion, Politics and Identity Among British Muslims*, London: I.B. Tauris, 2002.

———, *Young, British and Muslim*, London: Continuum, 2007.

Lieber, Alfred, 'Eastern Business Practices and Medieval European Commerce', *Economic History Review*, 1968 (Vol. 21, No. 2), pp. 230–243.

Lofland, John & Norman Skonovd, 'Conversion Motifs', *Journal for the Scientific Study of Religion*, 1981 (Vol. 20, No. 4), pp. 373–385.

Lopez, Fernando Bravo, 'Towards a definition of Islamophobia: approximations of the early twentieth century', *Ethnic and Racial Studies*, 2011 (Vol. 34, No. 4), p. 556–573.

Lopez, Robert, *The Commercial Revolution of the Middle Ages: 950–1350*, Cambridge: Cambridge University Press, 1987.

———, 'The Trade of Medieval Europe: the South' in: Stephan Broadberry & Kevin O'Rourke, *Cambridge Economic History of Europe*, Cambridge: Cambridge University Press, 2010.

Lorant, Karoly, *The demographic challenge in Europe*, Brussels: European Parliament, 2005.

Lowry, Heath W., *The nature of the early Ottoman state*, Albany: State University of New York Press, 2003.

———, *The Shaping of the Ottoman Balkans, 1350–1550: Conquest, Settlement & Infrastructural Development of Northern Greece*, Istanbul: Baçesehir University Publications, 2008.

Lucassen, L. & C. Laarman, 'Immigration, intermarriage and the changing face of Europe in the post war period', *The History of the Family*, 2009 (Vol. 14, No. 1), pp. 52–68.

Lüdke, Tilman, *Jihad Made in Germany: Ottoman and German Propaganda and Intelligence in the First World War*, Münster: Lit, 2005.

Lyons, Jonathan, *The House of Wisdom: how the Arabs transformed Western civilization*, London: Bloomsbury Press, 2009.

MacCulloch, Diarmaid, *A history of Christianity: the first three thousand years*, London: Penguin Press, 2009.

Macfie, Alexander, *Orientalism: A Reader*, New York: New York University Press, 2001.

Machiavelli, Niccolò, *The Prince*, London: Bantam Classics, 1984 (orig. 1513).

Magas, Branka, *The Destruction of Yugoslavia. Tracking the Break-up 1980–1992*, New York/London: Verso, 1993.

Makdisi, George, 'On the Origin and Development of the College in Islam and the West' in: Khalil Semaan (ed.), *Islam and the Medieval West. Aspects of Intercultural Relations*, Albany: State University of New York Press, 1980.

———, 'Scholasticism and Humanism in Classical Islam and the Christian West', *Journal of the American Oriental Society*, 1989 (Vol. 109, No. 2), pp. 175–182.

————, The Rise of Humanism in Classical Islam and the Christian West. Edinburgh: Edinburgh University Press, 1991.

Makdisi, John, 'The Islamic Origins of the Common Law', North Carolina Law Review, 1999 (Vol. 77, No. 5), pp. 1635–1739.

Malik, J. (ed.), Muslims in Europe-From the Margins to the Centre, Münster: LIT Verlag, 2004.

Mandaville, Peter, Global Political Islam, London: Routledge, 2007.

————, 'Muslim Transnational Identity and State Responses in Europe and the UK after 9/11: Political Community, Ideology and Authority', Journal of Ethnic and Migration Studies, 2009 (Vol. 35, No. 3), pp. 491–506.

————, 'Towards a critical Islam' in: Stefano Allievi & Jørgen Nielsen (eds.), Muslim Networks and Transnational Communities in and across Europe, Leiden/Boston: Brill, 2003, pp. 127–145.

————, Transnational Politics. Reimagining the umma, London/New York: Routledge, 2001.

Mann, Vivian & Thomas Glick (eds.), Convivencia: Jews, Muslims and Christians in Medieval Spain, New York: George Braziller, 1992.

Mantran, Robert, Istanbul dans la seconde moité du XVIIe siècle, Paris: Libaraire Adrien Maisonneuve, 1986.

————, 'The transformation of trade in the Ottoman empire in the eighteenth century' in: Thomas Naff & Roger Owen (eds.), Studies in eighteenth century Islamic history, Carbondale: Southern Illinois University Press, 1977, pp. 217–235.

Maréchal, Brigitte, 'Mosques, organisations and leadership' in: Brigitte Maréchal, Stefano Allievi, Felice Dassetto, Jørgen Nielsen (eds.), Muslims in the Enlarged Europe (Muslim Minorities, Volume 2), Leiden/Boston: Brill, 2003, pp. 109–111.

————, The Muslim Brothers in Europe: Roots and Discourse (Muslim Minorities, 8), Leiden: Brill, 2008.

————, 'The Question of belonging' in: Brigitte Maréchal, Stefano Allievi, Felice Dassetto, Jørgen Nielsen (eds.), Muslims in the Enlarged Europe (Muslim Minorities, Volume 2), Leiden/Boston: Brill, 2003, pp. 5–18.

Marks, Jon, 'High hopes and low motives: The new euro-mediterranean partnership initiative', Mediterranean Politics, 1996 (Vol. 1, No. 1), pp. 1–24.

Maussen, Marcel, Constructing Mosques: The governance of Islam in France and the Netherlands, Amsterdam: University of Amsterdam, 2009.

Merdjanova, Ina, Rediscovering the Umma. Muslims in the Balkans between Nationalism and Transnationalism, Oxford: Oxford University Press, 2013.

March, Andrew, Islam and Liberal Citizenship: The search for an overlapping consensus, Oxford: Oxford University Press, 2009.

Marriott, John, The Eastern Question. A Historical Study in European Diplomacy, Oxford: Clarendon Press, 1940.

Mas, Albert, *Les Turcs dans la littérature espagnole du Siècle d'Or: recherches sur l'évolution d'un thème littéraire* (2 Volumes), Paris: Impr. Follope, 1967.

Matar, Nabil, *Europe through Arab Eyes, 1578–1727*, New York: Columbia University Press, 2009.

———, *Islam in Britain, 1558–1685*, Cambridge: Cambridge University Press, 1998.

Matsuki, Eizo, 'The Crimean Tatars and their Russian-Captive Slaves. An Aspect of Muscovite-Crimean Relations in the 16th and 17th centuries', *Mediterranean World*, 2006 (Vol. 18), pp. 171–182.

Mattar, Philip, *The Mufti of Jerusalem: Al-Hajj Amin al-Husayni and the Palestinian national movement*, New York: Columbia University Press, 1988.

Mattingly, Garrett, *Renaissance Diplomacy*, Dover Publications, 1988 (first published by Houghton Mifflin Company, Boston, 1955).

Maussen, Marcel, *Constructing Mosques: The governance of Islam in France and the Netherlands*, Amsterdam: University of Amsterdam, 2009.

Maziane, Leïla, *Salé et ses corsaires, 1666–1727: un port de course marocain au XVIIe siècle*, Havre: Université de Rouen, 2007.

Mazower, Mark, *Salonica, City of Ghosts. Christians, Muslims and Jews, 1430–1950*, New York: Vintage, 2006.

———, *The Balkans. A short History*, New York: The Modern Library, 2002.

McCarthy, Justin, *Death and Exile. The Ethnic Cleansing of Ottoman Muslims, 1821–1922*, Princeton: The Darwin Press, 1995.

———, 'Muslims in Ottoman Europe: Population from 1800 to 1912', *Nationalities Papers: The Journal of Nationalism and Ethnicity*, 2000 (Vol. 28, No. 1), pp. 29–43.

———, 'Ottoman Bosnia, 1800–1878' in: Mark Pinson (ed.), *The Muslims of Bosnia-Herzegovina. Their Historic Development from the Middle Ages to the Dissolution of Yugoslavia*, Harvard: Harvard University Press, 1993, pp. 54–83.

McCormick, Michael, *Origins of the European Economy: Communications and Commerce AD 300–900*, Cambridge: Cambridge University Press, 2002.

McGowan, Bruce, *Economic Life in Ottoman Europe: taxation, trade, and the struggle for land, 1600–1800*, Cambridge/New York: Cambridge University Press, 1981.

McKee, Sally, 'Domestic Slavery in Renaissance Italy', *Slavery & Abolition*, 2008 (Vol. 29, No. 3), pp. 305–326.

McKinnon, Catriona, *Tolerance. A Critical Introduction*, London: Routledge, 2006.

McLoughlin, Sean, 'The State, New Muslim Leadership and Islam as a Resource for Public Engagement in Britain' in: Jocelyne Cesari & Sean McLoughlin (eds.), *European Muslims and the Secular State*, London: Ashgate, 2005, pp. 53–69.

McNeill, William, *Europe's Steppe Frontier 1500–1800*, Chicago/London: The University of Chicago Press, 1964.

McRae, Kenneth (ed.), *The six books of a commonweale*, New York: Arno Press, 1979.

Mehmet, Ozay, 'Turkey and the European Union: A Troubled Relationship or a Historic Partnership?' in: Tareq Yousif Ismael & Mustafa Aydin (eds.), *Turkey's Foreign Policy in the Twenty-First Century: A Changing Role in the World*, Aldershot: Ashgate Publishing Ltd, 2003, pp. 41–58.

Meijer, Roel & Edwin Bakker (eds.), The Muslim Brotherhood in Europe, New York: Columbia University Press, 2013.

Menocal, Maria, *The Ornament of the World: How Muslims, Jews and Christians Created a Culture of Tolerance in Medieval Spain*, Boston: Little Brown, 2002.

Metcalf, Barbara, *Making Muslim Space in North America and Europe*, Berkeley/London: University of California Press, 1996.

Metcalfe, Alex, *Muslims and Christians in Norman Sicily*, London: Routledge Curzon Taylor & Francis Group, 2003.

————, *The Muslims of medieval Italy*, Edinburgh: Edinburgh University Press, 2009.

Meyer, Eve, 'Turquerie and Eighteenth-Century Music', *Eighteenth-Century Studies*, 1974 (Vol. 7, No. 4), pp. 474–488.

Meyerson, Mark D. & Edward D. English (eds.), *Christians, Muslims, and Jews in Medieval and Early Modern Spain. Interaction and Cultural Change*, Notre Dame (I.): University of Notre Dame Press, 2000.

Minkov, Anton, *Conversion to Islam in the Balkans, Kisve bahasi petitions and Ottoman social life, 1670–1730*, Leiden/Boston: Brill, 2004.

Mintchev, Vesselin, 'External Migration and External Migration Policies in Bulgaria', *South-East Europe Review for Labour and Social Affairs*, 1999 (Vol. 3), pp. 123–150.

Mirdal, G.M., 'The Construction of Muslim Identities in Contemporary Europe' in: F. Dassetto (ed.), *Paroles d' Islam-Individus, Societes et Discours dans l' Islam Europeen Contemporain*, Paris: Maisonneuve et Larose, 2000, pp. 35–49.

Modood, Tariq, *Ethnicity, nationalism, and minority rights*, Cambridge: Cambridge University Press, 2004.

————, 'Introduction: the politics of multiculturalism in the new Europe' in: P. Werbner & T. Modood (eds.), *The Politics of Multiculturalism in the New Europe: Racism, Identity and Community*, London/New York: Zed Books, 1997, pp. 1–26.

————, 'The Place of Muslims in British Secular Multiculturalism' in: N. Alsayyad, M. Castells & L. Michalak (eds.), *Islam and the Changing Identity of Europe*, University Press of America: Lexington Books, 2000

Mohammad, Robina, 'Marginalisation, Islamism and The Production of the 'Other's' 'Other'', *Gender, Place and Culture*, 1999 (Vol. 6, No. 3), pp. 221–240.

Mondal, Anshuman A., *Young British Muslim Voices*, Oxford: Greenwood World Publishing, 2008.

Moore, Robert, *The Formation of a Persecuting Society: Power and Deviance in Western Europe, 950–1250*, London: Wiley-Blackwell, 2001.

Morrison, Kenneth, *Wahhabism in the Balkans*, Shrivenham: Cranfield University, Defence Academy of the United Kingdom, Advanced Research and Assessment Group, 2008.

Motadel, David, 'Islam and the European Empires', *The Historical Journal*, 2012 (Vol. 0, No. 3), pp. 831–856.

Muldoon, James, *Popes, Lawyers and Infidels*, Liverpool: Liverpool University Press, 1979.

Mun'im A. Sirry, 'Early Muslim–Christian dialogue: a closer look at major themes of the theological encounter', *Islam and Christian–Muslim Relations*, 2005 (Vol. 16, No. 4), pp. 361–376.

Naimark, Norman M. & Holly Case, *Yugoslavia and Its Historians. Understanding the Balkan Wars of the 1990s*, Stanford, California: Standford University Press, 2003.

Nalborczyk, Agata S., 'Islam in Poland: the past and the present', *Islamochristiana*, 2006 (Vol. 32), pp. 229–234.

Nebelsick, Harold P., *The Renaissance, The Reformation, and the Rise of Science*, Edinburgh: Edinburgh University Press, 1992.

Necipoglu, Gülru, 'The Life of an Imperial Monument: Hagia Sophia after Byzantium' in: R. Mark & A. Çakmak (eds.), *Hagia Sophia from the Age of Justinian to the Present Day*, Cambridge MA: Cambridge University Press, 1992.

Neumann, Iver B., *Uses of the Other. 'The East' in European Identity Formation*, Minneapolis: University of Minnesota Press, 1999.

———— & Jennifer M. Welsh, 'The Other in European self-definition: an addendum to the literature on international society', *Review of International Studies*, 1991 (Vol. 17), pp. 327–348.

Newman, David L., *An Imam in Paris: Al-Tahtawi's visit to France (1826–31)*, London: Saqi Books, 2004

Nicol, Donald, *Byzantium and Venice: A Study in Diplomatic and Cultural Relations*, Cambridge/New York: Cambridge University Press, 1988.

Nicosia, Francis R. *The Third Reich and the Palestine Question*, London: Tauris, 1985.

Nielsen, Jørgen S., 'Book reviews', *Journal of Muslims in Europe*, 2001 (Vol. 1), p. 217.

————, *Muslims In Western Europe*, Edinburgh: Edinburgh University Press, 2004 (3d ed.).

————, *Towards a European Islam*, Basingstoke: Macmillan, 1999.

———— & Lisbet Christiffersen (eds.), *Shari'a as a Discourse: Legal Traditions and the Encounter with Europe*, Burlington: Ashgate, 2010.

Nielsen, Jørgen S., Samim Akgönül, Ahmet Alibašić, and Brigitte Maréchal, Christian Moe (eds.), *Yearbook of Muslims in Europe*, Volume 1, Leiden: Brill, 2009.

Nielsen, Jørgen S., Samim Akgönül, Ahmet Alibašić, and Brigitte Maréchal, Christian Moe (eds.), *Yearbook of Muslims in Europe*, Volume 2, Leiden: Brill, 2010.

Nielsen, Jørgen S., Samim Akgönül, Ahmet Alibašić, and Hugh Goddard, Brigitte Maréchal (eds.), Yearbook of Muslims in Europe, Volume 3, Leiden: Brill, 2011.

Nielsen, Jørgen S., Samim Akgönül, Ahmet Alibašić, and Egdūnas Račius (eds.), Yearbook of Muslims in Europe, Volume 4, Leiden: Brill, 2012.

Nielsen, Jørgen S., Samim Akgönül, Ahmet Alibašić, and Egdūnas Račius (eds.), Yearbook of Muslims in Europe, Volume 5, Leiden: Brill, 2013.

Nieuwkerk, Karin van, Women embracing Islam: gender and conversion in the West, Austin: University of Texas Press, 2006.

Nirenberg, David, Communities of Violence: Persecution of Minorities in the Middle Ages, Princeton: Princeton University Press, 1996.

———, 'Sexual Boundaries in the Medieval Crown of Aragon' in: Salma Khadra Jayyusi (ed.), The Legacy of Muslim Spain, Leiden: Brill, 1992, pp. 141–160.

Nonneman, G., T. Niblock, & B. Szajkowski (eds.), Muslim Communities in the New Europe, Ithaca: Ithaca Press, 1996.

Nordbruch, Götz, Nazism in Syria and Lebanon: The Ambivalence of the German Option, 1933–1945, Routledge, 2009.

Norris, H.T., Islam in the Balkans. Religion and Society Between Europe and the Arab World, University of South Carolina Press, 1993.

———, Islam in the Baltic. Europe's early Muslim community, London: Tauris Academic Studies, 2009.

O'Brien, Peter, European Perceptions of Islam and America from Saladin to George W. Bush: Europe's Fragile Ego Uncovered, London: Palgrave Macmillan, 2009.

O'Callaghan, Joseph, A History of Medieval Spain, Cornell: Cornell University Press, 1983.

O'Connell, James, The Making of Modern Europe: Strengths, Constraints and Resolutions, University of Bradford Peace Research Report no. 26, Bradford: University of Bradford, 1991.

Öniz, Z., 'Globalization and Party Transformation: Turkey's JDP in Perspective' in: Peter Burnell (ed.), Globalizing Democracy: Party Politics in Emerging Democracies, London: Routledge, 2006, pp. 1–27.

Otterbeck, Jonas, 'The Depiction of Islam in Sweden', The Muslim World, 2002 (Vol. 92), pp. 143–156.

Özyürek, E., 'Convert alert: German Muslims and Turkish Christians as threats to security in the new Europe', Comparative Studies in Society and History, 2009 (Vol. 51, No. 1), pp. 91–116.

Pace, Michelle, 'Imagining Co-presence in Euro-Mediterranean Relations: The Role of Dialogue', Mediterranean Politics, 2005 (Vol. 10, No. 3), pp. 291–312.

Pagden, A. & J. Lawrence (eds.), Political Writings, New York: Cambridge University Press, 1991.

Pancevski, Bojan, 'Saudis fund Balkan Muslims spreading hate of the West', TimesOnline, March 28 2010.

Panzac, Daniel, *Barbary Corsairs: The End of a Legend, 1800–1820*, Leiden: Koninklijke Brill, 2005.

Parekh, Bhikhu, *Europe, Liberalism and the "Muslim Question"*, Leiden: ISIM & Amsterdam University Press, 2008.

———, *Rethinking Multiculturalism: Cultural Diversity and Political Theory*, Houndmills/London: Macmillan Press, 2000.

Pargeter, Alison, *The New Frontiers of Jihad: Radical Islam in Europe*, London/New York: I.B. Tauris, 2008.

Parvev, Ivan, *Habsburgs and Ottomans between Vienna and Belgrade, 1683–1789*, New York: Columbia University Press, 1995.

Peev, Y., 'Courants islamiques en Bulgarie', *Les Annales de l'Autre Islam*, 1997 (No. 4), pp. 183–197.

Perica, Vjekoslav, *Balkan Idols. Religion and Nationalism in Yugoslav States*, Oxford: Oxford University Press, 2002.

Perkins, Mary Anne, *Christendom And European Identity: The Legacy Of A Grand Narrative Since 1789*, Berlin/New York: Walter de Gruyter, 2004.

Perry, Mary Elizabeth, 'Moriscos and the Limits of Assimilation' in: Salma Khadra Jayyusi (ed.), *The Legacy of Muslim Spain*, Leiden: Brill, 1992, pp. 274–289.

———, *The handless maiden: Moriscos and the politics of religion in early modern Spain*, Princeton: Princeton University Press, 2005.

Peter, Frank (ed.), *Authorizing Islam in Europe* (Muslim World, special edition), 2006, (Vol. 96).

———, 'Individualization and Religious Authority in Western European Islam', *Islam and Christian-Muslim Relations*, 2006 (Vol. 17, No. 1), pp. 105–118.

Peters, Edward, *Inquisition*, Berkeley: University of California Press, 1989.

Peters, Rudolph, *Jihad in Medieval and Modern Islam*, Leiden: Brill, 1977.

Petrovich, Michael, *A History of Modern Serbia: 1804–1918*, New York: Harcourt Brace Javanovich, 1976.

Pfusterschmid-Hardtenstein, Heinrich, *A Short History of the Diplomatic Academy of Vienna*, Vienna: Diplomatic Academy of Vienna, 2008.

Pick, Thomas M., Anne Speckhard & Beatrice Jacuch, *Home-Grown Terrorism: Understanding and Addressing the Root Causes of Radicalisation Among Groups With an Immigrant Heritage in Europe*, Amsterdam: IOS Press, 2009

Pinson, Mark (ed.), *The Muslims of Bosnia-Herzegovina. Their Historic Development from the Middle Ages to the Dissolution of Yugoslavia*, Harvard: Harvard University Press, 1993.

Pirenne, Henri, *Mahomet et Charlemagne: Byzance, Islam et Occident dans le haut Moyen Age*, Paris: Jaca Books, 1987.

Pisoiu, Daniela, *Islamist Radicalisation in Europe: An Occupational Change Process*, London: Routledge, 2013.

Pogonowski, Iwo, *Poland: a Historical Atlas*, New York: Hippocrene Books, 1987.

Potz, Richard, 'Covenental and Non-Covenental Cooperation of State and Religions in Austria' in: Richard Puza & Norman Doe (eds.), Religion and Law in Dialogue, Leuven: Uitgeverij Peeters, 2006, pp. 11–19.

Poumarède, Geraud, Pour en Finir avec la Croisade: mythes et réalités de la lutte contre les Turcs aux XVIe et XVIIe siècles, Paris: Presses Universitaires de France, 2004.

Powell, James, Muslims under Latin Rule, 1100–1300, Princeton: Princeton University Press, 1990.

———, 'Frederick II and the Rebellion of the Muslims of Sicily, 1220–1224', Uluslararasi Haçli Seferleri Sempozyumu, 23–25 June 1997, Istanbul, pp. 13–22.

Powers, Gerard F., 'Religion, Conflict and Prospects for Peace in Bosnia, Croatia and Yugoslavia', Journal of International Affairs, 1996 (Vol. 50, No. 1), pp. 221–252.

Qaradawi, Yusuf Al-, Fiqh of Muslim Minorities: Contentious Issues & Recommended Solutions, Al-Falah for Translation Publications Distribution, 2003.

Quataert, Donald, The Ottoman Empire 1700–1922, Cambridge: Cambridge University Press, 2005.

Ragaru, N., 'Islam et coexistence communautaire en Bulgarie' in: Bougarel, X. & N. Clayer, Le nouvel Islam balkanique – Les musulmans, acteurs du post-communisme 1990–2000, Paris: Maisonneuve & Larose, 2001, pp. 241–288.

Rais, Mahmoud, The Representation of the Turk in English Renaissance Drama, Thesis Cornell University, 1973.

Ramadan, Tariq, Radical Reform: Islamic Ethics and Liberation, Oxford: Oxford University Press, 2009.

———, Western Muslims and the Future of Islam, Oxford: Oxford University Press, 2004.

Rambo, Lewis R., 'Theories of Conversion: Understanding and Interpreting Religious Change', Social Compass, 1999 (Vol. 46, No. 3), pp. 259–271.

Ramet, Sabrina Petra, Balkan Babel. Politics, Culture, and Religion in Yugoslavia, Boulder/San Francisco/Oxford: Westview Press, 1992.

Rath, J., R. Penninx, K. Groenendijk, & A. Meyer, Western Europe and Its Islam: The Social Reaction to the Institutionalization of "New Religion" in the Netherlands, Belgium and the United Kingdom, Leiden: Brill, 2001.

Rawls, J., 'The priority of rights and the idea of good', Philosophy and Public Affairs, 1988 (Vol. 17), pp. 251–276.

Raz, J., Ethics in the public domain. Essays in the Morality of Law and Politics, Oxford: Clarendon Press, 1994.

———, The Morality of Freedom, Oxford: Oxford University Press, 1986.

Reeber, M., 'Les khutbas de la diaspora: enquete sur les tendencies de la predication dans les mosques en France et dans plusieurs pays d'Europe occidentale' in: F. Dassetto, Paroles d' Islam – Individus, Societes et Discours dans l' Islam europeen contemporain / Islamic Words – Individuals, Societies and Discourse in Contemporary European Islam, Paris: Maisonneuve & Larose, 2000,

Rehman, Fatima Tabassum & Sophia F. Dziegielewski, 'Women Who Choose Islam. Issues, Changes, and Challenges in Providing Ethnic-Diverse Practice', International Journal of Mental Health, 2003 (Vol. 32), pp. 31–49.

Renan, Ernest, L' Islamisme et la Science, Paris: Calmann Levy, 1883.

Riley-Smith, Jonathan, The Oxford History of the Crusades, Oxford: Oxford University Press, 2002.

Roald, Anne Sofie, 'The conversion process in stages: new Muslims in the twenty-first century', Islam and Christian–Muslim Relations, 2012 (Vol. 23, No. 3), pp. 347–362.

Rodinson, Maxime, Europe and the Mystique of Islam, London: Tauris, 1988.

———, Muhammad: Prophet of Islam, London: I.B. Tauris, 2002

Rohe, Matthias, Muslim Minorities and the Law in Europe: Chances and Challenges, Global Media Publications, 2007.

———, 'Reasons for the Application of Sharia in the West' in: Maurits S. Berger (ed.), Applying Shari'a in the West. Facts, fears and figures, Leiden: Leiden University Press, 2013, pp. 25–46.

Roose, Eric, 'Fifty Years of Mosque Architecture in the Netherlands', Electronic Journal of Oriental Studies, 2005 (Vol. 8), pp. 1–46.

Rothman, E. Nathalie, 'Interpreting Dragomans: Boundaries and Crossings in the Early Modern Mediterranean', Comparative Studies in Society and History, 2009 (Vol. 51, No. 4), pp. 771–800.

Rotman, Youval, Byzantine slavery and the Mediterranean World, Harvard: Harvard University Press, 2009.

Rouillard, Clarence D., The Turk in French history, thought and literature (1520–1660), Paris: Boivin, 1940.

Roy, Jean-Henry & Jean Deviosse, La Bataille de Poitiers: Trente journées qui ont fait la France, Paris: Gallimard, 1966.

Roy, Olivier, 'A Clash of Cultures or a Debate on Europe's Values', ISIM Newsletter, 2005 (Vol. 15), pp. 6–7.

———, 'Islam in Europe: Clash of religions or convergence of religiosities?' in: Krzysztof Michalski (ed.), Religion in the New Europe, Volume 2, New York: Central European University Press, 2006, pp. 131–142.

———, Globalized Islam: The Search for a New Ummah, Columbia: Columbia University Press, 2006.

———, Secularism confronts Islam, New York: Columbia University Press, 2007.

———, Vers un islam europeen, Paris: Editions Esprit, 1999.

Runnymede Commission Report, 'Islamophobia: a challenge for us all', London: Runnymede Trust, 1997.

Ruthven, Malise, '"Born-again" Muslims: cultural schizophrenia', Open Democracy, 10 September 2009 (online publication: http://www.opendemocracy.net/faith-islamicworld/article_103.jsp).

Sabbides, Alexes, Byzantium in the Near East: its relations with the Seljuk sultanate of Rum in Asia Minor, the Armenians of Cilicia and the Mongols, AD c.1192–1237, Thessalonike: Kentron Buzantrinon Ereunon, 1981.

Sahas, Daniel, Byzantium and Islam: An Encounter of two Theocracies: mutual administration and exclusion, Toronto: Greek Canadian Association of Constantinople, 1993.

Said, Edward, Orientalism. Western Concepts of the Orient, New York: Pantheon Books, 1978.

———, Culture and Imperialism, London: Random House, 1993 (repr. by Vintage Books in 1994).

Saliba, George, Islamic Science and the Making of the European Renaissance, Boston: MIT Press, 2007.

Salvatore, Armando, 'Power and Authority within European Secularity: From the Enlightenment Critique of Religion to the Contemporary Presence of Islam', Muslim World, special edition 'Islam and Authority in Europe', 2006 (Vol. 96), pp. 543–561.

Samad, A. Yunas & Kasturi Sen (eds.), Islam in the European Union: Transnationalism, Youth and the War on Terror, Pakistan: Oxford University Press, 2007.

Savage, Timothy M., 'Europe and Islam: Crescent Waxing, Cultures Clashing', The Washington Quarterly, 2004 (Vol. 27), pp. 25–50.

Sayyad, Nezar Al- & Manuel Castells (eds.), Muslim Europe or Euro-Islam. Politics, Culture, and Citizenship in the Age of Globalization, Lanham: Lexington Books, 2002.

Sayyid, Salman, 'Beyond Westphalia: Nations and Diasporas – the Case of the Muslim Umma' in: B. Hesse, Unsettled Multiculturalisms: Diasporas, Entanglements, Transruptions, New York: Zed Books, 2000.

———, Thinking Through Islamophobia, London: Hurst & Co., 2010.

Shah, P., Legal Pluralism in Conflict: Coping with Cultural Diversity in Law, London: Cavendish, Glasshouse, 2005.

Shatzmiller, Maya (ed.), Islam and Bosnia. Conflict Resolution and Foreign Policy in Multi-Ethnic States, Montreal & Kingston/London/Ithaca: McGill-Queen's University Press, 2002.

Shmuelevitz, Aryeh, The Jews of the Ottoman Empire in the Late Fifteenth and the Sixteenth Century, Leiden: Brill, 1984.

Saunders, John, A History of Medieval Islam, London: Routledge, 1965.

Schechtman, Joseph, 'Compulsory Transfer of the Turkish Minority from Bulgaria', Journal of Central European Affairs, 1952 (Vol. 12), pp. 154–169.

Schlueter, E., B. Meuleman & E. Davidov, 'Immigrant integration policies and perceived

Group Threat: A multilevel study of 27 Western and Eastern European Countries', *Social Science Research*, 2013 (Vol. 42, No. 3), pp. 670–682.

Schwanitz, Wolfgang G., *Djihad made in Germany: Deutsche Islampolitik im 19. Und 20. Jahrhundert. Politik, Wirtschaft, Militär und Kultur*, Berlin: Trafo, 2005.

Schwoebel, Robert, *The Shadow of the Crescent: The Renaissance Image of the Turk*, Nieuwkoop: B. de Graaf, 1967.

Scott, H.M. *The Emergence of Eastern Powers 1756–1775*, Cambridge: Cambridge University Press, 2002.

Sedgwick, Mark, *Muhammad Abduh*, London: Oneworld Publications, 2009.

Selby, Jennifer, 'Hijab' in: Jocelyne Cesari (ed.), *The Oxford Handbook of European Islam*, Oxford: Oxford University Press, 2012.

Sell, Louis, *Slobodan Milosevic and the destruction of Yugoslavia*. Durham/London: Duke University Press, 2002.

Sells, Michael, 'Crosses of Blood: Sacred Space, Religion, and Violence in Bosnia-Hercegovina', *Sociology of Religion*, 2003 (Vol. 64, No. 3), pp. 309–331.

Setton, Kenneth M., 'Lutheranism and the Turkish Peril', *Balkan Studies*, 1962 (Vol. 2), pp. 133–168.

———, *Western Hostility to Islam and Prophecies of Turkish Doom*, Philadelphia: American Philosophical Society, 1992.

Shachar, Ayelet, 'Privatizing Diversity: A Cautionary Tale from Religious Arbitration in Family Law', *Theoretical Inquiries in Law*, 2008, (Vol. 9), pp. 573–607.

Shadid, W.A.R. and P.S. van Koningsveld (eds.), *Intercultural Relations and Religious Authorities: Muslims in the European Union*, Leuven: Peeters, 2002.

——— (eds.), *Islam and Muslims in the Margin: Political Responses to the Presence of Islam in Western Europe*, Kampen: Kok Pharos, 1996.

——— (eds.), *Religious Freedom and the Position of Islam in Western Europe*, Kampen: Kok Pharos, 1995.

——— (eds.), *The Integration of Islam and Hinduism in Western Europe*, Kampen: Kok Pharos, 1991.

———, 'The Negative Image of Islam and Muslims in the West' in: W.A.R. Shadid and P.S. van Koningsveld (eds.), *Religious Freedom and the Neutrality of the State: The Position of Islam in the European Union*, Leuven: Peeters, 2002.

Shah-Kazemi & Sonia Nurin, *Untying the Knot, Muslim Women, Divorce and the Shariah*, Nuffield Foundation, 2001.

Shaw, Stanford, 'The Ottoman Census System and Population, 1831–1914', *International Journal of Middle Eastern Studies*, 1978 (Vol. 9, No. 3), pp. 323–338.

Sholod, Barton, *Charlemagne in Spain: The Cultural Legacy of Roncesvalles*, Geneva: Droz, 1966.

Shryock, Andrew, *Islamophobia/Islamophilia: Beyond the Politics of Enemy and Friend*, Bloomington: Indiana University Press, 2010.

Silvestri, Sara, 'EU Relations with Islam in the Context of the EMP's Cultural Dialogue', *Mediterranean Politics*, 2005 (Vol. 10, No. 3), pp. 385–405.

Smit, Timothy James, *Commerce and Coexistence: Muslims in the Economy and Society of Norman Sicily*, (dissertation), University of Minnesota, 2009.

Sokolovic, Dzemal, 'How to Conceptualize the Tragedy of Bosnia: Civil, Ethnic, Religious War or ...?', *War Crimes, Genocide, & Crimes against Humanity*, 2005 (Vol. 1, No. 1), pp. 115–130.

Somun, Hajrudin, 'Wahhabism in the Balkans: a threat to regional stability?', *Today's Zaman*, 4 March 2010.

Southern, Richard, *Western views of Islam in the Middle Ages*, Cambridge: Harvard University Press, 1962.

Spencer, C., 'Europe and political Islam: defining threats and evolving policies' in: M. Kramer (ed.), *The Islamism Debate*, Tel Aviv: Moshe Dayan Center for Middle Eastern and African Studies, Tel Aviv University, 1997.

Stark, Rodney and Roger Finke, *Acts of Faith. Explaining the Human Side of Religion*, Berkeley/London: University of California Press, 2000.

Steyn, Mark, *Lights Out: Islam, Free Speech And The Twilight Of Europe*, Montreal: Stockade Books, 2009.

Stoianovich, Traian, 'The conquering Balkan Orthodox Merchant', *Journal of Economic History*, 1960 (Vol. 20, No. 2), pp. 234–313.

Stoye, John (1964), *The Siege of Vienna: The Last Great Trial Between Cross & Crescent*, London: Collins, 1964.

Sugar, Peter, *South-eastern Europe under ottoman Rule, 1354–1804*, Seattle/London: University of Washington Press, 1977.

Sunier, Thijl, 'Constructing Islam: Places of Worship and the Politics of Space in the Netherlands', *Journal of Contemporary European Studies*, 2005 (Vol. 13, No. 3), pp. 317–334.

———— & N. Landman, *Diyanet, the Turkish Directorate for Religious Affairs in a changing environment*, Amsterdam/Utrecht: VU University and Utrecht University, 2011.

Taggar, Yehuda, *The Mufti of Jerusalem and Palestine Arab Politics, 1930–1937*, New York: Garland Publications, 1987.

Tahzib-Lie, Bahia, 'The European definition of freedom of religion or belief', *Helsinki Monitor*, 1998 (Vol. 9), pp. 17–27.

Taylor, Charles, 'Multiculturalism and 'The Politics of Recognition'' in: A. Guttmann (ed.), *Multiculturalism and the Politics of Recognition*, Princeton: Princeton University Press, 1992.

Tebbakh, Sonia, *Muslims in the EU – Cities Report: France*, Open Society Institute, 2007.

Temel, Safiye, *Greek-Turkish Population Exchange: An Analysis of the Conflict Leading to the Exchange*, Thesis Standfort University, 1949.

Tenniswood, Adrian, *Pirates of Barbary: Corsairs, Conquests and Captivity in the Seventeenth-Century Mediterranean*, London: Riverhead Trade, 2011.

Thornton, Bruce, *Decline & Fall: Europe's Slow Motion Suicide*, New York: Encounter Books, 2007.

Tibi, Bassam, *Political Islam, World Politics and Europe*, New York: Routledge, 2008.

Tietze, Andreas, *Habsburgisch-osmanische Beziehungen*, Vienna: Verlag des Verbandes der wissenschaftlichen Gesellschaften Österreichs, 1985.

Tolan, John, *Saint Francis and the Sultan: the curious history of a Christian-Muslim encounter*, Oxford: Oxford University Press, 2009.

————, *Sons of Ishmael: Muslims through European eyes in the Middle Ages*, Gainesville: University Press of Florida, 2008.

————, *Saracens. Islam in the Medieval European Imagination*, New York: Columbia University Press, 2002.

————, *Medieval Christian perceptions of Islam: a book of essays*, New York: Routledge, 2000.

Toledano, Ehud, *The Ottoman Slave Trade and its Suppression, 1840–1890*, Princeton: Princeton University Press, 1982.

Toumarkine, Alexandre, *Les Migrations des Populations Musulmanes Balkaniques en Anatolie (1876–1913)*, Istanbul: Editions Isis, 1995.

Toynbee, Arnold, 'The Ottoman Empire in World History', *Proceedings of the American Philosophical Society*, 1955 (Vol. 99, No. 3), pp. 119–126.

————, *The Western Question in Greece and Turkey. A Study in the Contact of Civilizations*, New York: H. Fertig, 1970.

Treadgold, Warren, *A Concise History of Byzantium*, Basingstoke: Palgrave, 2001.

Trevor-Roper, Hugh, *The Rise of Christian Europe*, London: Thames and Hudson, 1965.

Tsitselikis K., *Old and New Islam in Greece: From Historical Minorities to Immigrant Newcomers*, Leiden: Martinus Nijhoff Publishers, 2012.

Tyler, Aaron, *Islam, the West, and Tolerance*, London: Palgrave Macmillan, 2008.

Udovicki, Jasminka & James Ridgeway (eds.), *Burn this House. The Making and Unmaking of Yugoslavia*, Durham/London: Duke University Press, 1997.

U.K. Government, *The Prevent Strategy: A Guide for Local Partners in England. Stopping people becoming or supporting terrorists and violent extremists*, HMSO London, 2008.

UK Home Office, *Improving Opportunity; Strengthening Society: The Government's strategy to increase race equality and community cohesion*, January 2005.

Vangeli, Anastas, 'Religion, Nationalism and Counter-secularization: The Case of the Macedonian Orthodox Church', *Identity Studies*, 2010 (Vol. 2), pp. 1–15 (available online at: http://identitystudies.iliauni.edu.ge/?page_id=11).

Varisco, Daniel Martin, *Reading Orientalism: Said and the Unsaid*, Seattle: Washington University Press, 2007.

Vasil'ev, Alexander, Henri Grégoire & Marius Canard (eds.), *Byzance et les Arabes*, Bruxelles: Éditions de l'Institut de philologie et d'histoire orientales, 1935.

Vaughan, Dorothy, *Europe and the Turk: A Pattern of Alliances*, Liverpool: University Press Liverpool, 1954.

Velikonja, Mitja, *Religious Separation and Political Intolerance in Bosnia-Herzegovina*, Texas: A&M University Press, 1992.

Verlinden, Charles, *L'esclavage dans l'Europe médiévale, Tome I: Péninsule Ibérique-France*, Bruges: Persée, 1955.

Versteegh, Kees, 'The Arab presence in France and Switzerland in the 10th century', *Arabica*, 1990 (Vol. 37, No. 3), pp. 359–388.

Vertovec, Steven, 'Diaspora, Transnationalism and Islam: Sites of Change and Modes of research' in: Stefano Allievi & Jørgen Nielsen (eds.), *Muslim Networks and Transnational Communities in and across Europe*, Leiden/Boston: Brill, 2003, pp. 312–326.

————, *Transnationalism*, London: Routledge, 2009.

———— & Alisdair Rogers (eds.), *Muslim European Youth: Reproducing Ethnicity, Religion, Culture*, London: Ashgate, 1998.

———— & Charles Peach (eds.), *Islam in Europe. The politics of religion and community*, London/Basingstoke: MacMillan & St. Martin's Press, 1997.

Vielau, Helmut-Wolfhardt, *Luther und der Türke*, Göttingen: Buchdruckerei von J. Särchen, 1936.

Vitkus, Daniel (ed.), *Piracy, Slavery, and Redemption: Barbary Captivity Narratives from Early Modern England*, New York: Columbia University Press, 2001.

Voetius, 'Over het mohammedanisme' in: J. van Amersfoort & W.J. van Asselt (eds.), *Liever Turks dan Paaps? De visies van Johannes Coccejus, Gisbertus Voetius en Adrianus Relandus op de islam*, Zoetermeer: Uitgeverij Boekencentrum, 1997.

Volpi, F., 'Regional community building and the transformation of international relations: the case of the Euro-Mediterranean Partnership', *Mediterranean Politics*, 2004 (Vol. 9, No. 2), pp. 145–164.

Vrcan, Srdjan, 'The War in ex-Yugoslavia and Religion', *Social Compass*, 1994 (Vol. 41, No. 3), pp. 413–422.

Vreg, F., 'Iluzije o evropskem multikulturalizmu', *Teorija in praksa*, 1993 (Vol. 30, No. 7–8), pp. 659–663.

Vryonis, Spyros, 'Religious change and continuity in the Balkans and Anatolia from the fourteenth through the sixteenth century' in: Speros Vyronis Jr. (ed.), *Islam and Cultural Change in the Middle Ages*, Wiesbaden: Harrassowitz, 1973.

————, 'Religious Changes and Patterns in the Balkans: 14th–16th Centuries' in: H. Birnbaum & S. Vryonis (eds.), *Aspects of the Balkans: Continuity and Change*, Paris/The Hague: Mouton, 1972.

————, *The Decline of Medieval Hellenism in Asia Minor and the Process of Islamization from the Eleventh through the Fifteenth Century*, Berkeley/Los Angeles: University of California Press, 1971.

Waardenburg, Jacques, *L'Islam dans le miroir de l'Occident: Comment quelques orientalistes occidentaux se sont penchés sur l'Islam et se sont formé une image de cette religion: I. Goldziher, C. Snouck Hurgronje, C.H. Becker, D.B. MacDonald, Louis Massignon*, Paris: Mouton, 1963.

————, *Muslims as Actors: Islamic Meanings and Muslim Interpretations in the Perspective of the Study of Religions*, Berlin: Walter de Gruyter, 2007.

————, *Muslims and Others – Relations in Context*, Berlin: Walter de Gruyter, 2003.

Walzer, Michael, *On tolerance*, New Haven/London: Yale University Press, 1997.

Warraq, Ibn, *Defending the West: A Critique of Edward Said*, New York: Prometheus Books, 2007.

Watson, Andrew, *Agricultural Innovation in the Early Islamic World. The Diffusion of Crops and Farming Techniques, 700–1100*, Cambridge: Cambridge University Press, 1983.

Watson, William, *Tricolor and Crescent: France and the Islamic World*, Westport: Praeger Publishers, 2003.

Waugh, Scott & Peter Diehl (eds.), *Christendom and its Discontents: Exclusion, Persecution and Rebellion, 1000–1500*, Cambridge: Cambridge University Press, 1996.

Werbner, Pnina, *Imagined Diasporas Among Manchester Muslims: The Public Performance of Pakistani Transnational Identity Politics*, Oxford: James Currey, 2002.

Wheatcroft, Andrew, *The Enemy at the Gate: Habsburgs, Ottomans and the Battle for Europe*, London: Pimlico, 2009.

Wintle, Michael (ed.), *Culture and Identity in Europe*, Aldershot: Avebury, 1996.

Wolf, Kenneth Baxter, *Christian Martyrs in Muslim Spain*, Cambridge: Cambridge University Press, 1988.

————, *Conquerors and Chroniclers of Early Medieval Spain*, Liverpool: Liverpool University Press, 1990.

————, 'Mohammed as Antichrist in Ninth-Century Cordoba' in: Mark D. Meyerson & Edward D. English (eds.), *Christians, Muslims, and Jews in Medieval and Early Modern Spain. Interaction and Cultural Change*, Notre Dame (I.): University of Notre Dame Press, 2000, pp. 3–19.

Woltering, Robert, *Occidentalisms in the Arab world: ideology and images of the West in the Egyptian media*, London: I.B. Tauris, 2011.

Yalcinkaya, Mehmet A., *The First Permanent Ottoman Embassy in Europe*, Istanbul: The Isis Press, 2010.

Ye'or, Bat, *Eurabia: The Euro-Arab Axis*, Madison (NJ): Fairleigh Dickinson University Press, 2005.

——, *The Dhimmī: Jews and Christians under Islam*, London/Toronto: Associated University Press, 1983.

Yıldırım, Onur, *Diplomacy and Displacement: Reconsidering the Turco-Greek Exchange of Populations, 1922–1934*, New York: Routledge, 2006.

Yilmaz, I., 'The challenge of post-modern legality and Muslim legal pluralism in England', *Journal of Ethnic and Migration Studies*, 2002 (Vol. 28), pp. 343–354.

Yurdusev, Nuri, 'Perceptions and Images in Turkish (Ottoman)-European Relations' in: Tareq Yousif Ismael & Mustafa Aydin (eds.), *Turkey's Foreign Policy in the Twenty-First Century: A Changing Role in the World*, Aldershot: Ashgate Publishing Ltd, 2003, pp. 77–100.

Ziaki, Angeliki, 'Greece: Debate and Challenges' in: Maurits S. Berger (ed.), *Applying Shari'a in the West. Facts, fears and figures*, Leiden: Leiden University Press, 2013, pp. 125–139.

Züricher, Erik Jan, *Turkey: a modern history*, London: Tauris & Co, 1993, repr. 2005.

Index